Counseling Ethics

Christin M. Jungers, PhD, LPCC, NCC is an Associate Professor of Counselor Education at Franciscan University of Steubenville. She obtained her doctoral degree in Counselor Education and Supervision from Duquesne University and has worked in the field as a counselor since 2000. Christin is a licensed professional clinical counselor, as well as a National Certified Counselor. Her clinical work spans a variety of issues and includes counseling with individuals, couples, and families. Currently, she offers pro-bono counseling services in Steubenville and Wintersville, Ohio through the Catholic Diocese of Steubenville. She is the editor of *The Counselor's Companion: What Every Beginning Counselor Needs to Know* (co-written with Jocelyn Gregoire), as well as numerous articles. Christin also has conducted trainings abroad in the Seychelles Islands and in Mauritius, which have been aimed at providing consultation to emerging counseling programs.

Jocelyn Gregoire, CSSp, EdD, LPC, NCC, ACS has been a Roman Catholic priest for 25 years and has been involved in the counseling field for many years. He is an Assistant Professor in the Department of Counseling, Psychology, and Special Education at Duquesne University in Pittsburgh, Pennsylvania. In addition to his doctorate in Education, he holds two other graduate degrees. Through his expertise as a professional counselor, Dr. Gregoire has helped thousands of people across the world in their journeys toward personal growth and healing. He is a National Certified Counselor (NCC), Licensed Professional Counselor (LPC), an Approved Clinical Supervisor (ACS), and a member of numerous counseling associations. He has co-authored several articles in refereed journals in the area of sexual addiction, racial and cultural identity development, and spirituality. He is also the co-author of *The Counselor's Companion: What Every Beginning Counselor Needs to Know*.

Counseling Ethics

Philosophical and Professional Foundations

Christin M. Jungers, PhD, LPCC, NCC
Jocelyn Gregoire, CSSp, EdD, LPC, NCC, ACS
Editors

SPRINGER PUBLISHING COMPANY
NEW YORK

Springer Publishing Company, LLC
11 West 42nd Street
New York, NY 10036
www.springerpub.com

Acquisitions Editor: Nancy Hale
Composition: Techset Composition Ltd.

ISBN: 978-0-8261-0851-7
E-book ISBN: 978-0-8261-0852-4
Instructor's Manual ISBN: 978-0-8261-9962-1
(Available upon request from textbook@springerpub.com)

12 13 14 15/5 4 3 2 1

Library of Congress Cataloging-in-Publication Data

Jungers, Christin M.
Counseling ethics : philosophical and professional foundations/Christin M. Jungers, Jocelyn Gregoire.—1st ed.
p. cm.
Includes bibliographical references and index.
ISBN 978-0-8261-0851-7—ISBN 978-0-8261-0852-4
1. Counseling–Moral and ethical aspects. I. Gregoire, Jocelyn. II. Title.
BF636.67.J86 2013
174'.91583—dc23

2012023493

Printed in the United States of America by Bang Printing.

This book is dedicated to all students who strive to embody ethical practices in professional counseling.

May you embrace for a lifetime the journey toward becoming virtuous and admirable helpers and persons.

Contents

PART III: TREKKING TO SPECIAL SITES IN COUNSLEING ETHICS

CONTRIBUTORS

Amy E. Alexander, MS Ed, Penn Hills Senior High School, Penn Hills, PA

Cecile Brennan, PhD, John Carroll University, University Heights, OH

Nancy G. Calley, PhD, University of Detroit Mercy, Detroit, MI

Kailla Edger, PhD, Walden University, Minneapolis, MN

Gina M. Gordon, MS Ed, Blackhawk Intermediate School, Beaver Falls, PA

Stephanie Helsel, PhD, Waynesburg University, Waynesburg, PA

Maura Krushinski, EdD, Duquesne University, Pittsburgh, PA

Christina I. Kumpf, MS Ed, Duquesne University, Pittsburgh, PA

Stephen Kuniak, PhD, NCC Unity Family Services, Leechburg, PA

Lynn E. Linde, EdD, Loyola University Maryland, Baltimore, MD

Helena K. Y. Ng, PhD, NCC, Duquesne University, Pittsburgh, PA

Thomas Petrone, EdD, Gestalt Institute of Pittsburgh, Pittsburgh, PA

Catherine A. Sherman, MEd, MFA, NCC, Washington & Jefferson College, Washington, PA

Stephen Southern, EdD, Mississippi College, Clinton, MS

Michael J. Taleff, PhD, University of Hawaii, Manoa, HI

Cristiana White, MSW, Aliquippa Elementary School, Aliquippa, PA

PREFACE

Cicero tells the story of Damocles, a courtier of a fourth-century-BCE tyrant named Dionysius. By all appearances, Dionysius was very rich, and he had all the luxuries money could buy, including tasteful clothing, jewelry, and delectable food. Seeing the king's wealth, Damocles commented regularly to the leader about his power and luxurious lifestyle, saying how truly fortunate the latter must be. One day, the king offered to switch places with Damocles so he could taste power and fortune first hand. Damocles readily agreed and immensely enjoyed being waited upon like a king. In the evening, a banquet was held for Damocles, but during the meal he looked up and noticed a sharpened sword hanging directly above his head that was dangling by a single horse-hair. Immediately, he lost all taste for the fine foods and beautiful girls and asked to take leave of the tyrant, saying he no longer wanted to be so fortunate.

For a number of years, we, the editors of this book, have been sharing conversations with one another, our students, and our colleagues about the place of philosophy in counseling. Sometimes these conversations have brought us to talk about how philosophy can inform our understanding of and approach to counseling techniques. At other times, it got us thinking about what philosophy has to teach counselors about the importance of coming to a shared anthropology of the human person and how this might benefit the development of counseling theories. In the spring of 2010, we engaged a discussion with a group of doctoral students at Duquesne University about the place of philosophy in counseling ethics. The excitement generated from that discussion eventually led us to write this book, which is aimed at offering readers a look at counseling ethics from positive and philosophical points of view. In our opinion, these perspectives go hand in hand and help counselors not to get stuck in fear-based or reactive approaches to ethics in which they might feel as if the sword of Damocles is dangling above them, ready to drop if they do not make the right ethical judgments. Unfortunately, the study of counseling ethics and the practice of working through ethical dilemmas can sometimes be experienced only as an exercise in learning one's ethical obligations and making sure one knows what not to do. Making good, ethical decisions is a stressful process, made even more so if counselors are concerned primarily about how to avoid lawsuits or sanctions (i.e., the Damocles sword). What we hope to do with this book instead is to introduce varying philosophical points of view that will stretch the reader's mind to an appreciation for the fact that there are many approaches to determining what is good and ethical. Indeed, philosophical ethics tend to push us to think beyond the minimum set of actions that keep us in compliance with codes of ethics or laws and invite us to look deeply at what constitutes good and professional behavior. There are many schools of philosophical ethics—some are well known and regularly used by counselors in decision making, such as ethical principles and social contracts (e.g., the codes of ethics and laws). Others are less well known or underutilized, such as existential phenomenology, care ethics, and virtues. Throughout this book, the various contributing authors describe these and other philosophical frameworks to give readers the chance to come to know how their philosophical leanings get implemented in ethical decision making.

In this book we also hope to emphasize the importance of counselors becoming ethically autonomous. Ethical autonomy is formed when each of us (counselors, educators, supervisors, researchers, and students) develops an appreciation for our own preferred set of philosophical ethics, embraces reflective and thoughtful decision-making processes, and has a sense of ownership for our ethical decisions. As counselor educators and practitioners, we are both very aware that becoming an autonomous and ethical practitioner is a journey of personal and professional discovery that begins in the classroom and continues throughout a counselor's professional career and personal life. We do not come to ethical autonomy overnight—it is forged by encountering a series of experiences (both hypothetical and real) that give us the opportunity to reflect on what being ethical means and what constitutes ethical choices. To help emphasize the developmental and discovery aspects of becoming an ethical counselor, we invited the various experienced counselors and counselor educators who contributed to this book to share not only their expertise about ethical issues, but also their insight into how they have become highly ethical decision makers. We hope you will take away some tidbits of wisdom from their sharing.

ORGANIZATION OF THE TEXT AND CHAPTERS

This book is the work of the editors and 16 contributing authors who have written about counseling ethics by drawing on their unique areas of interest and expertise. It is organized into three sections. The first section provides a philosophical context for understanding counseling ethics; the second addresses best practices with regard to ethical standards and obligations; and the third deals with ethical issues in various practice settings and counseling specialties. In keeping with our appreciation for the personal and professional discovery elements involved in becoming ethical counselors, each chapter is structured around the same "map"—or a set of similar headings that reflect the journey inherent to becoming virtuous practitioners. These are: (a) the foreseen destination (chapter objectives); (b) getting on the road (introduction); (c) exploring the territory (an examination of the chapter's content); (d) signposts for future treks (summary); (e) insights gained from the journey (an author's personal reflection on an ethical issues); and (f) moving forward (case study reflection and questions). Each chapter also contains example boxes, or landmarks, with mini case studies, points of professional reflection, or additional information that the reader might find of interest. Readers who would like to test their comprehension of the chapter content can do so by completing learning check questions that are available as an online tool from Springer Publishing Company at textbook@springerpub.com. Each chapter further offers suggested activities that can be used to help readers incorporate and interact with the content more personally. These activities are also available online in the Instructor's Manual at the same web address.

The prominent place of ethical, legal, and moral issues in mental health counseling, school counseling, marriage and family counseling, and related professions demands that practitioners be able not only to negotiate a maze of ethical codes and standards of care, but also to use good clinical judgment in decision making. We view this text as a resource that reminds readers about the most important fibers of the counseling profession: critical thinking, clinical integrity, client care, moral behavior, reflective practices, and a desire to do good for clients in all situations. Finally, we hope that readers will integrate the journey model of this book into their own understanding of how professional growth unfolds. In our experience, practicing ethically goes beyond figuring out the occasional ethical dilemma and is better described as the day-to-day way of being, living, and interacting with others that sets the course for counselors to develop, over time, into upstanding and admirable practitioners.

―――

Acknowledgments

We first would like to express our sincere gratitude to each of the contributors to this text who, through their contributions, have added to its quality. Without their hard work, dedication, insight, and personal reflections this book would not have met its aim to be a resource that helps readers learn about and reflect on the process of becoming an ethically competent counselor. Their cooperation and conscientiousness helped to ensure that the whole editing process unfolded smoothly and in a timely fashion.

We would like to extend a special thanks to Stan Wakefield, who helped to connect us to the wonderful team at Springer Publishing. We are grateful to Jennifer Perillo, who first appreciated our vision for this book and who helped us to form and shape that vision into this book's final product. We also could not have completed this text without the support of Nancy Hale, our Editor at Springer, and Kathryn Corasaniti, our Associate Editor, who was always at the ready to answer our questions.

We are grateful to our colleagues in the counseling programs at Duquesne University and Franciscan University who have given us support and encouragement as we worked toward completing this book, and to the students with whom we have had countless discussions about ethics quandaries and what it means to be a virtuous counselor. Finally, we are both grateful to our friends and family, especially our parents, who were our cheerleaders throughout the process. Thank you many times over!

Part I

Touring a Philosophical Landscape of Counseling Ethics

1

PHILOSOPHY AND COUNSELOR ETHICS

Christin M. Jungers and Jocelyn Gregoire

THE FORESEEN DESTINATION

This chapter aims to provide a short review of some key thinkers in the evolution of Western philosophical ethics and also attempts to draw connections between schools of moral philosophy and the practice of counseling. In addition, the chapter offers practical (clinical) points of consideration for counselors meant to help them think about their own ethical leanings. After reviewing this chapter, readers will:

- Be familiar with historical periods in the development of philosophical ethics.
- Be able to identify numerous important thinkers in the evolution of Western philosophical ethics.
- Be able to describe the four most influential schools of contemporary philosophy to influence the formation of the American Counseling Association (ACA) *Code of Ethics*.
- Understand the importance of coming to an individualized approach to using a set of philosophical ideas in counseling practice.
- Be able to apply various schools of philosophical ethics in the decision-making process surrounding counseling cases.

GETTING ON THE ROAD

It has been approximately 50 years since the counseling profession, under the guidance of the American Counseling Association, produced its first set of ethical standards in 1961. Creating the inaugural standard of practice in the form of an ethical code was important for counselors because it put a stamp of credibility on their profession when it was still in its infancy (Remley & Herlihy, 2010). Today, counselors look to the ACA *Code of Ethics* (2005) to give them some sense of the shared identity and values of the profession. Equally important, the code serves the express purpose of outlining guidelines for ethical behavior that assist counselors in making the best possible decisions in uncertain or compromising situations. In many ways, the ethical code fills the very pragmatic role of setting aspirational guidelines for the behavior of those who identify with and use the title "counselor." Indeed, we suspect that for many counselors and trainees the words "ethics in counseling" are closely linked to—if not synonymous with—the term "ethical code." In this introductory chapter, however, we want to take a step back from the practical guidelines outlined in the code and ask you to consider a more fundamental question: Where exactly are the ethical standards to which counselors adhere philosophically grounded?

To answer this question we will have to look much farther than 50 years into the past when our professional ethical code formally emerged, and we have to be willing to approach the question of ethics in counseling from a rather broad perspective, because, whether we think about it or not, every counseling interaction has a philosophical and ethical dimension. For example, consider the case of a counselor whose client invites her out for a cup of coffee after a session. To begin understanding and judging the counselor's ultimate decision, we have to ask some expansive questions, such as, How does the counselor use philosophy in making all kinds of clinical decisions, especially those that are *not* obvious dilemmas? How does the counselor use philosophy to form a personal and professional self concept?, and, How does the counselor's understanding of ethics contribute to her growth as a person and professional over time? In fact, the study of ethics as a philosophical discipline is concerned with much more than clinical dilemmas such as the one posed above; it is concerned with how to live a good life, how to become a moral and upright or virtuous person, and how to discern between lesser and greater goods (Betan, 1997; Jordan & Meara, 1990; Meara, Schmidt, & Day, 1996).

The big questions about what constitutes a good life and how one discerns between good and bad have been pondered by philosophers for several centuries. The amazing thing is these ponderings continue to have relevance for counselors today—in part because the ponderings form schools of thought that act as frameworks for making decisions about clinical situations (e.g., the coffee invitation) and in everyday moments. Perhaps more importantly, though, the ancient and contemporary philosophy greats help us not to take for granted the process of critical, informed thinking (and ultimately judging and acting) that is at the heart of ethics.

One of the most important reflections we believe you will have over the course of your professional career revolves around how you will deepen your practice of being. Many philosophers and religious figures have contemplated the *being-ness* of humanity with the hope of jump starting others to ponder seriously the state of their most important relationships and the ways in which they make decisions about how to live life. Although the question of human-being may seem abstract or even secondary to the concerns of counseling ethics, we believe it must be the central point of reflection for discussions surrounding ethics.

With all this in mind, the goals of this chapter are: (a) to situate the development of counselor ethics (including its most tangible product—the ethical code) inside a history of philosophical thought about morality that has been unfolding for centuries and (b) to help you think broadly about your own counselor professionalism from the point of view of various philosophical perspectives. Given these goals, we begin the chapter by providing a brief sketch of the evolution of philosophical ethics from ancient Greece to the 20th century. We then will examine more closely contemporary understandings of several major ethical theories, such as deontology, teleology, and virtue ethics, that have had the most profound effects on our current understanding of counselor ethics and professionalism. Finally, we will look at ethical principles. These are probably the most well-known backdrop to thinking about obligations related to client well-being, in part because the principles provide a bridge between ethical theory and the practical guidance counselors need to make decisions in the ambiguous situations that often arise in clinical work. The day-to-day ethical decisions you make emanate ultimately from the perspective, or balance of perspectives, you use to evaluate what is right, wrong, good, or moral with respect to your clinical work and your personal life.

EXPLORING THE TERRITORY

PHILOSOPHICAL ETHICS: A SHORT HISTORICAL OVERVIEW

Over the millennia, an untold amount of ink has flowed in an effort to capture the insights of great ancients, as well as contemporary philosophers, who have tried to provide a plausible answer to the questions, What is good and evil?, and, What makes a person good? Folktales, mythologies, legends, and even theological and philosophical treatises have attempted to solve the problem of good and evil for their own ages. Our aim in this section is to provide a short overview of the problem of good and evil, to which we refer as "ethics" or "the ethical problem," as it has evolved throughout Western history. Ethical thought, of course, has marked human development cross-culturally, and there is an expansive body of literature outside of the Western realm that addresses the big questions of life. We encourage you to study works by Eastern, Native American, Middle Eastern, and African philosophers. However, because the counseling profession was born and eventually grew up in a Western context, it tends to have been influenced by this context to a greater extent than others, and for that reason we delimit our discussion here to Western philosophical thought. Other chapters in this book will address areas of multiculturalism in ethics.

Landmark 1

ETHICS OUTSIDE OF THE WESTERN POINT OF VIEW

A story for your consideration . . .

The Buddha is credited with the *parable of the arrow*, a story that indicates a philosopher's right duty, which is to be occupied less with unanswerable questions and more with relieving suffering in the world.

A man was attacked with a poison arrow and was seriously wounded. When his friends and family offered to get a doctor to remove the arrow and help heal him,

(*continued*)

the man replied that he would not accept the doctor's assistance until he knew who shot the arrow, the physical characteristics of the attacker and where he came from, what material the arrow was made from, and so on. In the process of making such insistences, however, the hurt man died.

The lesson of this folktale is that doing philosophy has to have an element of moral reasoning, as well as an element of action for it to be relevant to day-to-day life (Boss, 1998).

A few non-Western moral philosophers:

- **Confucius (551 BCE–479 BCE)**: Chinese philosopher who taught that the pathway to a harmonious life comes through instilling in people a sense of duty to ancient Chinese elders. He also believed that duty to elders' values should be translated into public policy. Confucius' philosophy reflects a blend of virtue ethics and deontology.
- **Mo Tzu (about 470 BCE–391 BCE)**: Chinese philosopher who, like Confucius, lived during China's golden age of philosophy. Tzu's approach strongly de-emphasizes the adherence to tradition found in Confucius' teaching. Instead, he taught that people must seek good that benefits all—a somewhat utilitarian view on ethics.
- **Buddha**: proposed an intricate philosophy with many applications to contemporary ethics. In particular, Buddhism teaches that people and all elements of the earth are One and as such are interconnected and should live in harmony.

Ancient and Medieval Thought

We have referred several times already to "ancient greats" whose writings form a foundation for Western philosophical thought that informs how many people define the good life both in the private and public realms. Some of the most well-known of the early philosophers are the Greeks—Socrates (469 BCE–399 BCE), Plato (428/427 BCE–348/347 BCE), and Aristotle (384 BCE–322 BCE). Other influential figures include Heraclitus, Democritus, and Epicurus; a brief description of their thought is found in Landmark 2. Although each of these men expressed his unique ideas about ethics, several themes consistently mark the philosophy of Greek thinkers and stand as assumptions upon which they base their ethics. One such assumption was that one can discern right from wrong (morality) outside of the influences of religion by using human nature and reason (Johnson, 1999). In contrast, the influential ancient and medieval Christian thinkers, St. Augustine (354–430) and Thomas Aquinas (1225–1274), situated their ideas within the framework of Christian theology.

Early Greek Philosophers

One pair of concepts Greek philosophers generally embraced are harmony and moderation (Fox & Demarco, 2002). Harmony suggests that a well-ordered life is preferred over a chaotic existence, while moderation is the practice of avoiding extremes or excess. The good, harmonious life, therefore, is one that is ordered according to reason (primarily because reason is a uniquely human faculty). Plato, in particular, believed reason was the highest good because he saw the sensory world (think emotions, physical desires, etc.) as transitory and prone to change. The good world, conversely, is one of pure, fixed ideas, and, from Plato's point of view, it is the attainment of this world that ought to focus and direct the human life (Boss, 1998). Ultimately, Plato concluded that it is only when reason becomes the master of the appetites and the will that a person is able to live a good life. Likewise, the good life of the ancient Greek philosophers also is the life of moderation, an idea that is reflected in Aristotle's famous "golden mean." Living in moderation means that one balances the time and space for all necessary activities (e.g., eating, sleeping, spending time with family and friends, working, etc.) and in so doing develops a virtuous character (Fox & Demarco, 2002).

A second set of notable themes that emerges in the works of early Greek philosophers, though they are not uniquely embraced by the Greeks, are self-realization and the hierarchy of goods. Aristotle, for instance, believed self-realization or the obligation to improve oneself and embrace one's human potentiality is the highest good and should be the goal that is served by all other action. Because the human person is the only being in the universe with the ability to reason, the proper function or end toward which the person aims is the development of the intellectual capacity. Aristotle also recognized that people have physical needs and desires, though he believed that these must be balanced with reason. By developing a rational attitude, people are able to temper their desires and feelings and live according to the golden mean. Living according to the golden mean and aiming toward attaining a high level of self-realization (i.e., rationality) generally is considered virtuous by Aristotle. Living a virtuous life, moreover, involves the practice of developing habits that are guided by moderation. We will return to Aristotle's work and writings later in the chapter because they are particularly relevant to the modern field of virtue or character ethics, which encourages counselors to think about the importance of self-development to ethical and professional practice.

Early Christian Philosophers (About 354–1274)

The rise of Christianity strongly influenced ancient and medieval philosophy because it introduced a shift in conceptualizing ethics from a secular to a religious point of view. Like their Greek predecessors, Augustine and Aquinas affirmed the use of reason to discern differences between good and evil. Aquinas, moreover, incorporated the Greeks' ideas about human nature into his ethical stance in that he saw morality as grounded in human nature. However, both Augustine and Aquinas also believed that it is only within a theological framework that one can truly understand human nature and core ethical and human values. While the Greeks emphasized naturalism (human nature as emerging from and part of natural forces), Christian philosophers stressed the supernatural aspect of the human person because of their belief that the person is made in the image of a supernatural, spiritual God (Swindal & Gensler, 2005). The Christian philosophers, then, saw the person as fundamentally more than a natural being. A second major differentiation between philosophers such as Augustine and Aquinas and the Greeks is their proposition that the good life is not completed in this world; rather, they believed the life that begins after death is the one of most importance and highest value (Boss, 1998; Johnson, 1999).

Landmark 2

OTHER INFLUENTIAL EARLY GREEK PHILOSOPHERS

- **Heraclitus of Ephesus (535 BCE–475 BCE):** considered the concepts of good and evil as a pair of opposites that work in harmony with one another. He also considered life to always be changing and in motion such that one is not able to have the same experience more than once.
- **Democritus of Abdera (about 460 BCE–about 370 BCE):** happiness and cheerfulness are the key to a good life, and happiness is more about the pursuits of the mind than about physical appetites or material possessions.
- **Epicurus (341 BCE–270 BCE):** as an ethical egoist, Epicurus proposed that people ought always to do what brings them the most pleasure, because pleasure for the self ranks highest in the hierarchy of values. Epicurus believed, however, that it is not physical pleasure that brings the most happiness, but, rather, it is rationality that brings happiness (Boss, 1998).

Modern Philosophical Ethics

The long period of modernity begins somewhere in the 15th and 16th centuries and extends to the 20th century. It is tied to a number of important historical events, including the Renaissance in northern Italy, the Reformation ignited by Martin Luther, and the discovery of the Americas (Johnson, 1999). Philosophers who lived during this span of time contributed a diversity of ideas on ethics and include such figures as Thomas Hobbes, David Hume, Immanuel Kant, Jeremy Bentham, John Stuart Mill, Soren Kierkegaard, Karl Marx, and John Locke. The works of Kant, Bentham, and Mill will be explored further in the next section, as they represent two significant schools of ethical thought that have influenced the development of counselor ethics (i.e., deontology and teleology). Kierkegaard's philosophy prefigured the work of an influential body of thinkers known as existentialists and phenomenologists. Marx, though he did not consider himself an ethicist, nonetheless shaped the way numerous political leaders thought about the good life, and his ideas ultimately affected the quality of life for vast numbers of people (Boss, 1998; Johnson, 1999).

Social Contracts and Human Rights

One implicit assumption underlying much philosophical theorizing is that questions about what constitutes the good life are best considered with the *individual* person and his or her own needs in mind. By contrast, two figures in the modern world, Thomas Hobbes (1588–1679) and John Locke (1632–1704), grappled with the question of why men and women should be concerned with others' needs, as well as their own; they ultimately came to think of morality as closely tied to human rights and social obligations, which are concretized in the rules, regulations, or laws that help communities function well. Hobbes reasoned for the necessity of sovereign law. Largely because of what some would call his pessimistic outlook on human nature (Graham, 2004; Gould & Mulvaney, 2007; Johnson, 1999), Hobbes purported that in their natural state (i.e., without a governing body), people are fundamentally egoistic and will act only for their own good. To avoid the chaos and debauchery associated with basic human nature, he believed people agree to enter into social contracts in the form of laws. Laws ensure enough order to allow people to pursue their interests without being impeded by others' individual pursuits (Graham, 2004). Finally, Hobbes saw social contracts as necessary to protecting one fundamental human right—the right to life.

Locke also emphasized the social realm in his writings on ethics and morality; however, unlike Hobbes, Locke reasoned that human nature is fundamentally good and that people have inherent rights not only to life, but also to freedom and property. He also believed that civil law is put in place to protect and uphold, not limit, natural rights (Boss, 1998). Therefore, he argued for democracy over sovereign law as the preferred social contract.

Landmark 3

LICENSING BOARDS: OUR PROFESSION'S SOCIAL CONTRACT

The counseling license that most counselor trainees eventually seek after finishing a graduate degree and after completing several thousand hours of supervised clinical experience is, in fact, a privilege granted to trainees by a governing body: a state licensing board. State licensing boards create sets of rules and regulations that its licensees agree to follow in order not to lose the privilege of licensure. Hobbes believed that governing bodies help to keep order by promulgating laws that protect people from one another's self-centered acts.

1. *Whose rights do you believe are being guarded by state licensure boards?*
2. *Do you believe that it is necessary for counselors to be regulated by a governing body such as a licensure board?*
3. *What potential good or bad outcomes might be tied to the regulation of counselors by legal bodies known as licensure boards?*

Ethics in the 20th Century

One way of broadly characterizing ethics of the 20th century is to say that a certain skepticism is reflected in this era's thinking about what constitutes right and wrong (Johnson, 1999). Although early Greek and Christian philosophers and the multitude of thinkers in the modern world embraced a position of skepticism in order not to take their ideas about right and wrong for granted, they also supposed that one, indeed, can discern knowable truths about morality and immorality. A number of 20th-century philosophers have challenged this idea or at least limited what is defined as knowable. For example, anthropologist William Graham Sumner studied various tribal societies and concluded that the answer to the question of right and wrong depends largely on one's social context. His line of thought is associated with the ideas of cultural relativism, or the premise that what is knowable is discerned only through a cultural context, and, thus, it is impossible to make sweeping or absolute ethical statements (Sommers-Flanagan & Sommers-Flanagan, 2006). Another group of 20th-century philosopher-skeptics known as logical positivists see the knowable as that which is limited to its ability to be tested through scientific inquiry and verified through observable evidence.

Existentialism

Existentialism is not classified uniquely as a school of moral philosophy, yet, it finds a place in our discussion and comes into its own in the early and mid-1900s with the work of individuals such as Frederich Nietchze (1844–1900), Jean-Paul Sartre (1905–1980), and Martin Heidegger (1889–1976). Sartre proposed that the human person is condemned to a life of radical freedom in which he is responsible for every decision and choice he makes. It is choice, Sartre suggested, and not human nature or any type of essential quality to being human or essential quality of an act that belies what is of value. By choosing to engage in a particular act or behavior we give value to that act or behavior through our choice. A counselor, for example, who, though tired, sees her last client of the day and consciously chooses to set aside her desire to go home or "tune out" during the session communicates to herself, the client, and by extension all of her clients, that the clinical relationship is important, as is the sharing that will take place between counselor and client. Existentialists deepen the reflection on the relationship between choice and value by proposing that the attitude we take toward choice adds to or detracts from a well-lived human experience. According to Heidegger, the good life is the life that is lived authentically (Macquarrie, 1968) with an appreciation for the responsibility we have toward our freedom and with a sincere desire to do what is right for its own sake. Each choice we make, from the point of view of existentialists, is a participation in the creation of the world—a global statement about what is or is not valuable (Graham, 2004).

Care Ethics

Care ethics as a philosophical approach to understanding moral rightness and wrongness has been developed primarily in the 20th century, although the writings of Scottish philosopher, David Hume (1711–1776), foreshadowed the work of care ethicists. Philosophers who lean toward the ethics of care as a framework for making ethical decisions believe that the highest moral good is found in loving and being loved (cared for) by another person, and not in rationality as deemed by Plato, Aristotle, and many natural law ethicists, such as Aquinas (Sperry, 2007). Hume suggested that rationality is needed to discern the differences between right and wrong, but that sentimentality (emotion), especially sympathy, is required for people to be moved to act on what is deemed good or right (Boss, 1998). Philosopher Nel Noddings (b. 1929) views ethics as an active endeavor and believes that people are at their most human when they are actively engaged in caring for another person. She drew on the work of another well-recognized researcher and ethicist, Carol Gilligan (1993), who proposed that moral development is relational at its core, and not just rational or intellectual.

Landmark 4
CASE EXAMPLE

Terence, a community-based counselor, offers probono services from time to time to clients in need. Recently, he had a second session with a young woman who revealed that she had a history of abuse from a family member and had severed ties with her family due to the trauma. She was living with her fiancé in Terence's town but, apart from her fiancé, had few social support resources. Unexpectedly, Terence received a call from his client's boss who told him that his client was at work saying "odd things" and seemed to be in a state of mania. The boss, who was given Terence's phone number by his client, was concerned for the client's safety and asked him to come to the workplace to aid the client. Knowing that his client had few friends and no family in the area, and, upon learning from the client's boss that her fiancé was out of town, Terence pondered his options in this situation.

1. *How does accurate empathy or emotional astuteness potentially play a role in your understanding of the ethical elements of this clinical situation?*
2. *How does taking an ethic of care approach inform the decision-making process in this instance? Grounded in an ethic of care, what might you recommend that Terence do?*

CONTEMPORARY ETHICS AND THE COUNSELING PROFESSION

In this section, we examine four approaches to ethical study—deontology, teleology, virtue ethics, and principle ethics—that have their roots in the long history of philosophical thought that we briefly described above. Because these approaches are particularly influential in contemporary ethical study and in counseling ethics, we will spend more time considering how they might be applied in clinical practice. As you review this segment of the chapter, we encourage you, again, to consider which of these ethical theories, or balance of theories, best fits your approach to living a good life and practicing as an ethical clinician.

Deontology: Emphasis on Intrinsic Good

Deontology is a division of philosophical study that focuses on issues of morality, duty or obligation, and right action. It is commonly referred to as law ethics. Most often associated with the German philosopher, Immanuel Kant (1724–1804), deontological (or Kantian) ethics first adhere to the assumption that certain acts are, in themselves, either right and good or immoral and wrong (Meara et al., 1996). In describing how one would go about determining the rightness or wrongness of an act, Kantian ethics propose that the moral judgment one makes should be the very judgment that all other people who find themselves in the same circumstances would make. Thus, there is a quality to the deontological ethic that is universal in nature. Moreover, in the Kantian tradition, true moral judgments do not allow for human persons to be treated as a means to an end, but, rather, on principle, reflect the view that people are a good in and of themselves. This second precept for evaluating moral dilemmas points toward the virtue of justice that is both central to Kantian ethics and that gives it an other-oriented characteristic. Moral decision making requires that one considers the needs and the good of others to an equal extent that one thinks of his or her own needs.

To begin imagining how the deontological ethic might be put into practice, think about a counselor who is trying to decide the ethical merit of disclosing personal information to a client. Initially, that counselor would have to consider whether or not colleagues in the same situation also would make the decision to self-disclose. The counselor, additionally, would have to weigh the decision with a balanced consideration for the potential good that might be done for the client with regard to the self-disclosure and the potential good that would result for the counselor herself.

A second important component of deontological ethics has to do with obligation. Once a person has determined what is the morally right thing to do in a given situation that person has a duty to act on what is right. In Kantian ethics, the truly good act is the act that is intended. Although several different people may be faced with the same decision in the same circumstance, and although they may reach the same outcome, it is only the person who purposefully intended for the act to happen who has behaved most ethically. Using our earlier clinical example, once the counselor has decided about the moral rightness or wrongness of self-disclosure in a counseling session, she has an obligation to act on the decision. Moreover, by intending the decision she makes (given that it is one that is universally confirmed), the counselor truly acts ethically and to a greater degree than other clinicians who may have come to the same outcome simply by accident.

Because deontological ethics operate from the perspective that actions can be considered as basically right or wrong, there is a universalism that is communicated in this perspective. Thus, in determining how to make a decision or choose a course of action, this branch of ethical study tends to de-emphasize how situational factors affect outcomes. It is not the circumstances surrounding the decision, nor the consequences of the action taken that determine its ethical or moral quality—it is the act itself that is of most importance. For this reason, the deontological approach to ethics is said to support the idea that there are universal, moral principles (one might even say truths or, in Kant's words, *categorical imperatives*) that can be known, and once known, oblige one to act according to the principle.

If we return to our clinical example, we must consider what it is about self-disclosure that is essential; that is, what makes this act either moral or not in the counseling setting. Because of its emphasis on universalism over context, deontology as a framework for ethical decision making would not be overly interested in questions such as: What is the counselor's self-disclosure about?, How long has the counselor known the client and what is their level of mutual trust?, or What is the counselor's goal in making a personal disclosure?

As it may be becoming clear to you, there are ways in which the deontological approach to ethics is particularly applicable to counseling practice, and there are numerous situations in which counselors (at least in theory) would agree about the intrinsic rightness or wrongness of an act. Some of the most obvious that are outlined in the ACA *Code of Ethics* (2005) are: counselors do not have sexual relationships with their clients (A.5.a); counselors uphold clients' confidentiality (B.1.b, B.1.c.); and counselors disclose to clients the potential benefits and risks of participating in a counseling relationship (A.2.a). Deontological ethics is extremely relevant to these examples because they tend to have a high degree of social confirmability surrounding their moral rightness or wrongness. For instance, most counselors would agree that to initiate, pursue, or allow oneself to succumb to a sexual relationship with a client is a misuse of the power ascribed to the counselor role and a threat to a client's well-being. Very likely, you also can think of many situations from your own day-to-day life in which the concepts of intrinsic rightness or wrongness come into play (e.g., it is immoral to kill another person; it is immoral to cheat on a test; or it is immoral to betray a friend for one's own gain).

On the other hand, critics of a strictly deontological approach to ethics (e.g., Kitchener, 1984; Meara et al., 1996) point out that people often face conflicting obligations to moral judgments. In such instances, deontology may not go far enough in helping people in the decision-making process. Kitchener, who is well known for her work in the area of principle ethics, acknowledged this limitation of deontology through the description of numerous possible scenarios a counselor might face that raise questions as to what action is required. For example, counselors have a responsibility to protect the client's trust in the therapeutic relationship by keeping confidentiality. Yet, they also have a duty not to do harm to others by being complicit in a client's decision to intentionally harm another person. Keeping confidence and doing no harm, Kitchener points out, are both intrinsic goods to which a counselor is obligated. The split obligation seems to point toward a very real limitation of Kantian ethics in the area of its practical application.

Meara and her colleagues (1996), as well as numerous other virtue ethicists (e.g., Cohen & Cohen, 1999; Hill, 2004; Stewart-Sicking, 2008), raise another critique of deontology in that they suggest that it artificially pushes counselors into thinking about ethics primarily from the point of view of the quandary. These authors have suggested that being ethical is more about the personal virtues that guide and direct one's everyday decisions, whether or not those decisions are experienced as challenging dilemmas. Thus, every successive decision the developing counselor makes is important because it is formative of his or her character. Similarly, Betan (1997) pointed out that there is a wide gap between knowing what is the right thing to do and actually acting on it. A quick review of licensing board websites will reveal the names of clinicians who have been sanctioned due to unethical practice, and a browse of research findings related to unethical practice in counseling suggests that clinicians do, indeed, engage in unethical behaviors. Given these circumstances, we might say that virtue ethicists are concerned that in the branch of philosophy known as deontology, the person can too easily get lost inside of the problem.

Landmark 5
CASE EXAMPLE

Michelle is a counselor who runs her own private practice. For the past year, she has been counseling a woman whose daughter was killed in an automobile accident when a teen driver ran a stop sign while texting in the car. The client was devastated by her daughter's death and has been using counseling as a support network during her grieving process. In the most recent session, the client told Michelle that she has started to think about ways to turn her suffering into meaning and wants to write a book about the hazards of texting while driving and about her own story of loss and recovery. The client then tells Michelle that she would like her to co-author the book because of her expertise as a counselor and her understanding of the grief process. The client does not intend to terminate counseling at this time.

As you think about the counselor's options in this case, use the following questions, which reflect a deontological approach to determining ethical behavior:

1. *What would other people in Michelle's same situation decide to do if they also faced a similar dilemma?*
2. *In making this decision, how does the counselor consider the balance of needs of all people involved in the decision and its outcome?*
3. *What does the counselor need to do in order not to take any person for granted in this decision?*
4. *What is the counselor's obligation to act in this situation?*

Landmark 6
DEONTOLOGY AND THE ACA *CODE OF ETHICS*

The ACA *Code of Ethics* (2005) outlines both the minimal and aspirational requirements for counselor practice from a legal and ethical standpoint. Remley and Herlihy (2009) described the Code as the document to which licensing boards and ethics review committees will refer when making a determination regarding the ethical quality of a counselor's behavior. One important question review bodies will ask themselves is, What would other similarly educated and experienced counselors do in a similar situation? It becomes strikingly clear, in this instance, how deontological ethics affects judgments about the morality and legality of counselor behavior.

Teleology: Emphasis on Consequences

Teleology, or the study of the "final things," is another major branch of philosophical ethics in the Western tradition and is most closely associated with the writings and work of two figures, Jeremy Bentham (1748–1832) and John Stuart Mill (1806–1873). Teleological ethics, often known as utilitarianism, proposes that an act is not, in itself, moral or immoral. Rather, a moral quality is assigned to an act based on its outcomes. Teleological ethics, thus, is distinguished from deontological ethics in its emphasis on consequences rather than intrinsic moral values and obligations.

Bentham sought to develop an approach to morality that was scientific rather than religious. His ideas about how to determine what is good can be understood, to some extent, as a reaction against organized religions that placed value on suffering and self-sacrifice and, in part, as a response to injustices against his contemporaries who were poor and downtrodden (Boss, 1998). As a member of the hedonistic tradition, Bentham subscribed to the idea that pleasure is a natural good, while pain is a natural evil (Graham, 2004). He believed an act's utility, or usefulness, was based on its ability to bring forth happiness or to prevent pain.

Using his scientific leanings, Bentham proposed a concrete method of identifying an act's utility known as the Hedonistic calculus—a set of pains and pleasures against which an act was measured in order to determine its morality. The more happiness produced by the outcomes of an act, the more Bentham considered it to be good, moral, and worthy of endorsement. Utilitarianism, therefore, contends that something is morally good to the extent that it produces a greater balance of pleasure over pain for the largest number of people.

John Stuart Mill, a student of Bentham, was aware that utilitarianism was unpalatable to many people because it sanctioned actions that most people believed of be wrong simply because they produced pleasure—even if at another's expense. Therefore, Mill proposed that the good life, and the actions that uphold such a life, be evaluated by the quality (rather than just the quantity) of pleasures they produced. He acknowledged that some actions, though they may lead to happiness for some, still can be classified as immoral. In making distinctions between good and immoral acts, Mill contended that actions that produce high-quality pleasures, such as those that come from intellectual pursuits, being empathetic toward others, and maintaining a healthy lifestyle are of greater good than things that lead to low-quality pleasure, such as selfishness or ignorance (Graham, 2004).

Considering how utilitarianism might get applied to a counseling setting, we return to our earlier example about self-disclosure. From a deontological point of view, we determined that a counselor would have to imagine how other counselors also would decide to resolve the dilemma, mentally posit a universal statement about self-disclosure, and then resolve to act according to the obligation. Utilitarianism, however, demands that the counselor think about the potential benefits of self-disclosure: How likely is it that self-disclosure will result in some good for the client rather than harm? How intense will the good effects of self-disclosure be, and are the potentially beneficial effects likely to last over time? Will the self-disclosure in this instance be likely or not to lead to other, future benefits for the client? What decision surrounding self-disclosure will lead to the greatest number of benefits for all who are involved—both client and counselor? The preceding questions all tend to encourage the counselor to think not about the essential qualities of self-disclosure that merit it as a good or an evil, but about the outcomes and the effects of self disclosure for the client.

Landmark 7

UTILITARIANISM AT THE INTERSECTION OF COUNSELING AND DIVERSE SETS OF VALUES

Interestingly, utilitarianism seems to be increasingly influential in the counseling field as clinicians grapple with the intersection of diverse sets of values in counseling. Recent changes in the ACA *Code of Ethics* (2005) reflect a re-visioning of earlier standards of practice in a number of areas that traditionally were interpreted from a deontological point of view. For example, prior to 2005, the code strongly discouraged dual relationships between counselors and their clients because dual relationships were cast as something of an intrinsic wrong. The latest revision of the *Code of Ethics,* however, prompts counselors to consider the *potential benefits* for clients and clinicians of having contact outside of the clinical setting (A.5.d). In asking counselors to think about benefits, the code essentially invites counselors to reflect on the possible outcomes or consequences of their decisions and actions with regard to having limited, multiple relationships with a client—a reflection that is at the heart of utilitarianism.

Landmark 8

CASE EXAMPLE

Chad is a counselor at a community center that serves teenage boys who have a history of delinquency, drug use, and, to some extent, criminal behavior. In order to form an alliance with his male clients, Chad has begun thinking about selectively inviting the boys to accompany him to local diners or parks to play basketball. He hopes that by interacting with the boys outside of the center, the boys will open up to him more than they do when they talk in his office. Another counselor at the center expressed concern that Chad would be overstepping his boundaries and acting in an unprofessional manner. Putting yourself in Chad's position, consider the benefits or costs of engaging in this way with clients by using these questions that reflect a teleological approach to determining ethical behavior:

1. *What are some potential outcomes of Chad's decision to invite the boys to a park or diner?*
2. *How likely is it that escorting and interacting with clients outside of the center will result in some good for those involved rather than harm?*
3. *How intense will the good effects be, and are the potentially beneficial effects of the act likely to last over time?*
4. *Will Chad's clinical decision to interact with the boys outside of the center be likely or not to lead to other, future benefits for those involved?*
5. *What factors surrounding Chad's decision will lead to the greatest number of benefits for all who are involved?*

Virtue Ethics: Emphasis on Being and Character

The field of virtue ethics has a significantly different feel to it than deontological or teleological ethics in that the person takes center stage, while action and behavior are de-emphasized (Hill, 2004; Punzo & Meara, 1993; Stewart-Sicking, 2008). When considering the question of what constitutes the good life and how one makes moral decisions, virtue ethicists are interested in the qualities that comprise an individual's personhood, such as personal desires and goals and developed traits that sensitize one to others' needs (Punzo & Meara, 1993). Personal qualities are important to virtue ethics because they answer the central question of ethical inquiry that concerns virtue ethicists, namely, What *qualities* of the person's character make him or her good? Deontology and teleology seek to answer another question, What is the right thing *to do*? One can see the influence of the question of inquiry on the outcomes for ethics, with deontology and teleology's emphasis on duty, right behavior, and action, and virtue ethics' emphasis on personal characteristics (Rachels, 1993).

The connection between virtuous and ethical behavior is part of ancient Greek thinking, including that of Socrates, Plato, and Aristotle. Aristotle provided one definition of virtues when he suggested that a virtue is a habitual behavior that becomes a trait of one's character (Rachels, 1993). A more contemporary philosopher, Alasdair MacIntrye (1984), used a similar concept of *practices* to propose that virtue emerges from involvement in a variety of interactions and human activities in which a person consistently strives for excellence. Aristotle also drew on the concept of moderation to speak about virtue, suggesting that virtues are the mean between two extreme behaviors. Generosity, for instance is the mean between selfishness and unbounded self-sacrifice.

Because people can and often do develop habitual, destructive character traits, it is important to define more specifically examples of behaviors that are desirable for humans to develop. Some virtues include: benevolence, compassion, civility, dependability, fairness, honesty, justice, loyalty, self-control, and tolerance. Virtues commonly recognized as being central to the work of counselors are: prudence (or thoughtfulness), integrity, respectfulness, and benevolence (Meara et al., 1996). Meara and colleagues (1996) also described the virtuous counselor as:

- Motivated to do good
- Discerning as to ethical elements of clinical situations
- Tolerant of ambiguity.
- Self-aware and desirous of personal and professional development
- Willing to face one's biases
- Open to using knowledge about clients' cultural context in the counseling process

Given virtue ethicists' interest in the personal development of the individual, they tend to look broadly at ethical behavior, not limiting their understanding of ethics, for example, to the dilemma (Punzo & Meara, 1993). Virtue ethicists are concerned with how day-to-day decisions and habits form one's character because they believe a good character will help one to make ethical decisions that reflect the good life. Ultimately, virtue ethicists propose that counselors who are virtuous will be able to draw on their own internal qualities and motivation to do right in all kinds of clinical situations, even those that are not explicitly a dilemma.

Landmark 9

CASE EXAMPLE

Eduardo is a counselor who works at a drug and alcohol rehabilitation center. In a typical day, he has to make countless decisions related to his clinical work and the development of his personal and professional identity. For example, when he arrives in the morning, he finds five voicemail messages awaiting him from clients and family members of clients. He sighs as he thinks about when he will listen to the messages and return the calls. He then turns to his desk and notices a stack of client files from the past several days for which he has not entered notes. He wonders when he will make time for updating his client records. Eduardo then remembers that he is leading a new process therapy group today for a set of clients from the medical profession. This group is highly confidential due to the nature of the clients' medical work, but as he looks at the stack of files that need notes, he considers asking a colleague who is not involved in the group to help make reminder calls to the new members. At midday, Eduardo wanders into the staff lunchroom and overhears a couple of his coworkers remarking with hostility that the newly admitted clients are "so manipulative that it's unbelievable. They're just a bunch of druggies that will never change." Eduardo has also interacted with the new clients and opens his mouth to comment . . . .

If you were in Eduardo's position, what series of decisions might you make as you face a seemingly endless set of choices related to professional practice and personal being?

Virtue ethicists point out that we are faced with countless decisions each day, and the choices we make with regard to the small, seemingly mundane decisions are as important as the choices we make in more critical situations. Although virtue ethics tend not to provide concrete guidelines for action—a critique of virtue ethics made by those who lean toward the use of principle ethics or deontology—this school of philosophical thought suggests that the mannerisms and attitudes we develop as clinicians provide guidance that makes use of human relationships, care, and subjectivity.

Ethical Principles: Emphasis on Standards of Practice

Ethical principles in counseling are the most often referenced point of reflection when clinicians are trying to reason through a clinical dilemma (Kitchener, 1984; Urofsky, Engles, & Engebretson, 2008). The principles on which most ethical behavior is understood to rest were appropriated from Beauchamp and Childress's (1979) work on medical ethics and currently form the backbone for professional counselors' understanding about the minimal standard of practice required of licensed counselors (Corey, Corey, & Callanan, 2011; Remley & Herlihy, 2010). The five ethical principles to which counselors adhere (described here and elsewhere in the text) are:

- Nonmaleficence: the duty to do no harm to clients
- Beneficence: the duty to do something good for clients and to add to their overall welfare
- Autonomy: the duty to protect a client's right to live a free and self-directed life
- Fidelity: the duty to act with faithfulness in the relationship with a client
- Justice: the duty to treat all clients fairly and with the same level of goodwill

As Kitchener (1984) pointed out, drawing on intuition about good and bad is an excellent starting point for a clinician who is trying to make a decision in an ethical quandary. However, intuition does not always help counselors to reason through the many facets of a dilemma. She proposed that ethical principles are, therefore, useful tools to help weigh alternate options and decisions in ambiguous situations. For example, counselors can consider to what extent they are able to uphold (or would have to sacrifice) the basic principles of nonmaleficence, beneficience, autonomy, fidelity, and justice when making a decision of an ethical nature. In themselves, the principles that Kitchener described are equally important to maintaining and adding to client welfare. Thus, a challenge in using the principles as a guide for decision making is that in complex situations, one decision may help a counselor uphold a given principle while forcing him or her to sacrifice another.

Landmark 10

CASE EXAMPLE

Raj is a counselor who has been contracted to work at a large, multifacility long-term residential care center. The center provides housing for and meets the needs of older adults who are mobile and independent, as well as those who demand constant and critical care. Raj meets with older adults who request his counseling services, but he also frequently meets with the family members of residents when their loved one experiences a significant health problem (i.e., a fall, a medical problem, or rapid onset of dementia). Recently, Raj has been reflecting on a recurring struggle he faces in working with his clients and their families at points of crisis intervention. During a crisis, Raj sees family members who often demand to know what he has been talking about in counseling with their loved one. Moreover, the family members often overlook the desires of their loved one and instead ask his advice about the next appropriate level of care if their loved one suffered what

(*continued*)

appears to be a significant health problem. Raj often feels torn by the genuine concern he feels from family members to do good for their loved one and what he sees as his client's right to make her or his own decisions at all points of life.

Considering Raj's situation and his role as counselor:

1. *What ethical principles are at play in his situation?*
2. *What principles do you believe are most critical in this situation to follow?*
3. *What rationale do you give for reasoning through your decision?*

THE MEANING OF PHILOSOPHY TO COUNSELORS

At the beginning of this chapter, we asked you to step back from the ethical codes of our profession in order to take a look at their philosophical underpinnings. Our goal in asking you to engage in this exercise was not to devalue the codes, but, rather, to make two points. First, the codes of ethics that frame the various branches of professional practices (e.g., ACA, American School Counselor Association [ASCA], American Association for Marriage and Family Therapy [AAMFT], Association of Counselor Education and Supervision [ACES], etc.) emerge from schools of philosophical thought about what constitutes good action and what characteristics mark the virtuous person. As a profession, we have translated these broad philosophical questions into more specific inquiries: What are the right things for professional counselors to do?, and What qualities mark the admirable or upstanding clinician? In many regards, the codes provide concise and tangible answers to these two questions. Making reference to the role of personal characteristics (virtues) in ethical decision-making, the ACA *Code of Ethics* (2005, p. 3) states, for example, that "Inherently held values that guide our behaviors or exceed prescribed behaviors are deeply ingrained in the counselor and develop out of personal dedication, rather than the mandatory requirement of an external organization."

Practicing clinicians know, too, that the codes' answers to the above-mentioned philosophical questions are often experienced as incomplete (Corey et al., 2011; Welfel, 2010). Indeed, we might say that the codes' responses to common dilemmas of clinical practice invite as many questions as they answer. Most counselors with some clinical experience can share a story about a situation in which they needed guidance with decision making and found the code of ethics wanting. As Welfel said, the codes are not recipe books for how to make clinical decisions. This brings us to our second point. Counselors' professional interactions with one another, clients, and other key stakeholders in the systems within which they operate must assume responsibility for the day-to-day decisions they face, whether those decisions seem mundane and ordinary or are challenging and not fully addressed by the guidelines of the codes. It is here—the place of assuming one's own ethical autonomy—that one's philosophical leanings become evident. When facing either an ethical quandary or common, day-to-day decisions, for example, a counselor has to consider, first, her or his own value system and practices of living life well.

- Does the counselor, motivated by empathy, usually try to discern what action constitutes the most profound way to care for another (care ethics)?
- Does the counselor usually think it is important to determine the right thing to make in the situation, believing that there is an inherently right decision that can be made (deontology)?
- Does the counselor usually try to consider what will lead to the greatest happiness or benefit for all people involved by taking into account the relevant situational factors (teleology)?
- Does the counselor draw on her own set of habitually created virtues to guide her in decision making (virtue ethics)?
- Does the counselor consider ethical principles of doing good, doing no harm, protecting autonomy, and acting with justice and fairness toward clients (ethical principles)?
- Does the counselor refer to one of the profession's social contracts in the form of the ethical guidelines to offer guidance in decision making (ethical code)?

In practice, it may turn out that it is a balance of ethical perspectives, as well as one's intuition and way of living out relationships that provides the counselor with the most clarity in the area of ethical decision making. Most important, though, is that we counselors neither hide from our responsibility to think critically about our clinical decisions nor (as Hume would remind us) fail to draw on emotional intelligence in the forms of empathy and our subjective knowledge about human relationships in making ethical decisions. The ancient greats and contemporary philosophers, as well as many mentors within our own counseling profession, stand as reminders to us that we ought not take our clinical decisions for granted and that a little reflectivity always enhances our decision-making ability when it comes to the mundane or the dilemma.

SIGNPOSTS FOR FUTURE TREKS

This chapter was not devised to tell you which philosophical approach or approaches best fit the work of professional counselors and, certainly, it only skims the surface in presenting concepts of various schools of philosophical ethics. The concern, however, that we believe should be important to all counselors is: How do the insights of the ancient and contemporary philosophical thinkers factor into day-to-day decision making? With the emphasis in today's clinical environment on how to avoid legal wrong-doing, it is all too easy for clinicians to forget to ask the big questions about themselves, their professional development, and what it means to live the good life. The work and writings of Western, as well as non-Western thinkers, remind us to look critically and broadly at our work. As Aristotle proposed, our daily decisions create in us habits that put us on the path toward or away from living a truly human life. Every decision we make as professionals and personally has merit because it is part of the development of our personhood. To be an ethical helper is to enter into the practice of asking ourselves, What is the good life for ourselves and for our clients? Philosophy holds many insights for how we can answer this question, and reminds us that the personal and professional life are not far apart—rather they are different stages on which we play out our ethical leanings.

INSIGHTS GAINED FROM THE JOURNEY

One of the primary aims of this book is to help you, the reader, to appreciate the importance of taking a positive (i.e., generally a nonlegalistic) approach to ethical applications in clinical practice. We hope to highlight our point of view by inviting you to consider the role of philosophy in ethical decision making. We also hope to foster an appreciation for the ways in which the process of professional identity development interacts with one's ethical perspectives. As counselors and counselor educators, we both can attest to a noticeable transition that we have undergone in the past decades with respect to our relationship to counseling and ethics. Most notably, we both now appreciate more deeply our own responsibility to the ethical decision-making process in a way that we did not as novice counselors. Tangibly, this means that we are able to use our own critical reflections to make ethical judgments; we see ourselves at the center of the ethical decision or judgment. We contrast this current "lived experience" with the early years of our clinical practice during which we blindly (and most often out of fear and uncertainty) turned quickly to the code to tell us what to do! This is not to say that we do not now use the profession's codes of ethics as an important point of reference in challenging situations or that we do not consult with trusted colleagues before taking action in uncertain circumstances. The primary difference, it seems, is that as counselors, we realize we must own our decisions and not take for granted the opportunity that each ordinary and extraordinary decision holds for growth toward wisdom. Experience is a useful teacher and one that played a big part in the transition we are describing. Likewise, the study of philosophy, especially the existentialists, reminds us that we are always in the process of becoming—personally and professionally. We can embrace the opportunities that come our way or let them slip away. We both strive not to let them slip away and encourage you to do the same!

MOVING FORWARD: CASE STUDY AND REFLECTION QUESTIONS

Liselle is a second-year counseling student who is in the last half of her counseling internship at a site that services teen girls and boys who have a history of criminal behavior. Up to this point in her academic career, Liselle has performed well, and according to evaluations from her professors and her site supervisors at her internship placement, Liselle appears to be a good fit for the profession. She is capable of creating rapport with clients, she shows a genuine sense of empathy in her clinical interactions, and she makes the effort to research client issues with which she is unfamiliar.

Unfortunately, Liselle recently received news from her parents that her younger sister was beaten and raped by members of a local gang. Although she survived the attack, Liselle's sister was in critical condition due to severe trauma to the head. The police are considering it as a potential hate crime that was racially motivated. After learning this news, Liselle sought support from her family and friends, and then she shared the information with her internship-site supervisor. The site supervisor inquired about Liselle's emotional, physical, and spiritual well-being, and Liselle admitted that she was having a difficult time "holding it all together." Over the course of the next several weeks, Liselle's supervisor carefully observed Liselle's work, and became increasingly concerned with how she interacted with the clients. Whereas Liselle had formerly interacted in an upbeat, yet challenging and respectful manner with clients, she now seemed constantly lethargic and unresponsive to the teens. Moreover, on several occasions, the supervisor noticed that Liselle was verbally critical of clients in group interactions and judgmental toward them during what seemed like angry outbursts. At their next supervisory meeting, the supervisor decided to bring her concerns to Liselle. After sharing her recent observations, the supervisor told Liselle that she was very concerned that she was potentially operating as an impaired practitioner and recommended that she either reduces her client load or takes a leave of absence from her internship to allow her to be healed from her sister's trauma. Liselle appeared to listen to her supervisor but protested that she did not want to take time off from her internship, telling the supervisor, "I'm almost done with this internship, and I've performed well up to this point." She appeared distraught, even, when she told the supervisor that she had invested a lot of money and time into her program and did not want to jeopardize her investment by taking a leave of absence. Liselle adamantly insisted that she would be capable of not doing harm to any more clients and that she could put her own issues aside during clinical interactions.

REFLECTION QUESTIONS

- *Describe the key ethical issues in this case.*
- *What are the primary ethical dilemmas faced by the counselor and her supervisor?*
- *What decisions might you make to resolve the ethical dilemma's faced by Liselle and her supervisor?*
- *What did you learn from reflecting on this case?*
- *How did your response to the case exemplify a positive approach to ethics?*

REFERENCES

American Counseling Association. (2005). *ACA code of ethics*. Alexandria, VA: Author.

Beauchamp, T. L., & Childress, J. F. (1979). *Principles of bio-medical ethics*. Oxford: Oxford University Press.

Betan, E. (1997). Toward a hermeneutic model of ethical decision making in clinical practice. *Ethics and Behavior*, *7*, 347–365.

Boss, J. A. (1998). *Ethics for life: An interdisciplinary and multicultural introduction*. Mountain View, CA: Mayfield Publishing Company.

Cohen, E. D., & Cohen, G. S. (1999). *The virtuous therapist: Ethical practice of counseling and psychotherapy*. Pacific Grove, CA: Brooks/Cole.
Corey, G., Corey, M., & Callanan, P. (2011). *Issues and ethics in the helping professions* (8th ed). Pacific Grove, CA: Brooks/Cole.
Fox, R. M., & Demarco, J. P. (2002). *Moral reasoning*. Belmont, CA: Wadsworth Group.
Gilligan, C. (1993). *In a different voice: Psychological theory and women's development*. Cambridge, MA: Harvard University Press.
Graham, G. (2004). *Eight theories of ethics*. New York: Routledge.
Gould, J. A., & Mulvaney, R. J. (2007). *Classic philosophical questions* (12th ed.). Upper Saddle River, NJ: Prentice-Hall.
Hill, A. L. (2004). Ethical analysis in counseling: A case for narrative ethics, moral visions, and virtue ethics. *Counseling and Values, 48*, 131–147.
Johnson, O. A. (1999). *Ethics: Selections from classical and contemporary writers*. New York: Harcourt Brace College Publishers.
Jordan, A. E., & Meara, N. M. (1990). Ethics and the professional practice of psychologists: The roles of virtues and principles. *Professional Psychology: Research and Practice, 21*, 107–114.
Kitchener, K. (1984). Intuition, critical evaluation and ethical principles: The foundation for ethical decisions in counseling psychology. *The Counseling Psychologist, 12*, 43–55.
MacIntyre, A. (1984). *After virtue: A study in moral theory* (2nd ed.). Notre Dame, IN: University of Notre Dame Press.
Macquarrie, J. (1968). *Martin Heidegger*. Richmond, VA: John Knox Press.
Meara, N. M., Schmidt, L. D., & Day, J. D. (1996). Principles and virtues: A foundation for ethical decisions, policies, and character. *The Counseling Psychologist, 24*, 4–77.
Punzo, V. A., & Meara, N. M. (1993). The virtues of a psychology of personal morality. *Theoretical and Philosophical Psychology, 13*, 25–39.
Rachels, J. (1993). *The elements of moral philosophy*. New York: McGraw-Hill.
Remley, T., & Herlihy, B. (2010). *Ethical, legal, and professional issues in counseling*. Upper Saddle River, NJ: Prentice-Hall.
Sommers-Flanagan, R., & Sommers-Flanagan, J. (2006). *Becoming an ethical helping professional: Cultural and philosophical foundations*. Hoboken, NJ: John Wiley & Sons.
Sperry, L. (2007). *The ethical and professional practice of counseling and psychotherapy*. Boston: Pearson Education, Inc.
Stewart-Sicking, J. A. (2008). Virtues, values, and the good life: Alasdair MacIntyre's virtue ethics and its implications for counseling. *Counseling and Values, 52*, 156–171.
Swindal, J. C., & Gensler, H. J. (2005). *Anthology of Catholic philosophy*. New York: Rowman & Littlefield Publishers, Inc.
Urofsky, R. I., Engels, D. W., & Engebretson, K. (2008). Kitchener's principle ethics" Implications for counseling practice and research. *Counseling and Values, 53*, 67–78.
Welfel, E. R. (2010). *Ethics in counseling and psychotherapy* (4th ed.). Pacific Grove, CA: Brooks/Cole.

2

An Existential Approach to Understanding Counselor Identity

Jocelyn Gregoire and Christin M. Jungers

THE FORESEEN DESTINATION

The central topic of this chapter is counselor identity, which we explore by using an existential philosophical framework tied closely to the writings of Martin Heidegger. Our hope is that while reading the following text, you will:

- Become familiar with some definitions of counselor identity from the counseling literature.
- Get acquainted with common themes related to counselor identity, such as professional competence, professional community, and professional self.
- Learn about Martin Heidegger's philosophical anthropology of the human person and how it can expand our understanding of counselors' professional identity.
- Be introduced to the idea of professional competence as related to counselors' beliefs and attitudes, knowledge of the profession's history, and professional skill set.
- Learn about the importance of belonging to a professional community and collaborating with other related helping professionals.
- Be able to distinguish between the role of counselor-as-expert and counselor-as-professional.
- Be able to perceive counselor identity as related to the way counselors use their own unique self as the primary way of caring for clients.

GETTING ON THE ROAD

Any profession serious about its survival needs to undertake the essential task of searching to define its own identity. Identity quests often are characterized by moments of confusion, frustration, and ambiguity, as well as by periods of excitement, exhilaration, and insight. The mental health field as a whole cannot be exempted from the identity formation task, especially because it is home to a multiplicity of professions with various training standards, licenses, specialties, and histories. Likewise, mental health practitioners themselves must embrace an individualized meaning of their professional identity.

The need for a well-defined identity is particularly vital for professional counselors because of the considerable overlap that occurs for counselors and their counterparts with regard to the types of clients they see and services they provide (Van Hesteren & Ivey, 1990). Sharing a similar clientele and job tasks with other mental health professionals makes it difficult for many counselors to articulate a clear statement about their professional identity or account for the commonalities and distinctions that characterize counseling and other related helping professions (Cashwell, Kleist, & Scofield, 2009; Gale & Austin, 2003).

Role confusion and power struggles exist, moreover, within the counseling field itself, as evidenced by tension that sometimes has emerged between those supporting a unified counselor identity and those preferring a counselor identity based on area of specialization (Remley & Herlihy, 2010; Sweeney, 1995). For example, career counselors may identify themselves primarily by their specialization and, as a result, embrace an identity focused on career and lifestyle development; addictions counselors, clinical mental health counselors, and rehabilitation counselors may opt to identify themselves by the populations they most serve; while school or college counselors can choose to identify with the setting in which they work (Myers, Sweeney, & White, 2002). The contention between the American Counseling Association (ACA) and the American School Counselor Association (ASCA) as to whether or not counselors working in schools should identify as professional counselors rather than school counselors evidences to the challenges of specialization and professional identity (Mellin, Hunt, & Nichols, 2011). The elusiveness of counselor identity also is not constrained by the boundaries of its professional family unit for, in spite of counseling's nearly 100 years of existence in the United States (Ponton & Duba, 2009), a vast number of the public is still ignorant about who the professional counselor is. This is evidenced by the fact that many consumers, agency directors, school board members, and even our professional mental health counterparts are still asking (Hackney, 2000), *Who really is the professional counselor?*

Of course, the meaning of the professional counselor identity has been pondered for quite some time, and in response to the question posed above, the counseling literature has proposed various answers. One set of answers draws on the ideas that (a) there ought to be a reciprocal interplay between one's personal and professional selves, and (b) the professional self is part of a wider community. For example, some scholars view the incorporation of professional training into personal qualities within the setting of a professional community as attributes of counselor identity (Nugent & Jones, 2009). Similarly, Reisetter, Koreuska, Yexley, Bonds, Nikels, and McHenry (2004) viewed professional identity as the congruent integration of one's professional self (e.g., awareness and knowledge of one's values) with one's professional competence (e.g., skill development that emerges with training, practice, and supervision) within a professional community (e.g., participation in or identification with national, state, regional, or local counseling associations). Finally, Gibson, Dollarhide, and Moss (2010, p. 21) found that contemporary definitions of counselor professional identity revolve around three themes, namely, "self-labeling as a professional, integration of skills and attitudes as a professional, and a perception of context in a professional community." They concluded that professional identity development is both an intrapersonal and interpersonal process.

A second interesting response to the matter of counselor identity surrounds the concept of the therapeutic self. Auxier, Hughes, and Kline (2003) described the therapeutic self as the unique characteristics inherent to counselor identity that set it apart from other professional identities. Specifically, they suggested that, "counselors develop a therapeutic self that consists of a unique personal blend of the developed professional and personal selves" (Auxier et al., 2003, p. 25). The therapeutic self provides counselors with the professional contexts they can use as frames of reference for their counseling roles and decisions. Furthermore, the therapeutic self is the place from which counselors develop attitudes about responsibilities, ethical standards, membership within the profession, and learning styles that support higher levels of cognitive functioning (Auxier et al., 2003).

The above definitions are but a few examples of the many descriptions about professional counselor identity found in the literature. However, we find the themes of these definitions particularly useful to our exploration of counselor identity. The idea that professional identity of counselors comprises a necessary level of *competence*, involvement in a *community of others*, and a personal and professional therapeutic *self* reflects the philosophical framework we will use for our exploration of counselor identity.

Thus, our goal in this chapter is to engage you in the process of thinking about counselor identity—that of the wider professional community, but even more importantly, your own budding professional identity. Just as importantly, we hope that in reading this chapter you will embark on the professional identity formation process from a philosophical stance. In particular, we are appealing to the wisdom of existential phenomenologist, Martin Heidegger, to help us construct meaning around the concept of professional counselor identity.

Heidegger offers a sound philosophical anthropology of the human person, whom he describes as *Dasein* or *being-there* (Heidegger, 1927; Macquarie, 1968). Roughly translated, *Dasein* in the Heideggerian perspective means we are all *being-there-in-the-world-with-others-in-our-own-unique-way* (Macquarie, 1968). As we move through the chapter, we will break down the concept of *Dasein* and use it as a lens through which we can view our professional *Being* in the counseling world. Because this philosophical framework can seem a little overwhelming, we consider it piece-by-piece. First, we will look at what it means to *be-there-in-the-(counseling)-world* with a necessary level of competence. Competence is a broad concept that has multiple interpretations for counselors. Here, we understand counselor competence to refer to our personal attitudes and beliefs, as well as those we have toward our clients; knowledge of the history of our profession; and the skills that most counselors are expected to acquire through training. Next, we will explore the idea that we are always *being-with-others* in the counseling world. For example, the community of others to which we are attached as professionals comprises our own counseling community, other professional mental health and human services communities, and the public we are called to serve. Finally, we believe that *our-own-unique-way-of-being-in-the-(counseling)-world* is made possible through the integration of our professional therapeutic self into a world where we allow the voice of our conscience to express itself and call us to authenticity. The unique way being that each of us as counselors brings to the clinical endeavor will be our final area of exploration. Our aim here is not to encapsulate counselors' professional identity into an airtight or infallible definition that once and for all canonizes our understanding of who we are as counselors; rather, our humble purpose is to join our voices with the many others in our field and, in our own unique way, contribute to the process of making meaning of our professional identity.

EXPLORING THE TERRITORY

BEING-THERE-IN-THE-WORLD

As professional counselors, how are we to understand our *being-in-the-world*, and more precisely, our *being-there-in-the-(counseling)-world?* For Heidegger, the notion of *being-there-in-the-world* transcends a mere spatial concept of being physically planted in a particular place. He proposed that the way in which people are *being-in-the-world* is fundamentally different from the way in which other objects, such as a mountain, a tree, or a river, are in the world. The mountain or tree is, admittedly, located in the world, but neither can truly be understood to participate in its transformation. The human person, however, is in the world differently than all other objects—not merely as a spectator, but as a participant who has a responsibility to care for and positively change the world. Our *being-there* means that we have the ability to shape others and ourselves toward future possibility and to engage the process of becoming (Macquarie, 1968). Therefore, *being-there-in-the-(counseling)-world* does not refer merely to places where counselors work, such as a counseling agency or school. By extension, counselor identity cannot be tied simply to the settings where counselors operate. *Being-there-in-the-(counseling)-world* connotes that we counselors are always located in a world characterized first and foremost by a rich set of relationships with others, such as clients, coworkers, and other helping professionals. Moreover, our counselor identity is tied to these relationships and the responsibility we have to them. Our *being-there-in-the-(counseling)-world* thus calls us to transform others and ourselves toward positive, future possibilities.

Because we are *being-there* in a world where we also seek to be recognized and validated as professionals, we need to gain certain professional competencies in order to participate meaningfully and ethically in our counseling world. To honor our professional identity, we adhere to the right (virtuous) attitudes and beliefs in our dealings with people we encounter in the counseling world (Cohen & Cohen, 1999), possess a body of knowledge about the history and evolution of the counseling profession, and master the necessary skills held by counselors (Arredondo et al., 1996; Collisson, 2000). Let us take some time to examine each of these areas of competence.

Beliefs and Attitudes

Our *being-there-in-the-world* inevitably brings us to encounter other human persons who have ethical traditions, cultural and ethnic worldviews, and personal and professional values and standards both similar to and different from our own.

As counselors desiring to operate ethically, it is imperative that we be open to others' beliefs, values, and worldviews and be willing to examine our own. While we are not called to agree indiscriminately with our clients or support their every choice, we are expected to be open to their worldviews and traditions, as well as respect their autonomy, in order to guide productive conversations that enrich both our clients and ourselves (Fowers & Davidov, 2006). For example, we might not agree with a strictly patriarchal view of the family, but if we are working with clients whose culture values patriarchy, we need to be open to such a cultural worldview in order to be able to help the clients find ways to realize their own-most possibilities (Boss, 1988) within the framework of their beliefs and values. This holds true for every person we encounter in our counseling world.

A disposition of openness can help all those involved in the "human encounter" (Van Kaam, 1966, p. 16) that takes place in counseling to be free to realize their own unique possibilities. The relationship between our openness as counselors and our clients' move toward embracing their innate possibilities for becoming is, at its core, an ethical one. Heidegger reminds us that the good life is one in which we try consistently to be aware of our possibilities and to be responsible to our free nature. As counselors using an existential framework to examine our professional identity, we strive to be mindful of the extent to which our interactions with clients urge them toward their own possibility or get in the way of it (e.g., by our acting on our own conscious or unconscious agenda). The virtue of openness can be developed by the practice of reflection on one's professional work and personal life. Generally, reflectivity promotes increased sensitivity to our own traditions and fine-tunes our professional posture, as well as our ability to help clients cultivate the qualities that will lead them to live the good life.

Landmark 1

CASE EXAMPLE

Sherri, a 40-year-old Caucasian female individual, has been meeting with Charlene, a counselor in private practice in New Orleans, for nearly 2 years. At the recommendation of a friend, Sherri originally approached Charlene because she was feeling depressed but, more importantly, because the phantoms of sexual abuse issues from her childhood were beginning to resurface and haunt her adult life. Sherri reported that for the almost 2 years she was in therapy with Charlene, she made tremendous progress with regard to her issues, but she also commented that she felt trapped in the counseling relationship. Every time Sherri felt she was ready to stand on her own feet, Charlene brought up other issues that they had not explored or that Sherri believed were not related to her original problem in order to keep her coming back for counseling. Whether Charlene was acting this way because she did not want to see a good paying client slip away from her or out of some countertransference reasons still, to this day, is unclear to

(*continued*)

Sherri. However, when Sherri told Charlene that she was finally ending the counseling relationship because she was moving to Los Angeles, Charlene got very upset and tried to persuade Sherri that she would never be able to make it alone in a new place because their work is not over yet.

1. *How has Charlene been a hindrance to Sherri's fulfilling of her possibilities and achieving the good life?*
2. *How could Charlene have been more open to her own possibilities and helped Sherri embrace her innate free nature?*

Knowledge of History

Being in the counseling world as a competent practitioner requires counselors to take stock of their personal beliefs and attitudes related to countless facets of the human experience; it also demands that they know the history of the profession. You may be familiar with Robert Ludlum's novel *The Bourne Identity* (1984) that was made into a movie bearing the same name. Imagine for a moment that you, like Jason Bourne, are suffering from amnesia and have no memory of who you are, where you come from, your very name, or your personal history. For Jason Bourne, gaining knowledge about the history of the organization that made him was the key to understanding and reclaiming his personal and, we might add, professional identity. Similarly, as clinicians *being-in-the-(counseling)-world* our professional identity cannot be understood unless it is considered inside an accounting of how the counseling community was born and grew up. Knowing the historical dimension of the profession means we are (a) in touch with its past, including its founders and major social and political milestones; (b) informed of its present leanings, values, and practices; and (c) invested in its future by being aware of the dreams that the profession collectively has for itself and by dreaming ourselves about who we want to become as counseling professionals.

Looking to the past, we have to wonder, how can counselors possibly know what practices and virtues constitute the good life for clients if they are ignorant of the traditions and evolutionary landmarks of the community that helps define competent professional practice and virtues (Stewart-Sicking, 2008)? Consequently, it is imperative that we examine our history and become familiar with how counselors have understood good and proper or virtuous dealings with the public and with clients (Hackney, 2000). Ethical guidelines and codes are one set of documents that outline in specific terms what constitutes good and appropriate behavior for counselors. Turning our eyes to the past also helps us to be aware of the temporal dimension of our professional and human existence. We are a people, Heidegger (1927) reminds us, with limited time to be alive. The more in touch we become with our temporality, the more we can transcend an everyday, inauthentic, or taken-for-granted existence (Macquarie, 1968). In other words, in the counseling community's evolution as a body of professionals seeking to become more and more accountable to its own-most possibilities in relationship to the public it serves, we are given a chance to see our own evolution and understand that, on an individual level, we are always faced with opportunities to grow in professionalism. This might mean that we embrace a responsibility to help clients balance their own needs with those of others and, ultimately, make choices that lead to a coherent, good life (Stewart-Sicking, 2008). At its most basic level, growing in professionalism demands that we, as professional counselors, are aware of our ethical responsibilities, reflect regularly on our clinical work, and develop daily habits that form us into virtuous therapists.

Knowledge of the history of counseling is the foundation for an enlarged self-understanding of how past experiences (be them positive or negative) are significant in our development as professional counselors. More importantly, knowing the story of one's profession opens the eyes to the possibilities of future becoming. Recall the moment when you were first asked why you wanted to become a counselor. Frequently, the response to this question is, because I want to *help people.* As you started your journey into the counseling world, you may have understood the process of helping others to mean that you showed interest in them as persons, used attentive listening skills, and perhaps felt sympathy toward their plight. However, as you have learned more and more about the history of the profession, including such things as the development of counseling theories and/or the increasingly appreciated role of culture in counseling, has not your initial desire to *help people* become more grounded into new possibilities for how to act in ways that are helpful? In other words, the process of learning about the many facets of the counseling profession's history and development widens our understanding of our own professional identity and brings us in touch with the broad array of possibilities for how to exist and act competently as a counselor.

Landmark 2

KEY EVENTS IN THE SOCIAL, POLITICAL, AND HISTORICAL DEVELOPMENT OF COUNSELING

1890s	Sigmund Freud pioneered theory of psychoanalysis G. Stanley Hall founded the American Psychological Association (APA)
1896	Alfred Binet developed the first intelligence test in France
1900	Ivan Pavlov initiated the first behavioral models of learning
1907	Jesse Davis initiated the first guidance curriculum in public schools in Grand Rapids, Michigan
1908	Frank Parsons, "Father of Guidance," developed first comprehensive approach to vocational guidance Former Yale student, Clifford Beers, hospitalized for schizophrenia, exposed in a book, *A Mind that Found Itself*, the deplorable conditions of mental health institutions and advocated for mental health reforms
1913	Birth of the National Vocational Guidance Association (NVGA) which is considered the first counseling association and forerunner to the ACA
1925	First certification of counselors in New York and Boston in the mid-1920s

(continued)

1940s	Carl Rogers published *Counseling and Psychotherapy* and developed nondirective approach to counseling Division 17 of APA—the Division of Counseling Psychology, formally becomes part of APA
1952	The American Personal and Guidance Association (APGA) replaced NVGA
1961	APGA developed guidelines for Ethical Codes for counselors
1963	Community Mental Health Act was passed, allowing the establishment of community mental health centers nationally
1976	Virginia became the first state to pass a licensure law for counselors
1981	Council for Accreditation of Counseling and Related Programs (CACREP) was founded
1983	National Board of Certified Counselors (NBCC) began certifying counselors at national level APGA became the American Association for Counseling and Development (AACD)
1992	AACD became ACA
1996	ACA held its first world conference in Pittsburgh, PA
2009	California was the 50th and final state to enact legislation granting licensure for counselors
2010	Department of Veterans Affairs recognized licensed professional mental health counselors as eligible for positions and pay formerly restricted to clinical social workers

Landmark 3

"FORCES" IN COUNSELING AND PSYCHOTHERAPY: THEORY DEVELOPMENT

First force—psychodynamic theory

Sigmund Freud pioneered the development of the psychodynamic approaches to therapy that operate from the assumption that past experiences are the source of people's present emotional difficulties and that emphasize the place of unconscious processes in long-term treatment (Seligman & Reichenberg, 2009). Within the psychodynamic circle, it is worthwhile noting the contributions of Alfred Adler, Erik Erikson, Erich Fromm, Karen Horney, Carl Jung, Melanie Klein, Otto Rank, Harry Stack Sullivan, and others.

Second force—behavioral and cognitive-behavioral theory (CBT)

As the field of psychotherapy evolved, behavioral theory emerged with the work of B. F. Skinner. Skinner's behaviorism must be understood as a divergence from psychodynamically oriented therapy. It was a new way of understanding the nature of the human condition that was

(*continued*)

present-focused and interested in observable behavior rather than unseen mental processes (Blocher, 2000). By the 1970s, as counselors gradually opted to embrace a more eclectic approach to psychotherapy, cognitive-behavioral theories made their impact with the work of individuals such as Albert Ellis, Aaron Beck, William Glasser, and Donald Meichenbaum (Seligman & Reichenberg, 2009).

Third force—existential-humanistic theory

Reacting to the deterministic assumption in Freudian psychoanalysis and the mechanistic approach of behaviorism, humanistic psychology (which combines elements of humanism, phenomenology, and existentialism) took the stage (Gelso & Fretz, 2001). While Abraham Maslow, Carl Rogers, and Rollo May remain among the most respected intellectual leaders of the humanistic movement, the contributions of Fritz Perls and the Gestalt approach to therapy should not be undermined.

Forth force—multicultural counseling

By the turn of the 21st century, clinicians began to adopt a more integrated approach to therapy and treatment. They began to embrace a more multicultural-feminist-social justice worldview in their counseling practices and developed new competencies to sharpen their awareness and understanding of gender, culture, age, and other sociopolitical aspects in counseling (Ivey, D'Andrea, Ivey, & Simek-Morgan, 2007).

Skills

As noted previously, Boss (1988, p. 62) sees psychotherapy as being concerned with "freeing individuals to fulfill their own-most possibilities for being with things and with other human beings." Drawing on Boss's understanding of clinical work, we might say that counselors embrace a mission of helping people find the will to live a good life. Standing inside this definition, we are far from the mindset that psychology is the study of pathology or that counseling is a process of fixing what is broken (Stewart-Sicking, 2008). In an effort to distance itself from the medical model approach to mental health, the counseling profession tends to identify with prevention, health, strength, justice, and resilience instead of sheer pathology (ACA, 2005; Kleist & White, 1997). A challenge for all professional counselors revolves around learning how best to turn these values into humane clinical interventions that help clients cultivate the qualities essential to living a good life. In the end, it is imperative that we develop a set of skills inherent to the counseling profession. Why? Consider this. It is not because your local hairdresser works with scissors that you automatically assume you can entrust your new suit or wedding gown to be tailored by him or her. Similarly, it is not because people have a genuine desire to help others that we ought to assume they can skillfully guide a therapeutic conversation, identify core themes of treatment, or recommend treatment plans without the necessary training. As counselors, the skills we need in order to function professionally include the ability to be open to and respectful of others' traditions, listen reflectively and empathically, evaluate and assess typical and atypical behavior, identify problems, issues and strengths, exhibit care in the face of personal pain, create healing relationships, collaborate with clients and colleagues, notice and work through resistance, explore transference and countertransference, and so on. The knowledge and the mastery of these skills, however, should not turn us into counseling robots, but rather should help us become more and more agents of hope, empowerment, strength, and liberation for our clients.

Landmark 4

CASE EXAMPLE

Louis, a counselor educator at a university; Marta, a senior therapist and supervisor at a drug and alcohol facility; and, Larry, a counselor in private practice, were sharing a drink at their 25-year high school reunion. Louis and Marta, who over the years have seen each other several times at the annual conferences of the ACA, were enthusiastically discussing the latest books and articles they had read regarding research and interventions in counseling, the chapters and articles they were working on for publication, the workshops and training they recently attended, the presentations they had given, and the overall need for continuing education. During the conversation, Larry was present but nonparticipant, save some shy nods from time to time. When Marta very courteously tried to bring Larry into the conversation, both she and Louis were shocked to hear what he replied, "Well, folks, as far as I am concerned, as long as you have the heart and necessary disposition to help people, all these workshops, conferences, membership in organizations, continuing education units (CEU) and so on, do not matter. I got my credentials after I graduated 10 years ago with my master's in counseling, I am licensed in my state, and each year I take one of those online courses to secure enough CEUs to keep my license active, and that's it. I need my license in order to be able to get on insurance panels and make enough money to pay my bills and put food on my table. Otherwise, all these conferences and CEU requirements are only a means for some wise guys somewhere to make big bucks on genuine hardworking counselors like me."

While aiming at being as nonjudgmental as possible:

1. *What is your reaction to Larry's response?*
2. *What comment do you have about Larry's ethics based on his response to Marta and Louis?*
3. *Based on what has been discussed so far in this chapter, what do you have to say about the professional identities of Louis, Marta, and Larry?*

BEING-WITH-OTHERS

Heidegger opined that we are not alone in world. We coexist with other human existents without which our own existence would be insignificant (Macquarie, 1968). It is one thing to *be-there-in-the-(counseling)-world* with the right beliefs and attitudes, an informed knowledge of the history and traditions of our professional community, and the appropriate skills to perform our counseling tasks, but our competence would be worthless without the presence of other human beings. And so, in light of Heidegger's view of human existence, how do we understand the professional counselor as *being-there-in-the-(counseling)-world-with-others*? The second theme gleaned from the definitions of counselor professional identity that we discussed earlier, specifically, involvement in a *community of others*, helps us answer this question. In this section, we examine the professional counselor identity by appreciating the importance of counselors' involvement with (a) the intra-professional community, (b) the inter-professional community, and (c) the clients we serve.

Being-With-Others: The Intra-Professional Community

Our counselor identity will remain elusive if we are not *being-with-others* in our own professional community. By forming intra-professional relationships within the counseling community, we interact with fellow professional counselors who share a common training experience and credentials; hold membership in professional counseling organizations, such as the ACA, the American Mental Health Association (AMHCA), ASCA, Chi Sigma Iota (CSI), and the like; and obtain licenses and certification specific to the counseling profession. The view that identity is linked to *being-with-(professional)-others* in our own discipline is underscored by the fact that most definitions about counselor professionalism and identity are rarely given in terms of the service we perform. Rather, the definitions point toward commonalities that bind us with other members of our own professional counseling community (Ponton & Duba, 2009). Like any other distinct profession, counselors are identified by the development of their own mission statement, ethical code, accreditation strategy, competency standards, licensure, certification procedures, and other professional standards (Gladding, 2000). Our *being-with-others* in the intra-professional counseling community also provides us with a platform where knowledge can be shared, educational training is set, and advocacy works are done for the advancement and credibility of our profession (Glosoff, 1996). This very book is itself a testimony to the benefit of *being-in-the-(counseling)-world* with the intra-professional community. The fact of being able to garner the knowledge, talent, and insights of so many professional counselors who have contributed to its creation is a reminder that our vocation as professional counselors does not call us to be heroic lone rangers, but rather beckons us to be fully participant and integrated into our professional community where the sharing of our common roots and destiny can spring into a clearly defined identity.

Landmark 5

OUR MISSION AS PROFESSIONAL COUNSELORS

The Preamble of ACA *Code of Ethics* (2005, p. 3) affirms the mission of the professional counselors thus: "ACA members are dedicated to the enhancement of human development throughout the life span. Association members recognize diversity and embrace a cross-cultural approach in support of the worth, dignity, potential, and uniqueness of people."

Purposes for the code of ethics

ACA (2005) proposed five main purposes for its code of ethics: (a) to clarify the nature of ethical responsibilities, (b) to support the mission of the organization, (c) to establish principles that inform best practice, (d) to assist members in constructing a course of action, and (e) to serve as the basis for processing ethical complaints and inquiries.

Areas of ethical responsibilities

The ACA *Code of Ethics* (2005) provides broad guidelines to help counselors preserve their professional and ethical responsibilities around the following eight areas: (a) the counseling relationship; (b) confidentiality; (c) professional responsibility; (d) relationships with other professionals; (e) evaluation, assessment, and interpretation; (f) teaching, training, and supervision; (g) research and publication; (h) resolving ethical issues.

Being-With-Others: The Inter-Professional Community

Despite our struggle to articulate a unified professional counseling identity, our *being-there-in-the-world-with-others* is not limited only to our intra-professional community, but it also calls for inter-professional collaboration with other related professions (Mellin et al., 2011). Our *being-there-in-the-world* constantly brings us face-to-face with complex, multifaceted, and multidimensional social problems. Each day we are confronted with concerns, such as teenagers dropping out of school, women and men living in poverty, and varieties of individuals living with poor self-image, substance abuse, chronic mental illness, and disability. If we see ourselves as professional counselors trained to be agents of hope, empowerment, strength, and liberation for our clients, we need to acknowledge that we are not God Almighty endowed with the power to address all these issues in isolation. In order to achieve our full potential to effect positive social change, collaboration across numerous professional disciplines (i.e., the inter-professional community) remains the best practice strategy for addressing those complex and critical concerns we mentioned previously (Bemak, 1998; Brown & Lent, 1992; Lopez-Baez & Paylo, 2009). No wonder, then, that in some private practices, mental health agencies, schools, nursing homes, hospices, and hospitals professional counselors rub shoulders with psychologists, psychiatrists, medical practitioners, social workers, law enforcement personnel, judges, clergy, and lawyers in order to help the people entrusted to their care. The combined knowledge and skills of collaborators from multiple disciplines within the inter-professional community put to service for our clients and society as a whole will always yield better results than if we tried to apply only our own talents and resources (Brooks & Gerstein, 1990).

Landmark 6

CASE EXAMPLE

Juan, a 23-year-old devout Christian, came to the United States from Haiti to pursue a degree in business administration. Two months after his arrival in the country, Juan began to experience episodes of severe migraines, accompanied with lightheadedness and occasional blurred vision. Moreover, two or three times a week, he has terrible dreams about accidents, death, and deceased relatives. He called his mother, who advised him to seek the help of a pastor, for she attributed Juan's ailments to evil spirits. His mother believed that some jealous neighbors might have put a curse or cast a spell on him so that he would not succeed in finishing his degree. However, at the recommendation of one of his professors, Juan went to see David, a counselor from the university counseling center. After listening to Juan's story, including the recommendations of his mother, David decided that his client should not believe the superstitions about evil spirits and curses. He internally believed that consulting a pastor for an exorcism would only worsen Juan's situation. Instead, he consulted the *DSM* (in which he had formal training), formulated a diagnosis (which he suspected could be depression based on his initial projection that Juan might be suffering from homesickness), and prescribed a treatment plan that would put Juan back in shape again.

While being as nonjudgmental as possible:

1. *What can you say about David's action with regard to Juan?*
2. *Should you have been in David's place, how do you see your involvement with (a) the intra-professional community and (b) the inter-professional community playing out?*

Being-With-Others: The Clients We Serve

Our *being-there-with-others* refers to our involvement in both our intra-professional and inter-professional communities. However, we need not forget that our vocation as professional counselors calls us to use the competencies that characterize our profession to enter directly into a therapeutic relationship with another human being whose welfare is being entrusted to us. As we dedicate ourselves to therapeutic involvement in the personal life of other human beings, we are responding to some appeal of the *others* (our clients) who are reaching out to tell us that they need us in a very personal way at this phase of their life and development (Van Kaam, 1966). And, because our "being-there in the world, is never a fixed thing, but a light, a disclosedness, which brings all things to light" (Smith, 2010, p. 215), our *being-with-others* (our clients) commissions us to help them find light when they come to us plunged in the darkness of their human suffering by dispatching genuine concern and care (Smith). In essence, what really makes us professional beings is the fact that our vocation is primarily concerned with the direct care of another human person, and not a thing or an object. For example, a mechanic, a computer technician, or even a cabinet-maker all are undoubtedly experts in their respective disciplines. They can repair an automobile, fix a computer, or create a piece of furniture. They might even be said to have acted very professionally toward their clients by being courteous, hospitable, and on time with finishing the job in a neat and irreproachable way. However, the use of their expertise is directed to the things or objects they have been summoned to work on. With regard to us, professional counselors, however, we are not merely *experts* in the specific domains of counseling under which we have been well-trained, but we are primarily *professional beings* endowed with a deep sense of duty to care for and not to cause harm to another human person. In other words, our caring for the *others* (our clients), requires that we be motivated and committed to act for the good of other human persons, to be there when the *others* need our presence in the way that the *others* need it.

As agents of social change, caring in the way that others need it sometimes happens within a one-to-one dynamic between ourselves and our clients (i.e., the therapeutic relationship). However, caring can also be translated into works of advocacy as we intervene with systems and organizations or with other individuals or family members on behalf of our clients. The practice of advocating for clients has been associated with the counselor identity across counseling specialties (Perry & Locke, 1985; Smith, 2000; Vash, 1987; White, Thomas, & Nary, 1997) and since the earliest emergence of the profession (Brooks & Weikel, 1996). Indeed, Frank Parsons, the recognized patron of the counseling profession, is considered as a social and moral advocate to the unemployed and underemployed immigrant youth of his time.

Landmark 7

SOME EXAMPLES OF ADVOCACY WORK

Sometimes, new counselors shape their identity around the somewhat stereotypical image of the counselor welcoming clients to her office and offering them a seat on her couch. The image can project a womb-like atmosphere wherein counselor and client are removed from the rest of the world and from others. In reality, counselors often are called to interface with the inter-professional community and with significant others in the client's life. Consider these examples:

1. *A school counselor notices that one of her 2nd graders is always being pushed and picked on. Instead of simply asking the boy how he feels about the*

(continued)

situation, the counselor talks to the child's parents and organizes a bullying-prevention group.

2. *A community counselor works with teenagers who have past criminal records. He organizes job fairs with local employers and sometimes meets with employers before his clients go for interviews.*
3. *A counselor who works in a hospital regularly meets with older adult patients and their families to discuss the needs of the patient. He makes sure that the older adult patients play an active role in deciding about their follow-up care.*

IN-OUR-OWN-UNIQUE-WAY

We have grounded ourselves in Martin Heidegger's philosophical anthropology and thus far have tried to make sense of our counselor professional identity by observing the following: (a) *being-there-in-the-world* does not mean just being located as counselors somewhere in a private office, school, or agency, but rather, connotes a world characterized by a rich set of relationships and the acquisition of necessary competences and (b) *with-others* means involvement with the intra-professional, as well as the inter-professional communities, and the clients we are called to serve. Building on the third theme that we extrapolated earlier from the definitions of professional identity, namely, *professional self*, let us proceed by examining what we really understand by being there in the counseling world *in-our-own-unique-way*.

Our Professional Self

We situate the notion of selfhood within the framework of Martin Heidegger's philosophy. To exist, according to Heidegger, "is to 'stand-out' as the unique and distinctive being that is always mine and that expresses itself by the personal pronoun 'I'" (Macquarie, 1968, p. 17). We can choose to *stand-out* in the world in an authentic way, by taking total responsibility for the direction of our own life, or exist in an inauthentic way by choosing to let the direction for our life be determined by external factors (Macquarie, 1968). How does that apply to our counselor professional self?

As professional counselors, our *being-there-in-the-(counseling)-world-with-others* is conditioned by patterns imposed on our professional self from outside, and more specifically, from our professional counseling community with its code of ethics, training program, mission statement, and so on; from the expectations of other professional communities with whom we are collaborating; from society in general with its sets of rules and conventions; and from the clients we are called to serve (Lewis & Hatch, 2008). Consequently, our everyday professional existence inevitably has become what Heidegger (1927) would call an inauthentic one, as we diligently abide to the written codes and standards handed down to us by our professional organizations, follow the rules and guidelines determined by state and federal agencies that sanction our practices, and bow to the demands of society's conventions for fear of being out of line or not fitting in. Yet, given all this, we still can either choose our *professional self* or lose it; exist (stand out) as the distinctive beings that we are, or allow our professional self to "be submerged in a kind of anonymous routine manner of life, in which its possibilities are taken over and dictated to us by circumstances or by social pressures" (Macquarie, 1968, p. 14). In brief, we have a choice between living an *authentic* professional existence where our professional self takes possession of its own possibilities, or an *inauthentic* professional existence in which we relinquish or suppress all these possibilities.

As far as we are concerned, we want to believe that, in spite of our seemingly inauthentic professional existence in the counseling world (due to the many conventions to which we might feel obliged to follow), our professional self remains always unique, always ours. We are called to own it and be concerned about it. The call to own our unique, true professional self, our caring professional self, and our real possibilities realizes itself as the professional *conscience,* which is the voice of care urging us for freedom from the impersonal, inauthentic professional self. Macquarie (1968, p. 32) explains that:

> Conscience is the awareness of how it is with oneself. It has the character of a call or a summons, and this is simply the call of the authentic self to the self in its actual absorption in the world or lostness in the "they." We need not suppose that the call comes to one from outside of oneself. The call of conscience can be adequately understood in terms of the complex structure of the human existent himself.

The call from conscience to our authentic professional self is not the voice of the psychoanalytic super-ego policing our behaviors, thoughts, and feelings, nor is it necessarily the voice that urges us to *conventionally abide* to the moral standards or fixed codes of our professional communities and organizations (ACA, AMHCA, ASCA, and the like). Rather, our professional conscience is the voice that summons us to embrace virtue as the style of our professional life that will allow us to pursue our full potentials as professional beings, incline us to make the right decisions, and do the right thing in any given situation. Our professional conscience is the voice that summons us to practice our counseling profession for the sole love of it, rather than personal gain, and to revolutionize and expand its possibilities. While there is no denying that our professional self is inextricably tied to our *being-with-others-in-the-(counseling)-world,* we definitely can revolutionize and expand the possibilities of our counseling profession and, by the same token, reclaim and preserve the uniqueness of our professional self by heeding the voice of our professional conscience which echoes Heidegger's intuition: "moral progress takes place when individuals do follow insights of conscience that have broken free from conventional standards" (Macquarie, 1968, p. 33).

Actually, this book is an attempt to break away from an inauthentic professional existence to a more authentic one. Our purpose is to take a different direction from the negative conventional practices and application of the counseling ethical codes and standards, which can be summed up as "follow the rules in order to avoid trouble," to a more positive, philosophical approach where the uniqueness of the professional self is called to take center stage. From that standpoint, we can, as professional counselors, view relationships with others as authentic solicitude that beckons our professional self to deal with them not merely as experts handling a thing or an object, but as persons who have a responsibility to explore their future possibilities and who are endowed with the freedom to embrace a good life.

Landmark 8

CASE EXAMPLE

Sara is a newly graduated counselor working at a community mental health agency. She has developed her own caseload in the past year and during that time developed good working relationships with a number of clients. One in particular, LaTanya, has been coming to Sara for 8 months to work through self-image issues related to experiences of recurring discrimination in her personal life and work environment. In their last two sessions, Sara confronted LaTanya about her own behaviors that seemed to invite others to see LaTanya as a less thoughtful and intelligent woman than she really was. When LaTanya arrived for her next appointment, she greeted Sara with a smile and told her that although she stubbornly challenged Sara's insights during the last session, she later reflected on these and opened her eyes to Sara's confrontation. Moreover, LaTanya said she was so inspired that she confronted her boss when he made an insensitive comment to her about being "a spineless female wimp." After conveying this experience to Sara, LaTanya reached into her bag and pulled out a beautifully framed picture of an inspiring saying and handed it to Sara, saying, "I want you to have this. It will remind you of how much you helped me and is a sign of my gratitude toward you." Sara felt a twist in her gut as she thought about what to do. Wasn't she supposed not to take gifts from clients, especially ones that looked as expensive as this? What would LaTanya think if she refused the gift?

In light of what you understand by the professional self, how might you deal with the inner struggle Sara faced with regard to abiding to the ethical guidelines of her profession and wanting to show care to her client?

SIGNPOSTS FOR FUTURE TREKS

Looking back on the journey we just completed, we have to concede that our point of entry into the counseling world was quite shaky because it opened us up to the reality that our profession is struggling with an identity crisis. We have seen how, over the years, the counseling literature has made many attempts to come up with a unified understanding of counselor identity. Our purpose in this chapter was to contribute to the work of our colleagues by using an existential phenomenological perspective to lift yet another veil on the meaning of the professional counselor identity. Specifically, we gleaned three themes from current definitions of counselor identity—professional competence, professional community, and professional self—and examined them through Martin Heidegger's philosophical anthropology, which sees human persons as *being-there-in-the-world-with-others-in-our-own-unique-way*.

We would like to submit that our struggle to accurately articulate a unified definition of counselor identity is symptomatic of a deeper crisis that lies at the foundation of the profession itself. Counselors are not in agreement with each other about what counseling really is. They cannot agree on theory, goals, interventions, methods, and measures of effectiveness of counseling, which prompted Carl Rogers to lament in 1965, "The field of psychotherapy is in a mess." Our brief history survey about the different theoretical forces that have punctuated the evolution of the counseling field also evidences to this disagreement or fundamental crisis. By using Martin Heidegger's philosophical anthropology to journey through this chapter, we treasure the hope that our counseling profession will be able to develop a sound philosophical anthropology, that is, a unified understanding of who the human person really is. We believe that the counseling field can learn a lot from philosophy, and once we agree upon a unified philosophical anthropology, we might also come to a unified vision of counseling, its theory, goals, methods, interventions, and even the language that should be used to render it effective. By the same token, we suspect that a shared understanding of the human person also will lead us to a clearer definition of our professional counselor identity. Our hope is that someday we will no longer hear agency directors, board members, or the public ask the question: *Who really is the professional counselor?*

INSIGHTS GAINED FROM THE JOURNEY

After reflecting for a number of years on our own counselor identities, we want to share some of the insights we treasure with regard to our understanding of the professional counselor identity. These can be best introduced through a story, which we call "the restaurant experience."

One evening, we decided to have dinner at a Japanese restaurant and, as we walked in, we were warmly welcomed at the entrance by attractive waitresses dressed as lovely Geishas. These young ladies were beautifully groomed, mild-mannered, and welcoming, which prompted us initially to think of them as very professional. After we were seated, the waitresses shared their knowledge about the different dishes on the menu, the variety of sake available, and the desserts they recommended. During the course of the evening, while pouring our sake or taking our sushi orders, the ladies shared some tidbits about their families, their dreams, and their joys. That night, we left the restaurant saying: "Gee! We had a really genuine encounter today, not merely with 'a waitress,' but with other human beings."

The restaurant experience described briefly here has helped us to understand the depths of the professional counselor identity. When we first pondered this experience, we noticed that our initial impressions about the waitresses' professionalism came from the ways in which they operated at an organic, material, or body level with us. They smiled at us. They bowed. They extended their hands in a gesture of hospitality. Thinking about these waitresses, we realized that as counselors we, too, operate on a similar body or organic level with our clients, in that we welcome them with warm handshakes when they enter our offices. We give them our most affectionate smiles and talk with a soothing voice so as to make them feel comfortable. We dress well and have our offices nicely decorated. Our hope always has been that the initial encounter with our clients will leave the impression that we are professional helpers. Yet, over the years, we wondered if the warmth we expressed toward clients and our sincere desire to help them were really enough to connote the depth of meaning that was tied up with our professional counselor identity. So, we dug a little deeper.

Reflecting again on our memories of the restaurant experience, we noticed that the ladies who served us exhibited competence toward completing the various tasks of their job and interacted with us in ways that went beyond initial impressions and nice smiles. We realized we were struck by this encounter because the waitresses gracefully put into practice the techniques of their training. Not only did they know how to take our orders, but they also were able to make intelligent suggestions with regard to meal choices when we were overwhelmed by the menu. This part of our restaurant experience brought us to think again about our own identity as professional counselors. Continued interactions with clients has shown us that our competence in using the basic counseling skills and getting into clients' lived experiences is essential to rendering proper, professional service to our clients. We have learned to draw on our education and training, individualized theories of counseling, and mastery of therapeutic techniques, such as listening, evaluating, interviewing, identifying problems and issues, collaborating, working with resistance, and exploring transference and countertransference to evidence professionalism to our clients. But, again, with time, we were compelled to ask ourselves, is the material, organic level of encounter or technical competence enough to communicate the depth of our counselor professional identity? Thus, we dug deeper still.

Earlier in this chapter, we saw that to exist (stand out) implies that there is an intrinsic connection, a mutual implication, a reciprocal relationship between human beings and the world, which basically means that there is never a human being without a world and there is never a world without a human being (Murray, 2006). While we could call our waitresses very professional on both the level of the body and the level of technical competence, we finally realized that there was something more important to notice about that restaurant experience. Our encounter with the servers went beyond required acts of kindness (i.e., the initial, social smile) and spoke about the truth of their kind, compassioning selves that made each one of them unique among the others. The waitresses gave us more than a warm welcome or advice about menu. That evening, in sharing their hopes, dreams, and stories of their families, they revealed their humanity and helped us see who they were as persons, not just as "waitresses." In the same way, we have come to believe that counselors stand out in the world as unique professionals when they are able to integrate their professional selves into the organic and functional levels of participation in the reality of the counseling world. By listening to the voice of care calling into the professional conscience to commit ourselves to the appeal of our clients in need of our help, we are able to transcend our impersonal, conventional, and inauthentic professionalism, and embrace virtue that guides us to become authentic professionals invested in our clients' quest to achieve the good life. And so, what has this journey into the counseling world finally taught us about our professional identity? What answer do we give to the question, Who are we as professional counselors? Here it is:

> As professional counselors we virtuously stand out in the counseling world with our own professional community, and in collaboration with other professional communities, as authentic beings guided by a professional conscience that calls us to use our professional competence and our unique self to care for our clients by focusing on

prevention, health, and strength, instead of sheer pathology, and becoming agents of hope, empowerment, strength and liberation for the people we are called to serve.

MOVING FORWARD: CASE STUDY AND REFLECTION QUESTIONS

Roxanne is a 28-year-old Caucasian mother of two children, Shireen, who is 2 years old, and Jordan, 4 years old. Roxanne, who is Presbyterian, is married to Memoud, a Muslim from Pakistan. They are both nurses who work at two different hospitals. Because of their religious differences, they decided when they got married to go through a civil ceremony and forgo the religious wedding. They also decided not to impose their faith traditions on their children in order to allow them to make their own choice about the religion they would follow as adults. Recently, however, Roxanne made an appointment with a local counselor, Ryan, over emerging religious conflicts between herself and her husband. Roxanne confided to Ryan that Memoud, who in the past year underwent a religious conversion that led him to renew his faith, has started insisting that his children embrace Islam. He now believes that because he is the head of the family, the kids must follow his religion and has threatened to take the children to Pakistan if Roxanne does not comply with his demand.

After seeing Roxanne for three sessions, Ryan, recommended that it would be helpful if he could meet with her and Memoud as a couple. At Roxanne's invitation to join her in counseling, Memoud accepted. Then, after three sessions with the couple, Ryan decided it would be best to meet with them as a couple weekly and individually every other week in order to help them with some of their personal issues related to the presenting problem. During one of the individual sessions, Roxanne revealed to Ryan that she had arranged with her pastor to have both of her children secretly baptized in the Presbyterian church the following Sunday, and she asked him not to let her husband know. Meanwhile, Memoud similarly confessed to Ryan that on Friday of that same week, he intended to take his little boy, Jordan, to the mosque and have him initiated into the Muslim religion. He was adamant that his wife not know about his intentions. With all this information at his disposal, Ryan began to ponder, what might be in the best interest of his clients and what his decision might communicate to his clients about his professional identity.

REFLECTION QUESTIONS

- *Describe all of the key ethical issues in this case.*
- *What are the primary ethical dilemmas facing Ryan with regard to his professional identity?*
- *If you were in Ryan's position, what decisions might you make to resolve the ethical dilemmas you identified above in such a way as to be true to your professional identity?*
- *What did you learn from reflecting on this case?*
- *How did your response to the case exemplify a positive philosophical approach to ethics and to professional identity?*

REFERENCES

American Counseling Association (ACA). (2005). *ACA code of ethics*. Alexandria, VA: Author.

Arredondo, P., Toporek, R., Brown, S. P., Jones, J., Locke, D. C, & Sanchez, J. et al. (1996). Operationalization of the multicultural counseling competencies. *Journal of Multicultural Counseling and Development, 24*, 42–78.

Auxier, C. R., Hughes, F. R., & Kline, W. B. (2003). Identity development in counselors-in-training. *Counselor Education and Development, 43*, 25–38.

Bemak, F. (1998). Interdisciplinary collaboration for social change: Redefining the counseling profession. In C. Lee, & G. Walz (Eds.), *Social action: A mandate for counselors*. Alexandria, VA: American Counseling Association.

Blocher, D. H. (2000). *The evolution of counseling psychology*. New York, NY: Springer Publishing Company.

Boss, M. (1988). Recent considerations in Daseinsanalysis. *Humanistic Psychologist, 16*, 58–74.

Brooks, D. K., & Gerstein, L. H. (1990). Interprofessional collaboration: Or shooting yourself in the foot only feels good when you stop. *Journal of Counseling & Development, 68*, 477–484.

Brooks, D. K., & Weikel, W. J. (1996). Mental health counseling: The first twenty years. In W. J. Weikel, & A. J. Palmo (Eds.), *Foundations of mental health counseling* (pp. 5–29). Springfield, IL: Charles C. Thomas Publisher.

Brown, S. D., & Lent, R. W. (Eds.). (1992). *Handbook of counseling psychology*. New York: Wiley.

Cashwell, C. S., Kleist, D., & Scofield, T. (2009). A call for professional unity. *Counseling Today, 52*, 60–61.

Cohen, E. D., & Cohen, G. S. (1999). *The virtuous counselor: Ethical practice of counseling and psychotherapy*. Belmont, CA: Wadsworth Publishing Company.

Collisson, B. B. (2000). The counselor's professional identity. In H. Hackney (Ed.), *Practice issues for the beginning counselor*. Needham Heights, MA: Allyn & Bacon.

Fowers, B. J., & Davidov, B. J. (2006). The virtue of multiculturalism: Personal transformation, character, and openness to the other. *American Psychologist, 61*, 581–594.

Gale, A. U., & Austin, B. D. (2003). Professionalism's challenges to professional counselors' collective identity. *Journal of Counseling & Development, 81*, 3–10.

Gelso, C. J., & Fretz, B. R. (2001). *Counseling psychology*. (2nd ed.). Fort Worth, TX: Harcourt College Publishers.

Gibson, D. M., Dollarhide, C. T., & Moss, J. M. (2010). Professional identity development: A grounded theory of transformational tasks of new counselors. *Counselor Education and Supervision 50*, 21–37.

Gladding, S. T. (2000). History and philosophy of professional counseling. In H. Hackney (Ed.), *Practice issues for the beginning counselor*. Needham Heights, MA: Allyn & Bacon.

Glosoff, H. L. (1996). Counselor licensure laws: The role of the American Counseling Association. In J. W. Bloom (Ed.), *Credentialing professional counselors for the 21st century* (pp. 3–4). Greensboro, NC: ERIC/CASS.

Hackney, H. (2000). *Practice issues for the beginning counselor*. Needham Heights, MA: Allyn &Bacon.

Heidegger, M. (1927). *Sein und Zeit. Being and Time*. J. Macquarie, & E. S. Robinson, trans. (1962). New York, NY: Harper.

Ivey, A. E., D'Andrea, M., Ivey, M. B., & Simek-Morgan, L. (2007). *Theories of counseling and psychotherapy: A multicultural perspective* (5th Ed.). Boston, MA: Allyn & Bacon.

Kleist, D. M., & White, L. J. (1997). The values of counseling: A disparity between a philosophy of prevention in counseling and counselor practice and training. *Counseling and Values, 41*, 128–140.

Lewis, R. E., & Hatch, T. (2008). Cultivating strengths-based professional identities. *Professional School Counseling, 12*, 115–118.

Lopez-Baez, S. I., & Paylo, M. J. (2009). Social justice advocacy: Community collaboration and systems advocacy. *Journal of Counseling & Development, 87*, 276–283.

Ludlum, R. (1984). *The Bourne identity.* New York, NJ: Bantam Books.

Macquarie, J. (1968). *Martin Heidegger.* Richmond, VA: John Knox Press.

Mellin, E. A., Hunt, B., & Nichols, L. M. (2011). Counselor professional identity findings and implications for counseling and interprofessional collaboration. *Journal of Counseling and Development, 89*(2), 140–147.

Murray, E. L. (2006). *Imaginative thinking and human existence.* Pittsburgh: Duquesne University Press.

Myers, J. E., Sweeney, T. J., & White, V. E. (2002). Advocacy for counseling and counselors: A professional imperative. *Journal of Counseling & Development, 80*, 394–402.

Nugent, F. A., & Jones, K. D. (2009). *Introduction to the profession of counseling* (15th ed.). Upper Saddle River, NJ: Pearson.

Perry, J. L., & Locke, D. C. (1985). Career development of Black men: Implications for school guidance services. *Journal of Multicultural Counseling and Development, 13*, 106–111.

Ponton, R. F., & Duba, D. J. (2009). The ACA Code of Ethics: Articulating counseling's professional covenant. *Journal of Counseling & Development, 87*, 117–121.

Reisetter, M., Koreuska, J. S., Yexley, M., Bonds, D., Nikels, H., & McHenry, W. (2004). Counselor educators and qualitative research: Affirming a research identity. *Counselor Education and Supervision, 44*, 2–16.

Remley, T., & Herlihy, B. (2010). *Ethical, legal, and professional issues in counseling.* (3rd ed). Upper Saddle River, NJ: Prentice-Hall.

Seligman, L. W., & Reichenberg, L. W. (2009). *Theories of counseling and psychotherapy: Systems, strategies, and skills* (3rd ed.). Upper Saddle River, NJ: Prentice-Hall.

Smith, D. L. (2010). From passive psyche to dynamic dasein. *The Humanistic Psychologist, 38*, 203–220.

Smith, H. B. (2000). Counselor advocacy: Promoting the profession. In H. Hackney (Ed.), *Practice issues for the beginning counselor.* Needham Heights, MA: Allyn & Bacon.

Stewart-Sicking, J. A. (2008). Virtues, values, and the good life: Alasdair MacIntyre's virtue ethics and its implications for counseling. *Counseling and Values, 52*, 156–171.

Sweeney, T. J. (1995). Accreditation, credentialing, professionalization: The role of specialties. *Journal of Counseling & Development, 74*, 117–125.

Van Hesteren, F., & Ivey, A. E. (1990). Counseling and development: Toward a new identity for a profession in transition. *Journal of Counseling & Development, 68*, 524–528.

Van Kaam, A. (1966). *The art of existential counseling. A new perspective in psychotherapy.* Denville, NJ: Dimension Book, Inc.

Vash, C. (1987). Fighting another's battles: When is it helpful? Professional? Ethical? *Journal of Applied Rehabilitation Counseling, 18*, 15–16.

White, G., Thomas, R., & Nary, D. (1997). An empirical analysis of the effects of a self-administered advocacy letter training program. *Rehabilitation Counseling Bulletin, 41*, 74–87.

3

FRAMEWORKS AND MODELS IN ETHICAL DECISION MAKING

Cristina I. Kumpf

THE FORESEEN DESTINATION

After reading this chapter, students will be able to:

- Understand the basic tenets of ethical behavior.
- Integrate prior understanding with the knowledge acquired in this chapter.
- Use the moral principles to conceptualize an ethical dilemma.
- Come to see themselves as growing professionals who uphold ethical behavior.
- Identify an ethical dilemma within the context of an ethical decision-making model.

GETTING ON THE ROAD

Moments after receiving a call from the clinical supervisor, a counselor is informed that her 23-year-old female client has committed suicide. The client's parents arrive at the office demanding to meet with all those involved in their daughter's case and be told what she discussed with her counselor. Besieged with grief, the family is ushered into a private space. Before meeting with the family, the counselor and her colleagues talk about the deceased client's ethical and legal rights to confidentiality and her parents' rights to know what might have led to their daughter's death. The counselor assesses the situation, considers moral precepts, reviews ethical guidelines, and finally makes a decision.

In a nearby outpatient facility, a client who was diagnosed with cancer discusses the state of his physical health with his counselor. During the session, the counselor discovers that the client has decided to end all medical treatment and attempt to remedy his cancer only through a spiritual healing process. The counselor processes this decision further with the client, but despite their discussion regarding the effectiveness of chemotherapy and the potential for remission, the client seems convinced of his decision. He acknowledges the risks of discontinuing medical treatment but asserts his belief that the spiritual practices will work. During individual reflection on the case, the counselor experiences a sense of personal and professional helplessness. The counselor's mores conflict with the notion of hastening one's death, which is how she interprets the client's decision. The counselor also recognizes that ethical standards indicate that practitioners have the option of maintaining or breaking clients' confidentiality in such situations. Not certain whose values are of utmost concern in this case, and confused about her ethical responsibility to do no harm as well as to uphold the client's right to privacy, the counselor feels caught in a dilemma. Before the next session, the counselor consults with other trained and experienced clinicians, considers her moral and professional obligations, and makes a decision.

The preceding vignettes are examples of ethical dilemmas. Unlike day-to-day ethical occurrences, such as maintaining confidentiality when discussing cases with other professionals, ethical dilemmas emerge when potential resolutions to a quandary are either incompatible or seem equally viable. As Kitchener (1984, p. 43) described, an ethical dilemma is "a problem for which no course of action seems satisfactory. The dilemma exists because there are good, but contradictory ethical reasons to take conflicting and incompatible courses of action." Reference points, including ethical guidelines (e.g., the American Counseling Association [ACA] *Code of Ethics*, 2005), professional values, and moral precepts are in conflict in an ethical quandary.

In the example of the grieving family, for instance, ethical standards and virtues are potentially in conflict. The ACA *Code of Ethics* (2005) includes a standard (B.3.f) about confidentiality for deceased clients. The code recommends counselors to maintain confidentiality not only for their living clients but also for their *deceased* clients in line with appropriate legal mandates and agency policies. At the same time, however, the code's standard on confidentiality is potentially in conflict with the virtue of respectfulness, which might lead the clinician to want to share what her deceased client disclosed to her, especially if the client's family structure is strongly informed by group values and deemphasizes individual rights. The ethical, professional counselor in this (and all challenging cases) is expected to engage a thoughtful and careful process of decision making. Standards regarding confidentiality must be consulted; yet, it is also important to be mindful and considerate of familial practices and cultural customs, as well as the overarching values of the counseling profession. The resolution of any ethical dilemma is a recursive, multilayered process that requires counselors to have a thorough understanding of common ethical practices and codes of conduct, professional and personal values, moral principles, and one's philosophical approach to ethics, as well as training in one or more ethical decision-making models.

This chapter begins by looking at the foundations of ethical decision making, including moral principles, virtues, and codes of ethics that play into the process of working through ethical quandaries. (See Chapter 1 for additional descriptions of moral principles, virtue ethics, and other philosophical ethics that might inform the decision-making process.) It then explores two decision-making models that guide counselors through ethical dilemmas with a disposition of care, caution, and prudence. While similar in some respects, the models also highlight how differing philosophical leanings get integrated concretely into decision-making processes. Finally, I have included a personal testimony for the purpose of offering insight into the process of forging an ethical professional identity by willingly working through ethical ambiguities.

EXPLORING THE TERRITORY

MORAL PRINCIPLES IN ETHICAL DECISION MAKING

Very often, in trying to work through ethical dilemmas, counselors first turn to ethical codes for guidance on what they should do in the face of a quandary. However, counselors must recognize that ethical codes are themselves grounded in sets of philosophical ideas about what constitutes good and moral behavior for helping professionals. One set of philosophical ideas that have been used to construct and revise counselors' codes of ethics are known as moral principles. It is especially important for counselors to have a clear understanding of the moral principles that are valued by the profession because ethical codes, as extensive as they are, do not address all of the possible ethically ambiguous situations a practitioner might encounter (Bradley & Hendricks, 2008; Forester-Miller & Davis, 1996). In such instances, moral principles have a great deal of merit in helping counselors decipher what is likely to be the most caring, least harmful action. Forester-Miller and Davis (1996, para. 2) stated, "... by exploring [a] dilemma in regards to these [ethical] principles one may come to a better understanding of the conflicting issues." Ultimately, applying ethical principles to an ethical quandary can aid practitioners in designing a response to the dilemma that secures the welfare of both the client and the counselor. Numerous authors (e.g., Corey, Corey, & Callanan, 2011; Kitchener, 1984; Remley & Herlihy, 2010; Sperry, 2007; Welfel, 2010) have endorsed the following moral principles as central to the work of professional counselors.

Nonmaleficence

The principle of nonmaleficence suggests that moral behavior is behavior that does not cause harm to others, especially clients. In upholding this principle, professional counselors responsibly and actively refrain from inflicting intentional harm onto a consumer (Kitchener, 1984). Counselors also avoid activities that have the *potential* to result in harm for clients (Forester-Miller & Davis, 1996; Herlihy & Corey, 1996). Many of the guidelines in the ACA *Code of Ethics* (2005) either subtly or overtly reflect the principle of nonmaleficence. For instance, the Code states of group-level counseling, "in a group setting, counselors take reasonable precautions to protect clients from physical, emotional, or psychological trauma" (ACA, 2005; A.8.b). Elsewhere, the principle is reflected in a restriction on researchers to inflict harm on participants for the purposes of science (ACA, 2005; G.1.d). Although counselors may assume many roles, such as clinician, researcher, instructor, or supervisor, they must always strive to uphold this principle.

Beneficence

A symbiotic relationship exists between the principles of nonmaleficence and beneficence. If a clinician's primary task is to do no harm, then "doing good for other" immediately follows (Kitchener, 1984, p. 49). According to Kitchener, beneficence is a principle that is intricately interwoven into the counseling profession's ideas about highly ethical practice. A foremost aim of the therapeutic process, for example, is to promote human well-being in all its possible forms (Forester-Miller & Davis, 1996; Herlihy & Corey, 1996). When evaluating their work with clients, counselors ought to reflect regularly on the degree to which they have helped promote client change and growth, shown empathy, challenged and confronted where needed, encouraged distressed clients, and so on, as these are all indicators of the extent to which counselors are acting benevolently.

Landmark 1

CASE EXAMPLE

Brenda is a 52-year-old female attending treatment 5 days a week for drug and alcohol concerns. She is in her sixth week of treatment and has shown significant improvement. After a recent call from her insurance company, the client discovers she has exhausted her benefits for the year and is not eligible for other types of aid. The agency can continue to treat Brenda; however, the program will not receive any monetary compensation. Her counselor recommends transferring Brenda to a pro bono service that offers outpatient care 2 days per week. This will save the agency about $5,000 a week and relieve overcrowding in the group. During this discussion, the client tells the counselor that the agency is her only support system, and she does not want to leave. She begins exhibiting signs of severe depression and starts having thoughts of relapse.

1. *What ethical challenges does the counselor face?*
2. *While upholding the principles of beneficence and nonmaleficence, what decision do you believe the counselor should make?*

Autonomy

Autonomy is a moral principle that indicates a value for each person's freedom of choice. This principle, which is at the center of many ethical standards, also reflects broader sociocultural values on individualism. In most instances, counselors act in ways to protect and uphold clients' rights to govern themselves—this means they refrain from making decisions for clients and usually it means that they give advice infrequently and only with caution.

Although the principle of autonomy is meant to protect a person's right to self-directed behavior, it does not at the same time "imply unlimited freedom" (Kitchener, 1984, p. 46). Instead, the circumstances of a situation, as well as a person's ability to make rational decisions, factor into the degree of autonomy he or she is afforded. An absence of judicious behavior that appears likely to result in serious and foreseeable harm either for the client or for another identified person (see ACA, 2005, B.2.a) usually is grounds for a counselor to take actions that are intended to protect the client and other innocent persons; this may entail counselors in overstepping the boundaries of a client's self-governing privileges. For instance, when there are clear indications of serious and foreseeable harm, a counselor may have to assume the responsibility for notifying appropriate persons if a client is emotionally incapacitated or to request involuntary admission into a hospital or treatment facility for a client who is experiencing psychosis. Sovereignty is always to be respected, but it also ought to be assessed in light of a client's potential for harm and with regard to a client's immediate rational abilities.

Landmark 2

CASE EXAMPLE

Margery, a licensed professional counselor, prepares for her 11 o'clock evaluation. Before ushering in the client, Margery combs through the assessment packet and intake information to ensure that a thorough drug and alcohol assessment is conducted. She reviews a brief synopsis on the intake form that states the following:

Charles is a 55-year-old male who reports having concerns regarding alcohol consumption. He states ingesting 12 to 24 beers daily and believes his drinking is causing familial issues. No legal concerns were reported regarding current or past DUIs. Also, he denied a history of drug and alcohol treatment but believes outpatient care can be of benefit to him.

Margery invites Charles into her office. Almost immediately, Margery detects a strong odor of alcohol. Throughout the evaluation, the client has difficulty forming coherent sentences and exhibits short-term memory loss. Although the client denied recent consumption of alcohol, Margery administers an alcohol test. The results indicate intoxication—double the legal limit. Hearing the results, Charles confesses drinking alcohol earlier that morning. At the conclusion of the assessment, Margery conducts a second test to determine if Charles's alcohol levels have decreased. The results still indicate elevated levels of alcohol. In accordance with agency protocol and ethical guidelines, Margery informs the client that he must surrender his car keys and is not permitted to leave the facility unless he is picked up.

1. *How does the principle of autonomy apply in this example?*
2. *How would you feel and what would you think about your decision if you were in Margery's position?*

Justice, Fidelity, and Veracity

The final three principles address the place of equality, sincerity, and trustworthiness in every aspect of the counselor's work. Justice, or fairness, refers to the value counselors place on providing similar services of the same level of quality for all clients

(Corey et al., 2011; Forester-Miller & Davis, 1996; Welfel, 2010). For instance, a man makes an appointment with a local counselor, and when the counselor meets with the man, it becomes clear that the client is greatly distressed. However, the counselor discovers that the man's financial circumstances make it difficult for him to pay for therapy at a typical going rate. Enacting the principle of justice, the counselor may decide to offer pro bono service. Essentially, this principle "... suggest[s] that equal persons have the right to be treated equally, and nonequal persons have a right to be treated differently if the inequality is relevant to the issue in question" (Kitchener, 1984, p. 49).

Honesty and truthfulness characterize the principles of fidelity and veracity. When counselors are faithful to their clients, they place value on the trust that clients develop in them and seek to be good stewards of that trust by not betraying clients or taking advantage of their vulnerability as the less powerful members of the counseling relationship. Fidelity can be maintained by doing things such as establishing commitment to the therapeutic process, developing relevant goals, encouraging progress, and providing adequate and timely referrals (Corey et al., 2011; Forester-Miller & Davis, 1996). Alternatively, the principle of veracity urges counselors to be up front with their clients, especially with regard to, among other things, the costs and benefits of therapy, expectations for the client and counselor roles, use of specialized techniques or approaches, and confidentiality and its limits. Providing for a thorough informed consent process during which the limitations of the counseling process are discussed helps counselors to be truthful with clients.

VIRTUES IN ETHICAL DECISION MAKING

Virtues, like moral principles, are an equally valuable backdrop against which counselors can evaluate best courses of action in an ethical dilemma. These ideals underlie the aspirational elements of codes of ethics, that is, virtues point toward ways of being with clients, colleagues, supervisees, or students that go above and beyond minimal or expected ethical obligations. It is the professional counselor's responsibility to advocate for the welfare of clients by becoming informed about both the minimum *and* aspirational standards of practice. Ultimately, counselors aspire toward ideals and develop virtuous behaviors that enable them to behave altruistically (Cohen & Cohen, 1999; Meara, Schmidt, & Day, 1996).

Meara et al. (1996) suggested that just as there are certain moral principles by which counselors evaluate ethical dilemmas and which frame the profession's ideas about ethical behavior, there are also sets of virtues that characterize upstanding clinicians. Identifying virtues that are specific to oneself or one's personal or professional community is a philosophical process with subjective undertones. Each counselor, for example, likely has her or his own ideas about what character qualities she or he believes to be virtuous; however, according to Meara et al. (1996), there are some universal virtues that mark morally admirable therapists. Virtuous counselors practice discretion; are reasonable and thoughtful with decisions; are sensible, truthful, charitable, and kind; and are mindful and considerate of differences in beliefs, values, and customs. Often, a sincere desire to enact these virtues can help counselors decide between two courses of action that seem equally viable, guiding them toward a decision that upholds an ethical obligation and at the same time preserves or advances the therapeutic relationship.

Beginning with our training and continuing over the course of years of fieldwork, we forge our professional identity. In so doing, we gain clarity about personal propensities that either hinder or enhance the therapeutic process. Hopefully, we strengthen sets of values that aid in our professional development because values lie at the heart of virtue ethics and establish for us the ideals of professional behavior. Time, experience, self-awareness, and training all foster the development of virtuous behavior. Remember, virtues are not necessarily characteristics that are innate to our personalities. They are also skills or habits that can be learned by most.

ETHICAL CODES IN DECISION MAKING

Codes of ethics are probably the most often referenced documents in the ethical decision-making process. Professional counseling organizations, such as the ACA, American School Counselor Association (ASCA), International Association of Marriage and Family Counselors (IAMFC), Association for Specialists in Group Work (ASGW), and Association for Counselor Education and Supervision (ACES) among others, as well as state licensing boards, outline ethical standards for the purpose of guiding professionals toward best practices in community mental health or other settings and in work with specialized populations. Codes of ethics that inform the conduct of professionals in other sectors of the mental health field, such as the *Ethical Principles of Psychologists and Code of Conduct* (American Psychological Association [APA], 2010) and the *Code of Ethics* for social workers (National Association of Social Workers [NASW], 2008) can also be points of reference for counselors. Collectively, these sets of ethical codes help to promote continuity of care, uphold the integrity of the profession, and, like a navigational instrument, provide direction to counselors so that they can steer clear of ethical pitfalls when dilemmas arise.

The preeminent and most recognized set of standards for professional counselors is the ACA *Code of Ethics* (2005). Drawing on the above-mentioned principles and virtues, the code delineates mandatory expectations as well as aspirations for professional conduct. Therefore, all of a counselor's interventions and work are usually best contextualized within the basic tenets of the code. However, the code does not necessarily clarify the decision-making process required to resolve ethical concerns. For this reason, it is crucial that practitioners not only reference the profession's ethical codes, but also apply moral principles and virtues, seek consultation with colleagues, explore other credible sources of information, account for facility protocol, and be competent in using decision-making models.

Codes of ethics are regularly under revision as a way to keep them responsive to social, cultural, and even legal changes. Sometimes, new additions to the code surface because counselors and related helping professionals in large number begin to have similar concerns and questions about timely situations (Kaplan et al., 2009). Members of the 2002 ACA Ethics Task Force (see Kaplan et al., 2009) reviewed noteworthy changes to the 2005 *Code of Ethics*. In brief, the changes are:

- **Confidentiality** (B.2.a; A.9; B.3.f): The language about breaking confidentiality in the face of *clear and imminent danger* is replaced with *serious and foreseeable*

harm to allow for a broader range of situations in which confidentiality may be broken. Counselors are also free to determine whether or not to break confidentiality with terminally ill clients who want to hasten their deaths. Counselors are expected to keep confidentiality for deceased clients.
- **Sexual Relationships** (A.5.a): This standard prohibits sexual relationships with clients for at least 5 (rather than 2) years after termination and outlines a new ban on relationships with clients' family members or friends.
- **Multiple Relationships** (A.5.d; F.3.e.; F.10.f; G.3.d): Rather than prohibit dual relationships, the code permits multiple relationships with clients if the contact outside of therapy is determined to be beneficial to the client.
- **Cultural Issues** (A.10.e; B.1.a.; E.8; F.11.c): Receiving gifts from clients is not strictly prohibited and is best put into cultural context; reporting of suspected child maltreatment is put into cultural context to account for a range of parenting styles; and greater cultural sensitivity is urged for testing and assessment, as well as for counselor training.
- **Diagnosis** (E.5.d): Counselors now are permitted to refrain from diagnosis if the diagnosis will harm the client or others (e.g., be used against the client by another individual or organization).
- **Choosing Clinical Interventions** (C.6.e): Counselors are expected to use techniques and assessments that are empirically tested or theoretically grounded or to disclose to clients that their techniques are not proven or are still being developed.
- **Continuity of Care** (C.2.h): Counselors are required to have a plan in place for how to make referrals or transfer clients to identified practitioners should they leave their practice or become incapable of providing services.
- **Technology** (A.12): Multiple expansions and updates were made as a result of changing technology.

BASICS OF ETHICAL DECISION-MAKING MODELS

Excellence in clinical practice occurs within the cornerstones of moral principles, virtues, the standards outlined by codes of ethics, and other schools of philosophical ethics to which a practitioner might adhere (e.g., existentialism, social constructivism, or feminism). However, as already noted, putting ethics into concrete practice sometimes can be tricky. Applying moral principles to a clinical case may aid in clarifying the presenting issue (Forester-Miller & Davis, 1996) but may not provide an obvious or clear path for action during dilemmas. Indeed, a practitioner who exclusively adheres to one or another moral principle or virtue while resolving a dilemma may seem admirable, but, unbeknownst to the counselor, her actions may be laced with immoralities.

To account for the elusiveness that sometimes accompanies dilemmas, scholars have devised decision-making models. Decision-making models clarify and configure the *process* of coming to and enacting an ethical decision. Nearly all counselors can agree that ethical decision making is a recursive process that cannot be conducted with step-by-step instructions, even though most models propose sets of helpful steps or actions to take prior to and after committing to a decision.

For years, counselors and related helping professionals have recognized the need for organizing comprehensive, empirically based models that can be employed in therapeutic venues. In response, clinicians and researchers have developed an array of decision-making models. Though not all have been philosophically or theoretically grounded or scientifically tested (Cottone & Tarvydas, 2007), a number of them are informed by philosophical underpinnings, uphold theoretical schematics, or endorse pragmatic procedures (Cottone & Claus, 2000). One of the earliest and most often referenced models was outlined by Rest (1984), who grounded his approach in research about cognitive and moral development, especially that of Lawrence Kholberg. Since then, many decision-making models have surfaced. Forester-Miller and Davis (1996) and Corey et al. (2011) both offer models that outline practical steps in decision making that encourage counselors to apply ethical principles and to be reflective. Welfel (2010), making use of Kitchener's (1984) proposition that ethical decision making draws on intuition and critical, informed thinking, offered a model that emphasizes these elements in clinical decision making. Highlighting cultural elements, Garcia, Cartwrigtht, Winston, and Borzuchowska (2003) designed the *Transcultural Integrative Model*. Finally, there are numerous models that draw on the ideas that decision making ought to be less about the counselor's individual psychological or cognitive processes involved in coming to know what is right and more about relationships and social interactions (Cottone & Claus, 2000). These models include Cottone's (2001) social constructivist-based model of decision making and Hill, Glaser, and Harden's (1995) feminist model.

In the remainder of the chapter, I outline and exemplify two models of ethical decision making that can be put to use in most counseling settings. I chose these models because they highlight two differing philosophical points of entry to decision making. The models share many elements but also have their own nuances related to the schools of philosophical ethics upon which they draw. The first, Hill et al.'s (1995) model, draws on a set of feminist philosophical assumptions and values. You will notice that the model both emphasizes and values using the clinical relationship in decision making and that it attends to emotions, intuition, and collaboration. To some extent, the model reflects the philosophy of care ethics (Noddings, 2003). The second model, designed by Welfel (2010), is somewhat more pragmatic and emphasizes the importance of referencing moral principles and codes of ethics, as well as consulting with colleagues. As you familiarize yourself with these models, I invite you to reflect on the extent to which each approach resonates with your own philosophical approach to ethics. You might also find it helpful to review some of the other proposed decision-making models on your own to determine which model best fits your philosophical approach to ethics and counselor practices (see Cottone & Claus, 2000 for an overview of numerous decision-making models).

A FEMINIST MODEL OF ETHICAL DECISION MAKING

Hill and her colleagues (1995) described a feminist model for ethical decision making that involves using logic, intuition, and self-awareness, as well as collaboration with clients. Logic, in this model, refers to a counselor's practice of evaluating dilemmas in such a way as to refine and enhance one's moral assessment of the situation, as has been recommended by Kitchener (1984). Using logic in evaluating dilemmas also means that counselors understand moral principles and ethical guidelines and bring them to bear on the dilemma (Hill et al., 1995). Overall, the evaluative component requires the practitioner to operate using cognitive skills.

The feminist model also sanctions an intuitive component to decision making. According to Hill et al. (1995), conceptualizing events intuitively is an experiential and feelings-oriented process. Being able to identify ethical dilemmas demands that counselors have an instinctual reaction to a situation (often related to past, similar counseling occurrences) that indicates an ethical conflict has surfaced. Counselors sometimes also experience a gut sense for how to respond to the circumstance. In other words, the intuitive level of decision making is an uncensored process that assists the counselor in identifying personal and professional beliefs and assumptions, as well as an individualized interpretation of professional standards (Hill et al., 1995).

In addition, the feminist model highlights the role of self-awareness in the process of making good ethical decisions. Counselors, for instance, must be aware of the power differential between the client and themselves and how it could play a part in who ultimately resolves the ethical crisis. Awareness also refers to counselors' recognition that clinical issues and ethical quandaries emerge within sets of cultural values, which may differ between counselors and their clients (Hill et al., 1995). Knowing how their own cultural viewpoints influence how they see an ethical dilemma is important to counselors. Finally, when appropriate and feasible, counselors are encouraged to consult with clients from the start to the end of the decision-making process. Consultation underscores the collaborative element of the model. Below, I have summarized the steps of the model. The case of Frank and Mary (see Landmarks 3 through 7) is used to highlight how one would work through an ethical dilemma using a feminist-oriented process.

1. Recognize a Problem

The counselor's initial step in decision making is to recognize ethical problems. This may happen because a counselor logically evaluates a situation or because the counselor experiences feelings of discomfort, concern, or uncertainty that indicate a dilemma has surfaced. For example, a clinician may feel worried about a client's safety when he indicates that he has been depressed for weeks and thinks the people in his life would be better off if he were dead. However complicated or benign the situation, the counselor uses his or her feelings as a guide to knowing when a potential dilemma has emerged. Counselors also have to be careful that their feelings do not impede the therapeutic process or cause them to rush to a solution without evaluating the nature of the ethical problem.

Landmark 3

MARY AND FRANK CASE EXAMPLE

Mary, a counselor, is seeing Frank to address his marital frustrations. During the course of therapy, he reveals that he believes his wife is being unfaithful and then speculates about the man with whom he believes she is having an

(continued)

affair. Frank suddenly and angrily begins using strong profanity and racially insensitive language to describe the Hispanic man he thinks his wife is seeing. Nearly shouting, he exclaims, "You must know what I mean. Those people are worthless!" However, unbeknownst to Frank, Mary is married to a man of Mexican descent. Losing focus in the session, Mary says, "I'm not sure I want to spend the rest of our time today discussing your biases and unfounded opinions about Hispanics. How about we start fresh next week?" Frank abruptly stops but appears to be puzzled. He gives a nod and leaves the office. The following week, Frank, who has never missed a session in the past 2 months, fails to show for his appointment.

1. *What do you think is a potential ethical problem in this situation?*
2. *What feelings do you think Mary might be experiencing, and how might these inform her ability to recognize an ethical problem?*

2. Define the Problem

An essential characteristic of problem definition in the feminist model is that, where possible, a collaborative discussion about the potential problem unfolds between the counselor and client (Corey et al., 2011; Hill et al., 1995). The counselor may ask questions to explore the client's conceptualization of the problem. In addition, while identifying the issue, the clinician must consider the client's disposition, familial concerns, others who are involved in the case, facility regulations, codes of conduct, ethical principles, and laws. The clinician remains self-aware by appraising how his or her perceptions and feelings about the situation differ from those of the client and how cultural differences might be at play.

Landmark 4

MARY AND FRANK CASE EXAMPLE CONTINUED

After the missed appointment, Mary contacts Frank, who, with some persuading, agrees to come back at least for one more session. In preparation for the appointment, Mary reflects on what transpired with Frank. Mary questions whether it would have seemed she was condoning Frank's behavior if she had allowed him to continue with his racial profanities. She wonders what her responsibility is to work with clients on recognizing and challenging their stereotypes. She also ponders whether she was experiencing countertransference. Finally, Mary wonders how the level of trust that Frank had in her has been affected.

When Frank arrives for the next session, Mary begins by allowing him to discuss his reluctance to continue in counseling. Frank says he found Mary's behavior unprofessional and reveals that he is part of an extremist group that

(*continued*)

advocates for White supremacy. Furthermore, Frank indicates that based on Mary's response in the last session, he is certain Mary is for integration and he does not believe she can be his therapist. Mary remains attentive and, feeling discomfort, decides to share her own reflections and feelings with Frank. She tells him that she wants the best for him and would like to be able to help him work toward personal growth, but she also does not want to impose her own values upon him. They discuss the role of their values and cultural differences and the impact it is having and could continue to have on the therapeutic alliance.

1. *What potential ethical concerns do you believe are emerging in the case?*
2. *How invested might you be in collaborating with the client on problem definition in this and other cases involving ethical dilemmas?*

3. Developing Solutions

After recognizing and defining an ethical problem(s), the feminist model recommends counselors to brainstorm possible solutions to the quandary. Again, the clinician collaborates as much as possible with the client to generate solutions and conduct a cost-benefit analysis for each option. During this process, no options should necessarily be excluded.

4. Choosing a Solution

In choosing a solution to the dilemma, the clinician integrates the cognitive and emotional aspects of decision making to determine what seems to be the best course of action. Before committing to a decision, Hill et al. (1995, p. 30) recommend that counselors ask any of the following questions:

- Is this solution the best fit both emotionally and rationally?
- Does the solution meet everyone's needs, including the counselor's?
- Is the solution one that the counselor can implement and live with?

Landmark 5

MARY AND FRANK CASE EXAMPLE CONTINUED

As Mary and Frank discuss their values differences, Mary proposes a few alternatives for Frank to consider in light of his uncertainty about moving forward with their work. They talk about the possibility of continuing together and what each of them would need to have happen. They also discuss the possibility of Frank discontinuing treatment with Mary. Mary asks Frank what he thinks might be a feasible solution. Tentatively, Frank deliberates over the choices with Mary and decides that he wants to continue to work with her.

5. Reviewing the Process

Every decision made that aims at resolving an ethical dilemma ought to be carefully reviewed, especially because enacting ethical solutions does not always mean that the dilemma is over or quickly resolved. Hill et al. (1995, p. 30–31) propose the following questions to guide counselors in the assessment process:

- Are my values and personal characteristics influencing the solution choice?
- Would another clinician who has a cultural likeness to the client make a different decision?
- Does the power differential influence the choices being made?
- Would I feel comfortable subjecting the solution to the scrutiny of others?

Together, the therapist and the client discuss the solution to the dilemma. If appropriate and feasible, the client is asked to share his or her response to the choices being made.

Landmark 6

MARY AND FRANK CASE EXAMPLE CONTINUED

Mary remains somewhat unsettled about her work with Frank. She believes she is able to help him but is concerned about their values differences. Mary wonders how her personal beliefs about openness and diversity, as well as her own biases, will affect her ability to work with Frank. During the next session, Mary checks in with Frank about any lingering thoughts and feelings he might have had about their last session and the decision to continue working together. Frank admits he is still unsure about what to expect from Mary in upcoming sessions. He states, "I decided to continue with you because I trust your judgment, but I'm not sure you'll be on my side." Mary explores Frank's waning trust and ways to shore up his trust. They agree to check in from time to time about how their value differences are playing out in the relationship.

Mary and Frank have collaborated and decided to continue treatment. However, if the solution is unsatisfactory for the client or the counselor, they may decide to revisit alternative solutions (e.g., seeking an appropriate referral) until they reach a mutually agreeable outcome.

6. Implementing and Evaluating the Decision

At this point, Hill et al. (1995) propose that the counselor and client execute a solution and observe the outcomes of the decision. In other words, the clinician continues to engage the process by examining the consequences and, if need be, reevaluating the chosen solution. Counselors assess decisions and their own responses to them by considering whether or not they have acted within their best professional capacities and whether or not the decision continues to feel appropriate. Deciding on and implementing a solution to an ethical quandary may actually provide greater clarity to the issue being resolved, which, in turn, might require a redefinition of the ethical problem.

Landmark 7

MARY AND FRANK CASE EXAMPLE CONTINUED

After generating solutions and choosing one (i.e., engaging in regular discussion about their cultural differences in order to maintain the counseling relationship), Mary and Frank continually reassess the fit of the solution to the ethical dilemma. Trust and rapport have been reestablished, however, not without difficulty. Three months have passed and Frank has made significant progress, while Mary has grown professionally.

1. *How would you evaluate the decision to ensure that it is the most efficacious for the client?*

7. Continued Reflection

Hill et al. (1995) suggest that the final step requires counselors to consider how the process evolved and determine how the experience can enhance future understanding. Counselors may want to explore how resolving a current dilemma will factor into similar future quandaries and how they were personally and professionally changed by the experience. As seen, the feminist model emphasizes joint responsibility in coming to an acceptable solution to an identified ethical dilemma. The approach requires counselors to engage with their clients throughout the therapeutic process for the purpose of resolving an ethical dilemma.

A CRITICAL AND EVALUATIVE APPROACH TO DECISION MAKING: WELFEL'S MODEL

Welfel's (2010) model of ethical decision making, like the feminist model, is designed to help counselors navigate ethical dilemmas. However, Welfel's approach places less focus on the intuitive and relational facets of decision making and endorses a critical and evaluative process to decision making. This process involves considering professional standards, investigating the findings and wisdom of scholars, and engaging in a problem-solving approach that is based on ethical principles (Kitchener, 1984, 2000; Welfel, 2010). In addition, it is a step-by-step method of deliberating that must be grounded within the moral practices and virtuous agents sanctioned by the profession (Cohen & Cohen, 1999; Meara et al., 1996). The most recent iteration of Welfel's ethical decision-making model includes the following 10 steps.

1. Develop Ethical Sensitivity

Becoming ethically sensitive does not mean becoming diagnostically focused, theoretically grounded, or proficient in the techniques of a specific therapeutic approach. Although these are all essential in the practice of counseling, they do not necessarily, on their own, foster *ethical* sensitivity. Ethical sensitivity is what Welfel (2010) describes as a counselor's ability to identify blatant and, perhaps more importantly, subtle ethical problems that crop up in daily practice. Sensitivity is a virtue and, as previously mentioned, a virtue is a learned skill. When a 10-year-old child jokes about another child's misfortune, parents will often intervene and teach the importance of showing compassion. Children begin establishing a basic moral compass about what is right and wrong early in life through interactions with adults who can scaffold their moral development. Within the context of counseling, developing ethical sensitivity is a thought-provoking, reflective process in which a counselor practices recognizing how one's values, mores, and life experiences can impede or enhance the therapeutic process, especially when ethical uncertainties arise. It also means that counselors learn to look for ethical dimensions in all of their work, which requires them to be knowledgeable about virtues, ethical principles, standards of practice, and philosophical differences in determining good and ethical behavior from unethical and hurtful action. Consider the case of Rhonda and David (see Landmark 8).

Landmark 8

CASE EXAMPLE

Rhonda is a licensed professional counselor who has been a drug and alcohol therapist for 15 years. Within the recovery community she is recognized as a leader and a walking testament to how a 12-step program can foster change and sobriety. She advocates the 12-step model and requires that all clients attend at least two to three AA or NA meetings per week. One afternoon, prior to group, David (a client who was referred by his employer) arrives early to speak with her regarding his progress in the program. The following exchange occurs:

David: "Rhonda, when do you think I'll be finished? I need to get back to work."

Rhonda (with an edge to her tone): "David, what did I tell you when you started treatment?"

David: "Go to meetings . . . I know . . . but I don't have a way to get there."

Rhonda: "Have you reached out to any of the group members?"

David: "They don't live close to me . . . they probably won't be able to take me."

Rhonda: "Have you asked?"

David: "No, but . . . ."

Rhonda: "Then we're not having this discussion. I told you when you started what you needed to do to get done."

(continued)

David: "I know, but I can't pay my bills and don't have money to buy food. I don't know what to do."

Rhonda (raising her voice) states: "JUST GO TO MEETINGS."

David: "I know but I can't get there."

Rhonda: "JUST GO TO MEETINGS."

David: "Yeah, but I don't have money to feed my pets. What do you expect me to do?"

Rhonda: "HEY LISTEN, I'M NOT HAVING THIS DISCUSSION WITH YOU. GO TO MEETINGS."

David: "You know... YOU DON'T KNOW EVERYTHING. YOU'RE NOT THE ONLY PERSON WHO CAN HELP ME."

Rhonda: "GO TO MEETINGS. END OF DISCUSSION."

She walks away and in passing says to another therapist, "Those marijuana smokers, they just can't get it."

1. *What potential ethical concerns do you notice?*
2. *What information or resources did you use to determine that the ethical concern you pinpointed was valid and present?*
3. *In what areas might Rhonda need to hone her ethical sensitivity?*

2. Clarify Facts, Stakeholders, and Sociocultural Context of the Case

Being ethically sensitive helps counselors to identify potential areas of ethical concern in their counseling interactions. Once such a concern is noticed, Welfel (2010) suggests that counselors then deepen their understanding of the ethical dilemma by searching out all of the facts that are relevant to the situation (e.g., client disclosures, assessments, and the client's perspective on the situation) and making sense of the dilemma in its social and cultural context. If specific information is not available but is necessary for the case, the counselor should take every precaution to obtain the information without violating ethical guidelines (e.g., confidentiality). In addition, all individuals who are likely to be affected by the dilemma and eventual decisions will need to be identified (e.g., family members, psychiatrist, physicians, and guardians). Now, consider the case of Lauren (see Landmarks 9 and 10).

Landmark 9

CAROL AND LAUREN CASE EXAMPLE

Lauren is a 10-year-old who was recommended by school administration to seek counseling to address her bullying behavior. Reportedly, Lauren has started verbal altercations, blurted out obscenities, and posted derogatory Facebook comments about other students. Lauren's parents insist that their daughter is well

(*continued*)

behaved and believe she is the victim and not the perpetrator. Several teachers report observing Lauren's bullying other students, and the school counselor has documentation to prove bulling activity. Due to her parents' schedule, Lauren is at her grandparents' house every weekday evening, where she spends much of her time on Facebook.

When Carol, the counselor, meets Lauren for the first time, she asks her why she believes she is coming to counseling. Lauren responds, "Because of Facebook stuff and school stuff?" Carol asks, "Can you tell me about that?" Lauren says that she frequents Facebook much of the time at her grandparents. She admits to saying some mean things, but quickly insists that it is in response to classmates' cruel remarks. Furthermore, she indicates that she has received much taunting at school and has to respond back with "mean things." Carol asks, "What do other kids tease you about?" Lauren remains silent and eventually says, "I really don't want to talk about that." Moving forward and honoring Lauren's request, Carol asks about what her grandparents think about Facebook. She states, "They don't really care. My grandfather is drunk a lot and is mean if I bother him. So, my grandmother lets me go on the computer. My parents never talk about Papa's drinking." In Carol's efforts to gather additional information about this disclosure, Lauren states, "I don't want to talk about it."

1. *What ethical concerns might you initially have about this case?*
2. *How would you begin clarifying the facts and sociocultural aspects of this case and identifying the stakeholders?*
3. *What are the key pieces of information in the case?*
4. *What do you not know that you believe needs to be further explored?*

3. Define the Central Issues and the Available Options

Once all stakeholders have been identified, Welfel (2010) suggests that the central ethical concerns must be evaluated; there may be several. For example, a counselor may think about whether or not there is a need to breach confidentiality; how to ensure the greatest level of privacy for a client; and what actions may be required of her as a counselor who upholds values such as respect, discretion, honesty, and reflectivity. In trying to define the key ethical concerns, counselors consider what exactly the client has disclosed, the contextual factors, the persons involved in the dilemma, and whether or not the situation necessitates additional investigation from other service agencies (e.g., police, hospital officials, and child welfare personnel). When counselors gain clarity about the ethical issues at hand and can concisely express or classify the type of ethical concerns that are evident, they begin to explore available options. Welfel (2010) recommends that counselors begin brainstorming the range of alternatives without censoring ideas. Later, they can examine how their own personal propensities, beliefs, or attitudes may be influencing the decision-making process or their view of the most viable options (Treppa, 1998).

Landmark 10

CAROL AND LAUREN CASE EXAMPLE CONTINUED

During Carol's second session with Lauren, she asks if there is anything new about the bullying issues or her family life that she would like to share. She says, "My grandparents don't want me seeing you." Further inquiry reveals a startling revelation. Lauren claims that when she was age 7, her 35-year-old aunt, Debra, who is mentally handicapped, stroked her "down there" and then stroked herself. This happened on a few occasions. Lauren eventually told her grandmother, who insisted that she not tell this to her parents. A week after Lauren's disclosure, the grandmother placed Debra in a permanent care facility. Lauren never saw Debra again and never told her parents or another adult until now. She concludes, "My grandmother was afraid of what would happen if I told somebody. Please don't say anything. Will you?"

1. *Given Lauren's recent disclosure, what ethical dilemmas do you now see emerging?*
2. *Based on your assessment of the ethical concerns, what options are at Carol's disposal?*
3. *How do the contextual features of the case influence your conceptualizations and available options?*

4. Refer to the Professional Standards, Law, and Regulations

When counselors are able to clearly identify the ethical issues in an emerging dilemma, Welfel (2010) recommends that they review codes of ethics, laws, and agency policies to determine how they shed light both on the dilemma and on the available options. This step is the beginning of counselors seeking out the wisdom and experience of other counseling professionals as outlined in ethical standards and legal guidelines. Reviewing the *Code of Ethics* (ACA, 2005) may help counselors identify a best practice response to their situation that leaves them with little doubt about what they ought to do. For example, if Lauren, in the above case, told her counselor that her aunt was still living with her grandmother and still touching her inappropriately, the counselor could refer to the code's statements about serious and foreseeable harm, apply this to the dilemma, and determine that the case involves an instance in which confidentiality is limited. Welfel pointed out that, in such instances, this enables the counselor to move directly to implementing a plan and then reflecting on the decision. Considering the circumstances of Lauren's case, what do you believe the ethical code guides the counselor to do? What standards come into play? Are there any legal considerations the counselor would want to be aware of?

5. Reference Relevant Ethics Literature

If a determination about how to address the ethical dilemma is not clear after a review of the appropriate ethical codes and law, Welfel (2010) recommends counselors to broaden their reflections by referencing the body of relevant ethics literature to see how counselors have dealt with similar dilemmas. She points out that reviewing the literature can help counselors further identify the nuances of their case and look at the quandary from an unacknowledged point of view. Consulting ethics literature has the added benefit of normalizing a counselor's concerns and diffusing the emotional tension that can be felt while trying to reason through dilemmas.

6. Examine the Dilemma Using Moral Principles and Theories

Once counselors have collected and reviewed supporting literature, they examine their ethical concerns by using the moral principles (described earlier in this chapter) and virtues that underlie the codes (Welfel, 2010). For instance, in the case of Lauren, the counselor ought to consider under which circumstances a child's disclosure should be kept confidential. What would constitute harm to Lauren in keeping or revealing the disclosure about her aunt's abuse? What is Lauren's ethical right to autonomy? What actions would constitute the greatest good for Lauren? Appraising ethical dilemmas from this perspective can bring structure to and deepen one's understanding of a quandary that may seem insurmountable.

7. Consult With a Supervisor and Other Respected Colleagues

The task of resolving ethical dilemmas can sometimes be marked by uncertainty, frustration, fear, and concern. Moving through this process alone can be trying, leaving a counselor to feel emotionally and intellectually exhausted. Thus, Welfel (2010) proposes that counselors consult with colleagues throughout the process of working through ethical quandaries to reduce their feeling of being alone in the midst of facing ethical ambiguities. Moreover, consultation is a practice counselors should engage in with some regularity. It helps to ensure that their own beliefs, values, and worldviews are not obstructing the decision-making process. If you were consulting with the counselor in Lauren's case, what might you say to the counselor? In addition, if you were in the counselor's position, to whom would you turn for trustworthy and sound input about how to proceed?

8. Personally Deliberate and Come to a Decision

After critically evaluating an ethical dilemma in light of (a) one's intuitive sense of what issues are at the center of the quandary, (b) the codes of ethics and the law, (c) relevant literature, and (d) moral principles, and after consulting trusted supervisors or other professionals, Welfel (2010) considers that counselors must come to their own autonomous decision about what do. During one's individual deliberation, a counselor must weigh all the information, including the feedback received from other professionals; reexamine all possible options and their outcomes; and finally commit to a decision and construct a plan for action. Looking back on your assessment of Lauren's case, what decision do you believe is the best option for Carol and how might she implement the decision?

9. Inform Key Stakeholders About the Decision and Implement the Plan

Once a counselor comes to a decision and creates a plan for carrying it out, he or she must inform the necessary stakeholders and take steps to implement the resolution (Welfel, 2010). People who have a right to know of a counselor's decision typically include the client, the supervisor, any legal, school, or agency officials involved in the case, and possibly family members of clients (especially in the case of minors). It is also a good idea at this point to document the actions that will be taken to implement the decision, as well as other relevant pieces of information, such as the process the counselor used to arrive at his or her decision. Turning once again to the case of Lauren, what details of the case and your decision would you want to report to a supervisor? To the client, Lauren? To Lauren's parents and grandparents? Might you need to seek additional support before moving forward with the plan?

10. Reflect on the Decision

Reflection is not a foreign concept to most who aspire to be effective counselors. Welfel (2010) recommends that counselors conclude the decision-making process with a personal review and assessment of the entire process of dealing with a quandary. The reflection process helps counselors to add to their ethical sensitivity, and bolsters their confidence at working through future ethical quandaries.

SIGNPOSTS FOR FUTURE TREKS

Some of the most trying experiences for counselors involve resolving ethical dilemmas. Applying decision-making models helps counselors to come to thoughtful outcomes when obvious best solutions are elusive. As is evident from our review of the feminist and critical evaluative models, many aspects of good decision making are similar, despite differences models may have with regard to their philosophical assumptions. Both models that we reviewed contain best practices elements, such as becoming aware of ethical problems, naming and identifying elements of a dilemma, referencing the profession's ethical guidelines, seeking the wisdom of others, reflecting on moral principles and virtues, and coming to a decision. The uniqueness in decision-making models often surrounds how the model conceptualizes the problem. Some models see the ethical problem as primarily an issue for the counselor to work through and solve, while others see dilemmas as existing more within the therapeutic relationship and therefore demanding joint action on the part of the counselor and client in determining a resolution. These are philosophical issues that invite your reflection as a budding professional and are sure to influence how you will work through dilemmas. In the meantime, seek out other experienced professional counselors you admire and learn how they apply decision-making models and what assumptions they bring to the table. If I have found anything to be true about resolving ethical dilemmas, it has been that our reliance on each other as professional counselors is essential. Doing so promotes excellence in the profession, enables professional growth, and ensures the safety of those we serve.

In summary, this chapter was designed to inform readers about ethical decision making. The chapter highlighted the most well-recognized frameworks of decision making: ethical principles, virtues, and codes. Attention was given, furthermore, to:

- Defining and exemplifying ethical dilemmas
- Identifying and describing the six moral principles that are foundational to ethical decision making in counseling
- Introducing the place of virtues and virtuous behavior in ethical decision making
- Describing recent changes to the ACA *Code of Ethics*
- Discussing the purpose of decision-making models
- Providing examples of two decision-making models, a feminist and a critical evaluative model

INSIGHTS GAINED FROM THE JOURNEY

Throughout my journey as a licensed counselor, I have discovered that self-reflection is paramount to professional development. Ethical concerns and dilemmas present an opportunity for self-discovery because resolving an ethical issue requires counselors to examine their own values, motives, and preconceptions. In working through dilemmas, practitioners can identify what assets they bring to a situation and what potential impediments can disrupt the decision-making process. Developing self-awareness has prepared me to work through ethical concerns while enabling me to remain sensitive to the suffering and misfortunes of clients.

Although my journey has helped to foster professional competence, I began my voyage after graduate school with minimal experience and limited assurance. My first exposure to ethical concerns was during my work with adolescents. I conducted psychosocial evaluations to determine whether or not drug and alcohol treatment was necessary. It was a fact-finding process that required the clinician meet with the adolescent and guardian separately. In most cases, I would collect urine samples to determine the type and quantity of substance the adolescent was using. Once the facts were clarified and urine samples were collected, I established a diagnosis and made a treatment recommendation.

The diagnostic and recommendation aspect of the evaluative process was often a seamless procedure. Difficulties arose when parents were told that their child required drug and alcohol treatment. Despite being informed of the confidentiality policies, parents would often challenge the recommendation and demand evidence that their child had an issue. This was common in cases where the adolescent was recommended for a drug and alcohol assessment by law enforcement or school officials. Ethically, I was required to maintain the adolescent's confidentiality, which meant that despite the type, amount, or frequency of the adolescent's drug use, parents were not privy to this or drug screen results. In other settings, such as schools and medical facilities, parents maintain the legal right to access their child's records. However, drug and alcohol agencies endorse a policy that protects client privacy, even of minors. Often in difficult cases, I would rely on collegial and supervisory support. With experience, I became familiar with facility policies and how they corresponded to and differed from state law. I also referenced the ACA *Code of Ethics* to ensure I was upholding my professional obligations.

In time, I resolved ethical concerns by establishing a network of practitioners who were experienced and well informed on professional and agency policy, standards, and regulations. I became more skilled in my approach with families and learned how to therapeutically start, conduct, and end sessions. As my confidence and competence increased, self-doubt and anxiety decreased. This has led to advancement in terms of personal and professional growth. Essentially, my experiences during ethically challenging circumstances has strengthened my understanding, broadened my experiences, and expanded my knowledge base.

Counselors change, shape, and improve the quality of life for many. Remain motivated, show compassion, be culturally sensitive, and practice prudence throughout your journey as a counselor. Above all else, be mindful of ethical obligations and professional standards, and maintain connections with a community of professional counselors. We are all here to serve a common goal: to help promote personal growth in others and ourselves. This will make any ethical challenge manageable.

MOVING FORWARD: CASE STUDY AND REFLECTION QUESTIONS

Brad is a licensed counselor who has worked in community agencies for 10 years, mostly around drug and alcohol issues. One morning, Brad arrived at his office to discover he was receiving a new client, Melissa. Soon after therapy group began, Brad noticed that Melissa had 100% hearing loss and required a translator. Although the client agreed to remain in group, she was unable to understand much of the interaction among group members. Melissa's lip-reading abilities, although not helpful in the group setting, allowed her to understand Brad's questions. When he talked to Melissa about her situation, Brad learned that during her intake, she was told she would be afforded a translator during her treatment stay.

Later that afternoon, Brad met with the site supervisor, Michael, to discuss his concerns about Melissa's situation. Michael reviewed the intake information and assessment packet, and, after a quick scan, he indicated he did not have enough information to decide whether or not the facility had a responsibility to provide a translator. Brad indicated that Melissa's entrance into outpatient treatment was contingent upon the agency providing a translator, which she was told would happen. Brad voiced his frustrations regarding the agency's lack of follow-through. He also expressed concern regarding Melissa's addiction, which needed immediate attention and treatment. Michael claimed he would speak to the regional manager to determine an alternative solution. In the meantime, Brad was instructed to continue Melissa's treatment. Frustrated at Michael's lack of urgency, Brad indicated he did not believe it would be appropriate to bill the insurance company for services Melissa was not able to fully receive. Michael dismissed this comment and directed Brad to continue services and billing.

As the days passed, Melissa's engagement in group became minimal. She continued to express her frustrations regarding the agency's lack of follow-through and her inability to understand group discussions. Brad again addressed the site supervisor with urgency, who deferred his concerns to the regional manager, Dan. On the following day, Brad met with Dan, who claimed that the agency policy does not require the company to provide supportive services to the hearing impaired. Dan stated, "It's a costly service and not our responsibility to offer Melissa a translator." Brad disagreed, saying, "This may be true, but she was told she would receive a translator and entered the program with this understanding. We have had her in treatment for a week, billed her insurance company for services that have realistically not been rendered, and asked her to remain patient while the company makes a decision. Also, she appears to be regressing in her recovery and is having difficulty gaining traction in group because she is not able to follow the discussions. What do you suggest I do?" Dan instructed Brad to continue treatment with Melissa or as a last option refer her to an inpatient facility.

Melissa completed her first week in treatment but failed to show the next week. To follow up, Brad phoned Melissa's mother, who verbalized her disappointment in the program and voiced her concerns about Melissa's addiction. She also threatened to seek legal consultation regarding the agency's behavior. Concerned, Brad scheduled a meeting with Melissa and her mother.

REFLECTION QUESTIONS

- *What is the ethical dilemma?*
- *Identify the important aspects of the case as they pertain to ethical behavior and decision making.*
- *What parts of the code of ethics do you use to help reason through the dilemma? How might you apply ethical principles and values in your decision?*
- *What are the potential legal issues at play for the agency, Brad, Michael, and Dan?*
- *How might you have resolved the ethical dilemma presented?*
- *What did you learn personally and professionally in your discussion of this case?*

REFERENCES

American Counseling Association. (2005). *ACA code of ethics*. Alexandria, VA: Author.

American Psychological Association. (2010). *Ethical principles of psychologists and code of conduct*. Washington, DC: Author.

Bradley, L. J., & Hendricks, C. B. (2008). Ethical decision making: Basic issues. *The Family Journal: Counseling and Therapy for Couples and Families, 16*, 261–263.

Cohen, E. D., & Cohen, G. S. (1999). *The virtuous therapist: Ethical practice of counseling and psychotherapy*. Pacific Grove, CA: Brooks/Cole.

Corey, G., Corey, M. S., & Callanan, P. (2011). *Issues & ethics in the helping professions* (8th ed.). Pacific Grove, CA: Thomson Brooks/Cole.

Cottone, R. R. (2001). A social constructivism model of ethical decision making in counseling. *Journal of Counseling & Development, 79*, 39–45.

Cottone, R. R., & Claus, R. E. (2000). Ethical decision-making models: A review of literature. *Journal of Counseling & Development, 78*, 275–283.

Cottone, R. R., & Tarvydas, V. M. (2007). *Counseling ethics and decision making* (3rd ed.). Columbus, OH: Pearson Merrill Prentice-Hall.

Forester-Miller, H., & Davis, T. (1996). *A practitioner's guide to ethical decision making*. Retrieved from http://www.counseling.org/Counselors/PractitionersGuide.aspx

Garcia, J. G., Cartwright, B., Winston, S. M., & Borzuchowska, B. (2003). A transcultural integrative model for ethical decision making in counseling. *Journal of Counseling & Development, 78*, 275–283.

Herlihy, B., & Corey, G. (1996). *ACA ethical standards casebook* (5th ed.). Alexandria, VA: American Counseling Association.

Hill, M., Glaser, K., & Harden, J. (1995). A feminist model for ethical decision making. In E. J. Rave, & C. C. Larsen (Eds.), *Ethical decision making in therapy: Feminist perspective* (pp. 18–37). New York: Guilford.

Kaplan, D. M., Kocet, M. M., Cottone, R. R., Glosoff, H. L., Miranti, J. G., & , Moll...Tarvydas, V. M. (2009). New mandates and imperatives in the revised ACA *Code of Ethics. Journal of Counseling & Development, 87*, 241–256.

Kitchener, K. S. (1984). Intuition, critical evaluation and ethical principles: The foundation for ethical decisions in counseling psychology. *The Counseling Psychologist, 12*, 43–55.

Kitchener, K. S. (2000). *Foundations of ethical practice, research and teaching in psychology.* Mahwah, NJ: Lawrence Erlbaum.

Meara, N. M., Schmidt, L. D., & Day, J. D. (1996). Principles and virtues: A foundation for ethical decisions, policies, and character. *The Counseling Psychologist, 24*, 4–77.

National Association of Social Workers. (2008). *Code of ethics*. Washington, DC: Author.

Noddings, N. (2003). *Caring: A feminine approach to ethics & moral education*. Los Angeles, CA: University of California Press.

Remley, T., & Herlihy, B. (2010). *Ethical, legal, and professional issues in counseling*. Upper Saddle River, NJ: Prentice-Hall.

Rest, J. R. (1984). Research on moral development: Implications for training counseling psychologists. *Counseling Psychologist, 12*, 19–29.

Sperry, L. (2007). *The ethical and professional practice of counseling and psychotherapy*. Boston: Pearson Education, Inc.

Treppa, J. A. (1998). A practitioner's guide to ethical decision making. In R. M. Anderson, T. L. Needels, & H. V. Hall (Eds.), *Avoiding ethical misconduct in psychology specialty areas* (pp. 26–41). Springfield, IL: Charles C. Thomas.

Welfel, E. R. (2010). *Ethics in counseling & psychotherapy: Standards, research, & emerging issues* (4th ed.). Belmont, CA: Thomson Brooks/Cole.

Part II

Voyaging Through Best Practices in Counseling Ethics

4

Spiritual, Personal, and Cultural Values in Counseling Ethics

Helena K. Y. Ng

THE FORESEEN DESTINATION

Welcome to this part of your journey where you will examine the topics of spiritual values, personal values, and cultural sensitivity in the context of ethical counseling. As you start this trek, you will be given a compass that I recommend you use, as it will guide you on the ethical voyages you, no doubt, will take in your counseling career. Before familiarizing you with the compass and the rest of the terrain, let us look at what this journey will offer you:

- An opportunity to learn about the LOVE attitude—a disposition consistent with counselors' inherently held values and ethical aspirations.
- Discussion about the importance of spiritual, personal, and cultural values in the context of counseling.
- Help with developing awareness and understanding of one's own spiritual and personal values and cultural sensitivity.
- An invitation to become conscious of one's own biases toward others' values.
- A discussion about intervening skills pertaining to clients' spiritual, personal, and cultural values.

GETTING ON THE ROAD

The American Counseling Association (ACA) *Code of Ethics* (2005, p. 20) defines multicultural or diversity counseling as, "counseling that recognizes diversity and embraces approaches that support the worth, dignity, potential, and uniqueness of individuals within their historical, cultural, economic, political, and psychosocial contexts." Grounded in this definition, counselors who act ethically must appreciate and respect clients' diversities in background and personal attributes. In this chapter, we discuss a set of interrelated values—spiritual, personal, and cultural values—that are woven into the fabric of human existence. We explore these values and examine how they play a role in the dynamic interactions that unfold among counselors, clients, and the important others who participate in our clients' lives. Major goals of the chapter are to facilitate in counselors the development of sensitivity and understanding surrounding this unique set of values and, furthermore, to edge them toward greater competence in using intervening skills that are mindful of people's spiritual, personal, and cultural values.

Values are central to the human experience. They set parameters around the kinds of behaviors and lifestyles that are seen as good and appropriate, and they are rooted in a person's background, life experiences, and learning opportunities. The background that shapes values includes such things as a person's family, education, ethnicity, spirituality, and, as the *Code of Ethics* (2005) reminds us, such broad factors as economic situations and political atmospheres. Life experiences and learning opportunities, gathered as a person interacts with people and other elements of the environment, also form and re-form value sets. Egan (2010) argued that values drive our behaviors as they form the pragmatic criteria on which decision making is based. Knowing that values are of key importance to the human experience, it is essential that counselors approach values in an ethically appropriate manner.

EXPLORING THE TERRITORY

SPIRITUAL, PERSONAL, AND CULTURAL VALUES IN COUNSELING

In the counseling sphere, diversities in clients' backgrounds have the potential to enrich counselors' knowledge and experience. For instance, counselors may be fascinated by clients' accounts of their ethnic traditions. Diversities in clients' experiences also can open counselors to new horizons and broaden their perspectives. However, diversity can breed perplexity if not handled in a careful and ethically sensitive manner. The Preamble of the ACA *Code of Ethics* (2005) suggests members to identify and be familiar with their own cultural uniqueness. Counselors also are responsible for knowing about the differences in culture between themselves and their clients, especially those that may interfere with clinical work or the formation of a healthy therapeutic relationship. In particular, counselors must be conscious of biases that can stem from differences. At the center of the careful manner with which counselors manage their own values, those of their clients, and the differences that may lie within is a counselors' respect for clients' unique spiritual, personal, and cultural values. Counselors must honor rather than judge clients' values and work to learn about the sources of deeply held values. Indeed, understanding clients' values is an important basis that supports counselors' role as agents of change.

By truly caring for our clients, we likely will be motivated to embrace the code's recommendation for cultural sensitivity. I like to think of the process of living as culturally aware counselors as *working from the inside out*. Working from the inside refers to counselors' reflection on their spiritual, personal, and cultural values. Counselors explore and examine these values, as well as their biases toward others' values. Pedersen, Draguns, Lonner, and Trimble (2008) suggested that counselors cultivate their cultural awareness and sensitivity by exploring the impact of their own cultural biases and stereotypical inclinations. For example, a White counselor who is part of the dominant sociocultural group in the United States may need to be sensitive to socially transmitted negative beliefs about minority groups that one may harbor. A counselor who grew up poor may ask herself how her experience of poverty affects how she sees affluent clients. Likewise, counselors who come from middle-class or wealthy families might need to confront their views about the working poor. Working toward the outside refers to counselors' awareness and knowledge of clients' values, worldviews, and preferred behaviors and social structures. We will see later that working toward the outside sometimes demands that counselors engage in multiple forms of research about clients' traditions and heritage, some of which might include reading peer-reviewed material, engaging popular media, or having live experiences. Let us now turn our attention to the compass that helps us hone our inside-out skills.

CULTIVATING THE LOVE ATTITUDE

One of the primary aims of this chapter is to help you cultivate an ethical attitude of *concern*. Using terminology from the discipline of philosophical ethics, we can say that this approach is grounded in care ethics. Care ethics, associated with the work of psychologist, Carol Gilligan, and philosopher, Nel Noddings, propose that morality is understood relationally. The greatest good is expressed when we are compelled to act for others' benefit—when we *care* for them. In my own terminology, I propose that counselors develop the LOVE attitude, which is consistent with counselors' aspirations to operate professionally. The acronym LOVE stands for:

- **L**isten with the eyes and ears of our hearts
- **O**pen our attitude and avoid judging
- **V**alue clients' sharing of experiences
- **E**mpathize as if we were in clients' positions

Notice the attention we place on listening to clients with all our hearts. Freeman (2002, p. 172) contended that "We are disciples of what we pay attention to." Our care and concern for clients have drawn us into the discipleship of clients' well-being. Such discipleship resonates with our genuine longing to live out the essence of LOVE. This love comprises respect, authenticity, and truth. We endeavor to put into practice these key qualities as we cultivate our LOVE attitude. Simple as it may sound, it takes time to learn and nurture this attitude, let alone make it our natural demeanor.

The LOVE attitude prompts our sensitivity to and understanding of clients' spiritual, personal, and cultural values. It facilitates our hearts and minds to attend to clients, pondering their sufferings and learning about their pains. Putting the LOVE attitude into practice also strengthens our skills in exploring with clients the meaning of their human experiences with respect for their spiritual, personal, and cultural values. Most importantly, when we operate under the LOVE attitude, it helps us adhere not only to the mandatory aspects of the counseling ethical codes, but gears us toward practicing with the aspirational element of our ethics in mind. Aspirational ethics is a sophisticated level of ethical practice that directs counselors to center on the welfare of clients and act in the best interests of the entire profession (Cottone & Tarvydas, 2007).

The Preamble of ACA's *Code of Ethics* (2005, p. 4) states that, "Inherently held values that guide our behaviors or exceed prescribed behaviors are deeply ingrained in the counselor and developed out of personal dedication, rather than the mandatory requirement of an external organization." In effect, inherently held values refer to the virtues that lie within us. According to Geyer and Baumeister (2005) virtues invite individuals to practice self-control for the sake of society's interest. Such practice safeguards human beings from falling into immoral traps. In counseling, virtues inspire counselors to practice compassion for the sake of clients' interest. Virtues reveal the persons we are and illuminate the path that allows us to become the persons we desire to be (Cimperman, 2005). Meara (2001, p. 230) stated that "virtues connote habits, traits or qualities of a person that are somewhat stable and that encourage trust and confidence from others." The trust and confidence counselors earn from clients are a testimony to their genuine care for clients, as well as to their practice of virtue ethics. Hill (2004, p. 146) noted that virtue ethics "intentionally provides moral criteria for assessing the ethical qualities of counselor practices." In effect, virtues underscore the aspirational level of being ethical and inspire counselors' best practice.

Best practice in counseling does not just mean that counselors are in compliance with the ethical codes. Best practice entails a deeper level of engagement, the level associated with our aspirations, our genuine care for clients, and the practice of virtuous behaviors. The ACA's *Code of Ethics* is written in aspirational language, which implies ideal counselor behaviors (Hill, 2004). Counselors who follow their genuine desire to make a difference in people's lives operate on a sophistical level of ethical practice. Let us look at a counseling case that offers insights into the impact of the LOVE attitude on ethical practice. Out of respect for and protection of client privacy, fictitious names are used in the case studies, and some details in the vignettes are modified.

Landmark 1

CASE EXAMPLE

Carlos, a veteran counselor, has been seeing Rosa for almost a year. Rosa's values were quite different from those of her partner, Joe. One day, Rosa became angry at Joe because he told a potential buyer of their house about a water-leakage problem in the bathroom, which she did not think needed to be disclosed. As a result, they stopped talking to one another for several days, and Rosa insisted they see her counselor for a couples counseling session. Joe agreed. Two days before the session, Rosa called Carlos and told him that she wanted Joe to apologize. She asked Carlos to make that happen when they came to see him.

Carlos knew that he would not follow Rosa's request; however, he did want to empathize with his client and her partner. During the session, Carlos maintained an open mind and attitude and facilitated Rosa and Joe to talk about their perspectives and feelings. Specifically, Carlos explored with the couple the values they hold toward their lives, their marriage, and this conflict.

It was prudent of Carlos to comply with the ethical codes while also accommodating his clients' issues. Let us revisit this vignette using the lens of the LOVE attitude. In the counseling session, Carlos not only demonstrated his *listening* skills, but was *open* to both their points of view. Furthermore, he facilitated Rosa and Joe to open the eyes and ears of their hearts toward one another. As they made attempts to see things from each other's position, they were able to ascertain one another's *values*. The process of helping the clients eventually learn to appreciate one another's experiences and values was aided by Carlos's *empathy* for both Rosa's and Joe's position in the situation they shared. This vignette allows us to get a sense of the vigorous impact the LOVE attitude can have on the counselor and on clients. Such impact, in turn, empowers the clients to turn the struggle of their relationship into a dance. Cultivating the LOVE attitude at the outset of our counseling career will prepare us to deal with challenges while we learn to show concern and regard for clients. Now that you have the compass of the LOVE attitude on hand, we will embark further on our journey. Specifically, we will navigate three territories—spiritual, personal, and cultural values.

SPIRITUAL VALUES

According to the Association for Spiritual, Ethical and Religious Values in Counseling ([ASERVIC], 2009), the counseling profession needs to know that clients' beliefs (or absence thereof) about spirituality and religion are crucial to their worldview and can affect their emotional and social actions. Crook-Lyon and Wimmer (2005) similarly suggested counselors to develop awareness and sensitivity to clients' spiritual beliefs. Beck proposed that "psychotherapy professions are engaged in an impressive effort to humanize their work more broadly by paying unprecedented attention to spirituality" (2003, p. 24). To pay unprecedented attention to spirituality and spiritual values, let us begin by examining a series of definitions related to these two concepts.

Definitions of Spirituality and Spiritual Values

Numerous authors have tried to describe the meaning of spirituality. Chandler, Holden, and Kolander (1995, p. 41) maintained that, "spirituality is a natural part of being human and can be conceptualized in an understandable and practical fashion." Lambie, Davis, and Miller (2008) proposed that spirituality is a basic socializing strength that helps us to grow even in times of crisis. Savary (2007) perceived spirituality as a person's core values that determine that person's way of being, thinking, and behaving in the world. Lefebvre (2002) argued that spirituality helps people to meet the human need for meaning, integration, establishing roots, and transcendence, and likewise is related to one's longing for joy, peace, tranquility, and inner contentment. Finally, Sink and Devlin (2011) defined spirituality as it applied to the educational setting as, "simply an ongoing developmental process of positive meaning making and growth producing activities" (p. 132). Together, these definitions suggest to us that spirituality is at the core of human existence; it can be a strength in difficult times; and it is related to the desire to be virtuous and do something meaningful. Examples of spirituality include feelings of dedication, thoughts about a numinous experience, and gatherings among people who share similar purpose in life.

Speaking about a related concept, Haldine (2000, p. 53) described spiritual as "that pertaining to higher human characteristics or to non-earthly matters." Further, Haldine articulated that the spiritual "has something to do with how one experiences the world and with what one makes of that experience" (p. 62). Spiritual values inspire individuals to examine and reflect on the meanings of their actions and their relationships with self, others, and the transcendent. Also, spiritual values propel us toward introspective processes and help us tap into our undeveloped inner resources. Note that our spiritual values may change in accordance with our learning and experience in life. Both spirituality and spiritual values inspire human persons to turn interiorly, delving deeper into their personhood and their experiences in the world. Spirituality relates to our desires, thoughts, emotions, dreams, and hopes, while spiritual values connect with the qualities that lie within us.

Sometimes, clients bring their religious issues and beliefs into the session. Therefore, it is helpful to know some of the commonly held differences between spirituality and religiosity. According to Bailly and Roussiau (2010), spirituality is perceived to be a broader term than religiosity, even though the two constructs are closely connected. Underwood (as cited in Bailly & Roussiau) maintained that some people participate in religious activity which has no spiritual meaning, while other people engage in spirituality which is not tied to any religious belief. Counselors must be clear about the aspect clients want to address.

Awareness Related to Spirituality and Spiritual Values

Burke, Chauvin, and Miranti (2005) argued that a person's spiritual essence balances one's physical, emotional, social, and intellectual dimensions with equal weight, bringing meaning and depth to all aspects of life experience. Counselors, therefore, do well to examine their own spiritual values, and then work to become conscious about any bias they have toward others' spiritual values. Working *inside out* with regard to spiritual and religious values is in line with ASERVIC's (2009) recommendation: Counselors must examine the impact that their spiritual and/or religious beliefs and values have on the client and the counseling process. After developing awareness of the important aspects of one's own spiritual values, counselors cultivate sensitivity to clients' spiritual values. Such sensitivity does not mean that counselors must agree with or conform to clients' values. By the same token, counselors must be mindful of imposing their spiritual values on clients. What matters is counselors' respect for and openness toward clients' spiritual values. For example, a counselor who believes in the benefits of forgiveness may push his client to forgive the person who hurt her without considering the client's unresolved issue pertinent to the pain caused by her perpetrator. Although the counselor likely is acting on a good intention, his action may also reflect insensitivity to the client's experience and the process of working through emotions related to the painful experience.

Understanding Spirituality and Spiritual Values

ASERVIC (2009) endorses competencies for attending to and addressing spiritual and religious issues in counseling. Counselors must gain clarity about their spiritual values. Specifically, they need to know about the impact that their spiritual values may have on their counseling work. To learn about spiritual values, counselors can consult with colleagues and supervisors; attend professional seminars, workshops, conferences; and read associated journal articles. To strengthen personal spirituality, counselors can do reading, engage in spiritual practices and exercises, participate in spiritual activities, and reflect on the meaning of their life experiences.

Deepening knowledge does not necessarily require counselors to possess expertise in clients' spiritual values. According to Finn and Rubin (as cited in Richards & Bergin, 2000), "no special knowledge is required beyond the usual requirements of honesty, respect, and our appropriate level of openness" (p. 328). Counselors, however, do need to be honest with clients about their strengths and weaknesses in working with spiritual values in counseling. It is equally important for counselors to be open to and respect clients' spiritual beliefs, rather than criticize or coerce clients to go toward any specific direction. Essentially, counselors must know how spiritual values play a role in their clients' lives, and especially in their clients' presenting problems. Furthermore, counselors must be able to differentiate between integrating spirituality into the context of counseling and giving spiritual direction. Spiritual direction deals with helping people understand their life experiences almost exclusively in light of their relationship with God (Barry & Connolly, 1982). Integrating spirituality into the context of counseling is not nearly as centered on helping clients make sense of how God is working in their lives; rather, it more often involves an interweaving the spiritual dimension of the human experience into the working through of a clinical issue. Finally, counselors must steer clear of using counseling as a platform for promoting their own religious beliefs.

Intervening With LOVE

To help clients develop awareness and understanding of their spiritual values, counselors can use sensible questions. Posing thought-provoking questions is an effective intervening tool that helps clients to be more self-aware and even to become conscious of the spiritual elements in the problems they want to address in counseling. Questions also help clients gain clarity about how their values influence their lifestyle and their relationship with themselves and others. Some questions that counselors might use to illuminate the spiritual values at play in a client's experience are noted below in Landmark 2.

Landmark 2

QUESTIONS FOR EXPLORING SPIRITUAL VALUES IN COUNSELING

1. As you reexamine the dilemma you just described, what are the things you have learned from that experience?
2. Is there any positive side to this dilemma?
3. What are the things you feel grateful for after surviving this turmoil in your life?
4. What do you believe has helped you rise above the turmoil?

(continued)

5. What have you learned about yourself from this experience?
6. What have you learned about your relationship with others and perhaps the high power?

In adhering to the ethical principle of autonomy, which emphasizes preservation of people's freedom of choice, counselors help clients explore their own spiritual values rather than furnishing clients with their own values (Forester-Miller & Davis, 1996). Also, counselors do not judge clients' values lest their judgment cause harm to the client or the counseling relationship. Thus, in cases when counselors are not comfortable or competent in working with clients on issues that deal closely with spiritual values, they consider helping clients identify other, feasible options.

Landmark 3

CASE EXAMPLE

Keith is a devout Catholic who is working on his dual master's degrees in Social Work and Divinity. He works in a church setting for his internship. Agnes, one of his clients, just lost her husband to a brain tumor. Agnes belongs to a nondenominational church group. With pain in her voice, she often asks Keith, "Why did God give me such a miserable life?" Hearing Agnes's question, Keith decides that he will spend most of his time praying with Agnes and exploring answers from the Bible.

As we listen deeply to Agnes's question, we notice that Agnes was not necessarily looking for a theological answer. Rather, her question revealed strong emotions. Keith might need to explore with Agnes the primary and secondary emotions related to her question. What seemed to evoke those emotions? What seems to be Agnes's spiritual question or concern?

Counselors should take clients' words as significant communications about what they need or what is troubling them. While this implies respect for clients, counselors also need to help clients explore the connotations that lie beneath the surface. In the case of Agnes, her question seemed to point toward emotions tied to her experience of suffering. The counselor can use Agnes's question as a tool to help not just look for an answer to why her husband died, but as an opening to understanding her own emotional response to his death. Agnes's loss relates to her husband's death, and death certainly can overwhelm people, including helpers. According to Kübler-Ross (1969), fear of death is common, even though we believe we are able to deal with it on many levels. Keith seemed to have been overwhelmed by the death issue, and his underlying feelings might have made him shift topic or avoid talking about the issue. It is also possible that Keith knew little about loss and bereavement, and he avoided dealing with these aspects. What is more, Agnes's pain might have triggered some of Keith's own unresolved business with regard to his own losses. Applying the

LOVE attitude will enable Keith to listen to what is really bothering Agnes. For instance, Keith can use a caring and genuine lens to pay attention to Agnes's verbal and nonverbal behaviors, interpret those behaviors with an open mind, make an attempt to feel for Agnes's pain, and see to it that Agnes is permitted to mourn her loss in her own way. The LOVE attitude will help Keith open the eyes and ears of his heart, exploring with Agnes her suffering and offering regard toward her pain. Let us examine another vignette.

Landmark 4

CASE EXAMPLE

For the past year, Greg, a 71-year-old man, has been mourning the death of his eldest son who died of heart failure at the age of 40. Greg went to see Audrey, a 60-year-old female counselor. Greg talked about his sorrow over his loss and pondered what God wants him to learn from this loss. At the same time, he expressed his concern about his inability to stop crying and outwardly grieving. Audrey assured Greg that grief is a personal process which is unique to every individual. Furthermore, Audrey informed Greg that there is no strict rule about the depth and breadth of grief. Upon hearing that, Greg expressed a sigh of relief. Then, using the LOVE attitude, Audrey asked Greg to talk more about the suffering he is going through as a result of his son's death. Apart from offering caring responses to Greg from time to time, Audrey suggested that Greg pay attention to any positive aspects he has been experiencing pertaining to this loss. Greg expressed that his wife and his other two children have been worried about him. Yet, he has almost ignored them, as he was so focused on his grief.

Audrey was able to be present to Greg. Her statements about the grieving process spoke to Greg's experience. In addition, the LOVE attitude helped Audrey to gently lead Greg to see the positive side of things. If you were Audrey, what would you have done differently?

Audrey was sensitive to Greg's spiritual needs. She validated Greg's grieving process and informed him that grief is a personal matter. Quite often clients have only a faint idea about the "normal" period of mourning. Also, some clients do not feel comfortable or safe to cry in front of another person. Counselors must be aware of these phenomena and make an effort to understand clients' agony. Audrey was able to show care and support toward Greg. When she sensed Greg was ready, she explored the meanings related to his loss.

Death and dying are common clinical issues; however, more often than not, neophyte counselors are overwhelmed by clients' expression of grief, as well as clients' grief issues. In such circumstance, counselors are reminded of the principles of autonomy, nonmaleficence, and beneficence. Counselors must respect clients' autonomy, as clients possess the freedom to choose how to mourn. Also, counselors must adhere to the principle of beneficence, which requires them to work in clients' best interests. Finally, counselors strive not to harm clients. Counselors may hurt clients unintentionally if they direct clients only on the basis of their own spiritual values or say things which sound insensitive or cliché. For example, telling clients that "crying shows that we are weak" can add salt to clients' pain. Counselors have the potential to behave unethically if they are not ready to help clients sensitively or fail to make appropriate referrals.

PERSONAL VALUES

Generation after generation, people have discussed the topic of human values and ethical concerns (Doherty, 1992). Herr and Niles (as cited in Burke & Miranti, 1992) highlighted counselors' need to be aware of the impact their personal values have on the counseling process. Also, counselors must recognize that both their value systems and those of clients' are central to the maintenance of the therapeutic relationship. Recognizing the uniqueness of individuals, counselors must ponder the broad spectrum of personal values that seep into people's beliefs and attitudes, directly and indirectly affecting their way of living. Clients' values warrant respect and understanding. It is equally important that counselors are aware of and understand their own values.

Definitions of Personal Values

According to Anderson (2009) personal values are the things or behaviors people have a high regard for and treat as crucial. Bobowik, Basabe, Páez, Jiménez, and Bilbao (2011) maintained that "values guide one's personal intentional activities and provide means of altering one's happiness level" (p. 402). Personal values are unique to every individual; they are developed and shaped by the individual's experiences and learning opportunities and are subject to change across the lifespan. Shifts in one's personal values can be positive or negative, and they can benefit or deteriorate one's relationships. Some personal values that people embrace are honesty, freedom, justice, respect, and responsibility. Patterson (1992) cautioned us from necessarily paralleling personal preferences or tastes with values. Finally, personal values are intertwined with and shaped by spiritual and cultural values. For example, a Chinese man who decides to take care of his elderly parents is likely enacting a set of values that are personal but that also reflect an adherence to the values that stem from his collectivist cultural tradition. Likewise, an 18-year-old Caucasian, American male adolescent who decides to move to his own apartment may do so because he personally values adventure, but also because he aligns himself with a culture that sees forging an independent life as important.

Awareness Related to Personal Values

Ethical practice requires counselors to be familiar with the values they hold and be aware of the way their values influence the therapeutic dynamics. In addition, counselors are encouraged to become sensitive to biases they have with regard to others' values, worldviews, and life choices. Caring and ethically competent counselors are careful, therefore, not to submit to their spontaneous, values-based responses to clients' decisions. Instead, they reflect on the feelings, thoughts, and even judgments that can emerge when they hear clients talk about problems that are personally challenging for counselors due to values differences. Counselors might ask themselves why they are angry when they hear a client's account of her extramarital affairs with a married man. Or, why they feel disgusted when a male client reveals that he is gay. Or, why they shift focus whenever a teenaged client criticizes his stepfather. When sitting with clients, counselors must know that their verbal and nonverbal gestures can be interpreted as signs of affirmation, dislike, or disapproval of clients' values. Therefore, counselors who are caring and concerned about strengthening the therapeutic relationship are sensitive to their gestures in order not to cause nontherapeutic discomfort or outright harm to clients. At the same time, counselors need to help clients develop awareness of their values and recognize how those values affect their relationships, interfere with their way of living, and play a part in the therapeutic dynamics.

Understanding Personal Values

While developing awareness of their values, counselors usually benefit from exploring the sources of those values and understanding what impact personal values have on their ethical practice. For example, a counselor who grew up in a family that adheres to traditional values may disapprove of the idea of cohabitation. When sitting with a client whose presenting issues are about his relationship with the girl whom he has been living with for some time, the counselor must be aware of his own biases, which if left unexamined, may lead to judgment of the client's values and choices. Such bias could deter the counselor from focusing on the client's real issues because he is overly focused on how to tell the client not to live with a woman unless he is married to her. In a situation like this, the counselor must understand how his own values affect his work with the client. This example points toward the responsibility all caring counselors have not to let their own personal values blind them from seeing the most pressing clinical issues clients have to address.

Intervening With LOVE

The ACA *Code of Ethics* (2005) specifies that "counselors are aware of their own values, attitudes, beliefs, and behaviors and avoid imposing values that are inconsistent with counseling goals" (Standard A.4.b.). To observe this standard, counselors must be clear about the values they hold and how they get manifested. To this effect, counselors grapple deeply with any personal values that get in the way of their professional responsibilities (Mintz et al., 2009). For example, counselors do not extend the counseling process for the sake of attaining personal benefits, such as income or supervised client hours that can be counted toward licensure. According to Ford (2006, p. 3), "professionals' personal values also influence their view of human motivation and human behavior, thereby affecting their choice of theoretical orientation in their professional activities." Cottone and Tarvydas (2007) suggested counselors to identify personal values and, where needed, reconcile them with the profession's values. This is in line with the principle of beneficence, which is about serving clients and the profession in their best interests (Forester-Miller & Davis, 1996). We now examine a vignette about personal values.

Landmark 5

CASE EXAMPLE

Isabella, a 58-year-old single woman, holds a senior position with an auditing company. She is losing interest in her position and lacks motivation in her work, and therefore is thinking about retiring early. Yet, it is a difficult decision for her because if she retires before the age of 60, she will have to forego a big chunk of her retirement benefits. She is torn between doing what she thinks will make her happy and keeping her material lifestyle. She explains her dilemma to Grace, the counselor, who herself was formerly a corporate executive who enjoyed a luxurious lifestyle. Grace chose to follow her desire to help others, so she made a radical change to pursue counseling. Her current counseling position at a nonprofit community health counseling center provides her with a much lower income, yet, she finds herself living a much fuller life. Listening to Isabella's story, Grace can't help but see herself and uses her own values to make sense of Isabella's position. As Grace listens to Isabella, her facial expression and verbal comments suggest impatience and irritation. Grace even confronts Isabella in a condescending way.

In this vignette, we see that Grace imposed her values on Isabella instead of helping Isabella gain clarity about what she wants to do and how her values affect her decision making with regard to her career path. It is quite a challenge to sit with clients whose values conflict with ours. How would you work with Isabella on her dilemma?

The difference between Grace and Isabella's values created an unfavorable impact on the therapeutic dynamics. Grace needed to examine her personal values. Rather than making a judgment about Isabella's values and assuming to know what Isabella ought to do, Grace can explore personal values with Isabella and try to understand how those values play a part in her decision to retire early or not. In this case, the LOVE attitude would facilitate Grace to listen with an open mind, develop understanding of Isabella's dilemma, and delve into Isabella's internal struggle. If you were the counselor, what would you have done differently?

CULTURAL VALUES AND SENSITIVITY

According to Pedersen et al. (2008, p. 6), "All behaviors are learned and displayed in a cultural context." Furthermore, culture "controls our lives and defines reality for each of us, with or without our permission and/or intentional awareness" (Pedersen et al., p. 5). Ford (2006) suggested that most personal, ethical, and cultural values are acquired in childhood through living and socializing with people within the same culture. Truly, cultural background contributes immensely to the development of a person's values. Understanding a person's values begins with sensitivity to the aspects of that person's cultural background. It is important that counselors learn the features of clients' cultures in order to understand their issues.

In the United States, substantial social, cultural, and demographic changes have taken place in the last few decades, and these changes are ongoing. The influx of immigrants and visitors, students, and professionals add variety to the cultural mix. According to the latest report of the Citizenship and Immigration Services (USCIS) of the Department of Homeland Security (2010), people who were born in Mexico, India, the Philippines, the People's Republic of China, and Vietnam topped the list of new citizens. In working with clients who are new to this country, it is essential that counselors know about clients' level of acculturation and factors that interfere with their acculturation process.

Definitions of Cultural Values

The ACA *Code of Ethics* (2005, p. 20) defined culture as "membership in a socially constructed way of living, which incorporates collective values, beliefs, norms, boundaries, and lifestyles that are cocreated with others who share similar worldviews comprising biological, psychosocial, historical, psychological, and other factors." Culture is not restricted to race and ethnicity; it also encompasses gender, age, sexual orientation, socioeconomic status, and multiple other social constructs. In contemporary living, political, social, and economic changes have led to the emergence of new cultural groups. Examples of emerging cultural groups are people with AIDS, people struggling with obesity, and the aging population. Another group that emerges in the face of socio and political changes is the information technology culture. People in this culture embrace all sorts of electronic gadgets as their principal means of communication, and they have developed their own language. To work with clients from this and other emerging cultures, counselors must explore their cultural traits and their cultural language. Every family, school, and organization forms its unique culture. Thus, on a regular basis people confront multiple layers of culture, and these layers of culture follow people from one place to another. Examples of cultural values are respect for elderly persons, individualism, collectivism, and cooperation.

Awareness Related to Cultural Values

Counselors who know their own worldviews and stereotypical tendencies, who are conscious of clients' worldviews, and who demonstrate culturally appropriate practice are perceived as culturally proficient counselors (Cartwright & Fleming, 2010). To become culturally proficient, counselors need to develop sensitivity to clients' cultural values. Cultural sensitivity refers to awareness of values, beliefs, norms, and behaviors that pertain to a particular culture. To develop cultural sensitivity, counselors must be aware of their assumptions about other cultures (Pedersen et al., 2008). They also need to recognize their own stereotypical attributes and perspectives. Approaches that help to develop awareness include role-playing, reflection, probing, and supervision. Baruth and Manning (as cited in Garcia, Cartwright, Winston, & Borzuchowska, 2003) stated that counselors face more complex ethical dilemmas as they work with people with diverse worldviews. Cottone and Tarvydas (2007) suggested counselors be careful about standing at the crossroad of cultural encapsulation. Cultural encapsulation refers to seeing clients simply through one's own socially constructed lens. To avoid being encapsulated, counselors strive to see things from clients' perspectives. To develop sensitivity to clients' cultural values, counselors need to open their hearts and minds to clients' backgrounds and experiences.

Understanding Cultural Values

Following the inside out yardstick, counselors seek understanding of their family traditions and beliefs. Next, they learn about clients' cultural characteristics. Jun (2010) cautioned counselors to deconstruct inappropriate dichotomous, linear, and hierarchical thinking when they engage in multicultural counseling work. Reading is an effective means to enhance knowledge on diverse cultures. Newspapers, books, and scholarly publications form an excellent source of cultural knowledge. A Chinese saying, "To walk 10,000 miles is the same as to read 10,000 books" accentuates an important note: learning through reading is seeing and hearing about a culture through the eyes and ears of the writer. Learning through personal experience of a culture is also extremely informative and involves experiencing a culture and place with one's own eyes and ears. In the same way, working with clients from diverse backgrounds is an efficient means of acquiring cultural knowledge. Clients are some of the best teachers for culture-centered practice. The more counselors work with clients from diverse cultures, the less encapsulated they become.

Intervening With LOVE

The Association for Multicultural Counseling and Development (AMCD) recommends that counselors become aware of their own cultural values and biases, be sensitive to a client's worldview, and use cultural-specific intervention strategies (AMCD Multicultural Counseling Competencies, 1996). Having awareness and understanding of clients' cultural values sets the backdrop for counselors to work caringly with clients. Seeing the world through clients' cultural lens can be a challenging reality. Counselors who desire to shape and polish their culturally appropriate intervening skills must endeavor to be flexible and creative in their approaches because good counseling does not always look the same across cultures.

Landmark 6

CASE EXAMPLE

Frances, a Thai-Chinese female, has been seeing Ray, a Caucasian counselor, for about 2 months. Frances talked about memories of her early childhood which relate to her attributes of independence. Frances remembered her nanny put her atop

(continued)

a foldable table and walked away. This happened when she was a toddler. She recalled being frightened but dared not move lest she would fall from the table. Eventually, she developed strength and courage in coping with similarly alarming situations. When Ray heard those accounts, he asked Frances why it was the nanny and not her mother who took care of her. She told him it was (and is) part of the way of life and culture in her country that families who are financially capable employ helpers to do housework and babysit. Ray kept shaking his head as he said, "Your mother abandoned you." In a serious demeanor, he asked about Frances's feelings. Frances was taken aback by Ray's interpretation of the situation. Also, she was bothered by Ray's insistence on the discussion of the "abandonment issue."

Apparently, Ray interpreted Frances's experience using his own cultural lens. It is not easy to understand a person's position when one looks at things only from his or her own angle. It would be helpful for Ray to clarify with Frances the cultural aspects with which he was not familiar. From the perspective of the LOVE attitude, Ray needs to attune to Frances's worldview with an open demeanor and have regard for her experience.

SIGNPOSTS FOR FUTURE TREKS

Arriving at the last leg of your journey, I consider that you are seeing more clearly that spiritual, personal, and cultural values are of paramount importance to the ethical dimensions of counseling, as these values are inexorably interwoven into the fabric of people's lives. Clients' and our own values inform therapeutic dynamics, as well as the counselor–counselee relationship. The discussions in this chapter underscore the fact that values are refined by life experience, which includes experiences in counseling relationships. Sometimes we can alter even our most rigidly held values as we reflect on them in light of our social, spiritual, and clinical relationships. Our values have a significant impact on our lifestyle, our way of thinking, and our priorities. Burke and Muranti (1992, p. 1) argued that values "are placed on those things that can help persons achieve happiness and success." Meanwhile, Stein (1992) contended that values can make us weigh or judge things, with or without our knowing.

Culture in the United States is enriched by the diversities in our demographics. In response to this richness, counselors are giving higher priorities to cultural and personal values. On some occasions, clients desire to explore their spiritual issues. Integration of spirituality is a growing demand in counseling work. Counselors strive to be sensitive to and knowledgeable in the realm of spiritual, personal, and cultural values. To adhere to the ethical codes, counselors practice with respect and appreciation for the spiritual, personal, and cultural values clients hold. To live out the sophisticated level of ethical practice, counselors need to embrace the LOVE attitude.

The LOVE attitude creates the rhythm for our therapeutic dance with clients. Such an attitude frees us from using a one-size-fits-all lens to perceive clients, their values, and their experiences. Clients adhere to their spiritual, personal, and cultural values for an array of reasons. It is our responsibility to explore those reasons with clients. We need to be instrumental in helping clients confront the subtle, complex interplay of the value dynamics, and to channel those values into sources of change. Our experience is precious and helpful to our role as an agent of change. Yet, we have to be vigilant of using our experience as the major lens to perceive clients' values and their actions.

INSIGHTS GAINED FROM THE JOURNEY

In this section, I would like to share relevant insights I have gained from my counseling experiences. I reckon that my accounts will help deepen your learning about spiritual and personal values and cultural sensitivity in the ethical context of counseling. In addition, you will see how the LOVE attitude enhances ethical practice.

VICKY'S SPIRITUAL VALUES

The first account is about my work with Vicky, a Presbyterian female. As soon as Vicky settled into her chair, she complained about her daughter, who was dating a Catholic man. Vicky did not approve of her daughter dating any man who was not Presbyterian. At that particular moment, I was overwhelmed by her anger and was apprehensive about telling her about my Catholic faith. I went on to explore with Vicky her spiritual and personal values. In the third session, halfway into our conversation, Vicky asked about my faith. As soon as I told her I am Catholic, she became quiet. In the midst of silence, I felt her anger and disgust. For the rest of the session, she insisted on shifting to another topic. That was my last session with her.

As I reflected on my work with Vicky, I felt responsible for not revealing my faith beliefs to her early on in our relationship, which I avoided doing for fear of losing a client. I was still an intern, and I was fearful of not getting enough client hours for my internship. I failed to ascertain what my faith might mean for this client, and ultimately my not telling her about my faith might have made her feel embarrassed, betrayed, and angry. This experience inspired me to delve into my spiritual values, as well as clients' and examine possible outcomes that might be favorable or unfavorable to the therapeutic relationship. In hindsight, I did not comply with the principles of nonmaleficence, beneficence, and fidelity. My fear led me to obscure my own faith, which, in turn, injured my client's feelings. I neglected her best interest because I was not honest with her. My short-term concern (about losing a client) took precedence over other things, and my actions led our relationship to end on a sour note. Using the LOVE attitude would have helped me listen to what disturbed Vicky in this situation. My open attitude might have inspired me with the courage to disclose my own faith. I needed to respect Vicky's spiritual value and be sensitive to her struggle.

JENNY'S PERSONAL VALUES

The second anecdote is about my work with Jenny, a married woman in her mid-30s, who came to me to explore forgiveness regarding her extramarital affair with a married man. I resented what Jenny did. As she talked about her experiences, my nonverbal gestures might have indicated disapproval and even disgust. I did not realize that until Jenny asked if her deeds were unacceptable to me. Her remarks awakened me. It was difficult for me to tell her what was on my mind.

Looking back, I am conscious that my own values conflicted with Jenny's deeds. For a fleeting moment, I was judging her. Even then, I realized I was being unkind to her. I contemplated my values and my stance. I was positive that I could continue my work with her. She was remorseful about her infidelity and was determined to start her life anew. Her entire family, except her husband, treated her with disdain. Her extramarital affair was a serious mistake. Do not we all make mistakes? What matters is that we recognize and accept our weakness, learn from our mistakes and avoid committing the same hurtful deed. Jenny was able to convert her mistake into corrective measures and eventually forgive herself. My journeying with her in the sea of disdain, misery, and guilt humbled me and enriched my experience. Applying the LOVE attitude to this vignette, I see that I needed to offer undivided attention to Jenny and set aside my own values as I attended to her and considered her feelings.

WEI FANG'S CULTURAL VALUES

The third account underscores cultural values and sensitivity in my work with Wei Fang, a woman native to China. Wei Fang came to the United States several years ago, employed in the capacity of a nurse at the ICU of a private hospital. Wei Fang's dilemma was about her decision to sponsor her parents to immigrate to the United States. On one hand, Wei Fang enjoyed her free-spirited lifestyle living by herself. On the other, she wanted to observe her cultural tradition, which accentuates care and respect for parents. In some ways, my own ethnic tradition and way of living paralleled Wei Fang's. While I was wearing my counselor's hat, I was conscious of the possibility of imposing my values on Wei Fang. Using the LOVE attitude, I strived to see the issue from Wei Fang's cultural lens. I paid attention to her account of her own values, how those values affected her thoughts, feelings, and actions, and her relationship with self and others. With an open approach, I examined with her what she would like to do and identified various feasible options. She was pleased that we touched upon quite a number of potential scenarios. I encouraged her to continue to process those thoughts and feelings before making any decision.

As I reflected on my work with Wei Fang, I was pleased that I went with my conviction that clients are as unique as patterns of snowflakes. Although we share some similar cultural characteristics, our upbringing and other backgrounds can be quite different. Also, it would be unfair for me to give directions to clients because they are the ones who will live with the consequences of those directions.

DON'S VALUES

Don, a 40-year-old male adult, was admitted to the hospital due to episodes of pancreatitis. He was referred by a nurse to talk to me. He introduced himself as "a homeless man." When I asked how he was doing, he replied in a cheerful tone, "I'm very happy to be in a hospital!" He did not have to worry about finding a place to stay, enjoyed having his own bathroom, nice meals, and great service. Next, he expressed that he had applied for disability insurance. He was animated when he talked about the list of things he would buy when he received his first disability check. First of all, I was startled to hear that someone was happy about being hospitalized. Also, it was difficult for me to see how a seemingly decent man had got himself into all those situations. Except for the jaundice, which was reflected on his skin color and the white of his eyes, he looked physically fit for employment. I just could not accept the fact that an adult person was excited about receiving welfare payment rather than earning his own income. At that moment, I knew I was judging the client, and I sensed my vision becoming narrow. The information I gathered and the things I saw barely gave me details about the bigger picture of this person's values and difficulties.

I was glad that I caught my judgmental behavior and stopped that right there and then. I continued to work with Don on his future career plan and his purpose of life. Our session ended on the fifth day shortly before he was discharged. The LOVE attitude stimulated my internal process. I examined my stereotypical view which precipitated my culturally encapsulated demeanor. Re-attuning to the virtuous attitude opened my heart and mind to paths I have not yet traveled. Working with Don has not only broadened my cultural vision, but also enhanced my ethical counseling skills.

MOVING FORWARD: CASE STUDY AND REFLECTION QUESTIONS

Pat, a 27-year-old Caucasian, born and raised in the United States, was into her second year in a master's program in Buddhism at a university in Bangkok, Thailand. Pat met Danny in the weekly meditation workshop, and they started dating about nine months ago. Danny, a 25-year-old Thai man, received his college degree in English Language in the United Kingdom. He was pursuing his master's studies in Education in Bangkok. Danny was the only son in his family and lived with his parents and an older sister. Other than faith belief, Pat and Danny shared some common perspectives and values.

Every Sunday, Pat had dinner with Danny and his family. Pat found Danny's mother and sister controlling and too protective. Yet, Danny hardly said "no" to them. Last week, Pat asked Danny to move into an apartment with her. Danny said he had to talk to his parents about this. Pat was disappointed when she heard that. She did not talk to Danny for a week even though they saw each other in the workshop. More and more, she felt lonely, frustrated, and distressed. She sought counseling at her university's student service office.

The counselor, Melissa, was a Thai woman. Pat seemed uneasy to talk about her issue with Melissa as she had an impression that Melissa would not understand her feelings due to cultural differences. Pat challenged Melissa, asking her questions about North American and Western cultures. Melissa, in her calm and patient demeanor, explored with Pat what her confrontive attitude might mean and how that attitude related to her issues with Danny. That gentle confrontation facilitated Pat to examine her own values and her narrow vision toward others' values. Also, she learned from Melissa a calm way in interacting with people with cultural differences.

RELECTION QUESTIONS

- *Identify the pressing issue of the client.*
- *What challenges did Pat give to the counselor?*
- *How might you resolve the dilemmas by taking a positive approach to ethics?*
- *What did you learn personally and professionally from working through this case?*
- *How would you integrate the LOVE attitude when working with Pat?*

REFERENCES

American Counseling Association. (2005). *ACA code of ethics*. Alexandria, VA: Author.

Anderson, S. K. (2009). A proactive approach to teaching ethics from the inside out. *Career Planning and Adult Development Journal, 25*(1), 134–146.

Association for Multicultural Counseling and Development (AMCD). (1996). Alexandria, VA: Author. Retrieved from http://www.amcdaca.org/amcd/competencies.pdf

ASERVIC Spiritual Competencies. (2009). *Association for Spiritual, Ethical and Religious Values in Counseling*. Retrieved from http://www.aservic.org/competiencies.html

Bailly, N., & Roussiau, N. (2010). The daily spiritual experience scale (DSES): Validation of the short form in an elderly French population. *Canadian Journal on Aging, 29*(2), 223–231.

Barry, W. A., & Connolly, W. J. (1982). *The practice of spiritual direction*. New York, NY: HarperCollins Publishers.

Bobowik, M., Basabe, N., Páez, D., Jiménez, A., & Bilbao, M. A. (2011). Personal values and well-being among Europeans, Spanish Natives and Immigrants to Spain: Does the culture matter? *Journal of Happiness Studies, 12*, 401–419. doi: 10.1007/s10902-010-9202-1

Burke, M. T., Chauvin, J. C., & Miranti, J. G. (2005). *Religious and spiritual issues in counseling: Applications across diverse populations*. New York, NY: Brunner-Routledge.

Burke, M. T., & Miranti, J. G. (1992). Ethics and spirituality: The prevailing forces influencing the counseling profession. In M. T. Burke & J. G. Miranti (Eds.), *Ethical and spiritual values in counseling* (pp. 1–4). Alexandria, VA: ARVIC.

Cartwright, B. Y., & Fleming, C. L. (2010). Multicultural and diversity considerations in the new code of professional ethics for rehabilitation counselors. *Journal of Applied Rehabilitation Counseling, 41*(2), 20–24.

Chandler, C. K., Holden, J. M., & Kolander, C. A. (1995). Counseling for spiritual wellness: Theory and practice. In M. T. Burke & J. G. Miranti (Eds.), *Counseling: The spiritual dimension* (pp. 41–58). Alexandria, VA: American Counseling Association.

Cimperman, M. (2005). *When God's people have HIV/AIDS: An approach to ethics*. Maryknoll, NY: Orbis Books.

Cottone, R. R., & Tarvydas, V. M. (2007). *Counseling ethics and decision making* (3rd ed.). Columbus, OH: Pearson Education, Inc.

Crook-Lyon, R. E., & Wimmer, C. L. (2005). Spirituality and dream work in counseling: Clients' experiences. *Pastoral Psychology, 54*(1), 35–45. doi: 10.1007/s11089-005-6181-y

Doherty, W. J. (1992). Values and ethics in family therapy. In M. T. Burke & J. G. Miranti (Eds.), *Ethical and spiritual values in counseling* (pp. 74–80). Alexandria, VA: ARVIC.

Egan, E. (2010). *The skilled helper: A problem-management and opportunity-development approach to helping* (9th ed.). Belmont, CA: Brooks/Cole, Cengage Learning.

Ford, G. G. (2006). *Ethical reasoning for mental health professionals*. Thousand Oaks, CA: Sage Publications, Inc.

Forester-Miller, H., & Davis, T. (1996). *A practitioner's guide to ethical decision making*. Alexandria, VA: American Counseling Association. Alexandria, VA.

Freeman, L. (2002). *Jesus the teacher within*. New York, NY: The Continuum International Publishing Group Inc.

Garcia, J. G., Cartwright, B., Winston, S. M., & Borzuchowska, B. (2003). A transcultural integrative model for ethical decision making in counseling. *Journal of Counseling and Development, 81*(3), 268–277.

Geyer, A. L., & Baumeister, R. F. (2005). Religion, morality, and self-control: Values, virtues, and vices. In R. F. Paloutzian, & C. L. Park (Eds.), *Handbook of psychology of religion and spirituality* (pp. 412–432). New York, NY: The Guilford Press.

Haldine, J. (2000). On the very idea of spiritual values. In A. O'Hear (Ed.), *Philosophy, the good, the true and the beautiful* (pp. 53–71). Cambridge, UK: Cambridge University Press.

Hill, A. L. (2004). Ethical analysis in counseling: A case for narrative ethics, moral visions, and virtue ethics. *Counseling and Values, 48,* 131–148.

Jun, H. (2010). *Social justice, multicultural counseling, and practice: Beyond a conventional approach.* Thousand Oaks, CA: Sage Publication, Inc.

Kübler-Ross, E. (1969). *On death and dying: What the dying have to teach doctors, nurses, clergy, and their own families.* New York, NY: Scribner.

Lambie, G. W., Davis, K. M., & Miller, G. (2008). Spirituality: Implications for professional school counselors' ethical practice. *Counseling and Values, 52,* 211–223.

Lefebvre, S. (2002). The "crises of belief" in business and the need for a dialogue on the meaning of work. In T. C. Pauchant (Ed.), *Ethics and spirituality at work* (pp. 45–55). Westport, CT: Quorum Books.

Meara, N. M. (2001). Just and virtuous leaders and organizations, *Journal of Vocational Behavior, 58,* 227–234.

Mintz, L. B., Jackson, A. P., Neville, H. A., Illfelder-Kaye, J., Winterowd, C. L., & Loewy, M. I. (2009). The need for a counseling psychology model training values statement addressing diversity. *The Counseling Psychologist, 37*(5), 644–675.

Patterson, C. H. (1992). Values in counseling and psychotherapy. In M. T. Burke, & J. G. Miranti (Eds.), *Ethical and spiritual values in counseling* (pp. 107–119). Alexandria, VA: ARVIC.

Pedersen, P. B., Draguns, J. G., Lonner, W. J., & Trimble, J. E. (2008). *Counseling across cultures* (6th ed.). Thousand Oaks, CA: Sage Publications, Inc.

Richards, P. S., & Bergins, A. E. (2000). *Handbook of psychotherapy and religious diversity.* Washington, DC: American Psychological Association.

Savary, L. M. (2007). *Teilhard de Chardin The divine milieu explained: A spirituality for the 21st century.* Mahwah, NJ: Paulist Press.

Sink, C. A., & Devlin, J. M. (2011). Student spirituality and school counseling: Issues, opportunities, and challenges. *American Counseling Association, 55,* 130–148.

5

Standing Up to the Ethical Challenges Related to Boundaries in Counseling

Jocelyn Gregoire, Christin M. Jungers, and Cristiana White

THE FORESEEN DESTINATION

It is our hope that upon reading and reflecting on the themes of this chapter, you will be better able to:

- Describe what is meant by boundaries in professional counseling relationships.
- Discern between occasions of boundary crossings and boundary violations.
- Identify instances when counselors must be keenly aware of the potential for client harm due to boundary violations (e.g., as in the case of sexual relationships).
- Understand and reason through ethical dilemmas related to boundary issues using an existential and phenomenological philosophical framework.

GETTING ON THE ROAD

It is a common belief that human beings are social animals. Consequently, we are called to be in relationship with at least *an-other* in order to survive. The story of Robinson Crusoe is a good testimony to this fact. Robinson's need for relationship on the deserted island where he was cast away forced him to befriend a parrot, teach it how to speak, and interact with it until the day he met his new, human friend, Friday. Whether it is with members of our family, our friends, colleagues, complete strangers, or even with animals or nature, to be in relationship with at least *an-other* constitutes the very fabric of human personhood. It bestows on us a sense of identity, protects us from loneliness and insecurity, and invests us with a feeling of well-being and purpose (Cox, 2002).

The counseling field is primarily one of relationships, and more specifically, therapeutic relationships. A therapeutic relationship can be described as a truly authentic human encounter in which a counselor is totally present to *an-other* who is appealing to him or her for help. This other—the client—is the one to whom the counselor gives undivided and nonjudgmental attention and in whose personal existence, at least for a time, he or she participates. In brief, counseling necessitates that we share the life and way of *being-in-the-world* of our clients for whom we really care (van Kaam, 1966). As described in Chapter 2, counselors' professional identity, when seen from a phenomenological perspective on ethics, is characterized by *being-in-the-counseling-world-with-others*. In this world, counselors enter into therapeutic relationships with other human beings whose welfare is entrusted to them, and they are expected to use the knowledge and skills gained from training to act benevolently.

In this chapter, we aim to deal with ethical questions that arise as professional counselors wrestle with determining what constitutes healthy, therapeutic relationships. We begin our exploration of this ethical territory by expanding our understanding of concepts such as boundaries, boundary crossing, boundary violation, multiple relationships, gift-giving and gift-receiving, bartering, self-disclosure, and touch. The American Counseling Association's (ACA) *Code of Ethics* (2005) provides direction about how best to deal with these boundary dilemmas, and we encourage you to become familiar with the code. However, we also use this chapter to propose a model for ethical decision making grounded in existential and phenomenological philosophy. The model draws on the concepts of autonomy, dignity, and authenticity, which we believe are worth reflecting on when trying to make ethical decisions about boundary issues.

EXPLORING THE TERRITORY

UNDERSTANDING BOUNDARIES IN COUNSELING

A simple way to understand a boundary is to view it as the frontier that lies between therapeutic and nontherapeutic behaviors (Golden & Sonneborn, 1998). This statement implies that professional counselors maintain some degree of relational separation between themselves and their clients. Counselors' appreciation for and understanding of boundaries thus informs how they structure the therapeutic relationship, deal with occasions of nonprofessional contact, and determine what constitutes therapeutic content. For example, boundary issues are at play when counselors decide where counseling takes place (in an office, in the client's home, outdoors, etc.), how long sessions typically run, where they and their clients sit and how close they sit to one another, payment schedules, and so on. Boundary issues also are at the heart of determinations about what and who will be the primary focus of clinical conversations. Boundaries help counselors to be aware of their relational responsibilities to clients and be mindful about behaviors that help them to respond caringly to distressed clients (Haug, 1999). Training, consultation with colleagues and ethics-related literature, and the ACA *Code of Ethics* (2005) all help to inform counselors about where boundary lines are typically drawn in professional relationships with clients.

There is an ethical quality to judging boundaries. Stated simply, healthy and professional boundaries are growth-enhancing, while unhealthy or inappropriate boundaries can be destructive and have the potential to harm clients. Healthy boundaries are evident when counselors dually foster caring and supportive relationships with clients and also respect the need for the frontiers or relational separation from them. Because there are many varied ways in which boundaries can become blurred or nonprofessional interactions might unfold between helpers and their clients, counselors are encouraged to make the distinctions between professional and nonprofessional roles with clients as clear as possible. Clarity allows clients to know how far professional helping extends and where it ends. Being up front with clients about the limits one sets to keep relationships professional in nature is not unimportant, and it benefits both clients and counselors. Outlining the limits surrounding professional and nonprofessional interactions usually provides clients with a sense of physical and psychological safety and affords them the assurance that their welfare is not taken lightly and their vulnerability will not be misused. Counselors likewise profit from such discussions in that they are regularly reminded to reflect on and enact an appropriate balance of closeness and distance in clinical relationships (Nelson, Summers, & Turnbull, 2004).

Boundary Crossings

As stated, healthy boundaries are growth-producing for clients, and they allow counselors a degree of flexibility in determining how they actually live out the relational distance between themselves and clients. Not every counselor will interpret healthy boundaries in exactly the same way. Indeed, although the counseling field firmly upholds principles such as nonmaleficence (i.e., never harm or exploit clients), beneficence (i.e., treat clients with respect and dignity), and autonomy (i.e., allow clients to make their own decisions with regard to their life's direction), there nevertheless seems to be less agreement among professional counselors about what constitutes a concrete boundary crossing and when it is harmful. Practitioners generally agree that not all boundary crossings are boundary violations or exploitive to clients. Gutheil and Gabbard (1993) noted that crossings can benefit clients, be neutral, or be harmful. The latest revision of the ACA *Code of Ethics* (2005, A.5.d) acknowledges the potential benefits of nonsexual, nonromantic, nonexploitive boundary crossings for clients, former clients, or their families. Counselors operating from a variety of theoretical orientations also can testify to the benefic value of certain nonsexual boundary crossings. For example, some humanistic counselors may decide to self-disclose something about their personal lives, families, life experiences, and positive or negative feelings as a means to enhance the therapeutic alliance and outcomes. A counselor who adheres to a behavioral model of therapy might decide to take a person struggling with agoraphobia for a ride or a walk as part of the therapeutic process. Counselors who work with children may include in their therapeutic interventions the giving or receiving of small gifts from their clients, attending school plays in which the child is performing, or hugging or touching the client from time to time when warranted. Counselors who aim to be culturally sensitive may decide to see a client for one or more treatment sessions without charging a fee, accept to barter for their services, or respond positively to an invitation to attend a special event, such as a wedding or other culturally important celebration.

Boundary Violations

Boundary violations, in contrast to crossings, occur when counselors consciously or unconsciously use their position of power and authority as a vehicle to exploit or manipulate clients, thus causing significant damage to the client, counselors themselves, and the therapeutic alliance. The most obvious example of a boundary violation is a sexual relationship between a counselor and client (as well as between supervisors and supervisees and counselor educators and students). The literature describing ethical issues surrounding sexual relationships between counselors and clients utilizes a wide variety of terms, such as sexual contact, erotic contact, sexual activity, sexual intimacy, sexual relationship, sexual involvement, sexual boundary violations, and sexual misconduct (Berkman, Turner, Cooper, Polnerow, & Swartz, 2000). No matter what verbiage is used, there is no denying the offensive and abusive character of all sexual relationships, whether they are expressed explicitly through sexual contact such as kissing, fondling, sexual intercourse, and the like or through other, less overt manifestations of sexual behaviors, such as sexual gazes and seductiveness (Coleman & Schaefer, 1986).

Sexual relationships with clients are strictly forbidden and constitute a very serious offense. The *Code of Ethics* (2005, A.5.a) cannot be clearer on this particular matter when it stipulates, "Sexual or romantic counselor–client interactions or relationships with current clients, their romantic partners, or their family members are prohibited." (See Standard F.3.b and Standard F.10.a for statements about supervisors and educators.) The code also prohibits counselors from engaging in sexual relationships with former clients until at least 5 years after termination of the clinical relationship. Despite the fact that the codes of ethics of most professional mental health and human services organizations, including the ACA, the National Association of Social Workers (NASW), American Psychological Association (APA), and American Psychiatric Association, condemn sexual contact with current and newly formed clients as unethical, this transgression does occur with harmful consequences to clients. Detrimental effects have been shown to range from denial, guilt, shame, isolation, anger, depression, impaired ability to trust, loss of self-esteem, and difficulty expressing anger to psychosomatic disorders, sexual confusion, and increased risk of suicide (Brodsky, 1989; Feldman-Summers & Jones, 1984; Holtzman, 1984; Pope, 1990; Sonne, Meyer, Borys, & Marshall, 1985; Sonne & Pope, 1991). Other literature suggests that when sexual exploitation of a client by a counselor occurs, the family and friends of the client (Schoener, Milgrom, & Gonsiorek, 1989), as well as colleagues of the practitioner (Regehr & Glancy, 1995), are also negatively impacted upon.

Sexual exploitation of a client normally constitutes the most obvious and injurious form of boundary violation; however, nonsexual boundary violations are also potentially damaging. For example, counselors may bill their clients for missed appointments, phone conversations, and preparing reports or lengthy insurance claim forms even though clients have never been made aware of such fees during the informed consent process. Some counselors may barter their services for expensive gifts, such as a car, jewelry, or property, or they might take advantage of a client's expert knowledge or skill in a particular area for personal gain (e.g., seeking inside information from a client who is a stock broker or banker to turn a large profit). Harmful consequences of nonsexual boundary violations can include shame, fear, guilt, self-blame, isolation and emptiness, disengagement from services, identity confusion, mistrust of authority, paranoia, depression, and self-harm.

MULTIPLE AND NONPROFESSIONAL RELATIONSHIPS IN COUNSELING

Setting professional boundaries does not necessarily mean that counselors will never expect to encounter the possibility of having other, outside relationships with clients. Because as counselors we are professional *beings-there-in-the-world-with-others*, it is inevitable that, on occasion, we will have connections other than therapeutic ones with our clients or people connected to our clients during the course of therapy or after termination. In our profession, these other connections are what constitute multiple and nonprofessional interactions or relationships. When these additional relationships are nonsexual in nature, we can think of them as boundary crossings that call for careful evaluation. The ACA *Code of Ethics* (2005, A.5.d) recommends that counselors generally avoid nonprofessional relationships with clients or their family members.

The ethical issues surrounding multiple relationships have registered a lot of attention in the counseling and other human sciences literature (e.g., Borys, 1994; Borys & Pope, 1989; Coleman & Schaefer, 1986; Corey, Corey, & Callanan, 2011; Gottlieb, 1993; Kagle & Giebelhausen, 1994; Moleski & Kiselica, 2005; Pearson & Piazza, 1997) and have highlighted many instances in which multiple relationships between counselors and clients might occur. Examples of nonprofessional interactions include but are not limited to (a) friendships between the professional counselor and the client; (b) social interactions and events that happen because the counselor and client belong to and attend events organized by the same club, gym, church, or philanthropic association; (c) business or financial relationships in which one party may be a former employer or employee of the other; (d) collegial or professional relationships in which the professional counselor and the client are colleagues in an academic institution and may be collaborating on scholarship activities, such as publications or presentations at conferences; and (e) supervisory or evaluative relationships in which the supervisor may be the former counselor of the supervisee (Anderson & Kitchener, 1996; Zur, 2011a).

Examples of multiple relationships are boundless; yet, there is agreement that there are a few common types of overlapping or multiple relationships in which counselors and clients might find themselves. Cottone (as cited in Kaplan, 2006) suggested that these include (a) sexual and/or romantic relationships (described previously as a boundary violation), (b) any nonprofessional relationships, and (c) relationships that undergo a role change (e.g., a counselor shifts from providing couples counseling to individual counseling for the same clients). Pearson and Piazza (1997) reviewed the literature and identified five sets of circumstances in which counselors, as well as educators, supervisors, and researchers, might experience multiple professional or nonprofessional roles. They described these as follows:

1. *Circumstantial multiple roles* happen by sheer happenstance and are unintended by both the counselor and the client. For example, a counselor goes out for dinner at a restaurant and the waiter who has been assigned to his table is one of his clients.
2. *Structured multiple professional roles* emerge due to the nature of the professional activities and responsibilities of counselors, educators, or supervisors. For some, such as educators, there is an almost inherent expectation that they will play multiple roles with students, including teacher, advisor, and even clinical supervisor. Similarly, counselors who are *being-there-in-the-world-with-others* interact and consult with colleagues, such as psychologists, social workers, doctors, or clergy in order to best help clients. Structured multiple professional roles are generally not considered problematic if clear and appropriate boundaries are maintained by the counseling professional.
3. *Shifts in professional roles* often arise with organizational restructuring, which alters relationships among workers within the organization. For example, a student who graduates from a counselor education program and is later hired as faculty in the same program becomes the colleague of former professors. In another example, a counselor might have a client who is a seminarian, and upon his ordination, he is posted as the parochial vicar of the parish where the counselor goes to church.
4. *Personal and professional role conflicts* occur when a professional relationship evolves into a personal relationship of either a sexual or a nonsexual nature. Conversely, a role conflict might emerge when a preexisting personal relationship becomes professional in nature. The first instance usually is seen as more problematic if the professional counselor misuses the power position of his professional role; however, not all role conflicts are necessarily detrimental to clients. For example, a counselor might become a godparent for a client's child, and that gesture might be extremely meaningful to the client.
5. *Predatory professionals* deliberately try to take advantage of the clinical encounter to cater to their own personal needs instead of those of the client. For example, a counselor or counselor educator might recruit students, supervisees, or emotionally fragile clients to meet her sexual needs or for financial gain.

The potential for counselors and clients to share multiple relationships with one another is always present. For this reason, counselors are strongly encouraged to think through the possible impact that overlapping relationships can have on clients and the clinical encounter. This is where ethical decision making comes into play. Though we will look at a phenomenological and existential decision-making model later in the chapter, it is important to note that decisions about how to address the reality of multiple, nonprofessional interactions with clients involve a careful weighing of the potential benefits or possible harm that might come to clients through outside interactions.

Landmark 1

CASE EXAMPLE

Will is a counselor educator at a small university in a rural community. After he moved to the area with his family, he decided to open a private practice to offer a needed service to the community, as well as to stabilize his finances. A devout Catholic, he soon found himself involved in various activities in his parish. One day, Will was approached by the parish priest, who told him that he urged a member of the parish's pastoral council, Mikela, to contact him for grief counseling. Will knows of Mikela because he purchased a car from her husband's dealership shortly after he relocated and because Mikela's husband is a member of the St. Vincent de Paul Society, for which Will volunteers each month. Mikela herself is also a member of the lady's guild with Will's wife. Moreover, Mikela's son is one of Will's students in his professional ethics class.

1. *What are some potential benefits to Mikela and the counseling relationship should Will take her on as a client?*
2. *What are some potential harms to Mikela and the counseling relationship should Will decide to take her on as a client?*
3. *What decision would you recommend for Will and why?*

GIFT-GIVING AND GIFT-RECEIVING

Gift-giving is a social and universal ritual that conveys gratitude, altruism, appreciation, and love (Saad & Gill, 2003); yet, the decision about whether or not to participate in this ritual with clients is a point of confusion for many in the counseling field. Indeed, counselors react to clients' gift-giving behavior with a range of emotions and ethical judgments, from those that are positive and endorsing to those that are negative and disapproving (Spandler, Burman, Goldberg, Margison, & Amos, 2000). Lazarus and Zur (2002) suggested that therapists tend to be very discreet about gift-receiving from clients out of a concern that they might be accused of committing a boundary violation or exploiting a client. Until recently, the ethical judgments assigned to giving and receiving gifts have tended to indicate a general disapproval of the practice. This ethical judgment, which largely reflected a deontological approach to ethics, highlighted a preference among counselors to keep the professional role as clear and objective as possible—uncontaminated by any confusion that might be brought on by trying to determine the meaning behind the gift-offering. A more current consensus among counselors, however, is that gift-giving can be a meaningful gesture that, when properly handled, has the potential to boost the therapeutic relationship and pave the way for positive clinical outcomes (Brendel et al., 2007; Corey et al., 2011; Hahn, 1998; Spandler, et al., 2000; Zur, 2004, 2007). In fact, many clinicians and ethicists even believe that to reject gifts that are offered by clients, especially when the act is culturally appropriate and sanctioned, can be potentially harmful to the therapeutic alliance and process (Knox, Hess, Williams, & Hill, 2003; Spandler et al., 2000). From this contextually oriented and teleological perspective, the practice of giving gifts is evaluated with an appreciation for diverse cultural meanings that might be attached to the offering. For example, a client's gift might be viewed as something akin to a tip offered to the therapist as an expression of satisfaction for the good services provided or in gratitude for unexpected benefits that were garnered from the counseling relationship. Very often, clients' gift-giving can also take on a ritualistic meaning, as in a "parting gift" that marks the termination of the therapeutic relationship (Gerig, 2004; Shapiro & Ginzberg, 2002).

The ACA *Code of Ethics* (2005, A.10.e) reflects the more contemporary consensus on how to interpret and judge the ethical appropriateness or inappropriateness of gift-giving, stating that "in some cultures, small gifts are a token of respect and showing of gratitude." The code thus suggests that gift-giving by clients does not always pose a detriment to the therapeutic relationship or clinical work. However, the code also provides at least a few guidelines by which a counselor can evaluate whether or not to take a client's gift. These guidelines recommend counselors to consider the value of the gift, as well as the client's motivation for offering the gift and the counselor's motivation for accepting it. Usually, small, symbolic, inexpensive gifts are considered appropriate. Examples of these gifts include items such as cards; homemade cookies or bread; flowers; homegrown fruits; a framed picture; and even small monetary donations. Expensive gifts, such as a piano, a car, a paid vacation, a membership to a luxurious club, as well as gifts that are sexually suggestive or that have racist or sexist innuendos typically are deemed inappropriate and unethical. When counselors consider the motivation behind a client's gift, they should reflect on the possible meanings of the gift-offering in light of a client's therapeutic goals and desired areas of personal growth. For example, clients who feel unappreciated, unloved, or uncared for, or those with low self-esteem who generally feel undeserving, may offer a gift as a subtle way of enticing their counselor into liking them (Zur, 2011b). Similarly, counselors themselves should carefully evaluate their own interests in accepting gifts from clients, especially those that appear to be more than a small token of gratitude.

Landmark 2

CASE EXAMPLE

Daniela is a counselor at an HIV/AIDS clinic. She has been working for a few months with Michelle and her young son, Ben, who has been diagnosed with HIV. During much of that time, Michelle has spent their sessions complaining to Daniela about her personal problems and the difficulties she has in providing for Ben's medical needs. Michelle also has a history of not bringing Ben to his doctor's appointments and not administering medication that he needs to maintain his health. However, after the most recent sessions, when Daniela challenged Michelle about her choices regarding her son, Michelle seems

(*continued*)

more invested in her son's welfare and is complying with doctors' recommendations regarding his medical needs. Happy with her own sense of empowerment and her son's welfare, Michelle, who is a freelance artist, excitedly offered to paint a picture for Daniela that she could hang in her office. Daniela is concerned that if she refuses this gift, Michelle might be discouraged and return to her old noncompliance patterns.

1. *What ethical principles and issues are involved in the situation?*
2. *What are the potential benefits or harm that can occur if Daniela agrees to accept the painting?*
3. *What course of action might you take to resolve this situation and why?*

BARTERING PRACTICES IN COUNSELING

Long before the use of gold and silver coins, paper money, checks, or credit cards were common ways to pay for goods or services, bartering was an ordinary practice. Bartering refers to the exchange of goods and/or services in lieu of money. Tribal societies such as those in Papua New Guinea, Irian Jaya, Indonesia, and some areas in Africa, still barter their goods and services, as do many of our Western contemporaries who live in agricultural, farming, and rural communities (Canter, Bennett, Jones, & Nagy, 1996; Koocher & Keith-Spiegel, 1998). The counseling profession is not untouched by the practice of bartering. Many professional counselors accept nonmonetary goods or services from their clients in return for their therapeutic services. Bartered services can include things such as mechanical repairs, housework, babysitting, or secretarial work, while bartered-for goods can include items such as chickens, cabinetry, produce, sculpture, and so on (Zur, 2006).

The revisions to the ACA *Code of Ethics* in 2005 indicated a subtle move away from the code's earlier position that bartering be strongly discouraged in order to embrace a more reasonable and flexible stance. Standard A.10.d (ACA, 2005) states:

> Counselors may barter only if the relationship is not exploitive or harmful and does not place the counselor in an unfair advantage, if the client requests it, and if such arrangements are an accepted practice among professionals in the community. Counselors consider the cultural implications of bartering and discuss relevant concerns with clients and document such agreements in a clear written contract.

This standard cautions counselors from engaging in bartering practices without careful thought and planning and, concurrently, recognizes that the exchange of goods and services might be acceptable and usual practice for some client groups. Moreover, the standard highlights the importance of acting on behalf of clients' well-being in all aspects of the therapeutic process, even payment practices.

At the same time, bartering, like gift-giving, raises concerns with regard to boundaries in a therapeutic relationship (Corey et al., 2011). Because this practice can potentially generate conflicts, exploitations, and corruption of the professional relationship, most counselors prefer to shy away from it (Gerig, 2004). Bartering arrangements imply, at the very least, boundary crossings and, in some instances, they initiate multiple relationships. For example, when goods are bartered for therapeutic services, no new relationship is generated aside from the therapeutic one, and this type of exchange merely constitutes a boundary crossing. However, when a client provides services in exchange for counseling, a more significant boundary crossing occurs because the client takes on the additional role of employee to the counselor (Zur, 2006). If services exchanged are not perceived as competently provided or equal in value, this may leave the counselor and client in a precarious situation and having to make a determination about how to resolve their differences. Counselors have an ethical duty not to abandon their clients, and, thus, they may face challenges in upholding fidelity to the client while also trying to advocate for fair payment.

Landmark 3

CASE EXAMPLE

Luana, a 4th grade teacher, complained about feelings of stress and anxiety to her school principal. The latter advised her to seek counseling and referred her to Sylvia, a therapist with whom she was acquainted. Luana followed her principal's recommendation and began to see Sylvia, with whom she formed a very good rapport. After one of their counseling sessions, Sylvia casually mentioned to Luana that her son, Logan, who is in the 3rd grade, was having difficulties at school and that his grades had been declining since the last semester. Luana acknowledged how difficult it can be for children when they get behind in their work and then suggested to Sylvia that perhaps she could take on the task of tutoring Logan until his grades were better. Luana hesitantly admitted that she was struggling to afford counseling, but would be open to tutoring Logan in exchange for counseling sessions or a reduced counseling fee.

1. *Considering the circumstances of the case, what do you believe are the possible benefits or harms to Sylvia and Luana's counseling relationship should they agree to this bartering arrangement?*
2. *What would you advise Sylvia to do if she consulted you about the case?*

SELF-DISCLOSURE

Self-disclosure, or the unveiling of personal information by professional counselors about themselves to clients, can be viewed as an act that is deliberate, unavoidable, or accidental. Deliberate self-disclosure takes place when counselors intentionally communicate personal information to their clients. This type of disclosure may be verbal, such as when a counselor tells a client where she grew up, or about her favorite hobbies, or about life experiences that mirror those that a client is going through. It might also be nonverbal and communicated, for instance, in a counselor's mannerisms and how he chooses to dress or decorate his office (Barnett, 1998; Gutheil & Gabbard, 1998; Mahalik, Van Ormer, & Simi, 2000). Deliberate self-disclosures are self-revealing, as in the case of counselors disclosing information about themselves, or self-involving, which occurs when counselors reveal personal reactions or emotions (e.g., anger, compassion) to incidents that happen during counseling sessions (Knox, Hess, Petersen, & Hill, 1997).

Unavoidable self-disclosure refers to a variety of information about counselors that is obvious and inescapable to their clients. These disclosures usually include things such as counselors' gender and race, physical appearance (e.g., visible tattoos or facial hair), tone of voice, accent, apparent disabilities, marital status when indicated by a wedding ring or photos, and pregnancy (Barnett, 1998; Tillman, 1998). Unavoidable self-disclosures become even more extensive if therapists provide services from their homes where their economic status, family situation, and even information about their pets, hobbies, habits, and neighborhood are visible.

Accidental self-disclosure typically occurs when, by happenstance, counselors' personal preferences and lifestyle choices or valued activities overlap with those of their clients in social settings. For example, accidental self-disclosure takes place when counselors find themselves dining at the same favorite restaurant or shopping at the same preferred fish market as that of their clients. Counselors also can self-disclose something about themselves in counseling sessions through spontaneous verbal or nonverbal reactions, such as surprise, appreciation, anger, and so on (Stricker & Fisher, 1990).

Based on the above descriptions, we get a sense of how counselors can intentionally or unintentionally share bits of their personal selves with clients. We also must realize that self-disclosure, or personal revelations, encompass more than what we tell clients with regard to the details of our lives. There is a certain amount of personal disclosure that happens simply by our clients encountering us in our bodily selves and professional surroundings. When seen from an existential and phenomenological viewpoint, the counseling relationship is an authentic human encounter in which we share in the way of *being-in-the-world* of clients who appeal to us for help. Counselors, therefore, cannot respond to that appeal without being wholly present to the other, which suggests that they cannot respond to clients merely with cool or unembodied responses, although these might look like proper counseling techniques or skills. A genuine therapeutic encounter entails a kind of *being-in-the-world* of our clients that opens the door for them to be privileged in sharing, to some extent, in our own way of *being-in-the-world*. Viewed through the lens of genuine therapeutic encounter, a certain amount of self-disclosure seems inescapable.

Landmark 4

CASE EXAMPLE

Latifa, a 30-year-old Eastern European woman, told her therapist, Olivia, that she just discovered that she is pregnant with her sixth child. She is completely overwhelmed and is certain that this child will be a burden on her and the family. She

(*continued*)

confessed that she is contemplating having an abortion. Olivia unhesitatingly started to tell Latifa how she herself came from a huge family of 10 children and that she was the seventh among her siblings. Olivia continued that one day her mother told her that she had planned to abort her while she was only 2 weeks old.

1. *How would you evaluate Olivia's decision to use self-disclosure in this case?*
2. *How might Olivia's disclosure affect Latifa's relationship to her?*
3. *Do you believe Olivia's boundary crossing was beneficial, neutral, or harmful? Why?*

THERAPEUTIC AND NONTHERAPEUTIC TOUCH

Touch constitutes an important aspect of nonverbal communication in human relationships. Messages sent between humans through physical touch are powerful and are often remembered more intensely even than words that are shared. Touch has been efficaciously used in most healing traditions throughout history (Zur & Nordmarken, 2011); it is significantly important to healthy human development; and it has been shown to provide valuable benefits in medical treatment, as well as some psychotherapeutic interventions (Floyd, 2000). As much as counselors affirm the place of nonverbal cues and messages in their work, the use of touch in therapy often generates concern and poses dilemmas for counselors. The main concern about physical touch is that it can be misused for sexual exploitation by unscrupulous therapists, or it can connote sexual intents to vulnerable clients. Following Freud, who viewed touch as a threat to the reputation of psychoanalysis and an obstacle to the cure of neurosis, many risk management guidelines, consumer protection agencies, insurance companies, and ethical and legal experts issue warnings about the perils of touch. Their perception is that any nonerotic touch can potentially lead therapists to embark on the slippery slope toward a sexual relationship (Zur & Nordmarken, 2011).

On the other hand, verbal communication coupled with touch has the potential to enhance expressions of empathy, safety, and comfort and provide clients with an increased feeling of being heard, noticed, and understood by the therapist (Hunter & Struve, 1998). Sometimes therapists intentionally utilize various means of touch as strategies to enhance a positive connection and trust within the therapeutic alliance (Phalan, 2009; Smith, Clance, & Imes, 1998), to greet or sooth clients, to help them relax or quiet down, or even to reassure them. These forms of therapeutic touch can include a hug; light touch; stroking of a client's head; rubbing of a client's back, shoulder, or arm; rocking; or hand-holding (Zur & Nordmarken, 2011). Nontherapeutic touches that are counterclinical, clearly unethical, and even illegal in some states and that need to be avoided are:

1. Sexual touch in which the intent is to create sexual arousal by touching the client's sexual organs, buttock, breasts, stomach, or mouth.

2. Hostile–violent touch that involves a counselor being physically hostile to a client and even violently assaulting the latter.
3. Punishing touch in which a counselor uses punitive measures, such as slapping a young client on the buttocks or slapping a young client on the hand as punishment for "undesired behavior."

DIGNITY, AUTONOMY, AND AUTHENTICITY: CONCEPTS FOR ETHICAL DECISION MAKING

As we have seen, the counseling field has evolved in how it judges relationship boundaries between professionals and clients. The move toward describing potential benefits of multiple relationships, as well as gift-giving and bartering that is evidenced in 2005 ACA *Code of Ethics* are examples of how interactions that traditionally were seen as taboo are now more open to counselors' careful appraisal for possible advantages to clients. However, this seemingly more open approach communicated in the code does not mean that counselors need not carefully evaluate the ethical quality of boundary crossings. In the sections that follow, we describe several concepts, including autonomy, dignity, and authenticity, that can be used in conjunction with the ACA *Code of Ethics* (2005) to help counselors discern outcomes for boundary dilemmas. We then adapt these concepts to a decision-making model counselors can use to reach ethical decisions.

Protecting the Dignity and Autonomy of Clients

The first section of the ACA *Code of Ethics* states, "The primary responsibility of counselors is to respect the dignity and promote the welfare of clients" (2005, A.1.a). Respecting clients' dignity means that counselors view them as human beings who are ends in themselves and not means to satisfy their own personal egos or desires (Brenner, 2009). The idea that people are *ends* was championed by Immanuel Kant, an 18th-century German thinker (1724–1804). Kant postulated that human dignity is reflected in the right each person has to be autonomous and, thus, to make choices and create precepts by which he or she will live, provided that those choices and precepts, when enacted, do not infringe on others' similar right to be self-directed (Brenner, 2009). Stated differently, autonomy suggests that each person (rather than an outside entity such as a government, a religious group, or even a counselor) has a right to determine what is ethical and good. To provide balance to people serving their own needs and desires in creating their moral codes, Kant also proposed that the conclusions a person draws about what is ethical must be able to be confirmed as a universal law to be followed by others. Thus, the test of what is good and ethical is that one's personal decision can be turned into a universal precept.

Counselors readily embrace the connection Kant makes between dignity and autonomy. For instance, when a counselor helps a client work through the options related to a decision she has to make and is able to help her come to her own course of action without imposing judgment or personal values onto the client, that counselor is said to have shown respect for the client's dignity and to have treated her as an end in herself. On the other hand, when counselors treat clients as objects that they can use for their own personal gain, they are seen as diminishing clients' dignity. For example, if a counselor educator avows that he quit his teaching job to pursue full-time private practice primarily because he makes more money from clients than he does at teaching, the counselor can seem to be using clients as means (to making more money) rather than as ends.

Although Kant recommended that people subject their "laws" or ethical decisions to a court of public opinion (even if only in their imagination), his decision-making model based on the notion of autonomy is, admittedly, limited. The problem is that when it comes to creating personal laws, it is doubtful that, in all circumstances, people will abide strictly to the laws that they themselves create or that they will punish themselves for not upholding their laws. In a sense, it is easier to forgive oneself for a transgression against a personal precept than it is to forgive oneself for breaking someone else's law. To put this to a boundary-related example, consider a counselor who determines for herself that to touch her clients is unethical. When this same counselor meets a client who has just experienced a tremendous loss and is crying while telling her story, that counselor may suddenly reach out and grasp her client's hand. She has made a decision not to live up to her own precept, but in evaluating her choice, the counselor might find many reasons why she touched her client and treat her own "transgression" lightly.

Acting With Authenticity in the Counseling Relationship

Kant provided us with two important concepts: the dignity of the person and autonomy (the protection of which is a confirmation of a person's dignity). Upholding a client's dignity and protecting his or her right to autonomy are both seen as goods in the counseling profession. Likewise, from Kant's perspective, counselors are afforded the right to determine (autonomously) what constitutes ethical behavior with regard to their professional endeavors. However, because it is sometimes easiest to bend or break the moral precepts that we ourselves make, autonomy itself is not a flawless means by which to appraise what is or is not ethical. To help account for the limits of autonomy, existentialists and phenomenologists, Soren Kierkegaard (1813–1855), Martin Heidegger (1889–1976), and Jean Paul Sartre (1905–1980) drew on the concept of authenticity as a way to help people sincerely do what is good and ethical. In a sense, being authentic is a remedy for just making individual laws and trying unsuccessfully to live up to them.

Before we look at how these philosophers understood authenticity, we consider what is not implied in the term. Despite what we might think about authenticity, Kierkegaard, Heidegger, and Sartre do not equate this concept to uniqueness of character, individual integrity, or personal fulfillment. Moreover, authenticity does not mean *being true* to oneself, and neither does it mean being honest or inwardly sincere to oneself. Furthermore, the mere fact of telling the honest truth about oneself is not proof of sincerity (Carman, 2009). To be sincere means to spontaneously and naturally *present oneself* sincerely, without a calculated or deliberate effort that could appear manipulative. Indeed, as Sartre observed, even when one is telling the truth about oneself, the fact of making a deliberate effort to be sincere can be self-defeating (Carman, 2009). If these common-sense definitions of authenticity do not connote what the philosophers understood by authenticity, what then is authenticity and what is it to be an authentic counselor?

Being Authentic According to Kierkegaard

For Kierkegaard, the authentic person is one who can wholeheartedly commit to something or someone in a holistic, concrete, and unconditional manner. Authenticity is only possible when we fully embrace the present moment and set of circumstances in which we happen to be and make the best possible ethical decision while being open to the outcomes of our decisions without making excuses for them or avoiding responsibility for them by hiding behind membership in a group. (An example of hiding behind a group might occur when a counselor says, "I wanted to accept that small gift from my client, but the *Code of Ethics* advised me not to.") Being authentic means that one is not afraid to take a strong "leap of faith" completely independent from reason in order to commit blindly and personally to something or someone in every moment of one's life. While for Kierkegaard, this blind personal commitment or "leap of faith" was to God (Carman, 2009), counselors who are striving to be authentic can ask themselves to what or to whom is their personal commitment as professionals. The moment one chooses to embrace the counseling profession, he or she makes a commitment to a mission clearly spelled out in the Preamble of the ACA *Code of Ethics* (2005). This mission affirms that counselors commit to fostering the development of the human person throughout the lifespan and embrace diversity and multiculturalism in support of the worth, dignity, and uniqueness of the human person. Hence, being an authentic counselor entails that, come what may, the counselor takes a leap of faith to commit to the welfare of clients, even if it demands crossing some boundaries like visiting a client in the hospital or attending a religious or secular event that is part of a client's cultural tradition.

Being Authentic According to Heidegger

For Martin Heidegger, authenticity is understood as that which is most *my own* and has to do with my unique relationship to myself as opposed to my relations to others or the way others see me. Authenticity defies conformism and comprises two distinct features, namely *resoluteness* and *forerunning*. Being resolute means possessing the practical wisdom to respond intelligently, skillfully, and with finesse to the exigencies of concrete situations without minimizing their importance or treating them as a mere general state of affairs that are better dealt with by following rigid generic rules (Carman, 2009). In other words, to be an authentic professional counselor is to avoid falling into what Heidegger terms the *everydayness* or *averageness* of the counseling world that urges us to bow unthinkingly or without self-reflection to authority figures and mainstream views within the field. To be an authentic professional counselor entails that we break free from actual situations we happen to find ourselves in and resolutely confront and pursue *possibility*, that is, our potential for becoming. As described in Chapter 2, being authentic means that we use our professional consciences and sets of virtues to orient us toward the right decisions in any given circumstances, to respond to the demands of our counseling profession just for love of it, and to revolutionize and expand its and our possibilities.

Forerunning is a concept that suggests that a person must take full and uncompromising ownership of personal commitments, even when they diametrically oppose ethical norms that apply to everyone, including oneself. Forerunning, which for Heidegger means "running against or even into death" (Carman, 2009, p. 234), implies that professional counselors choose to firmly uphold their personal commitments against all odds and accept to face the vulnerability of the counseling world, as well as their identity, while being willing and ready to embrace future possibilities, however fragile they may be and assume the anxiety such commitments produce.

Being Authentic According to Sartre

For Jean Paul Sartre, authenticity entails that we stop acting in *bad faith* (*mauvaise foi*) or self-deception. In order to conceal a fear of the potential consequence of making a choice, Sartre suggested that people prefer to deceive themselves by thinking that they do not have the freedom to make choices. They pretend that they are not responsible by believing that their choices are already predetermined by their character or circumstances, or they will refuse to make *personal commitments* arguing that their possibilities are indefinitely open ended (Carman, 2009). Thus, by acting in bad faith, and by just going with the flow and sticking with the safest, easiest choice while remaining oblivious to the innumerable options available to them, inauthentic people submit themselves to the whims of circumstances they find themselves in. Consequently, they are more objects than conscious human beings; or, to use Sartre's metaphysical distinctions; they are more "being-in-itself" than "being-for-itself."

AN EXISTENTIAL PHENOMENOLOGICAL FRAMEWORK FOR DECISION MAKING

We invite you now to think about how the concepts of autonomy, dignity, and authenticity help counselors to take full and committed responsibility for their ethical choices surrounding boundary issues. However, we first must acknowledge that there is much wisdom propagated by the counseling literature with regard to ethical awareness and decision making. The following helpful tips should be considered throughout any decision-making process: (a) be perpetually ethically alert through constant questioning and assuming of personal responsibility; (b) be cognizant of ethical codes and legal standards and use them critically during any ethical decision-making process; (c) be constantly up to date on new research and theory development in the scientific and professional literature; (d) be aware of one's own fallibility with regard to being an ethical professional counselor; (e) be humble enough to question one's own decisions and behavior and open to the questioning of others; (f) be able to second-guess one's own convictions or certainties; and (g) be aware and make use of the crucial role of consultation with trusted colleagues (Pope & Keith-Spiegel, 2008). To these practical recommendations, we now add a set of questions grounded in existential and phenomenological philosophy that counselors can use to make ethical decisions when boundary dilemmas arise.

1. Am I Using My Client as an End or as a Means for Personal Gain?

Kant enjoins us to "act in such a way that you always treat humanity, whether in your own person, or in the person of any other, never simply as a means, but always at the same time as an end" (Grassian, 1992, p. 89). Thus, in any ethical dilemma, counselors should consider the extent to which their preferred decision respects a client's dignity, and by extension, his or her autonomy. For example, when making boundary-related decisions, such as whether to hug or touch a client, to have a meal with a client, to strike up a friendship with a client's relative, and so on, counselors need to evaluate whether their actions account for the client's evaluation of the decision (e.g., whether or not he or she wants to be hugged) and respect the client's desires or whether their decisions are motivated by their own personal needs or desires and subtly treat clients as a means to meet their own ends (e.g., a counselor might want to be seen as sympathetic and so, without garnering consent, decide to hug a client to feel personally assured that she is perceived as caring). Because of the inherent power differential between counselors and clients, counselors need to take into account the possibility that a client's consent to accept a hug or not to protest the counselor's friendship with a family member might not reflect the client's true wishes.

2. Am I Allowing My Client to be Autonomous?

The notion of autonomy is at the heart of Kant's moral theory. People are autonomous when they are bound only by the authority of their own will and not by the will of others. Each person's rational will is thus the sole authoritative legislator and executioner of his or her moral law. Based on this principle, counselors do well to ask themselves if they are allowing their clients to be self-governing. A key question in determining the ethical quality of an action therefore is: Does the counselor's course of action respect and uphold a client's right to decide what she wills or does not will, what she seeks to avoid or not avoid, or what course of action she wants to pursue or not pursue? For example, when a counselor tries to dissuade her male client from moving to another state under the pretense that he will be deprived of the helpful and nurturing environment he was getting in counseling, but also with the quiet knowledge that she will greatly miss this invigorating client, the counselor is not respecting her client's autonomy. She is, in fact, subtly blocking her client's right to be self-governing and can be seen as trying to impose her own will on a self-determinant human being capable of making his own choice.

3. Am I Authentically Honoring My Commitment to My Profession and My Client?

Counseling is an authentic encounter that necessitates that counselors share the life, existence, and way of *being-in-the-world* of clients. The professional counselor's vocation demands that helpers be concerned primarily with the direct care of other human beings and motivated and committed to act for their good. In light of Kierkegaard's view of the authentic self, counselors can ask themselves how much they are concretely and unconditionally committed to their professional vocation and to the good of clients entrusted to their care. When it comes to self-disclosure, gift exchanges, bartering services, or any form of nonsexual multiple relationships with clients, counselors do well to reflect on the extent to which the decision to cross a boundary truly is grounded in genuine client care. If the crossing does seem intentionally to care for a client, counselors then must ask if they are ready to allow their commitment to a client's care to lead them to take the "leap of faith" and cross the boundary, even if ethical codes advise against it.

4. Am I Authentically Resolute or Am I Acting as a Conformist?

To be authentic, Heidegger calls us not to get stuck in *everydayness* or *averageness*, but to confront and break free from every circumstance we find ourselves in and to resolutely pursue future possibility, that is, our potential becoming. To help in the process of making a decision about whether or not to get involved in a business partnership with a client, give a ride to a client, or take a walk outside the office with the client, counselors might ask themselves: Am I in this situation embracing virtue as the style of my professional life? Am I pursuing my full potential as a professional being? Am I responding to my client out of sole love and wholehearted commitment to my counseling profession? Am I really trying to revolutionize the profession and expand its possibilities?

5. Am I Authentically Being a Forerunner or Acting as a Risk Manager?

To be authentic professionals, counselors need to make their personal commitments to the profession and to clients their "most own." Forerunning implies "running against or even into death." When counselors hear the genuine call from their professional conscience to cross a boundary with a client in order to provide a comforting touch or a reassuring hug, or to attend a client's celebratory event, or to sit in the same church or on the same school committee as clients, they may ask themselves: Am I being a conformist or running against the odds come what may? They might also ask themselves whether they will listen only to the voice of professional authority telling them to avoid crossing the boundary or also heed the wisdom of their personal commitments to the profession and the welfare of their clients.

6. Am I Acting in "Good Faith" or in "Bad Faith"?

Taking a risk-management approach definitely does not propel professional counselors to authenticity. The fear of lawsuits or of embarking on a *slippery slope* continues to deter numerous counselors from taking a genuine leap of faith when it comes to crossing some boundaries in order to help their clients. Hence, when faced with situations in which they need to cross some boundaries, such as receiving a small gift, disclosing some personal information, or even providing some counseling sessions for an exchange of goods due to a client's extraneous circumstances, counselors may evaluate the decision by asking: Am I not responding to a client's need because I only wish to abide by the conventional moral standards or fixed codes of our professional communities and organizations? In that regard, counselors must ask: Am I acting in "good faith" or in "bad faith?" Am I really standing up to my responsibility vis-à-vis my professional calling as a counselor and the clients whose welfare I am supposed to care for, or am I merely acting more as an object rather than a conscious human being?

SIGNPOSTS FOR FUTURE TREKS

This journey we have undertaken into our professional counseling world brought us to explore the complex territory of boundary crossings and boundary violations. We hope that as we come to the close of our trek you have been enriched with the awareness that not all boundary crossings are necessarily violations of our *Code of Ethics* and that in some circumstances boundary crossings can be beneficial. However, in all cases of possible boundary crossings, counselors do well to reflect carefully on the potential benefits and harms that might come to clients from the crossing, as well as on their motivation for engaging in a boundary crossing, especially when it might be deemed by others as a violation. Moreover, we hope that you will keep in mind the concepts of autonomy, dignity, and authenticity (garnered from Kant and from an existential and phenomenological understanding of ethics) when dealing with boundary dilemmas. Here are some handy points of reflection that reflect these concepts:

- Am I using my client as an end or as a means for personal gain?
- Am I allowing my client to be autonomous?
- Am I authentically honoring my commitment to my profession and my client?
- Am I authentically resolute or am I acting as a conformist?
- Am I authentically being a forerunner or acting as a risk manager?
- Am I acting in "good faith" or in "bad faith"?

INSIGHTS GAINED FROM THE JOURNEY

When dealing with ethical dilemmas related to boundary issues, we must first acknowledge that there is a certain amount of flexibility in how professionals determine what is and is not a helpful boundary crossing. Moreover, each of us who participates in the counseling profession must humbly recognize that human beings, including ourselves, are not infallible. Without a doubt, the majority of professional counselors respond to the call to enter the profession with a genuine desire to care for the welfare of the clients, act on good intentions, and readily abide by the *Code of Ethics*. Yet, we are aware that counselors do engage in boundary violations and abuse the power differential that exists between themselves and clients.

The truth from which no one can escape is that counseling professionals are made of flesh and blood, wholly and fully human. We are not made of wood, glass, stone, or marble. As human beings, we are endowed with feelings, emotions, and desires. Because counseling is primarily about relationships and genuine encounters between two human beings that mutually take part in the way of *being-in-the-world-of-each-other*, there is little chance of being able to escape personal attractions or temptations to misuse the counseling relationship at times for one's own gain. It would be naïve for any professional to think that just going by the book, following the rules, or dogmatically abiding by the code will allow him or her to always sail to safety without violating or even crossing any boundary. The *Code of Ethics* is not an airtight shield against violations. The code does not say it all. The code is not and will never be finite. What, then, is the code? It is the lighthouse that can lead the ship to safety in a stormy night, but the captain of the ship has to do all the maneuvers to avoid crashing against rocks and reefs and get to safe harbor.

Hence, this is why, without undermining the importance of our *Code of Ethics*, we have proposed along this journey a framework that can help counselors navigate dilemmas without risking the life of the therapeutic relationship by crashing it against the rocks and reefs of boundary violations. Grounding the decision-making process in serious philosophical reflections will help us discern how best we can help our clients whenever we are faced with the decision to engage in sexual or nonsexual boundary crossings or violations. By sincerely and genuinely asking ourselves how authentic we are in our therapeutic encounter with our clients, we might have a clearer idea how to proceed, even when the code does not provide us with every possible answer.

MOVING FORWARD: CASE STUDY AND REFLECTION QUESTIONS

Jobina, a 22-year-old single mother from India, is in counseling with Koreta because of stress-related issues. Jobina regularly complains to Koreta that she is a bad mother to her 3-year-old only daughter and that she sometimes does not know how to handle her. Koreta, herself a mother of two young children aged 4 and 6, offered that Jobina and her daughter could join her and her family on outings to the beach in view of encouraging socialization for Jobina's daughter and modeling parenting. As time went by, Jobina's daughter started to get attached to Koreta's family, and Jobina herself felt that she was functioning much better than in the time before she started counseling with Koreta. However, Koreta recently found out that she was pregnant with her third child and decided that she needs to terminate the counseling relationship with Jobina. Upon hearing that news, Jobina told Koreta, "You have helped me a lot with regard to my stress, and I feel like I'm a much better parent. My daughter seems to love to be with you and your children. I feel like I owe you more than I can repay. During your pregnancy, could I come to your home and help you with chores around the house and even babysit your kids when you need a break? It would give my daughter a chance to continue to see your children, with whom she has grown so close, and would help me feel like I'm giving back for all you have done." Koreta asked for some time to think about it.

REFLECTION QUESTIONS

1. *What options do you believe Koreta has at her disposal to show that she is not trying to use Jobina only for personal gain?*
2. *What potential response could Koreta give that would show that she is not infringing on Jobina's autonomy?*
3. *What could Koreta do to show that she is authentically honoring her commitment to the counseling profession and to Jobina?*
4. *What could Koreta do to show that she is authentically resolute and not acting as a conformist?*

5. *What could Koreta do to be a forerunner and not a risk manager?*
6. *What could Koreta do to show that she is acting in good faith rather than in bad faith?*

REFERENCES

American Counseling Association. (2005). *ACA code of ethics*. Alexandria, VA: Author.

Anderson, S. K., & Kitchener, K. S. (1996). Nonromantic, nonsexual posttherapy relationships between psychologists and former clients: An exploratory study of critical incidents. *Professional Psychology: Research and Practice, 27*, 59–66.

Barnett, J. E. (1998). Should psychotherapists self-disclose? Clinical and ethical considerations. In L. VandeCreek, S. Knapp, & T. Jackson (Eds.), *Innovations in clinical practice: A source book*, Vol. *16* (pp. 419–428). Sarasota, FL: Professional Resource Exchange.

Berkman, C. S., Turner, S. G., Cooper, M., Polnerow, D., & Swartz, M. (2000). Sexual contact with clients: Assessment of social workers' attitudes and educational Preparation. *Social Work, 45*, 223–235.

Borys, D. S. (1994). Maintaining therapeutic boundaries: The motive is therapeutic effectiveness, not defensive practice. *Ethics and Behavior, 4*, 267–273.

Borys, D. S., & Pope, K. S. (1989). Dual relationships between therapist and client: A national study of psychologists, psychiatrists, and social workers. *Professional Psychology: Research and Practice, 20*, 283–293.

Brendel, D. H., Chu, J., Radden, J., Leeper, H., Pope, H. G., Samson, I. et al. (2007). Price of a gift: An approach to receiving gifts from patients in psychiatric practice. *Harvard Review of Psychiatry, 15*, 43–51.

Brenner, A. (2009). The lived-body and the dignity of human beings. In H. L. Dreyfuss, & M. A. Wrathall (Eds.), *A companion to phenomenology and existentialism*. Blackwell Companions to Philosophy (pp. 478–488). Chichester, West Sussex: Wiley-Blackwell.

Brodsky, A. M. (1989). Sex between patient and therapist: Psychology's data and response. In G. O. Gabbard (Ed.), *Sexual exploitation in professional relationships* (pp. 15–25). Washington, DC: American Psychiatric Press.

Canter, M., Bennett, B., Jones, S., & Nagy, T. (1996). *Ethics for psychologists*. Washington, DC: American Psychological Association.

Carman, T. (2009). The concept of authenticity. In H. L. Dreyfuss, & M. A. Wrathall (Eds.). *A companion to phenomenology and existentialism*. Blackwell Companions to Philosophy (pp. 478–488). Chichester, West Sussex: Wiley-Blackwell.

Coleman, E., & Schaefer, S. (1986). Boundaries of sex and intimacy between client and counselor. *Journal of Counseling and Development, 64*, 341–344.

Corey, G., Corey, M. S., & Callanan, P. (2011). *Issues and ethics in the helping professions*. Pacific Grove, CA: Brooks/Cole.

Cox, Frank. D. (2002). *Human intimacy: Marriage, the family, and its meaning* (9th ed.). Belmont, CA: Wadsworth/Thomson Learning.

Feldman-Summers, S., & Jones, G. (1984). Psychological impacts of sexual contact between therapists or other health care practitioners and their clients. *Journal of Consulting and Clinical Psychology, 52*, 1054–1061.

Floyd, K. (2000). Affectionate same-sex touch: The influence of homophobia on observers' perceptions. *The Journal of Social Psychology, 140*, 774–788.

Gerig, M. (2004). Receiving gifts from clients: Ethical and therapeutic issues. *Journal of Mental Health Counseling, 26*, 199–210.

Golden, R. L., & Sonneborn, S. (1998). Ethics in clinical practice with older adults: Recognizing biases and respecting boundaries. *Generations, 22*, 82–86.

Gottlieb, M. C. (1993). Avoiding exploitive dual relationships: A decision-making model. *Psychotherapy, 30,* 41–48.

Grassian, V. (1992). *Moral reasoning: Ethical theory and some contemporary moral problems.* Englewood Cliffs, NJ: Prentice-Hall.

Gutheil, T. G., & Gabbard, G. O. (1993). The concept of boundaries in clinical practice: Theoretical and risk-management dimensions. *American Journal of Psychiatry, 50,* 188–196.

Gutheil, T. G., & Gabbard, G. O. (1998). Misuses and misunderstandings of boundary theory in clinical and regulatory settings. *American Journal of Psychiatry, 155,* 409–414.

Hahn, W. K. (1998) Gifts in psychotherapy: An intersubjective approach to patient gifts. *Psychotherapy; Theory/Research/Practice/Training, 35,* 78–86.

Haug, I. (1999). Boundaries and the use and misuse of power and authority: Ethical complexities for clergy psychotherapists. *Journal of Counseling & Development, 77,* 411–417.

Holtzman, B. L. (1984). Who's the therapist here? Dynamics underlying therapist-client sexual relations. *Smith College Studies in Social Work, 54,* 204–224.

Hunter, M., & Struve, J. (1998). *The ethical use of touch in psychotherapy.* Thousand Oaks, CA: Sage Publications.

Kagle, J. D., & Giebelhausen, P. N. (1994). Dual relationships and professional boundaries. *Social Work, 39,* 213–220.

Kaplan, D. (2006). The end of "clear and imminent danger." *Counseling Today, January.* Retrieved from http://ct.counseling.org/2006/01/ct-online-ethics-update

Knox, S., Hess, S. A., Pedersen, D. A., & Hill, C. E. (1997). A qualitative analysis of client perceptions of the effects of helpful therapist self-disclosure in long-term therapy. *Journal of Counselling Psychology, 44,* 274–283.

Knox, S., Hess, S. A., Williams, E. N., & Hill, C. E. (2003). Here's a little something for you: How therapists respond to clients gifts. *Journal of Counseling Psychology, 50,* 199–210.

Koocher, G. P., & Keith-Spiegel, P. (1998). *Ethics in psychology: Professional standards and cases* (2nd ed.). New York: Oxford University Press.

Lazarus, A. A., & Zur, O. (Eds.). (2002). *Dual relationships and psychotherapy.* New York: Springer.

Mahalik, J. R., van Ormer, E. A., & Simi, N. L. (2000). Ethical issues in using self-disclosure in feminist therapy. In M. M. Brabeck (Ed.), *Practicing feminist ethics in psychology.* Washington: American Psychological Association.

Moleski, S. M., & Kiselica, M. S. (2005). Dual relationships: A continuum ranging from the destructive to the therapeutic. *Journal of Counseling & Development, 83,* 3–11.

Nelson, L. G., Summers, J. A., & Turnbull, A. P. (2004). Boundaries in family-professional relationships: Implications for special education. *Remedial and Special Education, 25,* 153–165.

Pearson, B., & Piazza, N. (1997). Classification of dual relationships in the helping professions. *Counselor Education and Supervision, 37,* 89–100.

Phalan, J. E. (2009). Exploring the use of touch in the psychotherapeutic setting: A phenomenological review. *Psychotherapy: Theory, Research, Practice, Training, 46,* 97–111.

Pope, K. S. (1990). Therapist-patient sexual involvement: A review of the research. *Clinical Psychology Review, 10,* 477–490.

Pope, K. S., & Keith-Spiegel, P. (2008). A practical approach to boundaries in psychotherapy: Making decisions, bypassing blunders, and mending fences. *Journal of Clinical Psychology, 54,* 638–652.

Regehr, C., & Glancy, G. (1995). Sexual exploitation of patients: Issues for colleagues. *American Journal of Orthopsychiatry, 65,* 194–202.

Saad, G., & Gill, T. (2003). An evolutionary psychology perspective on gift-giving among young adults. *Psychology & Marketing, 20,* 765–784.

Schoener, G., Milgrom, J., & Gonsiorek, J. (1989). Therapeutic responses to clients who have been sexually abused by psychotherapists. In G. Schoener, & J. Milgrom (Eds.),

Psychotherapists' sexual involvement with clients: Intervention and prevention (pp. 95–112). Minneapolis: Walk-In Counseling Center.

Shapiro, E. L., & Ginzberg, R. (2002). Parting gift: Termination rituals in group therapy. *International Journal of Group Psychotherapy, 52*, 319–335.

Smith, E., Clance, P. R., & Imes, S. (Eds.). (1998). *Touch in psychotherapy: Theory, research and practice*, New York: Guilford Press.

Sonne, J., Meyer, C., Borys, D., & Marshall, V. (1985). Clients' reactions to sexual intimacy in therapy. *American Journal of Orthopsychiatry, 55*, 183–189.

Sonne, J. L., & Pope, K. S. (1991). Treating victims of therapist-patient sexual involvement. *Psychotherapy, 28*, 174–187.

Spandler, H., Burman, E., Goldberg, B., Margison, F., & Amos, T. (2000). "A double-edged sword": Understanding gifts in psychotherapy. *European Journal of Psychotherapy, Counseling and Health, 3*, 77–101.

Stricker, G., & Fisher, M. (Eds.). (1990). *Self-disclosure in the therapeutic relationship.* New York: Plenum.

Tillman, J. G. (1998). Psychodynamic psychotherapy, religious beliefs, and self-disclosure. *Journal of Psychotherapy, 52*, 273–286.

Van Kaam, A. (1966). *The art of existential counseling. A new perspective in psychotherapy.* Wilkes-Barre, PA: Dimension Books.

Zur, O. (2004). To cross or not to cross: Do boundaries in therapy protect or harm. *The Psychotherapy Bulletin, 39*, 27–32.

Zur, O. (2006). Therapeutic boundaries and dual relationships in rural practice: Ethical, clinical and standard of care considerations. *Journal of Rural Community Psychology. E9/1.*

Zur, O. (2007). *Boundaries in psychotherapy: Ethical and clinical explorations.* Washington, DC: APA Books.

Zur, O. (2011a). Dual relationships, multiple relationships & boundaries in psychotherapy, counseling & mental health. Retrieved from http://www.zurinstitute.com/dualrelationships.html

Zur, O. (2011b). *Gifts in psychotherapy.* Retrieved from http://www.zurinstitute.com/giftsintherapy.html

Zur, O., & Nordmarken, N. (2011). *To touch or not to touch: Exploring the myth of prohibition on touch in psychotherapy and counseling.* Retrieved from http://www.zurinstitute.com/touchintherapy.html

6

Ethical and Legal Considerations for Confidentiality in Counseling

Catherine A. Sherman, Gina M. Gordon, and Kailla Edger

THE FORESEEN DESTINATION

After reading this chapter, it is our hope that students will:

- Understand the purpose, practice, and value of maintaining confidentiality in counseling.
- Begin to develop clinical awareness of when confidentiality should be broken.
- Be able to articulate how confidentiality differs in individual and group therapy settings.
- Appreciate issues of confidentiality in the school setting.
- Be able to engage in thoughtful discussion regarding issues of confidentiality.

GETTING ON THE ROAD

One of the bedrocks of the counseling relationship is the practice of maintaining a client's confidences. Confidentiality is a counselor's ethical duty to safeguard client disclosures shared during counseling sessions, except under certain circumstances or provisions. This duty, however, is more than an ethical or legal obligation; it is an essential therapeutic condition. Confidentiality speaks directly to the nature of the counseling relationship, and its value is universally affirmed both by individual practitioners and all prominent counseling associations and professional organizations. The American Counseling Association (ACA) *Code of Ethics* (2005) devotes an entire section to the issues of confidentiality, privileged communication, and privacy. Though the code addresses nuances and limits of confidentiality, its underlying message to counselors is that the professional practice of maintaining confidentiality is elemental to the therapeutic alliance. For example, the Code states, "Counselors recognize that trust is a cornerstone of the counseling relationship. Counselors aspire to earn the trust of clients by creating an ongoing partnership, establishing and upholding appropriate boundaries, and maintaining confidentiality" (ACA,

2005, p. 7). In service to the trust counselors strive to gain from clients, they refrain from sharing client disclosures without a client's consent or other justified reason (ACA, 2005, B.1.c). Likewise, the American School Counselor Association (ASCA) recognizes in its *Ethical Standards for School Counselors* (2010) that the primary obligation with regard to confidentiality is to students, though this code also acknowledges the inherent rights of students' parents. For example, the ASCA *Ethical Standards* (2010, A2.d) states that professional school counselors "recognize their primary obligation for confidentiality is to the students but balance that obligation with an understanding of parents'/guardians' legal and inherent rights to be the guiding voice in their children's lives, especially in value-laden issues." Confidentiality, thus, is firmly acknowledged to be the scaffolding onto which the counseling enterprise is constructed.

Because confidentiality is such a foundational element of clinical practice, we use this chapter to explore the sometimes complex practice of keeping confidences. First, we invite you to think about confidentiality from various philosophical points of view that encourage counselors to adopt best practice behaviors and attitudes. This means that counselors think not only about what *not* to do that will keep them in compliance with guidelines (e.g., not talk to friends or family about clients' disclosures), but they also ponder how they can adopt positive daily practices, as well as careful, thoughtful, and respectful dispositions toward keeping confidentiality. Next, we consider what ethical codes and the law have to say about confidentiality because counselors are obliged to be familiar with both. Legally, for instance, practitioners must educate themselves about state and federal laws on privacy, privileged communication, and duty to warn and protect. Finally, we wrap up the chapter by sharing a personal testimony about an ethical dilemma surrounding the topic of confidentiality and provide a case study with discussion questions as a way for you to apply this chapter's information.

EXPLORING THE TERRITORY

UNDERSTANDING CONFIDENTIALITY THROUGH PHILOSOPHICAL ETHICS

Philosophical ethics tend to bring us in touch with the aspirational elements of counselor behavior. In the following sections, we consider what is good or ethical about keeping clients' disclosures private and reflect on how philosophy can help us to reason through dilemmas related to confidentiality, especially when there seem to be other goods competing with our desire to maintain confidentiality. Though we discuss several schools of philosophical ethics, we start by looking at Heidegger's philosophy.

Heidegger's Philosophy and Confidentiality

As we noted above, the practice of confidentiality has both legal and ethical elements. Before turning directly to ethics, we want to point out that philosophers themselves often express appreciation for the law and its place in moral decision making.

Existential phenomenologists, William Luijpen and Henry Koren (1969), for example, noted something very important about legal principles. They stated that "the legal order takes the necessary steps to effectively establish humanity" (p. 196). What a powerful concept! They explained that the law "guarantees a certain stability to the humanity that has already been attained. This stability is the expression of a society's firm will not to sink below a certain level of humanity" (p. 196). In essence, the law sets a standard or "minimum" of humanity, and while one may be disgusted by the process of litigation, one cannot deny that "engaging in a lawsuit is a great advance over settling matters with fists and daggers" (Luijpen & Koren, 1969, p. 196). One's good will, coupled with the reality of litigation, is very often enough motivation for counselors to abide by ethical standards and legal mandates related to confidentiality. Yet, philosophers are known for pushing us beyond the minimum, taken-for-granted aspects of our existence and for proposing creative frameworks that add value and meaning to our intuitive sense about right and wrong. Heidegger (1889–1976) does just this by taking the concept of ethics beyond mere obedience to the law.

In his work *Being and Time,* Heidegger introduced the concept of "thrownness," which he explained to mean that all human beings are "enmeshed in a particular context" (Guignon, 1993, p. 225). We are *thrown* into a situation, Heidegger (1927/1962) suggested, and we find ourselves engaging. When we are born, we already exist in a storied world. We are immediately faced with certain givens, such as familial expectations, responsibilities, religious affiliations, and social and political realities. Some liken this idea to walking onto the stage of a play mid-act with certain actors and props already in place and having to decide how to engage (Savickas, 1997). The world in which we live and our being are inextricably linked—there is no being without also *being-in-the-world.* We are always there in the world and in the circumstances of existence. The concept of *being there* is what Heidegger called *Dasein,* or literally, *there-being* (Edger & Meyer, 2010). *Dasein* has certain essential structures, the most important of which to consider for our purposes is that of *being-toward.* This means that *Dasein,* or our human condition of being thrown into a storied world, always projects into the future. Everything we do contributes to making us who we are, and because of this, our decisions about how to behave and relate to others are affected. (See Chapter 2 for additional discussion on Heidegger's philosophy.)

How do these ideas contribute to our understanding of the ethics of maintaining confidentiality? Counselors who see laws and standards about confidentiality as relevant to their work, and who carefully reflect and seek supervision during dilemmas involving confidentiality, relate to clients in a certain manner that involves "a commitment toward the future" (Guignon, 1993, p. 225). Such counselors understand that they make themselves *to be* people who are responsible, or caring, or supportive, or trustworthy to clients because they behave in a certain manner. Specifically, they make themselves caring, supportive, and trustworthy because they decide hourly and daily not to expose clients' most painful or even ordinary disclosures with others, and because, when breaching confidentiality seems necessary, they do not take such decisions lightly. As long as they keep acting the way that they do (that is, responsible to the trust formed in the therapeutic alliance that comes from keeping confidences), they make themselves into the sort of counselors who are viewed as highly professional, honorable, and trustworthy, and the people with whom they engage come to expect that of them. Thus, decisions counselors make in the present moment to keep personal disclosures private begin to shape how they will be viewed in the future by their clients.

Another important concept to consider in this discussion is the notion that ethical guidelines are based on common values, such as fairness, honesty, and dignity. Ethical guidelines are not merely subjective creations of a counselor's own making. Rather, counselors share a common human existence with others and have solidarity with them. Universal values, such as those seen in the principles of fidelity, beneficence, justice, and nonmaleficence (Welfel, 2010), are held by counselors and noncounselors alike—they surface through our shared history as a human race. Attunement to shared values goes beyond lifestyle options—it is much more universal than that. "Given that we have become the kind of people we are—people who, for example, care about children and believe in justice—there is now no way to drop these commitments without ceasing to be who we are" (Guignon, 1993, p. 233). We are embedded in and indebted to the wider context of a culture that shares some universal values. Participating in sets of universal values is what Heidegger (1927/1962) calls *authentic historicity*. As ethical counselors, we must make our authentic historicity known to clients in order to create a therapeutic environment that feels safe in its predictability that moral commitments play a fundamental role in our practice and that we uphold the minimum level of humanity outlined in the law. Thus, by following the laws and ethical standards that address confidentiality, we participate in a shared set of values that ensures people the right to seek help from another (e.g., a counselor) without being exposed to gossip or judgment.

Care Ethics and Confidentiality

An ethics of care (Gilligan, 2003; Noddings, 2003) perspective invites counselors to demonstrate genuine care—and one might even say love—for clients. Initially introduced by Carol Gilligan and Nel Noddings, and further elucidated by Annette Baier, Virginia Held, Eva Feder Kittay, Sara Ruddick, and Joan Tronto, care ethics is defined as a moral theory grounded in the idea that there is an ethical significance in all human relationships. Clients entrust us with their most personal information, and protecting confidences is a vital way of communicating this care and concern. Confidentiality, in the context of a counseling relationship, creates an environment of uncommon personal and emotional safety, thereby freeing clients to express themselves in ways that they may not feel secure doing outside the counseling room. It is through this safe environment that clients are able to take the first steps from self-disclosure towards self-awareness, and, ultimately, to personal growth. Indeed, without the promise of confidentiality, clients are not likely to speak openly, express feelings genuinely, or connect authentically with their counselor, which can result in superficial, irrelevant, or worse, false dialogue, and little to no therapeutic gain. Ultimately, from an ethics of care point of view, not to maintain a client's confidences short of recognized exceptions does harm to the relationship. It may indicate that a counselor has been unable to empathize fully with his or her client or the vulnerability that comes with disclosure.

Virtue Ethics and Confidentiality

Philosophers such as Elizabeth Anscombe, John McDowell, and Bernard Williams introduced the concept of virtue ethics in our contemporary era. In short, virtue ethics states that there is no definite set of rules or obligations that cover every situation (Hursthouse, 1999). Rather, in determining what is good or ethical, individuals should "always act in accordance with the hierarchy of [their] values and never sacrifice a greater value to a lesser one" (Rand, 1964, p. 44). To some extent, then, values are personally defined. The proper method of making ethical decisions from a virtues perspective thus begins with an assessment of one's personal hierarchy of values and self-interest (Rand); personal investment makes a difference in virtue ethics. For example, a man who greatly values his marriage and the love he has for his wife may decide to spend a lot of money trying to save her when she becomes very sick. In theory, he could have used the money to save 10 other women he did not know. According to a utilitarian view, which suggests that the most ethical decisions provide for the greatest happiness of the greatest number of people, the lives of 10 are worth more than the life of one. However, virtue ethicists believe that valuing the interests of loved ones over strangers is noble and an essential part of humanity.

Taking this reasoning to the ethic of confidentiality, we get a feel for why maintaining confidentiality is seen by professional helpers and their clients as virtuous. Counselors keep confidences of those with whom they enter into relationship. Though we may have differing levels of intimacy or closeness with our clients, we nonetheless have interactions and conversations with each of them that are outside of the ordinary, social realm. In their sharing, our clients move from stranger to known other—one for whom we are thus called to care by virtue of our relationship. Our and our clients' personal investment in the counseling endeavor makes our decision to safeguard their disclosures both honorable and necessary.

Virtue ethics also proposes that certain sets of shared values inform counselors' behaviors and decisions with regard to their professional work (Meara, Schmidt, & Day, 1996). For example, upholding confidentiality requires counselors to enact values such as respect, discretion, and diligence (Cohen & Cohen, 1999). It can be difficult not to share information with others. Welfel (2010) pointed out that one of the most frequent breaches of a client's privacy occurs when counselors talk to their family members about clients' cases. Cohen and Cohen discussed the virtue of discretion as having broad applicability to counseling duties; discrete counselors take measures to protect various aspects of a client's privacy. The ACA *Code of Ethics* (2005) points out numerous areas in which counselors do well not to reveal more than is necessary about a client or his or her situation (see Standard B.3). When faced with the prospect of breaking confidentiality, a counselor who is disposed toward virtue ethics also will likely approach the decision with diligence. Diligent counselors are neither careless nor nonchalant about issues related to a client's welfare, especially one as critical as breaching confidentiality (Cohen & Cohen, 1999). Such counselors reflect on the reasons for breaking a client's confidence, and their reasoning is based on clear evidence, sound judgment, and ethical and legal requirements. In addition, they will be mindful of the personal dimensions that accompany the decision to break confidentiality, including their own and their clients' feeling responses.

Interestingly, the notion that counselors act to protect their own professional well-being is also viewed favorably in virtue ethics. The virtue of self-protection may seem egocentric, but it is linked with the care and well-being of both the client and counselor. Remember that from a Heideggerian perspective everything counselors do projects into the future. If a counselor repeatedly breaks confidentiality, even for a perceived higher cause, the helping relationship will crumble, and clients will be hurt. By not enacting shared values on discretion, respect, and diligence upon which confidentiality is based, counselors fail to protect their professional reputations, and ultimately they will not be able to convince clients to invest in the relationship.

Principle Ethics and Confidentiality

In principle ethics, theory is directed toward a common set of goals or obligations (Meara et al., 1996). This philosophical approach proposes that human beings (and more specifically, counselors), are obligated to act under the guidance of ethical principles, such as beneficence, nonmaleficence, autonomy, fidelity, and justice (Welfel, 2010), that direct us in making moral decisions. Beneficence and nonmaleficence reflect the counselor's intentional will to do no harm to clients. Careless breaches in confidentiality have the potential to harm because they can shatter a client's trust in the counselor and the counseling process, leaving a client feeling shocked, angered, and betrayed (Glosoff & Pate, 2002). A client may even cease to reveal additional private material or end therapy (Glosoff & Pate, 2002). Respect for autonomy validates each individual's right to choose what is disclosed and to whom it is disclosed. The principle of fidelity, meanwhile, encourages counselors to make a conscious effort to build a trusting relationship by explaining the parameters of confidentiality through informed consent. Finally, justice requires that counselors treat clients fairly in their use of discretion. Counselors do not randomly select clients whose disclosures they will protect. All clients have the right to know that their information will be kept secure, unless specific circumstances warrant a breach.

Landmark 1

CASE EXAMPLE

Karen is a licensed professional counselor who specializes in couples work. She has been seeing a married couple, Rob and Lanie, for 6 months, and they have progressed positively in treatment. Yesterday, Karen received a panicked phone call from Rob who asked if he could speak with her alone. Karen set up an individual session with Rob the following day. When Rob arrived, he told Karen that he was very distressed because he had met with an ex-girlfriend a few days ago and had sex with her in her apartment. He mentioned that he had been talking to her casually for the past 3 months online after she

(continued)

found him on Facebook. The conversations had become more intimate, and they decided to meet for dinner. The night quickly turned sexual. He told Karen that he did not want his wife to find out and revoked his written consent that allowed Karen to disclose any information to his wife Lanie. Shortly after, Rob left in a panic and told Karen that he will see her in their next couple's session, which is scheduled in 4 days.

1. *How does Rob view Karen's authentic historicity?*
2. *How can Karen respond to Rob in terms of Care Ethics?*
3. *Within the conditions of Virtue Ethics, how could Karen deal with this situation?*
4. *What actions should be taken that would comply with Principle Ethics?*
5. *Based on the decisions that Karen will make, how is she being-toward?*

LEGAL ASPECTS OF CONFIDENTIALITY

To this point, we have been reflecting on the aspirational elements of confidentiality. As discussed above, ethics push counselors to see confidentiality within the frameworks of what is good for the client, the clinical relationship, and even the counselor's professional well-being. However, the ethical aspects of confidentiality often overlap or intersect with privileged communication and privacy, two legal terms also addressed in the ACA *Code of Ethics* (2005).

Privileged Communication

Privileged communication is "the client's right to prevent a court from demanding that a mental health professional reveal material disclosed in a confidential professional relationship ..." (Welfel, 2010, p. 116). Knowing about the right to privileged communication and how it applies to clinical work is important for counselors, who often are called to testify in court about clients who are facing a variety of circumstances that demand legal interventions (e.g., child custody cases, divorce proceedings, etc.). Privilege protects a client's privacy by requiring counselors not to disclose personal information to a judge or in a court of law. The extent of a client's legal protection varies from state to state. States outline in the law their own exceptions to privilege; thus, exceptions found in one state may not be identified in another. Given the variation in state laws, counselors are encouraged to become familiar with the bounds of privileged communication in the states within which they practice. In an important 1996 case, *Jaffee v. Redmond*, the U.S. Supreme Court ruled that privilege also extends to the federal level. In this case, the Court asserted that "the psychotherapist-patient privilege must be as reliable and unequivocal as possible so as to promote an atmosphere of 'confidence and trust' within the psychotherapeutic relationship" (Mosher & Swire, 2002, p. 577). Clients' rights to privileged communication thus are broad, as they are safeguarded in state and federal courts.

Both confidentiality and privileged communication protect clients' rights and aim to make mental health services as effective as possible; yet, it is important to know that neither confidentiality nor privileged communication are absolute rights (Remley & Herlihy, 2010). Sometimes for the good of others or for the good of the client (e.g., to ensure safety), a counselor is obliged to divulge confidential information. Limits to privileged communication typically include: client permission to disclose information, child or elder abuse, cases of serious and foreseeable harm to self or others, legal mandate, and lawsuits against the counselor (Stone, Conte, & Antkowiak, 2007). Thus, it is always in a counselor and client's best interest to have a discussion during the informed consent process about confidentiality and privilege, including how they benefit the client and when they are limited by laws and ethical standards.

Counselors may wonder if privilege is afforded only to their adult clients and what legal rights are granted to minors. Numerous authors (Ledyard, 1998; Younggren & Harris, 2008) have pointed out that children and minors under age 18 (and in some states age 14) tend to be granted fewer legal rights than adults. There is, moreover, support for the idea that parents should have access to their children's health and mental health care information as they are largely responsible for their well-being. However, it is also evident that minors ought not to be excluded from claiming their constitutional rights to privacy based on age. The case of *Daniel v. Daniel O. H.* (1990), which involved a 6-year-old boy who was seeing a psychologist due to possible sexual abuse and custody issues, shows how far a child's privilege rights can extend. When the boy's therapist stated that he did not want to testify for fear of destroying the therapeutic relationship, the courts ruled in favor of the 6-year-old boy. When reviewing the case, the Sixth District Court of Appeals in California determined that the young boy had "privilege rights that were independent of his parent's guardianship . . ." (Younggren & Harris, 2008, p. 594). The outcome of this case shows how critical it is for counselors to be familiar with their minor clients' rights to privacy, privileged communication, and confidentiality, as well as to be able to advocate for these rights. This case also reinforces the importance of counselors reflecting holistically on individual clients' issues and concerns. For example, when reasoning through a dilemma related to confidentiality, counselors might ask themselves questions such as, If private information about my client is disclosed to the court, could this cause more harm than good and how might it affect the counseling relationship I have created?

Privacy

Privacy is a legal concept that refers to an individual's constitutional right not to have personal information exposed without consent, as well as the right to control information in health-related records (Stone et al., 2007). (For a discussion on the legal aspects of privacy and health records, see Chapter 8.) The ACA *Code of Ethics* (2005) addresses the ethical dimension of client privacy from the perspective of the profession's value on respect. To show respect for clients, the code obliges counselors to uphold privacy laws, and when disclosure is necessary, to reveal only the minimum amount of privately shared information as is necessary to the circumstances. Standard B.1.b further recommends counselors only to solicit information during sessions that is germane to counseling goals and treatment (ACA, 2005). In other words, clients have rights to privacy even in the counseling process itself, and counselors should consider their clients' comfort level and willingness to disclose personal material. Respectful counselors are mindful of the purpose of their questions, considering fully if their requests serve their clients' well-being and further the counseling process.

PROTECTING CLIENTS THROUGH INFORMED CONSENT

Informed consent involves a discussion between counselors and clients about the purposes, benefits and risks, and expectations of the counseling process. It is an opportunity for counselors to introduce themselves to clients, answer questions about the counseling process, and begin to build a therapeutic alliance. Informed consent documents usually address the counselor's philosophical approach to counseling, relevant professional information, typical length of treatment, costs of the service, a statement of clients' rights, an explanation about the use of supervision and consultation, and a description of confidentiality rights and limitations. The informed consent process is the client's first assurance that the counselor will not share or transfer personal or diagnostic information unless they have the client's written permission.

Gathering a client's initial informed consent with a carefully thought out disclosure statement introduces the client to typical or standard professional practices such as supervision, consultation, or treatment teams that may pose limits to their right to confidentiality. Being up front and transparent about the use of supervision, consultation, and/or treatment teams indicates honor and respect for the vulnerability of a client's position in the counseling relationship, and concurrently, allows counselors to take advantage of valued input from other helping professionals who can aid in the therapeutic process. Counselors who do seek supervision or consultation in their work with a client show care and concern for the relationship by protecting as much client privacy as possible throughout the process. Only necessary details ought to be exposed, and clients should be assured of a counselor's sensitivity to their privacy.

The process of gathering a client's informed consent has three main components: (a) the explanation of the nature, benefits, risks, and limitations of counseling; (b) a disclosure process ensuring clients' understanding; and (c) free consent (Welfel, 2010). Discussing confidentiality is essential to the informed consent conversation because the counselor discloses relevant information the client needs to know in order to make an educated decision about whether or not to participate in counseling (Corey, Corey, & Callahan, 2011). Likewise, counselors use informed consent to convey to the client that (in most instances) the decision to engage in counseling services is a free choice made without any coercion or pressure from the helper (Welfel). With this in mind, informed consent conversations should be carried out in a spirit of openness, invitation, and transparency. Counselors will want to introduce clients to the counseling experience in a way that empowers the client to make the best possible decision about participating in the process.

Cultural Considerations in Informed Consent

Ethical codes and best practices require counselors to explain confidentiality in ways that are sensitive to their clients' cultural, spiritual, and developmental backgrounds. Developing multicultural competency is more than just learning about other cultures; it involves knowing one's own worldview, values, and cultural assumptions. An important piece to self-understanding is realizing that there may be dissonance between one's own worldview and that of a client's. Clients from collectivist cultures who value interdependence over individuality may interpret the limits of confidentiality more generously than clients whose values are formed in an individualistic culture. For example, when discussing confidentiality with clients from South Asia, Abrahams and Salazar (2005) noted that confidentiality as conceptualized in Westernized ethical guidelines may not resonate with this client group. A traditional family from South Asia may expect to participate in their adult family member's counseling (Abrahams & Salazar, 2005). A culturally competent counselor will want to acknowledge this client's cultural orientation and find solutions for addressing the client's therapeutic needs without dishonoring or alienating the family. Gaining an appreciation for how different cultural groups perceive confidentiality and privacy is important, though such knowledge should not be made into blanket assumptions or stereotypes. At the same time, Abrahams and Salazar's findings highlight how ethical dilemmas surrounding confidentiality can arise. Counselors may find themselves torn between the best practice recommendations of ethical codes and sets of values that conflict with the code. Counselors who lean toward care and virtue ethics as their primary way of determining ethical goods may be keenly aware of being caught in a dilemma as they attempt to uphold ethical obligations and relational virtues that suggest loosening the boundaries of confidentiality.

Informed Consent With Minors

A client's age can influence both our understanding of confidentiality and the ways in which confidentiality is explained at the outset of the counseling process. Counselors working with students or minors under the age of 14 in a community or school setting typically obtain their assent as opposed to consent. Assent refers to a minor's willingness or agreement to participate in counseling, while consent—a right reserved for adult parents or legal guardians—refers to the adult's permission for the minor to begin counseling (Welfel, 2010). Thus, parents, not minor clients, legally agree to informed consent (Glosoff & Pate, 2002). Counselors must be particularly aware of a minor's custodial arrangement in the informed consent process, especially when the child's parents are divorced. All parents who have legal (not residential) custody of a minor client are entitled to informed consent. Moreover, because parents of minors legally consent to their child's participation in counseling, they appreciate informed consent information and expect counselors will share information with them throughout the counseling process in a sensitive manner (Welfel, 2010). Finally, in obtaining assent from minors, counselors can best serve their potential clients by making their discussion about the process developmentally appropriate. For instance, counselors may want to limit their use of technical terms and/or provide concrete, age-specific examples to illustrate concepts.

Landmark 2
PROFESSIONAL REFLECTION

One of my (Gina Gordon [G.G.]) 9-year-old female students with mild mental retardation began meeting with me once per week. We worked on feelings exploration and interpersonal skills. She also participated in a group for social skills interventions. When I obtained her assent (along with her parents' consent), I used pictures to supplement my verbal communication. I knew she was a more visual student, so I used pictures of clocks to let her know what times we would meet during the day. I used pictures of a heart and different facial expressions to illustrate that we were going to talk about her feelings. Lastly, I used puppets and role play to convey the meaning of "confidentiality."

LIMITS TO CONFIDENTIALITY AND PRIVILEGED COMMUNICATION

As we have already mentioned, a discussion about confidentiality must touch on its limitations. Ethical codes and federal and state laws provide guidelines outlining circumstances in which counselors may be permitted or required to break confidentiality. Even with these guidelines, however, counselors do well to seek consultation and supervision when they are considering breaking confidentiality (Corey et al., 2011; Remley & Herlihy, 2010). In addition, it is good practice for counselors to document in writing the client's situation, the outcome of the consultation or supervision discussions, and the actions taken when a decision to break confidentiality is being made. Written documentation should be clear, straightforward, and focused on factual content. The following are some examples of instances when confidentiality may be breached without client consent:

- In the case when a client poses a danger to self or others
- In the case of suspected child or elder abuse or neglect
- If a client seriously risks infecting others with HIV/AIDS
- If a court mandate has been issued

In practice, counselors may experience feelings of anxiety or guilt and may even question their level of competence when they are faced with a decision to break confidentiality. These feelings should not be ignored, but acknowledged and explored. Such an exploration can provide rich material for personal growth and discovery. For instance, a counselor may discover that she has strong personal beliefs about family violence that she had not fully recognized until she had to break confidentiality in order to protect her client's safety.

Counselors may wish to discuss with their clients the intent and purpose for breaking confidentiality so as to reinforce the caring relationship that exists. For example, if a counselor needs to report a client to child protection services, the counselor may want to make the call with the client present. Doing so can help the client feel part of the decision-making process and perhaps strengthen the therapeutic alliance. Counselors who work with minors may find it beneficial to involve parents in the initial meeting to discuss the types of information shared, as well as the parameters around confidentiality. Lawrence and Robinson-Kurpius (2000) recommend parental involvement as an effective way to ensure counselor self-protection and clarify policies regarding confidentiality.

Both ACA and ASCA, in the most recent versions to their codes of ethics, chose to revise the language outlining exceptions to confidentiality in cases of harm or danger. Rather than talking about *clear and imminent danger*, the codes now limit confidentiality in instances of *serious, foreseeable harm* because this language embraces a more collective perspective on client welfare and safety (Kaplan, 2006). The ACA *Code of Ethics* (2005, B.2.a) states, "The general requirement that counselors keep information confidential does not apply when disclosure is required to protect clients or identified others from serious and foreseeable harm . . . ." Likewise, the ASCA *Ethical Standards for School Counselors* (2010, A.2.c) states, "Keep information confidential unless legal requirements demand that confidential information be revealed or a breach is required to prevent serious and foreseeable harm to the student . . . ." The change in language provides all counselors with more opportunities to make decisions that would be considered those of a reasonable person, especially in the case of an emergency. In the school setting, the language modification has been seen as especially helpful because it provides school counselors with opportunities to discuss questionable areas of concern for safety with parents and legal guardians in a more comfortable manner. Carolyn Stone (2011) mentioned that the notion of *serious and foreseeable harm* helps "to limit the liability of a party to those acts carrying a risk of foreseeable harm" (p. 6).

Landmark 3

PROFESSIONAL REFLECTION

Near the end of the school day, a young male student was referred to me (G. G.) by his teacher as a result of a disagreement he had with a peer. In meeting with him, he seemed noticeably irritated and angry, and after assessing both his verbal and nonverbal communication, it became clear to me that riding the bus home may not be in his best interest. I talked with him about the possibility of getting a ride home from a family member. Given his current state of emotions and his previous involvement with the principal over a physical altercation, I was concerned that he may do or say something on the bus that could negatively affect him, the other students, and perhaps even the bus driver. In this case, the student was not presenting any clear, imminent danger, but there was definitely the potential for future harm on the bus. Therefore, we called his parents together, explained the situation, and his mother picked him up.

Harm to Others: The Duty to Warn and to Protect

The ACA *Code of Ethics* (2005, Standard B.2.a) is often applied to instances in which a client appears to pose a serious threat of harm to himself or herself or another person. In such cases, a counselor has both an ethical and legal duty to break confidentiality in order to intervene on behalf of the vulnerable party (Remley & Herlihy, 2010). In this section we will consider the duty to warn and protect in the case of clients who seem likely to hurt others.

It is helpful, when looking at this limit to confidentiality, to appreciate its nuanced interpretations by codes of ethics and the law. Welfel (2010) noted that while ethics *permit* counselors to break confidentiality, the law often *requires* counselors not only to breach their promise of confidentiality, but also to warn and protect innocent third parties. Court rulings have played a significant role in shaping counselors' understanding of their dual responsibility to clients and the public; when translated into law, these rulings are an example of how the legal system seeks to prevent mental health professionals from sinking below minimum expectations of human behavior and universal values. Yet, as much as the law has unequivocally mandated counselors to value the safety of clients and the public more highly than confidentiality (under certain provisions), it also lacks in clarity with regard to counselors' practical obligations when they face real dilemmas about how to balance the right to confidentiality with a duty to public safety (Pabian, Welfel, & Beebe, 2009). Before we turn to a closer discussion of the duty to warn and protect, consider what you believe constitutes a clear case of duty to warn: under what circumstances would you be reasonably certain that the good of protecting another person outweighed your client's right to privacy? For example, what if your client threatened harm to no one in particular but said that she wants to kill all persons of a particular race? Or, what if your client, who has a history of committing violent acts, expressed continuous rage toward a particular family member? Or, finally, what if your client described fantasies of killing people on various occasions? With the guidance of the law, the input of other professionals, and your own ethical compass, these are questions that, should you face, will require an informed and diligent clinical response. Let us turn now to the duty to warn.

The legal duty to warn stems from the landmark 1974 court case *Tarasoff v. Regents of the University of California.* Essentially, in this case, California's lower courts found that a counselor has an ethical duty to break confidentiality in order to notify, or warn, a third party of immediate danger posed by a client. The case centered on determining the degree of responsibility a psychologist had to Tatiana Tarasoff, a romantic interest of the therapist's client, Prosenjit Poddar. The client expressed to the therapist his intent to kill Tarasoff and, in response, the therapist, who saw Poddar at a university clinic, informed campus police who questioned and then released him. The therapist did not inform Tarasoff of the threat, and later, Poddar followed through with his threat and killed her. Two years after the judgment, in 1976, California's Supreme Court reconsidered the initial *Tarasoff* ruling and replaced the "duty to warn" responsibility with a "duty to warn and protect" (*Tarasoff v. Regents of the University of California,* 1976). Duty to protect is a broader obligation than duty to warn, and, in practice, it implies more legal responsibilities on the part of the counselor. This duty urges mental health professionals to "use reasonable care to protect the intended victim" (as cited in Pabian et al., 2009, p. 2). Despite the change issued by the 1976 *Tarasoff* ruling, "duty to warn" language continues to be used widely even though it misrepresents and often too narrowly defines counselors' legal and ethical obligations to those who are not their clients (Pabian et al., 2009).

Since the landmark ruling in *Tarasoff*, there have been numerous other court decisions about the issues of confidentiality and duty to warn and protect. Some of these have fallen in line with *Tarasoff* and even extended mental health professionals' legal obligations to warn and protect. Examples include *Jablonski v. United States* (1983) and *Davis v. Lihm* (1983) (later overturned) (Walcott, Cerundolo, & Beck, 2001). The most important finding in these cases is that the courts understood mental health professionals to have a duty to warn and protect when a client has a history of violent behavior because such a history may be enough to indicate future serious and foreseeable harm, even if a client has not made any specific threat (Walcott et al., 2001). The *Jablonski* case, in particular, has prompted counselors to evaluate clients' past violent behaviors carefully when conducting risk assessments, making decisions about appropriate clinical responses, and determining how to protect others from foreseeable harm. On the other hand, numerous court rulings have limited the expansive duty to protect that was established by *Tarasoff*. Among many others, these include *Leonard v. Iowa* (1992) and *Boynton v. Burglass* (1991). The *Boynton* case specifically rejected the findings of *Tarasoff* and found that mental health professionals engage in work with human persons whose behaviors are never fully predictable and that such professionals should not be held liable to another person's decision to enact harm. Walcott and his colleagues (2001) pointed out that, in fact, the general movement of the courts since the 1980s and 1990s has been to limit rather than expand *Tarasoff*.

Because of the range of court findings and the confusion for mental health professionals about their legal obligations with regard to warning and protecting potential victims, many states have established statutes that codify a counselor's duty to warn and/or protect clients and possible victims. Twenty-three states have statutes in place that require therapists to warn and/or protect, while nine have a common law duty (Pabian et al., 2009). Other states either have not ruled on the issue or allow counselors to break confidentiality but do not legally obligate them to warn and protect (Pabian et al., 2009). For example, in Pennsylvania, a duty to warn law exists. In 1998, the Pennsylvania Supreme Court addressed the issue of whether or not mental health professionals have an obligation to warn a third party of potential harm. In *Emerich v. Philadelphia Center for Human Development, Inc.*, the court ruled that mental health professionals in Pennsylvania have a duty to warn a third party when the professional is made aware of an immediate, specific threat of serious harm to an identified individual (Wettstein, 1999). A counselor who practices in a state whose law binds counselors to warn *and* protect those at risk of harm from a client have to take reasonable measures to help intended victims stay out of harm's way; usually, this requires more than a call to proper authorities (e.g., police) (Welfel, 2010). It also may include working with potential victims to distance themselves from a client or encouraging the client who is likely to inflict harm to be voluntarily hospitalized. Involuntary hospitalization, additionally, may be an option that therapists consider in their plan to protect (Pabian et al., 2009; Walcott et al., 2001). Each of these actions suggests that counselors have made a conscious decision about what they believe good counseling and the role of a good counselor to be. Ultimately, ethical practice involves counselors being aware of the larger context (e.g., legal system) within which they work, and so we strongly encourage you to review the statutes and laws of the state in which you will practice. On a final note, in determining when a duty to warn and protect emerges, Walcott and his colleagues pointed out that most states follow two guidelines: (a) a client must specifically name or otherwise identify a person against whom he or she means to commit violence, and (b) the client has a history of violent actions that would suggest he or she is likely to engage in serious and foreseeable harm. These guidelines reflect the spirit of rulings in cases that have outlined a counselor's duty to safeguard the public.

Discharging a duty to warn must be done with care. The literature outlining care ethics reminds counselors of the relational component of any ethics decision and encourages the use of one's own sense of compassion, empathy, and concern (in this case, for clients and possible victims) when dealing with a quandary. Concretely, counselors can show care by helping a client understand how exercising a duty to warn serves both the client and the person under threat; notification protects both persons from unsafe actions. Truly caring acts are also thorough in nature, which is why is it ethically important for counselors to conduct complete risk assessments when they believe a client has the potential to follow through on an expressed intent to harm. A careful assessment is based on clinical observations and interviews (e.g., mental status exam), historical evidence (e.g., review of client's files for evidence of prior violent acts), and determination about whether or not the client has access to weapons. A thorough threat assessment most often involves consultation, as well. Through the assessment process, the counselor is recommended to document critical information, such as the results of the mental status, the observed behaviors of the clients (e.g., obvious agitation and pacing), statements made by the client, and outcomes of consultation. Most important, counselors who are reflective and caring remember that even in crisis situations, their role is primarily to act as clinician, keeping in mind the good of the client and others.

Landmark 4

CASE EXAMPLE

Jose is currently counseling a young man, Bryan, who served two tours in Iraq with the Marines and saw substantial amounts of combat time. For the past year, Bryan has been working on two primary treatment goals. First, he is trying to manage explosive bouts of anger that accompany flashbacks from combat and that sometimes involve physical aggression, usually toward objects (e.g., throwing or toppling furniture). He has been in several bar fights, as well. Second, he is learning to control drinking that has gotten to the point of abusive. Recently, Bryan has expressed disgust with his boss, who confronted him twice about his drinking. When Bryan arrives for his latest

(continued)

session with Jose, he is clearly agitated as he reveals that he was just fired from his job for alcohol abuse. Using many expletives, he exclaims that he cannot believe his boss fired a veteran and that he needs to be taught a lesson.

1. *Assessing Bryan's behavior, what observations do you make that concern you?*
2. *Is there any other information you want to know about Bryan as you assess risk?*
3. *How would you describe Bryan's level of threat to others or himself?*
4. *What might you decide to do in light of the circumstances? Why?*
5. *What philosophical approach to ethical decision making do you draw on?*

Harm to Self: The Suicidal Client

There is widespread agreement among counselors that they have a professional duty to safeguard the lives of their clients, especially when clients seem intent on killing or harming themselves (ACA, 2005; Corey et al., 2011; Hyldahl & Richardson, 2011; Remley & Herlihy, 2010; Welfel, 2010). The legal responsibilities and ramifications associated with a counselor's duty to protect in circumstances of suicide are not as evident as in cases when a client poses a threat of harm to another person (Bongar, 1991; Corey et al., 2011). However, ethical principles, such as beneficence and nonmaleficence, virtues, an ethic of care, and the law clearly spur counselors to protect clients from taking their own lives. In practice, this means counselors likely will have to reason through a dilemma related to breaking confidentiality.

To encounter a suicidal client is without doubt stress-provoking (Hendin, Lipschitz, Maltsberger, Haas, & Wynecoop, 2000). All counselors, especially novice clinicians, should therefore take steps to manage these cases with a reasonable standard of care and deal with the personal stress that accompanies them. Similar to ethical decision making with regard to the homicidal client, decision making with the suicidal client involves counselors in conducting a careful assessment of a client's risk for acting out his or her suicidal impulse; this often entails seeking consultation and supervision. Counselors should only disclose essential information when breaking confidentiality in order to protect suicidal clients. When individually identifiable information in educational records must be released, this disclosure does not extend past the duration of the time of emergency (USDE, 2007). Lastly, counselors should familiarize themselves with their state's voluntary and nonvoluntary hospitalization or commitment procedures.

School counselors must be sensitive to both a student's needs and parental rights in cases when a student threatens serious self-harm. Given that parents have inherent rights over their children, they should be notified when their son or daughter discloses suicidal ideations and/or plans—even if the counseling relationship is compromised because of a break in confidentiality. *Eisel vs. Board of Education of Montgomery County* (1991) concluded that school counselors must notify parents in cases where suicide or harm to others is mentioned (James, 2008). School counselors have a duty to use reasonable means to attempt to prevent a suicide or homicide when they are aware of a student's intent. We find it helpful to use a decision-making model, seek supervision, and ultimately, reflect on the decision and its possible outcome. Will the outcome of the decision, for instance, be in the best interest of the student? Carolyn Stone (2009) developed the STEPS Model for ethical decision making in school settings. You can learn more about STEPS by looking at the 2010 ASCA *Ethical Standards*. Chapter 14 of this text also reviews the STEPS Model.

Landmark 5

CASE EXAMPLE

A 3rd grade teacher recommends that one of her students meet with you. The student, Jack, has been displaying off-task behaviors, such as: keeping his head down on the desk and not participating in class, isolating himself from his peers at recess and lunch, and drawing pictures that represent death (coffins, knives, and blood). As you meet with Jack, you learn very quickly that he misses his father. His father committed suicide 2 years ago. In processing his feelings, Jack reports that he "hates his life," and he "wishes he was dead." He "wants to see his dad."

1. *As a school counselor, how would you react to these statements?*
2. *What are your ethical responsibilities to Jack? What are your legal responsibilities to Jack and his parent/guardian?*
3. *What thoughts might be circulating in your mind?*
4. *How would you seek support if you found yourself in this ethical dilemma?*

Harm Posed by Abuse or Neglect

Principle ethics recommend counselors evaluate their actions in light of the duty to do no harm. A case can easily be made that the stakes in not causing harm are no higher than in situations involving potential abuse to a child or vulnerable adult. A large body of research (e.g., Anda et al., 2006; Cicchetti, Rogosch, & Toth, 2006) establishes the relationship between persistent abuse and risk of various, long term pathological outcomes for children. Armed with this knowledge, counselors have good reason to be invested in preventing abuse of children. States and the federal government together oblige counselors to speak up when they are aware of cases of abuse toward children and elders. Counselors themselves, desiring not to do harm to the most defenseless, often find themselves, through the process of reporting, acting as advocates on behalf of children and elders who are abused or neglected.

In cases in which a child reveals to a counselor that he or she is being abused or neglected, and in cases in which an adult discloses that he or she is abusing or neglecting a child, counselors are required to report such information to appropriate authorities. Although states differ in terms of the language used to outline the legal mandate to report and thereby protect children, all states identify counselors as mandated reporters of child abuse (Remley & Herlihy, 2010). At the federal level, the Federal Child Abuse Prevention and Treatment Act (1987) also demands the same level of intervention by counselors. It is important to note, however, that because states use their own guidelines and language around mandated reporting, counselors should investigate the details of these statutes. Often, counselors only have to have a suspicion of abuse or neglect to be required to report. Before releasing confidential information, counselors practice diligence in assessing the evidence of abuse, seeking supervision or consultation, discussing concerns with clients if possible, and making a report to law enforcement or other appropriate social services agencies.

Abuse encompasses physical, sexual, and emotional and verbal acts of violence and aggression. It is not always easy to determine whether or not abuse is occurring in the life of a minor client or to a minor by a counselor's adult client. This uncertainty makes the process of breaking confidentiality to report what one may not confidently know feel like a risky endeavor. Moreover, counselors sometimes look at abuse that is reportable and abuse that is suspected as posing different levels of risk and therefore requiring different levels of action (Kennel & Agresti, 1995). The literature points out various other reasons why counselors hesitate to report, one of which is concern related to how the report will affect the counseling relationship in the future (Welfel, 2010). Without diminishing counselors' legitimate hesitancies, we suggest that they balance their knowledge of legal obligations with reflections on aspirational ethics. Again, counselors keep in mind that the law itself demands the minimum of humanity. In wanting to become the kind of counselor who is not willing to do harm and who is seen as trustworthy and caring, counselors must participate in upholding universal values, such as protecting vulnerable persons. Heidegger's concept of *historic authenticity* is exceptionally relevant here.

Issues Related to Communicable Diseases

There are approximately 1.2 million people in the United States who have been diagnosed with the HIV infection, and that number continues to grow by nearly 50,000 per year (Centers for Disease Control and Prevention, 2009). It is not unlikely that counselors will find themselves working with clients who are diagnosed with HIV/AIDS during their professional lifetime. Of these, some counselors will also see clients who decide not to disclose their diagnosis to people who they may put at risk of being infected, leaving counselors with the burdensome decision of whether or not they should break confidentiality (Wong-Wylie, 2003). Because of the life-threatening and communicable nature of AIDS, clinicians have questioned whether or not there is an ethical duty to warn in such cases (Garcia, Forrester, & Jacob, 1998). As with the limits to confidentiality already discussed, underlying this dilemma is an ambiguity about the extent to which an individual's right to privacy supersedes the concern for public safety. Further complicating decisions to disclose is the stigma that historically has surrounded HIV/AIDS diagnoses, which can lead some to have a strong sense of protectiveness around privacy for a group of people who have been shunned and publically feared.

When considering the ethical quandaries that can arise with regard to HIV/AIDS, it is important to be mindful of the implications of autonomy. Guided by this principle, counselors consider that an automatic breach of confidence of those who are diagnosed with HIV/AIDS is usually discouraged. It has been compellingly documented that individuals who are of sound mind have the right to make their own decisions about their bodies (Harding, Gray, & Neal, 1993). These arguments are strong declarations against immediately breaching a client's confidentiality to warn a third party. Indeed, the 2005 ACA *Code of Ethics* favors upholding confidentiality (Garcia et al., 1998), stating that counselors *may* be justified in disclosing information to third parties (e.g., sex partners), but only when those third parties are identifiable and known to be at a verifiable high risk of becoming infected with the disease. Before making any kind of a disclosure, counselors must first confirm that the diagnosis exists and then thoroughly assess the intent of the client. In addition, counselors must confirm that the client has not already told the third party about his or her diagnosis and that the client does not intend to tell that third party in the future (Herlihy & Corey, 2006). Ethically, counselors might best aid clients by helping them think globally about their diagnosis, including the risks they can pose to others, precautions they can take to protect others, and decisions to refrain from high-risk behaviors (Harding et al., 1993).

The legal obligations surrounding duty to warn and HIV/AIDS are themselves unclear, especially in terms of outcomes found in case law. For instance, while the *Tarasoff* case generated a push toward warning third parties of imminent danger, the concept of duty to warn, when applied to clients who are diagnosed with HIV/AIDS, is more complex. Wong-Wylie (2003, p. 38) pointed out that in *Tarasoff*, "Poddar [the perpetrator] made a 'specific and active' intent to kill Ms. Tarasoff, whereas clients with HIV are 'passive' and without intent." Because of inconsistencies such as that surrounding active or passive intent to harm, the *Tarasoff* case has not been entirely relevant to HIV/AIDS cases, and in most instances *Tarasoff* has not be applied (Garcia et al., 1998). With regard to state laws, many states have clear mandates that, in cases of HIV/AIDS, counselors are not permitted to enact the duty to warn without a client's consent. Releasing personal information thus can expose a counselor to legal sanctions (Corey et al., 2011; Welfel, 2010). Best practices suggest that counselors who are faced with a dilemma surrounding threat to harm from HIV/AIDS seek legal counsel before consummating a decision.

Landmark 6

CASE EXAMPLE

Jennifer is a licensed counselor working at a community mental health facility. During an individual session, her client, Andy, tells her that he just returned from the free clinic and that he tested positive for HIV. Andy is noticeably distraught; he is crying as he tells Jennifer about his experience, but his sadness quickly turns to anger. Andy states that he only had sex with three individuals in his lifetime and that he was very careful about not sharing needles when he used heroin with his friends. In his anger, he tells Jennifer, "I'm just going to infect

(*continued*)

everyone I can. Might as well! Whoever infected me didn't care so why should I?"

1. *Does Andy pose a foreseeable risk of danger to himself or others? Why or why not?*
2. *Does Jennifer have an ethical duty to warn? Why or why not?*
3. *Considering this information about clients with HIV/AIDS, how could Jennifer respond?*

Court Mandates

Another commonly encountered limit to confidentiality involves counselors in being mandated by a court to release private client information, often in instances when a client is being tried for a crime or in custody disputes. The court request is made through a subpoena, or an order directed at a person to appear in court on a certain day with the expectation that he or she will either testify or produce documentation for a particular lawsuit. While the expectations tied to being subpoenaed may seem relatively straightforward, there are a number of conditions a counselor must consider before testifying or producing documents for a lawsuit.

When counselors are subpoenaed by the courts to disclose confidential information without their clients' permission, they should consider the order in light of the profession's value on respect for client privacy, as well as ethical principles such as autonomy and nonmaleficence. State and federal laws that uphold individual privacy rights, as well as court rulings, such as *Jaffee v. Redmond* (1996) should also be reviewed in dilemmas involving court orders. Thus, counselors who testify in court should first and foremost obtain written permission from their clients to do so. If they cannot obtain written permission, counselors may still be mandated to testify in court or send confidential records. If counselors cannot take steps to prohibit disclosure to the courts (and ethically, they need to take this step), then they should limit the release of confidential information as narrowly as possible to minimize the potential harm to the client and the counseling relationship (ACA, 2005).

Not all court orders are created equally, so counselors must understand the legal policies of court mandates before disclosing information. "A subpoena, search warrant, or arrest warrant, even when it is signed by a judge, is not sufficient, by itself, to require or even permit a program to make a disclosure" (SAMHSA, 1994, para. 26). In the substance abuse field, for example, a court order must be a *Good Cause Court Order*. Before a court can mandate a counselor or treatment program to share a client's private material, the court has to show that there is a viable reason for making the request and that the good to be achieved through release of confidential information is greater than the harm that potentially will befall the counselor-client relationship. The information it seeks from the order also cannot be obtained elsewhere (SAMHSA, 1994).

A 2010 ruling in Ohio recently upheld patients' right to privileged communication even in the case of a grand jury subpoena. In *Turk v. Oiler*, a patient sued the Cleveland Clinic for violating his privacy rights when the clinic released his medical records in response to a grand jury subpoena (Weiss, 2011). The patient claimed that Ohio's statutes did not limit doctor–patient privileged communication so as to allow the release of his private health information, including mental health and substance abuse records, to the grand jury. This case further compels clinicians to take all laws into account before responding to a grand jury subpoena or any other legal request that requires the disclosure of confidential information.

Other Circumstances That Limit Confidentiality

In addition to the instances already described, there are a number of other circumstances that limit a client's right to confidentiality; these typically involve legal action, such as when a client begins litigation against a counselor, or a client's own request to waive confidentiality. Looking briefly at the second instance, counselors should know that while it is the client's right to waive confidentiality and leave the counselor with no legal grounds for withholding requested confidential information, there are certain laws that protect the client regardless of their waiver. For example, in Pennsylvania, under drug and alcohol law, a counselor cannot disclose any information beyond the dates of treatment and the nature of the treatment to a client's employer. Regardless of the client's waiver of confidentiality, the law still stands and employers (who often have an interest in their employees' progress in addictions treatment) are not ever privy to information beyond the two noted elements. This state law is written to protect the client from potential employee discrimination. As a result of this law, Employee Assistance Programs (EAP) are used as moderators between employers, clients, and treatment program personnel. Above all, counselors must understand that confidential client information is the client's. Unless ethically or legally restricted, counselors should not put up barriers when their clients ask them to share their clinical information with others. In Section A.6.b, Confidentiality and Advocacy, counselors are informed that they aspire to advocate for their clients by working to remove any potential obstacles that inhibit their growth and development (ACA, 2005). Counselors thus continuously consult with their supervisors and team members in ethical dilemmas in order to determine how best to provide consistent, helpful, and ethical services.

CONFIDENTIALITY IN GROUP WORK

Confidentiality in the group setting presents additional issues counselors need to address with clients. Jacobs, Masson, and Harvill (2009) outlined two issues concerning confidentiality of which group leaders must be aware. First, group leaders should be mindful of "the leader's ethical responsibility for keeping material confidential and the leader's lack of total control regarding members' keeping matters confidential" (Jacobs et al., 2009, p. 440). Given the uniqueness of a group setting, it is essential for counselors to maintain their ethical standards and consult with other professionals if issues emerge within the group.

Practically, group leaders will want to process with members the limits of confidentiality in a group setting. Group leaders ultimately cannot ensure that members will not divulge confidential material outside of group. It is good practice to discuss this possibility during the very first group session or perhaps even during the group formation or planning stage. Talking about confidentiality is a component of the group's informed consent process. Counselors should expect that some group members will find the possible limits of confidentiality a source of anxiety, and in some instances, a potential barrier to group work. Discussing members' feelings and concerns early, as well as revisiting the role of confidentiality in the group experience, are important leader tasks. What is more, group leaders may want to help members understand the therapeutic benefits of maintaining confidentiality; it is not just a rule to follow. Confidentiality in group helps to create a safe space for all members to participate actively and authentically.

Landmark 7

SUGGESTIONS FOR ADVANCING CONFIDENTIALITY IN GROUP COUNSELING

At the start of a new group, a counselor may want to ask group members to reflect on a time when their confidences were shared without their knowledge and permission. Some members may want to do this in writing; others may be comfortable discussing their experiences. The goal of this activity is to help members appreciate the importance of protecting others' confidential information. Some questions to pose include:

1. *How did you learn your confidences were shared without your permission? What did you do?*
2. *How did this breach make you feel? List the feelings you experienced.*
3. *Did your relationship/friendship with the person who broke your confidences change? If so, how?*
4. *Did the situation influence your willingness to share personal information?*

Obtaining a minor's assent is equally important in group work. Children and adolescents need to be aware of what their participation in the group will be like. Developmentally and cognitively, they may or may not be able to fully understand the information discussed through the assent process. Carolyn Stone (2009, p. 203) stated, "Competence, volunteerism, and knowledge are necessary elements if students are to give us informed consent to participate in a group." Regardless of their developmental and cognitive level, it is still the counselor's ethical duty to prepare the minor for the counseling process, specifically with understanding the realms of confidentiality as best as is possible.

Landmark 8

PROFESSIONAL REFLECTION

In creating a group counseling intervention for students whose parents are divorced, I (G. G.) had a parent ask me about confidentiality within the group. He said, "How can I know for

(*continued*)

sure that when my daughter leaves the group the other girls aren't going to repeat everything she said? My daughter can participate in the group if you can guarantee nothing will ever be repeated." I validated his feelings and explained that I could not promise that because confidentiality is never guaranteed in a group setting. I explained that I would reiterate the significance of that to the students in the group setting, but once they left the group, neither he or I could control their actions. As one could assume, that young lady did not participate in the group. I was somewhat disappointed because I believed the power of the group would have benefitted her greatly.

Confidentiality in Schools

Confidentiality in school counseling presents challenges to counselors who must balance the privacy of students, the legal rights of parents/guardians, and the reality of working alongside other professionals in an educational setting. School counselors may feel like they are serving multiple constituencies with sometimes competing or conflicting needs. In order to best meet the needs of students, school counselors educate themselves on concepts of confidentiality, privacy, informed consent, and the legal rights of minors (Glosoff & Pate, 2002). Students, even if they are minors, should be afforded the ethical right to confidentiality. Minors are no different than adults in benefiting from a therapeutic alliance that protects personal information and communication. An important caveat lies in the distinction between ethical and legal rights. While minors have the ethical right to confidentiality in counseling, their legal rights to privacy and informed consent belong to their parents (Glosoff & Pate, 2002). As such, parents control their children's access to counseling services, although exceptions exist in some states (Glosoff & Pate, 2002). Minors do not gain "ownership and control of their privacy rights" until they reach 18 years of age, the age of maturity (Glosoff & Pate, p. 21).

Isaacs and Stone (1999) reported that a student's age is an influential variable in deciding how to handle an ethical dilemma involving confidentiality. Wagner (1981) stated that the degree to which confidentiality was maintained varied by grade level. "The younger the client, the greater the counselor's allegiance to the parents" (Wagner, 1981, p. 308). Bodenhorn (2006) found the five most common areas in which school counselors encountered ethical dilemmas were:

- Confidentiality of personal disclosures
- Confidentiality of student records
- Acting on information of danger to self or others
- Parental rights
- Dual relationships with faculty

School counselors may wish to work collaboratively and proactively with parents when juggling the ethical and legal duties of counseling children (Glosoff & Pate, 2002). Educating parents on their roles and responsibilities embedded within the framework of the ASCA National Model can foster positive alliances. Counselors need not wait until the process of informed consent to do so. Glosoff and Pate (2002) suggested that school counselors communicate with parents on a regular basis, such as at PTA meetings. Other ways to advocate for one's counseling program and address issues such as confidentiality and informed consent include monthly newsletters, guidance department websites, and students' agenda books. Clarifying the nature and limits of confidentiality in the counseling relationship is one essential aspect of communication to parents.

Another sensitive aspect of counseling minor clients in the schools involves determining when and what to share with noncounseling staff. School counselors work alongside teachers, administrators, coaches, and other staff members. However, counselors have limits to what they can disclose regarding students, and noncounseling staff may not understand, or appreciate, these limitations. As with parents, school counselors should consider educating their colleagues regarding the purpose and therapeutic imperative of protecting client confidences, as well as discussing appropriate disclosure. Educating colleagues can be done formally, such as offering a staff training session during orientation for new employees, as well as informally, like brown-bag lunches. Regardless of the method, returning to these issues with colleagues on a periodic basis is good practice.

Landmark 9

PROFESSIONAL REFLECTION

Teachers frequently used to ask me (G. G.) about my meetings with their students. "Who did Sam say he was mad at?" or "What did Manuel tell you about his family?" There were times when I felt as if teachers perceived me as a "secret-keeper" and saw me as trying to have more power than them with their students. My principal gave me the opportunity to address this at a faculty meeting. I articulated to the faculty the meaning of confidentiality in counseling, specifically how it pertains to children in school. I also gave them a copy of the ASCA *Ethical Standards* and highlighted the sections relevant to confidentiality. Since then, I have not had teachers ask me to reveal students' disclosures.

SIGNPOSTS FOR FUTURE TREKS

Guiding counselors in their decision to break confidentiality goes beyond professional ethical codes and legal mandates. Maintaining client confidentiality should transcend compliance and tap into the spirit of honoring client dignity and the counseling enterprise. Counselors will want to ask themselves if compromising confidentiality is in their clients' best interest and if disclosing private information will help and not hurt clients' well-being. As evidenced in this chapter, there are a plethora of factors that contribute to developing a sound ethical decision. Reading and understanding the ethical and legal parameters of confidentiality is one piece to the puzzle, but it can undoubtedly present challenges and moments of emotional exhaustion when attempting to fit the puzzle pieces together to create one final product—a decision. It was our intention to disseminate personal and professional experiences that will help you along your journey of ethical, professional, and personal development.

INSIGHTS GAINED FROM THE JOURNEY

As a professional school counselor, I (G. G.) am mindful of the significance of maintaining confidentiality in the school setting. I often ask myself: What information should I disclose to a teacher and what should I keep within the walls of my counseling room? These questions tend to create ethical dilemmas for me. As a professional school counselor, I have always been cognizant of the ASCA *Ethical Standards* (2010) with regard to confidentiality. I keep a copy of the standards posted in my counseling room, disseminated the revised 2010 edition to members of our counseling department, posted a link on my website so parents could access it, and even spent time at a faculty meeting educating my staff about the *Ethical Standards*, specifically with a discussion around confidentiality. After a student leaves my room, his or her teacher will frequently stop in and ask, "So how is she doing?" or "What did he have to say about that ...?" These are questions that I find challenging to answer, as I do not always know how to best respond in a professional manner. With my experiences in the school setting, I have found some teachers genuinely want to know how their students are doing while other teachers simply want information to "gossip" or to pass judgment about the students.

One example of this involved a student, Leanna,[1] who was suspected to be a victim of child abuse. I met with Leanna individually to determine more about the alleged report of child abuse. Although there were no physical marks on her body, there was enough information that seemed to warrant a phone call to the local Children and Youth Services (CYS). Based on the unique needs of this case, I consulted with another counselor in the district and decided it would be in Leanna's best interest to make a report to CYS. After making the report to CYS, a case worker came to the school that afternoon and spoke with Leanna privately. At the end of the day, Leanna's teacher came to my room and asked me what was going on with her. I remember feeling a slight pull in my stomach because I knew this teacher genuinely cared for Leanna, but I also wanted to protect Leanna's rights and privacy. After acknowledging this feeling, I responded to the teacher with the following comment: "I appreciate your concern for Leanna, and I know how much you care about Leanna. Given some recent events, you should know that there could be some things happening at home that may be affecting Leanna academically and socially. For now, please monitor her closely and let me know if you notice any changes in her behavior."

During peer supervision, we referenced the ASCA *Ethical Standards* again and discussed how only pertinent information needs to be shared with teachers. I believe I provided the teacher with adequate information relevant to the situation.

This is an example of one of many situations involving ethical dilemmas around confidentiality. I am aware of how these situations will continue to surface. As they

[1] *Name was changed to protect the student's identity.*

do, I will continue to consult, seek supervision, and refer to the ASCA *Ethical Standards* for ways to resolve the ethical dilemma. Although I have gained confidence in communicating pertinent information to teachers, I know that I will use the resources available to strengthen my expertise and comfort in this area.

MOVING FORWARD: CASE STUDY AND REFLECTION QUESTIONS

Mr. Manning, a U.S. history teacher, is concerned about one of his students, Emily. Emily, a sophomore, is not submitting her homework on time and failed her last test, leaving the final page completely blank. Mr. Manning contacts the school counselor, Ms. Lewis, to request that she schedule an appointment with his student. Emily meets with Ms. Lewis, and they develop a good rapport. Over several meetings, Emily discloses her overwhelming feelings of not being loved by her mother. Emily says that her mother focuses all of her attention on her new boyfriend who is "creepy and a loser." To relieve her sadness and anger, Emily burns herself with cigarettes. Ms. Lewis sees the burn marks and urges Emily to see a doctor immediately—and to tell her mother. Emily agrees, even though she knows that her mother will be "pissed and not very understanding" about her self-injurious behavior. A week later, Ms. Lewis contacts Emily, asking her to stop by the office. Emily says she does not have time and that everything is "okay" now. Everything is not, as Emily continues to receive failing grades. Soon after report cards are issued, Emily's mother calls Ms. Lewis and wants to know what is happening with her daughter. It has been a couple months since Ms. Lewis has seen Emily. She wonders what she should say to Emily's mother.

REFLECTION QUESTIONS

- *What are the main ethical dilemmas presented in this scenario?*
- *Discuss Ms. Lewis's actions with Emily.*
- *What should Ms. Lewis's share with Emily's mother? With Mr. Manning?*
- *Identify and discuss relevant ACA and ASCA ethical code.*
- *How will you resolve this quandary using a positive approach to ethics?*

REFERENCES

Abrahams, S., & Salazar, C. (2005). Potential conflicts between cultural values and the role of confidentiality when counseling South Asian clients: Implications for ethical practice. In G. R. Walz, & R. K. Yeps (Eds.), *VISTAS: Compelling perspectives on counseling, 2005* (pp. 145–148). Alexandria, VA: American Counseling Association.

American Counseling Association. (2005). *ACA code of ethics*. Alexandria, VA: Author.

American School Counselor Association. (2010). *Ethical standards for school counselors*. Retrieved from http://asca2.timberlakepublishing.com//files/EthicalStandards2010.pdf

Anda, R. F., Felitti, V. J., Bremner, J. D., Walker, J. D., Whitfield, C., Perry, B. D. et al. (2006). The enduring effects of abuse and related adverse experiences in childhood: A converging of evidence from neurobiology and epidemiology. *European Archives of Psychiatry in Neuroscience, 256*, 176–186.

Bodenhorn, N. (2006). Exploratory study of common and challenging ethical dilemmas experienced by professional school counselors. *Professional School Counseling, 10*(2), 195–202.

Bongar, B. (1991). *The suicidal patient: Clinical and legal standards of care*. Washington, DC: American Psychological Association.

Boynton v. Burglass, 590 So2d. 446 (Fla. App. 1991). Centers for Disease Control and Prevention. (2009). *HIV surveillance report: Diagnoses of HIV infection and AIDS in the United States and dependent areas, 2009*. Retrieved from http://www.cdc.gov/hiv/surveillance/resources/reports/2009report.

Cicchetti, D., Rogosch, F. A., & Toth, S. L. (2006). Fostering secure attachments in infants in maltreating families through preventive interventions. *Developmental Psychopathology, 18*, 623–649.

Cohen, E. D., & Cohen, G. S. (1999). *The virtuous therapist: Ethical practice of counseling and psychotherapy* (2nd ed.). Belmont, CA: Wadsworth Publishing Company.

Corey, G., Corey, M., & Callahan, P. (2011). *Issues and ethics in the helping professions* (8th ed.). Pacific Grove, CA: Brooks/Cole.

Danial v. Daniel, O. H. (1990).

Davis v. Lhim, 335 N. W. 2d 481 (Mich. Ct. App. 1983). Edger, K., & Meyer, E. (2010). Considerations for teaching existential–phenomenological counseling theory. *ACES Spectrum, 71*(1), 17–29.

Edger, K., & Meyer, E. (2010). Considerations for teaching existential-phenomenological counseling theory. *ACES Spectrum, 71*(1), 17–29.

Eisel vs. Board of Education of Montgomery County, 597 A.2d 447, 456 (Md. 1991).

Emerich v. Philadelphia Center for Human Development, Inc. (1998). 554 Pa. 209 720 A.2d 1032.

Federal Child Abuse Prevention and Treatment Act. (1987). 42. U.S.C. 1232g.

Garcia, J. G., Forrester, L. E., & Jacob, A. V. (1998). Ethical dilemma resolution in HIV/AIDS counseling: Why an integrative model? *International Journal of Rehabilitation and Health, 4*, 167–181.

Gilligan, C. (2003). *In a different voice: Psychological theory and women's development*. Cambridge, MA: Harvard University Press.

Glosoff, H. L., & Pate, R. H., Jr. (2002). Privacy and confidentiality in school counseling. *Professional School Counseling, 6*(1), 20–27.

Guignon, C. B. (1993). Authenticity, moral values, and psychotherapy. In C. Guignon (Ed.), *The Cambridge companion to Heidegger* (pp. 215–239). New York: Cambridge University Press.

Harding, A. K., Gray, L. A., & Neal, M. (1993). Confidentiality limits with clients who have HIV: A review of ethical and legal guidelines and professional policies. *Journal of Counseling and Development, 71*, 297–305.

Heidegger, M. (1962). *Being and time*. New York: Harper & Row.

Hendin, H., Lipschitz, A., Maltsberger, J. T., Haas, A. P., & Wynecoop, W. (2000). Therapists reactions to patients' suicides. *American Journal of Psychiatry, 157*, 2022–2027.

Herlihy, B., & Corey, G. (2006). *ACA ethical standards casebook* (6th ed.). Alexandria, VA: American Counseling Association.

Hursthouse, R. (1999). *On virtue ethics*. New York: Oxford University Press.

Hyldahl, R. S., & Richardson, B. (2011). Key considerations for using no-harm contracts with clients who self-injure. *Journal of Counseling & Development, 89*, 121–127.

Isaacs, M. L., & Stone, C. (1999). School counselors and confidentiality: Factors affecting professional choices. *Professional School Counseling, 2*(4), 258–266.

Jablonski v. The United States. 712 F.2d 391 (9th Cir. 1983).

Jacobs, E. E., Masson, R. L., & Harvill, R. L. (2009). *Group counseling strategies and skills*. Belmont, CA: Brooks/Cole.

Jaffee v. Redmond. (1996). 1996 WL 315841 (U.S. June 13, 1996).

James, R. K. (2008). *Crisis intervention strategies*. Belmont, CA: Brooks/Cole.

Kaplan, D. (2006). The end of "clear and imminent danger." *Counseling Today, January*. Retrieved from http://ct.counseling.org/2006/01/ct-online-ethics-update/.

Kennel, R. G., & Agresti, A. A. (1995). Effects of gender and age on psychologists reporting of child sexual abuse. *Professional Psychology: Research and Practice, 26*, 612–615.

Lawrence, G., & Robinson-Kurpius, S. E. (2000). Legal and ethical issues involved when counseling minors in nonschool settings. *Journal of Counseling & Development, 78*, 130–136.

Ledyard, P. (1998). Counseling minors: Ethical and legal issues. *Counseling and Values, 42*, 171–177.

Leonard v. Iowa, 491 N. W. 2d (Iowa Sup. Ct. 1992).

Luijpen, W. A., & Koren, H. J. (1969). *A first introduction to existential phenomenology*. Pittsburgh, PA: Duquesne University Press.

Meara, N. M., Schmidt, L. D., & Day, J. D. (1996). Principle and virtues: A foundation for ethical decisions, policies, and character. *The Counseling Psychologist, 24*(1), 4–77.

Mosher, P. W., & Swire, P. P. (2002). The ethical and legal implications of *Jaffee v. Redmond* and the HIPAA medical privacy rule for psychotherapy and general psychiatry. *Psychiatric Clinics of North America, 25*, 575–584.

Noddings, N. (2003). *Caring: A feminine approach to ethics & moral education*. Los Angeles, CA: University of California Press.

Pabian, Y. L., Welfel, E., & Beebe, R. S. (2009). Psychologists' knowledge of their states' laws pertaining to Tarasoff-type situations. *Professional Psychology: Research and Practice, 40*, 8–14.

Rand, A. (1964). *The virtue of selfishness*. New York: Signet.

Remley, T. P., & Herlihy, B. (2010). *Ethical, legal, and professional issues in counseling*. Upper Saddle River, NJ: Pearson Education.

SAMHSA. (1994). *Technical assistance publication (TAP) Series 13: Confidentiality of patient records for alcohol and other drug treatment*. Rockville, MD: U.S. Department of Health and Human Services.

Savickas, M. L. (1997). The spirit in career counseling: Fostering self-completion through work. In D. P. Bloch, & L. J. Richmond (Eds.), *Connections between spirit and work in career development: New approaches and practical perspectives* (pp. 3–25). Palo Alto, CA: Davies-Black.

Stone, C. (2011). Serious and forseeable harm or clear, imminent danger. *ASCA School Counselor, 48*(4), 6–8.

Stone, C. (2009). *School counseling principles: Ethics and law* (2nd ed.). Alexandria, VA: American School Counselor Association.

Stone, C., Conte, C., & Antkowiak, E. (2007). The legal intrigues of counseling practice. In J. Gregoire, & C. Jungers (Eds.), *The counselor's companion* (pp. 32–50). Mahwah, NJ: Lawrence Erlbaum Associates, Inc.

Tarasoff v. Regents of the University of California, 529 P.2d 553 (Cal. 1974).

Tarasoff v. Regents of the University of California, 551 P.2d 334 (Cal. 1976).

U. S. Department of Education. (2007). Balancing student privacy and school safety: A guide to the Family Educational Rights and Privacy Act for colleges and universities. Retrieved from http://www2.ed.gov/policy/gen/guid/fpco/brochures/postsec.html

Wagner, C. A. (1981). Confidentiality and the school counselor. *Personnel and Guidance Journal, 59*, 305–310.

Walcott, D. M., Cerundolo, P., & Beck, J. C. (2001). Current analysis of the Tarasoff duty: An evolution towards the limitation of the duty to protect. *Behavioral Sciences and the Law, 19*, 325–343.

Weiss, N. F. (2011). To release or not to release: An analysis of the HIPAA subpoena exception. *Journal of Medicine and Law, 253*.

Welfel, E. R. (2010). *Ethics in counseling & psychotherapy: Standards, research, and emerging issues*. Belmont, CA: Brooks/Cole.

Wettstein, R. M. (1999). *Emerich v. Philadelphia Center for Human Development*: The new duty to warn in Pennsylvania. *Journal of the American Academy of Psychiatry and the Law, 27*(2), 309–313.
Wong-Wylie, G. (2003). Preserving hope in the duty to protect: Counselling clients with HIV or AIDS. *Canadian Journal of Counseling, 37*, 35–43.
Younggren, J. N., & Harris, E. A. (2008). Can you keep a secret? Confidentiality in psychotherapy. *Journal of Clinical Psychology, 64*(5), 589–600.

7

Record Keeping and Technology in Counseling Ethics

Gina M. Gordon, Stephen Kuniak, and Catherine A. Sherman

THE FORESEEN DESTINATION

After reading this chapter, students will aspire to:

- Recognize and apply ethical standards with regard to record keeping in counseling.
- Identify the purpose(s) and types of record keeping.
- Understand ways to maintain records of clients/students.
- Acquire knowledge of what information should and should not be included in records.
- Be familiar with common methods of incorporating technology into counseling.
- Be knowledgeable about common ethical concerns related to technology and counseling.
- Reflect upon one's ethical journey as a counseling professional.

GETTING ON THE ROAD

What does it mean to become competent at the task of record keeping? What is the role of advancing technologies in counseling practice? Both of these questions may not immediately surface when one ponders the tasks of professional counselors. Yet, both are worthy of attention when we consider the multifaceted roles and ethical responsibilities of clinicians. Careful record keeping long has been considered an essential part of clinical practice for counselors, while technological advancements more recently have led to a closer integration of technology into counseling, presenting new ethical concerns for professionals. The goal of this chapter is to address ethical issues surrounding the areas of recording keeping and technology by providing relevant information and practical examples. Furthermore, we invite you to read the chapter with the philosophies of care and virtue ethics in mind, because these ethical frameworks help to propel us outside of a legalistic approach to ethics. Finally, we provide personal testimonies based on insights we have gained from our own professional journeys and encourage you to think about the information in this chapter in light of your own clinical experiences.

EXPLORING THE TERRITORY

EXPLANATION OF RECORDS

Remley and Herlihy (2005, p. 119) defined records as "any physical recording made of information related to a counselor's professional practice." Schrier (1980, p. 452) stated that a record could include "any item, collection, or grouping of information about an individual, including education, financial transactions, medical history, and identifying numbers or symbols." Mitchell (1991, p. 12) shared that records are "any written documents, audio or video recordings, or other tangible items that contain client information . . . [and are] any compilation of information for the purpose of diagnosis and treatment." These brief descriptions of records suggest that professional counselors use various types of documents that help them work competently. Often, records are associated with counselors' handwritten notes taken during or after a counseling session; these are known as clinical case notes (Remley & Herlihy, 2005). However, client records also refer to administrative documents, such as appointment books, intake forms, billing information, and communication logs (Swartz, 2006). In a school setting, counselors oversee two additional types of records: educational records and personal records. Educational records include a variety of different student and academic information, such as grades, information about disability and accommodations, and financial data. School counselors' personal case notes are akin to clinical case notes and typically include the date, student's name, and a few details about the student that serve as a memory aide. These case notes are kept separate from a student's educational record. "Handwritten notes about a student written by a counselor, teacher, or administrator are not considered to be an education record under FERPA [Family Educational Rights and Privacy Act] and are therefore not subject to access or disclosure rules" (Merlone, 2005, p. 372). Whether in a community or school setting, counselors aspire to work in accordance with the highest ethical standards and help clients in a positive way; in other words, they enact the principle of beneficence. With regard to record keeping, this means, among other things, that counselors maintain confidential records and document sessions appropriately and in a timely manner.

PURPOSE OF RECORDS

Counselors have a responsibility to care for their clients' welfare. The responsibility to care involves counselors in drawing upon virtues, such as integrity, diligence, and trustworthiness (Cohen & Cohen, 1999). These virtues play an integral part in the counselor's record-keeping practices and help to highlight its aspirational purposes.

Caring for a client and showcasing integrity means that counselors are honest about the information they include in a client's record. Conveying diligence means they will provide reliable counseling services, which usually is aided by reviewing a client's record prior to a session. Both of these practices help clients to instill trust in the counselor, which furthers the authenticity of the counseling relationship and makes it a safe place for the client to openly discuss personal issues.

Other reasons for maintaining adequate records are to provide meaningful services for clients, ensure continuity of care, and protect the counselor from lawsuits (Luepker, 2003; Piazza & Baruth, 1990). Clients benefit when counselors maintain precise and thorough notes because, under these circumstances, clinical work is more likely to be clearly defined (Remley & Herlihy, 2005) and in keeping with therapeutic goals. Reciprocally, counselors reap rewards from keeping good records. Diligent counselors are mindful to include significant details related to verbal and nonverbal communication and about the relationship dynamics. Having a document that highlights the progress and process of each counseling session helps to strengthen counselors' ability to meaningfully guide future sessions. In addition, counselors use records to ensure continuity of care for clients, and, thus, they are cognizant that a coworker, supervisor, or another professional colleague may be examining their client records at some point. It is helpful, then, for counselors to document about client progress, effectiveness of certain techniques or programs, and overall impressions about follow-up care (Mitchell, 1991; Soisson, VandeCreek, & Knapp, 1987). In an elementary, middle, or high school setting that can have several hundred students, it may be difficult for counselors to record information each time they meet with a student, which poses a challenge to ensuring continuity of care. Nonetheless, it is in the best interest of school counselors to create a record-keeping system that intentionally serves this purpose. For example, if a parent requested to know how one's child was progressing in a friendship group, a counselor could refer to her record-keeping system and let the parent know how many group sessions the student attended and topics of discussion, as well as her observations about the student's behavior. Maintaining good records helps strengthen direct client care, as well as communication with key stakeholders, such as parents and teachers—all part of providing continuous, helpful service.

Note-taking also serves the goal of protecting a counselor's own welfare. Looked at from this point of view, counselors need to be mindful of why they are including particular information in their records. Remley and Herlihy (2005) encouraged counselors to ask themselves not only why they are including something in their client's record, but who could possibly read this information and for what purpose they may read it. Using this mental framework as a guide, counselors may feel more confident in their decision about what to include or omit from their clients' records. While not undervaluing the importance of counselors' personal and professional welfare and their need to be legally aware, we also agree with Cohen and Cohen, who suggested that careful documentation "be guided primarily by concern for clients' welfare" (1999, p. 95). Thus, when counselors ponder what to include in a record, they might equally weigh legal and virtue considerations.

Landmark 1

PROFESSIONAL REFLECTION

I (G. G.) recall a professor's wise statement: "Anything you document should be written as if a lawyer was reading it." This comment, at first, made me feel somewhat anxious about the practice of record keeping because I did not want to document anything that may end up misinterpreted. Initially, for me, the significance of writing case notes was to ensure self-protection. As I became more aware of my own values and morals, I came to realize that while it was critical to document information in the event that a lawyer were to read it, it was equally, if not more important, to document information because of underlying care and virtue ethics. Was I being a fair counselor when I chose to include certain information in one client's file but not in another client's file? Was I displaying discretion with deciding what information to share with a colleague? Did I resemble a competent counselor when I chose to shorten part of the case note because I was tired of writing that day? Now, when I reflect upon the comment made by the professor, I find myself feeling less anxious and more appreciative, and I realize that there is so much more to record keeping than just the legal ramifications.

CONTENT OF RECORDS

What do you write in a case note? What information do you include and what do you leave out? These are questions counselors face in determining the appropriate content of a case note. There seems to be minimal time spent in graduate counseling programs on creating clinical case notes, which may add to novice professionals' confusion. Mitchell (1991) purported that records need to address the type of counseling service provided, how clients' goals were addressed, and the counselor's perceived level of attainment toward goals. Mitchell noted, further, that it is important to write case notes succinctly, yet thoroughly. Relatedly, whether counselors record notes during a session with a client or immediately after is a decision that usually reflects their personal style, though they ought carefully to consider how their in-session note-taking might be perceived by a client and how it might detract from direct client care. Landmark 2 summarizes some of Mitchell's helpful guidelines regarding ways to communicate effectively in case notes.

Landmark 2

RECOMMENDATIONS FOR KEEPING RECORDS (MITCHELL, 1991)

1. **Since some words have similar meanings, be clear and specific with the choice of words used in the case note.**
Case Example: A client arrives for his session 15 minutes

(continued)

late. He enters the room, visibly upset, yelling about how his lateness is not his fault. He sits down and has difficulty focusing on your questions. It would *not* be recommended to write in your case notes that client was in a bad mood. The word "bad" has too many meanings. Instead, it may be more advantageous to write about observable behaviors: *Client arrived late to session, spoke loudly in a fast way, sat in chair with a sigh, and ignored questions.*

2. **Eliminate opinions and adjectives that allude to judgmental statements. Keep your writing bias-free and specific.**
   Case Example: An 8th grade student is referred to you due to ongoing disruptive behavior in class. Although the teacher describes this student as obnoxious, uncooperative, disrespectful, and abnormal, these words would *not* be recommended to use in your records. These are reflective of the teacher's opinion. Instead, you might choose to write: *Student referred to me by homeroom teacher on February 24, 2010 due to teacher's concerns with behaviors displayed in the classroom setting.*
3. **Discard technical professional jargon and only document concrete information.**
   Case Example: As a licensed professional counselor working at a community agency, you referred a 9-year-old child suffering from what appears to be severe depression to another colleague in your agency who has more experience working with children and adolescents. You provide your colleague with this child's records, which states that you believe she is suffering from severe depression. Since there was not a formal diagnosis given with regard to criterion set forth in the *DSM*, it would be more beneficial for your colleague to know some of the behaviors that would warrant this possible diagnosis of depression. Some of these behaviors might include: *isolated from peer group, decrease in academic grades, withdrawn from social activities like cheerleading and soccer, and so on.*

Knowing what to address in a note is as important as knowing the nuances of how to write a good note. Schrier (1980, p. 456) recommended that certain information be included in routine case notes. Some of this information includes:

- Relevant demographic data, such as age, sex, race, income, legal status (court ordered or voluntary admission)
- Statement of the problem as seen by the client
- Relevant historical information necessary for proper diagnoses
- Assessment procedures, including home visits, tests, interviews, evaluations, consultations, and referrals
- Diagnoses and their factual basis
- Proposed treatment plans and objectives
- Ongoing assessments of problems and treatment plans as they relate to planned objectives, needed modifications, and so on
- Record of discharge, transfer, and termination and of the basis for these actions

The American Psychological Association (APA) recently revised its record-keeping guidelines. Although these guidelines have not been adopted by the American Counseling Association (ACA), they appear to be a helpful frame of reference for counselors. The APA recommended including the following information (Drogin, Connell, Foote, & Sturm, 2010):

- Client-identifying information
- Billing information
- Informed consent
- Authorization for release of confidential information
- Plan for service
- Historical information of client's functioning
- Assessment results
- Behavior rating results
- Crisis management documentation
- Theory-based intervention
- Client's current status and objective behaviors

In summary, there are multiple guidelines surrounding which information to include in a record. Among the examples listed in this section, it would be helpful to highlight the content you think best represents your client and accurately meets the needs of the setting in which you work.

WRITING CASE NOTES

There are numerous formats by which to structure case notes. Some counselors use a template provided to them by their counseling agency. Others create a case note format that fits the needs of their clients and setting. We discuss two formats common to community mental health settings in this section: the SOAP format and the STIPS format. You will also read about an additional format, COP, which was designed specifically for school counselors.

SOAP Format

SOAP notes are derived from a medical records approach and aim to provide ongoing assessment of client treatment and progress (Cameron & turtle-song, 2002). The SOAP note format enables counselors to use a problem-solving structure in conceptualizing their cases and is considered by some to be a way to document relevant information "thoroughly and holistically" (Cameron & turtle-song, 2002, p. 286). Remley and Herlihy (2005) identified four components to SOAP notes:

- S—Subjective
- O—Objective
- A—Assessment
- P—Plan

Landmark 3

A SUMMARIZATION OF SOAP DEFINITIONS AND EXAMPLES (CAMERON & TURTLE-SONG, 2002, p. 290)

Section	*Definition*	*Examples*
Subjective (S)	What the client tells you What pertinent information others tell you about the client Basically, how the client perceives the world	Client's feelings, concerns, plans, goals, and thoughts Client's orientation to time, place, and person
Objective (O)	Factual What the counselor personally observes/witnesses Quantifiable: What was seen, counted, smelled, heard, or measured	The client's general appearance, affect, behavior Client's demonstrated strengths and weaknesses Test results, materials from other agencies
Assessment (A)	Summarizes the counselor's clinical thinking	For counselor: Include clinical diagnoses and clinical impressions
Plan (P)	Describes the parameters of treatment Consists of an action plan and prognosis	Action plan: Include interventions used, treatment progress, and direction. Counselors should include the date of next appointment. Prognosis: Include the anticipated gains from the interventions

Landmark 4

EXAMPLE OF A SOAP NOTE

3/15/11 1:00 p.m.

(S) J reports feeling overwhelmed with busy work schedule. Indicates how schedule over the last 3 weeks has been making him have to go to bed late and get up early. Attempted to go to bed early on some nights but can't seem to go to bed early all nights because of studying for upcoming national exam.

(O) Generally anxious throughout the session. At the beginning, J was pacing back and forth in the room. By the middle of the session, J was sitting on chair, tapping foot. By the end of the session, J was sitting in a different chair, chewing gum loudly and quickly.

(A) More information is necessary before diagnosing, but J is displaying anxiety-related behaviors and struggling with adjustment to new work and school schedule.

(P) Rescheduled for 4/5/11 at 2 p.m.; prognosis somewhat low to medium. Continue reality therapy. Referred to Men's Coping Group. Next session, introduce use of cognitive behavioral therapy and explore solution-focused therapy.

Counselor's Signature

STIPS Format

The STIPS format was developed largely to assist counselors-in-training. With this audience in mind, Prieto and Scheel (2002) created the STIPS format primarily to help counselor trainees develop the ability to conceptualize cases and write case notes consistently. STIPS format is divided into five useful categories:

- S—Signs and symptoms
- T—Topics of discussion
- I—Interventions
- P—Progress and plan
- S—Special issues (Prieto & Scheel, 2002)

Landmark 5

EXAMPLE OF A STIPS NOTE

Date: 4/7/11

(S): H entered the room about 15 minutes later than expected. He shared that he had to wait for his girlfriend to drive him to the appointment. H was wearing his work clothes (construction worker), which were dirty. H reported feeling exhausted from the physical work he did that day. H's speech was fluent and average tone. H stated that he has been taking his medication and has noticed an elevation in his mood. H reported sleeping well and eating well. H's mood appeared to have been more energetic as compared to the last session.

(T): Topics for the session included: (a) reviewing homework assignments, and (b) further discussing H's feelings toward girlfriend and girlfriend's family. H openly discussed his cognitions and feelings of inadequacy and incompetence as a boyfriend. H examined his feelings toward his girlfriend's family. Feelings were explored and H participated in some role plays to practice assertiveness skills. H reported that he went out to dinner with his girlfriend and her parents and was able to cognitively reframe his thoughts about girlfriend's family. H also shared the way he has been using assertiveness skills at work.

(I): H responded well to the CBT training where he has learned to identify some irrational thoughts and challenge them. Behavioral interventions, such as role playing, has helped H increase his own awareness toward his strengths in handling situations. H will continue to maintain his journal of cognitions, feelings, and reflections.

(P): H has responded well to the interventions. H is using CBT to challenge irrational beliefs. His participation in role plays has empowered him to increase his confidence toward being assertive with others, especially at work. I will continue to help H explore his cognitions and feelings about his girlfriend and her family. If he chooses to continue using the journal, then this can also be used to process.

(S): Given H's progress and current state of productivity, a psychiatric evaluation is not warranted at this time.

Counselor's Signature

COP: A Possible Format for School Counselors

All counselors are trained to maintain confidential records. Although the aforementioned examples could apply to the school setting, school counselors do not usually use a specific format for case notes. Merlone (2005) surveyed school counselors' record-keeping practices and found that they document their work in vastly different ways. The study revealed that school counselors mostly use a daily log, file cards, or some type of computer program, but some also use a notebook or an information sheet to log counseling goals and topics of discussion.

Landmark 6

EXAMPLE OF SCHOOL CASE NOTE—COP

As a professional school counselor, I (G. G.) have attempted several ways to record information about students. I have used blank pieces of paper and a computer to take down my impressions. Neither of these techniques seemed to work for me. As a result, I created my own record-keeping form to document meetings with students. Below is an example of a possible case note, **COP (Content, Observable Behavior, and Plan)**, that I adapted from SOAP. I use this format in the school setting as a memory aide.

Student's Name: James **Grade**: 3rd **Date**: October 12, 2010
Referred By: X Self ____ Parent/Guardian ____Teacher _____Other Staff

Content: James requested to meet to discuss conflict with classmate. He and his classmate argued over what game to play at recess. James sought ways to solve problems and manage conflict.

Observable Behaviors: James seemed focused throughout the session. He was open to sharing his thoughts and feelings about the situation. May have felt somewhat anxious because his face turned blotchy-red at the beginning of the session—this blotchy-red color went away as we continued talking.

Plan: James is going to try out two strategies discussed: (1) Talk to classmate at recess about compromising and (2) Offer classmate other activities that they both like to do.

Will meet with James next week to see how his situation is progressing.

The COP format, like the SOAP and STIPS formats, is a way for counselors, first, to highlight the most significant information that will help direct student care. In addition, the template encourages users to be brief and succinct in note taking, which serves the dual purposes of helping counselors keep up with notes in a demanding school environment and ensuring that they are not overly revealing in the event that their notes would be subpoenaed.

Writing for Self-Development

We want to end this section by pointing out that writing case notes can be a powerful aid in the process of professional and self-development. Writing notes helps counselors form the habit of reflectivity, without which professional development may not occur. If counselors fail to reflect on their work after each therapeutic encounter, it is possible that they can get stalled in the novice phase of development, even with years of clinical work behind them (Skovholt & Ronnestad, 1992). However, the potentially mundane practice of documenting records gets transformed to self-development when counselors embrace note-writing as an opportunity to reflect upon themselves and their clinical work. Writing for reflectivity helps counselors move step-by-step toward mastery of the craft called counseling. Some questions to consider when writing for self-development include the following: Was this the most respectful way to elicit a response from the client?; Were there any other observable behaviors noted that could have been processed even further?; Was information documented in a fair, honest manner?; and Was information written with integrity? No matter what format is used, counselors advance their professional development when writing is taken as an opportunity for challenging and confronting themselves and critically evaluating the level of care they offer to clients. Good note taking can help us become better counselors.

Landmark 7

SUMMARY GUIDELINES FOR WRITING CASE NOTES

Documenting for Self-Protection (Remley & Herlihy, 2005)

1. Keep in mind that documents may need to be viewed within the context of a legal proceeding.
2. Specific situations (i.e., abuse, suicide/homicide, illegal, or unethical behaviors) require documentation.
3. Document sessions as soon as possible.
4. Keep all original notes and relevant papers in a secure, locked drawer.

Documenting for Self-Development

1. Take the time to reflect upon your written case notes.
2. Be mindful of care ethics as you write down pertinent information.
3. Use the writing process to help you identify your own areas of strength and weakness.

MANAGING RECORDS

Professional counselors are accountable for maintaining succinct, accurate case notes; moreover, they are equally responsible for monitoring how they store and access records. The ACA *Code of Ethics* (2005), Section B.6 outlines several guidelines for managing records. For example, counselors are required to keep all records in a confidential, safe place, such as a locked filing cabinet or drawer (B.6.a); clients' records should only be shared with a third party if the client has given written consent for disclosure (B.6.f); and clients' records must be retained for a segment of time mandated by federal, state, and local laws (B.6.g). There seem to be varying suggestions on how long clients' records should be kept. Amato, Blase, and Paley (2000) suggested that maintaining records beyond the minimum 15 years is at the discretion of the counselor, in conjunction with the site's policies. Amato et al. further recommended that records of minors be kept for 3 years beyond the majority age. Schrier (1980) endorsed keeping records for at least 6 years for clients over the age of 18 and 6 years after the minors reach the age of majority. Merlone (2005) found that school counselors reported keeping their notes for 1 to 10 years after a student left their school. Although the national standards set forth by the American School Counselor Association (ASCA) do not concentrate on documentation, Sealander, Schwiebert, Oren, and Weekley (1999) reported that school records should be maintained for 5 years as long as there is no outstanding request to inspect or review them. ASCA released a position statement on the professional school counselor and confidentiality with regard to records:

> Professional school counselors keep records of their counseling relationships separate from academic records and do not disclose the contents of their counseling records except when privacy exceptions exist. When professional school counselors receive court orders they believe might lead to the disclosure of private information they gained in counseling relationships with students, they should request legal advice from their supervisors and should follow the legal advice provided to them. (ASCA, 2008)

Finally, agencies and schools should determine a process for destroying case notes and records after a reasonable and appropriate amount of time has passed that upholds confidentiality of clients (ACA; Schrier, 1980).

Family Educational Rights and Privacy Act (FERPA)

The 1974 Family Educational Rights and Privacy Act, also known as the Buckley Amendment, is a federal privacy law protecting educational records generated in primary and secondary schools, as well as colleges and universities. FERPA regulations apply to any school receiving funds administered by the U.S. Department of Education (USDE, 2011a, 2011b). Under FERPA, school counselors must protect the privacy of students' educational records. An educational record is specific information about a student kept by an educational institution or its designee (USDE, 2011b). It is not a "single file" but an "aggregate" of information stored electronically and in written form (Jed Foundation, 2008, p. 8). While an educational record can include academic work, financial information, disciplinary records, and requests for disability accommodations, it does not, according to the Jed Foundation, cover the following:

- Personal notes not shared with, or accessible to, others
- Health-related records used for treatment purposes and shared only with others connected with such treatment
- Observations and conversations with a student—if such observations are recorded with the intention of sharing with others, they become an educational record
- Security records

- Employment files unless such employment is related to having student status, such as a work-study job
- Alumni files except for information related to a student's period of enrollment

Counselors should be aware that their handwritten, personal notes used as "memory aids" are not automatically exempted from FERPA regulations (ACA, 1999, p. 6). Once a counselor records comments made by others, such as parents and teachers, these notes are no longer exempt from FERPA protection even if such notes are in the counselor's "sole possession" (ACA, p. 7). In addition, the physical location of personal notes can determine whether such documents are exempted from FERPA regulations. It is best practice to store personal notes in a location in which only the counselor has access (ACA).

School counselors should be aware of parental access to child abuse reports. When a school counselor documents suspected cases of child abuse, this information becomes part of a student's educational record, and, as such, may be accessed by parents (ACA, 1999). Schools do not need to provide immediate access to requests to review records; they have 45 days before access must be given (USDE, 2011b). Moreover, the Family Policy Compliance Office (FPCO) allows schools to "delete the name of the school employee who initiated the report from the documentation that is shared with a parent" (ACA, p. 12).

Directory information is not considered part of a student's educational record, and thus is not protected information under FERPA. Schools do not need written permission to share directory information, which can consist of a student's name and contact information, dates of attendance, date of birth, and awards (USDE, 2011a). Yet, schools must inform parents and eligible students about the content in directory information and that they have a right to decide not to have such information shared (USDE).

Parents or eligible students (students 18 years or older or enrolled in a postsecondary institution) have the right to inspect educational records, correct or insert a statement contesting information in educational records, and consent to disclosure of information in educational records through written consent (USDE, 2011a). Schools do not need to mail copies of educational records unless it is unreasonable for eligible students or parents to access them physically. In such cases, institutions may request payment for duplicates (USDE, 2011a). Finally, schools do not need written permission to share educational records with the following parties:

- "School officials" who have "legitimate educational interest"
- Institutions to which a student plans to enroll
- School auditing officials
- Offices and institutions associated with student's financial aid
- Accrediting groups
- Judicial order or subpoena
- In cases of emergency when a student is a threat to self or others
- Relevant juvenile justice authorities (USDE, 2011a)

Parents and eligible students must receive annual notification of FERPA rights; such notification does not need to be individualized. A school may determine the means of notification, such as including FERPA guidelines in a school newspaper or handbook (USDE).

The FPCO extends parental rights of access to both biological parents, even if separated or divorced, and those with legal custodial rights, including foster parents (ACA, 1999). Biological parents may provide written permission to schools to extend parental rights to step-parents, partners, or other relatives (ACA). FERPA rights transfer to the "eligible" student once that student turns 18 years old or enrolls in a postsecondary institution. Schools are permitted, but not required, to share information with parents if their eligible student is declared as dependent on their federal income tax forms (ACA).

FERPA and Higher Education

The 2009 FERPA revisions ushered in a fresh understanding between colleges and universities and the Department of Education, particularly with regards to the limits of confidentiality in order to protect the safety of campus communities (Lake, 2009). Behind these changes is the specter of the 2007 Virginia Tech massacre. Reports following the shooting spree call into question whether FERPA privacy regulations interfered with school officials' ability to share information regarding students in distress. Clarification to FERPA language addresses these concerns. College officials now have greater purview in deciding when to break confidentiality and with whom (Lake, 2009). School counselors, as a result, should feel more empowered to share information in cases of health and safety emergencies, even if such circumstances are not "imminent, just significant—like a menacing statement to others, or the availability of a weapon" (Lake, para. 14). In addition, the Department of Education will not second-guess a school's decision to share private information as long as "there is a rational basis" for such action (USDE, 2008, "Dear Colleague Letter," para. 3). Furthermore, schools cannot be sued for monetary damages, as articulated in the 2002 Supreme Court case, *Gonzaga University v. Doe*. Schools may be sanctioned, and federal aid may be withheld, especially if there is a history of FERPA violations (McDonald, 2008).

Health Insurance Portability and Accountability Act (HIPAA)

HIPAA is a 1996 federal privacy law that protects personal health records that are transmitted electronically for the purposes of treatment and payment. Clients provide consent to have their health records shared by signing a privacy notice. The notice, given to a client on the first day of services, includes information regarding access and use of health records as well as the client's rights to review, copy, and change records (Annas, 2003). HIPAA regulations do not cover school treatment records, even if shared (Jed Foundation, 2008).

The 2000 Privacy Rule issued by the Department of Health and Human Services extends privacy protection for medical records, most notably for psychotherapy notes (Mosher & Swire, 2002). Notes taken by a counselor in the process of therapy and stored apart from a client's health record are considered psychotherapy notes (Mosher & Swire, 2002). Some information is excluded from the definition of these notes, including medication history, diagnoses, and service dates (Mosher & Swire,

2002). In addition, general consent for services does not authorize disclosure of psychotherapy notes; rather, "more specific and limited authorization" must be obtained from the client (Mosher & Swire, 2002, p. 583). Moreover, "no third-party payer can condition enrollment in a health plan or payment of a claim on a patients' agreement to sign such an authorization" (Mosher & Swire, 2002, p. 583).

TECHNOLOGY AND COUNSELING

To this point, we have been looking at the ethics surrounding record keeping. We now turn our attention to another topic: the place and practice of technology in counseling. Technological advances affect a wide range of counselors' work, from the more periphery aspects of service, such as billing and record keeping, to direct service, as in telephone and online counseling. Technology refers to devices as common place as telephones, voicemail, and computers, as well as the Internet, web cameras, email, and electronic or online assessment tools (ACA, 2005). Given our tech-based culture, we invite you to consider how counseling would appear if it was completely based in the virtual world. Though this notion may seem like science fiction to some, the truth is that online counseling practices are springing up with increasing frequency (Shaw & Shaw, 2006; VandenBos & Williams, 2000). The ability of the Internet to reach virtually anyone provides significant gains to the scope of a counselor's practice. Some aspects of the counseling process, and certain underserved segments of the population, such as those in rural areas, those who would typically feel uncomfortable about seeing a counselor, and those with disabilities that prohibit easy access to a counselor's office, seem poised to benefit from the integration of technology and counseling (Alleman, 2002; Mallen, Vogel, & Rochlen, 2005). Although technology can provide significant improvements to our day-to-day and professional lives, as with anything else, convenience has to be tempered with responsibility. As professionals who use or consider using technology, it becomes our role not to stray too far from the ethics that guide us in our physical offices. Being a virtuous practitioner extends into all aspects of our work, even that which takes place in a virtual world.

Methods of Technology-Assisted Counseling

Technology-assisted counseling can be defined broadly as any actions that mirror a traditional counseling relationship but that take place through a technology-based medium, rather than face to face in an office setting (e.g., phone counseling and online counseling). Many online counseling practices currently market and offer their services through a web page that acts as the "face" of the agency. Like all counselors, however, cyberclinicians who use the Internet to provide counseling have to consider what constitutes the most responsible parameters and modalities of practice.

Two prominent methods of interacting with clients online are asynchronous communication (e.g., email) and synchronous communication (e.g., live chat that can include the use of webcams). Email-based counseling can be helpful for individuals who are introspective or motivated by the process of writing (Murphy & Mitchell,

1998). For clients who use email, counseling can become like a living journal. Like traditional methods of counseling, the process of using email has to be well defined, especially as email communication is not necessarily a time sensitive interaction (Rochlen, Zack, & Speyer, 2004). In addition, in the informed consent process, the counselor ought to contract with the client on how emails are processed and in what way responses and clinical data (i.e., email correspondence) will be safely and confidentially handled (ACA, 2005, A.12.g).

Synchronous counseling using live chat or a webcam is an alternative to email counseling. Webcams create the sensation of "telepresence," which is the feeling that an individual is in the presence of a person even when they, physically, are not (Fink, 1999). The phenomenon of telepresence provides opportunities to develop a therapeutic relationship with the client through the computer. In addition to understanding usual ethical concerns, counselors who use this medium must address practical issues, such as making provisions for what happens if an Internet connection is lost and learning how to use a camera effectively. Webcams, like any other camera, have a given viewing area for their aperture. Careful focusing of the camera helps to make certain that the interaction is as much like a face to face, "in the office," counseling session as possible. In addition, it may be easy for counselors who use web cameras in their homes to grow careless around the obligations to confidentiality within the more relaxed environment of an online office. This in mind, informed consent documents help clients know their rights and understand the nuances of a counseling relationship based on web-camera interaction. Perhaps more importantly, clinicians ought to review their practices regularly to evaluate the extent to which they are acting with diligence to protect clients' well-being regarding confidentiality and other related rights.

Practice and Ethics Issues in Online Counseling

Counseling in the traditional sense requires no physical tools. Items such as assessments, workbook activities, and play therapy toys are optional attachments to the therapeutic process. Just as with most things, the more attachments we add to something, the more complex the process can become. Below we look at some of the potential ethical concerns counselors need to consider when venturing into the online counseling world.

Informed Consent

Members of the 2002 ACA Ethics Revision Task Force (Kaplan, 2006) suggested that, among the many changes to the 2005 Code related to technology, the guidelines for informed consent are paramount. The code points out that in all counseling, even cybercounseling, it is the counselor's role to be up front about the benefits and risks of counseling, as well as its processes and procedures. The uniqueness of technology-assisted counseling calls for counselors to be conscientious about informed consent issues they otherwise might not encounter in a traditional setting. For example, cybercounselors ensure that clients are aware of (a) the limits of confidentiality when using electronic communication, (b) how a counselor will handle private electronic information, (c) legal rights or constraints clients face when they are in a different state than the counselor, (d) limitations related to crisis management, and

(e) impact of time zone differences on communication. Much has been written, in particular, about challenges surrounding confidentiality in technology-assisted counseling (ACA, 2005; Alleman, 2002; Mallen et al., 2005; Shaw & Shaw, 2006). As a response to the very public nature of information shared over the Internet, the code recommends that, in the informed consent process, counselors encourage clients to take measures to protect their own technology devises from outside users in order to maintain privacy and that they use encryption where possible. Counselors themselves are recommended to use secure websites and encryption software. Finally, of utmost importance is the way in which a counselor handles the informed consent process. Maheu and Gordon (2000) noted that less than half of psychologists surveyed used a formal informed consent procedure for start-up of online services. As well, only half made appropriate recommendations ahead of time for crisis and safety contingencies. A virtue-based approach to cybercounseling that invites counselors to reflect on how to gather informed consent with thoroughness and care for the client can help diminish such instances and empower clients to be educated consumers of cybercounseling.

Crisis Management and Duty to Warn and Protect

Crisis management is an ethical concern in any agency, private practice, or school. In settings where localized service is offered, making decisions related to client and community safety and breaking confidentiality involves challenging questions about serious and foreseeable harm, crisis assessment, and type of intervention needed. These same issues are relevant in technology-assisted counseling, but concurrently, counselors have to grapple with other layers of complexity. How, for example, could a counselor in Pennsylvania assess the potential for serious and foreseeable harm and, if needed, guarantee crisis management for a client in Idaho? Counselors who practice online ought to address this limitation concretely before they establish an online counseling office or begin to offer services. The ACA *Code of Ethics* (2005, A.12.g) and most literature endorse the idea that consent forms used for clients of online counseling clearly spell out crisis management procedures and document personal, as well as emergency contact information gathered from clients (Kraus, 2004; Mallen et al., 2005). The service provider can also list 911 as a crisis-response option when clients are not in session. Mallen and colleagues further recommend gathering local police contact information from clients at the start of counseling relationships. Finally, counselors do well to consider the level of risk they are willing to incur given the limitations surrounding crisis management. Some clients may not be suitable candidates for online services (Childress, 1998). Based on information provided in a disclosure statement, counselors can determine whether or not the client may need more intensive services than the Internet counseling arena can provide. In such instances, counselors can help clients locate more appropriate services in their area. The versatility of the Internet can aid in this referral process (Grohol, 2003).

Licensure and Scope of Practice

Professional license requirements tend to vary by state. Portability of a license is not guaranteed across states or disciplines. In contrast, online counseling has very few discernable boundaries (Barnett, 2005). When examining online counseling and licensure, counselors arrive at one dominant question: If a counselor is licensed and practicing in one state and a client is in another state, how are ethical practice boundaries established? Embedded in this question not only are ethical concerns related to practicing within the boundaries of one's competence, but also legal questions related to counseling beyond the scope of one's license.

The ACA *Code of Ethics* (2005, A.12.e) obliges counselors to know and abide by the laws governing licensure when offering technology-assisted counseling. As Shaw and Shaw (2006) pointed out, however, there is some debate and confusion about where online counseling occurs—in the state of the counselor or that of the client. Thus, counselors may be subject to laws and regulations surrounding online mental health services not only in their own state, but that of their clients. Other similar gray areas and loopholes exist in how to apply existing laws for counselors who use technology (Koocher & Morray, 2000). With this in mind, counselors are best served by learning to be diligent, thorough practitioners who value being informed about state licensing laws. With this information in hand, they will be able to make educated decisions about their own and clients' rights when engaging in cybercounseling. Barnett (2005) suggested that it may be best to practice within a familiar jurisdiction (i.e., state) and one in which a counselor is already licensed. However, others seem to view this as an unnecessary limitation of the potential reach and benefit of cybercounseling (Alleman, 2002). When counselors have questions about how rules and regulations of their license interface with technology-assisted practice, it is best to check with other practitioners or the state board (Mallen et al., 2005).

Therapeutic Alliance

The therapeutic alliance is arguably the most important part of a clinical relationship (Horvath & Luborsky, 1993). The therapeutic alliance is often characterized by the establishment of common goals and is fostered by the interactions between the counselor and client. There is very little baseline information on how these interactions may be different in online counseling. According to Horvath and Luborsky, a necessary feature in the development of therapeutic alliances is to establish trust between counselor and client. Establishing trust in professional relationships has to do, in part, with instilling trust through competence, trustworthiness, and accountability (Cohen & Cohen, 1999; Shaw & Shaw, 2006). Formal and accurate informed consent procedures can help to establish a cybercounselor's competency. Shaw and Shaw also recommended that counselors who practice online provide clients with a way to verify their credentials, respond to clients in a timely fashion, be available between online meetings, and arrange for continuous service if the counselor is temporarily unavailable.

Advocacy

Although technology-assisted counseling potentially makes this service available to many more underserved client groups, it is also true that some client populations who may benefit the most from online counseling may be the most difficult to engage through this medium (Kaplan, 2006). People who are limited by personal resources may not have the ability to connect to a counselor via a home computer. Thus, when counselors think broadly about the meaning of their professional identities, recognized by many to include an advocacy role, it becomes relevant for them to think about advocating on behalf of clients in need of greater access to technology.

There are many creative ways to help funding sources and organizations become educated about the benefits of making technology-related resources available to underserved individuals. As well, organizations, such as insurance companies, may give online practices greater access to reimbursement of services if these are not already covered (Barnett, 2005).

Social Networking

The popularity of social networking sites has exploded in recent years. These websites allow individuals to post personal information about themselves on a page for friends and colleagues to view. Many users go beyond the social aspect of these sites by making use of the networking opportunities for their businesses. The very nature of social networking sites is to make private information public. The tech savvy, trustworthy, and diligent clinician will think carefully about how to put proper safeguards in place around social networking media to ensure personal safety and boundaries online. Indeed, a core ethical concern with social networking media is that a great deal of personal information can be provided in very public and easily accessible locations. Counselor professionalism requires careful attention to personal and professional boundaries (Welfel, 2010). Social networking sites, when not used with care, can blur and trample these boundaries. In making ethical decisions around the way social networking sites are used for marketing and personal purposes, counselors need to be well informed about available safety measures built into many popular, well-used sites. Many, for example, have privacy settings that restrict the level of information made available to others. It would be worthwhile for counselors to weigh their understanding of professional boundaries with the potential good that might be gained by restricting access to personal information only to close, personal friends, and family that are listed by the site as "friends."

Landmark 8

CASE EXAMPLE

John is a new counselor working out of his own private practice. He has begun offering an online component to his practice which he advertises through a web page and a dedicated social networking page. John meets with a client weekly through webcam-based counseling. He believes that he has taken all necessary precautions with regard to informed consent, privacy, methods of payment online, and professional boundaries. One morning when checking his email, John notices an odd message. His regular online client has requested to be added to John's personal social networking page. John considers this proposition briefly but decides this would not be appropriate and so declines the request. At their next scheduled session, the client is a virtual no-show and does not respond to any of John's efforts at follow-up. Later, when John reviews his office social networking site he sees a distressing message posted. The wayward client has left unhappy feedback on the site indicating

(continued)

that John is not a good counselor. Though John deletes this post, the angry client continues to periodically post rude comments to other clients' testimonials on John's professional social networking page. John makes the decision to reevaluate and reorganize his online practice.

1. *How do you evaluate John's decision to delete the client's friend request? What might you have done differently?*
2. *Aside from social networking, what other current technology would you have to evaluate when constructing an online practice?*
3. *Given your review of John's case study, would you feel comfortable opening an online practice? What are the pros? What are the cons?*

"Tech"niques in Therapy

Technology-assisted counseling refers to methods of service delivery (i.e., phone and online counseling) but also can include the use of specific technology-based techniques in counseling practice. Integrating technology-based media into therapy requires critical evaluation, especially as the ACA *Code of Ethics* (2005) recommends that counselors be wary of using treatment interventions without positive, evidence-based effects. Consider the increasingly popular technology, video games, and its potential therapeutic value in counseling.

Video games have become a multibillion-dollar industry, having reached record high sales in 2000 with a reported $20 billion profit (Cohen, 2000). Despite the strong presence of video games in American culture, this form of media has been seen primarily negatively by mental health professionals due to research that points out a connection between video game use and enhanced, aggressive feelings and sometimes behaviors in the player (Anderson, 2004; Griffiths, 1999). Others discuss such concerns as addictive behaviors that might develop with extensive gaming (Griffiths & Davies, 2005; Griffiths & Hunt, 1998).

More recently, though, an emerging body of literature also indicates health benefits related to gaming. Some games, for instance, seem to help in pain management by diverting attention from pain or discomfort (Griffiths, 2005). Certain games seem to help young people develop social and spatial abilities (Griffiths, 2005). Other benefits could be garnered from game use. Some video games, for example, rely on specific kinds of voice interface to manipulate game characters; these might be used to teach different types of communication skills. Similar to film, which can provide clients with a means to experience emotion vicariously through characters or intriguing plots, games with realistic graphics or tasks might also elicit emotional reactions that can be therapeutically relevant or prompt clients to work on therapeutic goals as a result of playing the game.

With potential benefits and harms associated with video game use, counselors ought to carefully sift through the literature about gaming when coming to a determination about the ethics of games as a therapeutic technique. Because there is still only minimal research surrounding the effectiveness of video games as a mental health tool, it is difficult to discern its potential benefits or harm as a therapeutic technique. We offer the following points of consideration for counselors who consider building an intervention around video games into treatment:

- Concerns about aggression and violence found frequently in this form of media ought not be overlooked, and counselors should carefully evaluate how a client may react to the dramatic imagery and challenging scenarios presented in modern video games.
- As with the use of films, counselors who use video games should consider the relevance of the game to a client's therapeutic goals, review the game before use, and debrief the gaming experience in light of therapeutic aims (Lampropoulos, Kazantzis, & Deane, 2004).
- Aspects of cultural sensitivity, sensitivity to trauma, and violence should be considered thoroughly. A therapist can review the video game's rating online or on the back of the game packaging before considering its use.

SIGNPOSTS FOR FUTURE TREKS

It is our hope that this chapter provided practical support for those beginning their journey into the counseling profession. We believe that good counselors practice competently with regard to all aspects of clinical work, including record keeping and technology. As you reflect on what it means to be a competent clinician, we invite you to keep in mind the themes of this chapter, such as balancing legal concerns in record keeping with virtues considerations, using record-keeping practices to ensure continuity of care, and, finally, turning writing into a self-development opportunity. We have also suggested that technology-assisted counseling be grounded in diligent and careful practice that aims to support the best interests of clients. Counselors need to be ever vigilant of the responsibilities of beneficence and nonmalficence in this still-emerging area of counseling. Being reasonably versed in currently existing technology is helpful in understanding the meaning it plays in our clients' lives. We hope this chapter provided a background against which you can evaluate decisions when dilemmas related to record keeping and technology-based counseling arise. Remember, supervision and consultation help to ensure that appropriate steps in ethical decision making are taken. Most importantly, maintain an optimistic outlook toward the counseling field and all of the challenges, frustrations, and joy that accompany it. You chose this field for a reason. Believe in yourself and know that you can overcome any obstacle that presents a barrier.

INSIGHTS GAINED FROM THE JOURNEY

PERSONAL TESTIMONY 1

As a professional school counselor, I (G. G.) have always been mindful of maintaining adequate personal notes reflective of meetings with students. However, one area of record keeping that has posed a challenge for me involves determining what information to include in students' educational records (i.e., Special Education Evaluation Reports) based on my personal notes.

A number of years ago, several students were referred for special education evaluations. When students are referred for an evaluation to determine if special education is warranted, our instructional support teacher elicits input from a variety of staff, including me. In order to gain a holistic view of the student, she asks us to provide a snapshot narrative on how the student is currently performing, making sure to include any academic or social concerns or strengths. This input is then included in the Evaluation Report, which is generated by the school psychologist. The Evaluation Report is a detailed report highlighting the student's background information, educational history, concerns, observations, as well as results of assessments administered by the school psychologist. The Evaluation Report is made part of the child's educational record, and a copy of the Evaluation Report is also sent home to the child's family. My dilemma has always been: what information should I include in these reports? How do I accurately convey information pertinent to the child's success as a student without providing too much information or too little information? What is the most effective way to present my personal notes?

I resolved this dilemma by seeking supervision and consultation. Not only did I consult with our school psychologist, but I also consulted with other school counselors within the school counseling department. During peer supervision, we referenced the ASCA *Ethical Standards for School Counselors*. In addition, I brought this to the attention of my clinical supervisor. Given the implications of FERPA, my personal notes are sole possession records and not education records because they are private notes used as a memory aid that only include observations and professional opinions. However, once I include information from the "sole possession records" in the Evaluation Report, they will become educational records, thus providing a parent with full access to retrieve. During individual supervision with my clinical supervisor, we reviewed the content of my personal case notes and determined which information would be the most critical to include. I "practiced" writing short paragraphs that communicated the essential information, and my clinical supervisor shared her feedback and suggestions on ways to make it even more succinct, objective, and professional.

Not only did I gain confidence in submitting information for Evaluation Reports, but from this experience I also learned vital lessons about ethical development of a professional school counselor. I learned to ask myself the questions: What are my ethical obligations to the student? What are my ethical obligations to the school? Thus far as a school counselor, I have intersected many ethical dilemmas. As I continue to serve in the role as a school counselor, I know various ethical dilemmas will continue to emerge. Being cognizant of that, I need to approach each ethical dilemma in a positive manner. Referencing the ASCA *Ethical Standards for School Counselors* and seeking supervision are two positive ways I handled dilemmas related to record keeping.

PERSONAL TESTIMONY 2

I (S. K.) have been interested in electronics since I was very young. My uncles introduced me to video games as a child, and since then I have been an avid "gamer." When I relate to my clients, I try to make use of my knowledge of technology, as well as interactive media, to help build rapport and use meaningful interventions. Something I had not considered when I first began counseling was how I would have to safeguard my own boundaries in these minimally discussed areas.

One ethical dilemma that has emerged for me related to technology and counseling revolves around the termination process with younger clients who are aware of my gaming hobby, either because of how it plays a role in counseling sessions or because they hear me give a lecture on technology at educational events. Often, I get the request to begin an online relationship after my clinical relationship has closed. I have made it a point to ensure that the professional–personal boundary is not broken, as incidental as it sounds. If I would not meet a former or current client for dinner socially, I would not meet that same client for a few rounds on my Microsoft Xbox, either. Clients tend to understand that counselors are not willing or able to be both the professional helper and their personal friend. However, when there is a lack of discussion around technology and counseling, I have found that they may not be clear about boundaries related to being my friend on Facebook or XBox Live. Having conversations about this topic has actually become something that I incorporate into opening and closing discussions with many clients, in order to avoid uncertainty about what I have learned can be a grey area for them. Furthermore, as a precaution, I ensure that my personal information is hidden on all of my online social networking accounts. While this may seem as if it could have a negative impact on my social life, it, in fact, sets a very clear boundary that makes my professional tasks as counselor much easier. I ensure that my work stays separate from my personal life and in so doing I enhance both.

MOVING FORWARD: CASE STUDY AND REFLECTION QUESTIONS

Danicka is a 9-year-old 4th grade student at Whiteville Elementary School. She was initially referred to you, the elementary school counselor, due to changes occurring within her family. Her mother, Jamie, contacted you to explain that she and Danicka's father were filing for divorce, and she requested that you "check in" with Danicka to make sure she is handling the adjustment well. As a thorough, ethical practitioner, you document every parent contact, teacher consult, and student meeting as part of your personal case notes. You keep these personal case notes in a separate filing cabinet in your office. For this particular phone call, you take note of the following: *Danicka's mom contacted me on 10/27/09 at 9:30 am to report changes in family dynamics (divorce). Wants me to check in with Danicka. Explained to mom how my role as a school counselor works in the school setting; discussed referral opportunities if warranted. Reminded her of confidentiality issues, as referenced in the ASCA* Ethical Standards. After consulting with Danicka's homeroom teacher, you document the following: *On 10/28/09, teacher reports that Danicka is performing well with her academics. She has all A's and one B. Teacher's concerns are that Danicka seems distracted at times by other students. Often, she has difficulty with female peer interactions.* You arrange with the teacher a convenient time to begin meeting with Danicka. Since you have been doing 4th grade classroom guidance lessons, you already have established rapport with Danicka. During your initial meeting with Danicka, you are attempting to build a more trusting relationship. In doing so, Danicka opens up about some of the changes she is experiencing, but in your professional opinion, she really seems to be handling things well. You document in your personal case notes: *Met with D. on 11/2/09 at 2:30 pm due to parent request. D. reports feeling sad at times with her dad not living at home anymore, but glad that she still gets to see him. States she likes talking to her one friend about it because her friend's parents are divorced, too. D. was comfortable and appeared generally at ease with talking about the changes. Arrange to meet with her some time the following week. She was glad about that.*

Two days after your initial meeting with Danicka, her father, Noah, who still has legal custody and rights as a father, contacted the school secretary and requested copies of her educational records. Noah told Mrs. Gearson, the secretary, "I will be in tomorrow to pick up Danicka's records, including anything from that counselor that she has been talking to." Mrs. Gearson relayed the message to you. She then asked you to prepare copies of Danicka's records so they would be ready when Noah arrived.

REFLECTION QUESTIONS

- *Describe the main ethical issue(s) of the case.*
- *What would you include as part of Danicka's educational records? How did you go about your decision of what to include and what not to include?*
- *How would you handle Noah's request of ". . . including anything from that counselor that she has been talking to"? What would you include, if anything?*
- *Describe how you could take a positive approach to this situation.*

REFERENCES

Alleman, J. R. (2002). Online counseling: The Internet and mental health treatment. *Psychotherapy: Theory, Research, Practice, & Training, 39*, 199–209.

Amato, L., Blase, C., & Paley, S. (2000). Ethics. *American Journal of Art Therapy, 39*, 12–15.

American Counseling Association. (2005). *ACA code of ethics*. Alexandria, VA: Author.

American Counseling Association. (1999). *Professional counselor's guide to federal law on student records*. Alexandria, VA: Author.

American School Counselor Association. (2008). Position statement: Confidentiality (Rev.). Retrieved April 19, 2010, from http://asca2.timberlakepublishing.com//files/PS_Confidentiality.pdf

Anderson, C. A. (2004). An update on the effects of playing violent video games. *Journal of Adolescence, 27*, 113–122.

Annas, G. J. (2003). HIPAA regulations—A new era of medical-record privacy? *The New England Journal of Medicine, 348*(15), 1486–1490.

Barnett, J. E. (2005). Online counseling: New entity, new challenges. *The Counseling Psychologist, 33*(6), 872–880.

Cameron, S., & Turtle-Song, I. (2002). Learning to write case notes using the SOAP format. *Journal of Counseling & Development, 80*, 286–292.

Childress, C. (1998). Potential risks and benefits of online psychotherapeutic interventions. Retrieved from http://www.ismho.org/potential_risks_and_benefits.asp

Cohen, A. (2000). New game [Playstation 2]. *Time, 156*, 58–60.

Cohen, E. D., & Cohen, G. S. (1999). *The virtuous therapist: Ethical practice of counseling and psychotherapy* (2nd ed.). Belmont, CA: Wadsworth Publishing Company.

Drogin, E. Y., Connell, M., Foote, W. E., & Sturm, C. A. (2010). The American Psychological Association's revised record-keeping guidelines: Implications for the practitioner. *Professional Psychology, Research and Practice, 41*(3), 236–243.

Fink, J. (1999). *How to use computers and cyberspace in the clinical practice of psychotherapy*. Northvale, NJ: Aronson.

Griffiths, M. (1999). Violent video games and aggression: A review of the literature. *Aggression and Violent Behavior, 4*(2), 203–212.

Griffiths, M. (2005). Video games and health: Video gaming is safe for most players and can be useful in health care. *BMJ, 331*, 122–123. doi: 10.1136 Retrieved from http://www.bmj.com/content/331/7509/122.full.pdf

Griffiths, M. D., & Davies, M. N. (2005). Videogame addiction: Does it exist?J. Goldstein, & Raessens (Eds.). *Handbook of computer game studies* (pp. 359–368). Boston: MIT Press.

Griffiths, M. D., & Hunt, N. (1998). Dependence on computer game playing by adolescents. *Psychological Reports, 82*(2), 475–480.

Grohol, J. M. (2003). *The insider's guide to mental health resources online*. New York: Guilford Press.

Horvath, A. O., & Luborsky, L. (1993). The role of the therapeutic alliance in psychotherapy. *Journal of Consulting and Clinical Psychology, 61*(4), 561–573.

Kaplan, D. (2006). Ethical use of technology in counseling. *Counseling Today, December*. Retrieved from: http://ct.counseling.org/2006/12/ct-online-ethics-update-4/.

Koocher, G. P., & Morray, E. (2000). Regulation of telepsychology: A survey of state attorneys general. *Professional Psychology: Research and Practice, 31*, 503–508.

Kraus, R. (2004). Ethical and legal considerations for providers of mental health services online. In R. Kraus, J. Zack, & G. Stricker (Eds.), *Online counseling: A handbook for mental health professionals* (pp. 145–160). San Diego, CA: Academic Press.

Lake, P. (2009). Student-privacy rules show a renewed trust in colleges. *Chronicle of Higher Education, 55*(22), A72. Retrieved from http://web.ebscohost.com

Lampropoulos, G. K., Kazantzis, N., & Deane, F. P. (2004). Psychologists' use of motion pictures in clinical practice. *Professional Psychology: Research and Practice, 35*(5), 535–541.

Luepker, E. T. (2003). *Record keeping in psychotherapy & counseling: Protecting confidentiality & the professional relationship*. New York, NY: Brunner-Routledge.

Maheu, M. M., & Gordon, B. L. (2000). Counseling and therapy on the internet. *Professional Psycholoogy: Research and Practice, 31*, 484–489.

Mallen, M. J., Vogel, D. L., & Rochlen, A. B. (2005). The practical aspects of online counseling: Ethics, training, technology, and competency. *The Counseling Psychologist, 33*, 776–818.

McDonald, S. (2008). The Family Rights and Privacy Act: 7 myths—and the truth. *Chronicle of Higher Education, 54*(32), A53–A54. Retrieved from http://web.ebscohost.com

Merlone, L. (2005). Record keeping and the school counselor. *Professional School Counseling, 8*, 372–376.

Mitchell, R. W. (1991). *Documentation in counseling records*. Alexandria, VA: American Association for Counseling and Development.

Mosher, P. W., & Swire, P. P. (2002). The ethical and legal implications of *Jaffee v. Redmond* and the HIPAA medical privacy rule for psychotherapy and general psychiatry. *Psychiatric Clinics of North America, 25*, 575–584.

Murphy, L. J., & Mitchell, D. L. (1998). When writing helps to heal: E-mail as therapy. *British Journal of Guidance and Counseling, 26*, 25–32.

Piazza, N. J., & Baruth, N. E. (1990). Client record guidelines. *Journal of Counseling & Development, 68*, 313–316.

Prieto, L. R., & Scheel, K. R. (2002). Using case documentation to strengthen counselor trainees' case conceptualization skills. *Journal of Counseling & Development, 80*, 11–21.

Remley, T. P., & Herlihy, B. (2005). *Ethical, legal, and professional issues in counseling.* Upper Saddle River, NJ: Pearson Education, Inc.

Rochlen, A. B., Zack, J. S., & Speyer, C. (2004). Online therapy: Review of relevant definitions, debates, and current empirical support. *Journal of Clinical Psychology, 60*(3), 269–283.

Schrier, C. J. (1980). Guidelines for record keeping under privacy and open-access law. *Social Work, 25*(6), 452–457.

Sealander, K. A., Schwiebert, V. L., Oren, T. A., & Weekley, J. L. (1999). Confidentiality and the law. *Professional School Counseling, 3*, 122–127.

Shaw, H. E., & Shaw, S. F. (2006). Critical issues in online counseling: Assessing current practices with an ethical intent checklist. *Journal of Counseling & Development, 84*, 41–53.

Skovholt, T. M., & Ronnestad, M. H. (1992). Themes in therapist and counselor development. *Journal of Counseling & Development, 70*, 505–515.

Soisson, E. L., VandeCreek, L., & Knapp, S. (1987). Thorough record keeping: A good defense in a litigious era. *Professional Psychology, 18*(5), 498–502.

Swartz, S. (2006). The third voice: Writing case notes. *Feminism Psychology, 16*(4), 427–444.

The Jed Foundation. (2008). *Student mental health and the law: A resource for institutions of higher education.* New York, NY: Author.

U. S. Department of Education. (2008). *Dear colleague letter about the Family Educational Rights and Privacy Act (FERPA) final regulations.* Retrieved from http://www2.ed.gov/policy/gen/guid/fpco/hottopics/ht12-17-08.html

U. S. Department of Education. (2011a). *Family Educational Rights and Privacy Act (FERPA).* Retrieved from http://www2.ed.gov/policy/gen/guid/fpco/ferpa/index.html

U. S. Department of Education. (2011b). *FERPA general guidance for parents.* Retrieved from http://www2.ed/gov/policy/gen/guid/fpco/ferpa/parents.html

VandenBos, G. R., & Williams, S. (2000). The Internet versus the telephone: What is telehealth, anyway? *Professional Psychology: Research and Practice, 31*, 490–492.

Welfel, E. R. (2010). *Ethics in counseling and psychotherapy* (4th ed.). Pacific Grove, CA: Brooks/Cole.

8

Ethical Features Related to Developing and Sustaining Professional Excellence

Christin M. Jungers and Jocelyn Gregoire

THE FORESEEN DESTINATION

It is our hope that after reviewing this chapter, readers will be prompted to think deeply about how their own character development is a central part of becoming an ethical helper. In particular, we invite readers to aspire to:

- Value habits and practices that lead to the formation of character excellences, such as courage, moderation, sense of self-worth, and open-handedness.
- See self-development as an integral part of lifelong professional development.
- Embrace opportunities for continuing education, supervision, and consultation.
- Use countertransference productively in the therapeutic relationship and seek counseling when unresolved personal issues cloud the prospects for client progress.
- Identify personal strategies for self-care and take measures to build environments that contribute to professional sustenance.

GETTING ON THE ROAD

In this chapter, we look at what it takes to become an excellent professional counselor and to thrive long term in the work that counselors do. As noted elsewhere in this text, ethics in counseling is as much about the personal development of the helper as it is about the helper's ability to reason through ethical quandaries. Thus, we want you to consider first and foremost the duty helpers have to their own personal and professional formation. Such formation is not random or without a backdrop—we will use a few of Aristotle's ideas about individual excellence to prompt our thinking. We also provide discussion about the kinds of experiences that contribute over time to making counselors as masterful as possible, including personal counseling, lifelong learning opportunities, and supervision. We look at how the person of the counselor intersects with a number of important clinical topics, such as transference, countertransference, and termination. Finally, we examine some of the ethical implications related to counselor wellness, self-care, burnout, and impairment, as they are tied intricately to a counselor's personhood. Taking a long view on the process of being and becoming a counselor, we accentuate the developmental aspects of these topics.

EXPLORING THE TERRITORY

EXCELLENCE IN SELF-DEVELOPMENT

What does it look like to develop and then sustain excellence as a therapist? If you had to characterize the essence of such an experience, how would you describe it? To be and to become a helper who others would describe as ethical and as embodying excellence is a lifelong work forged by the reciprocal interaction among one's personal life choices, professional experiences and decisions, and reflection on both. In the early phases of counselor development, when much energy is spent on managing the anxiety that accompanies learning new skills and professional roles, the personal elements that comprise excellence are often underestimated and sometimes even dismissed. It is not unusual for counselor trainees or new professionals to focus primarily on how to use certain techniques or correctly facilitate practical tasks that they see as essential to the professional counselor identity, such as leading groups, knowing what questions to ask clients, learning how to fill out an intake form, and so on. Indeed, this type of focus is developmentally appropriate and necessary for those who are putting on the counselor role for the first time and deciding exactly how they will make the identity their own (Skovholt & Ronnestad, 1992, 2001). The place of personal or character qualities, thus, can get deemphasized early on in counselor development because forming other professional skills takes precedence. In addition, character qualities can be overlooked because the uniqueness of counselor training and development as a personal journey is under-recognized. Becoming a counselor is not the same as entering a profession in which one can thrive just on cognitive abilities, or on competitiveness, or even on technical finesse. Rather, counseling is a profession in which the helper's whole self is immersed in the work one does. The work is grounded in a human encounter (van Kaam, 1966) with another person, and this provides a good rationale for why who a counselor is matters as much as what one does.

The issue of personhood was described long ago by Aristotle (trans. 2002), who suggested that living a good life involves developing character excellences. Stewart (2010, p. 190) summarized this concept as sets of personal qualities that "convey a sense of well-ordered balance and discernment." The excellences in character include such things as courageousness, moderation, a genuine sense of one's own dignity, a willingness to contribute to the betterment of the community that is balanced by a desire to receive from others, and mild mannered-ness (Stewart, 2010).

These are hard-won traits for many of us in the counseling field who come to the profession with our own shortcomings, blind spots, or scarred sense of self. If we want to talk about ethics in counseling, however, we must not overlook the self-development aspect of the work. Consider for a moment how a few of the excellences described previously benefit counselors and their clinical work in practical ways or, conversely, how a counselor might be hindered in one's work without having cultivated excellences in character.

Courage

In what ways do you believe it takes courage to assist clients in clinical encounters? While it is true that in their professional work counselors are not expected to overcome feats of endurance or battle physical threats to their or their clients' lives (metaphors often equated to courage), they do, however, frequently find themselves mustering the nerve to confront others' defensive responses to traumatic or trying life experiences (e.g., denial about an addictive behavior). To do good for clients, counselors are also expected to broach sensitive topics that they themselves would prefer to avoid because it might lead to a strong negative reaction from the client or because they are afraid it might make them uncomfortable. Sometimes, the safest route in a clinical conversation is to let the sleeping giant lie; yet, this route may not be the most ethical when one goal toward which counselors aspire is to do good for others. A counselor, for example, might not know how to ask a young woman about the impact on her current life experiences of her having been raped. If the young woman herself seems hesitant to talk about the topic, the counselor might lead the conversation to a less scary topic, never to reinitiate this painful issue again. To broach socially taboo subjects such as rape, death, addiction, sexual or gender identity confusion, racial identity, racial and ethnic differences between counselors and clients, poverty, discrimination, social privilege, and the like is not always easy and does indeed require personal courage on the counselor's part.

Sense of Self-Worth

Next, ponder how the character excellence of having a genuine sense of one's own dignity and worth might be relevant to good counseling. Stewart (2010) described this trait as neither an overinflating nor an undervaluing of one's own worth. Worth is not equated, moreover, with material objects, money, fame, or reputation. Professional training, and the clinical encounters that follow in the years after training is complete, helps counselors to feel settled and at home in the technical duties of their work. Yet, it is equally as important that helpers feel at home in their own selves, with a healthy appreciation for their personal goodness. Insecurity (or an exaggerated negative perception about an aspect of oneself) can lead to all kinds of unhelpful diversions in relationship dynamics that do not benefit therapeutic work. Those familiar with client-centered therapy will recognize Rogers (1961) ideas coming alive here, as he described the good counselor as living a congruent life in which the counselor sees both himself and the client with eyes of unconditional positive regard. Believing in our own self-worth, we are prompted to appreciate the dignity of our clients—persons with life struggles rather than sets of symptoms strung together and comprising one diagnosis or another.

Open-Handedness

Finally, imagine how the character excellence of open-handedness (Stewart, 2010), or the ability to help the community that is balanced with a willingness to be cared for by others, plays a role in ethical practice for counselors. What ethical missteps might unfold for counselors who tend to overindulge a passion for helping others? This question is one that has often been discussed in counseling literature and involves the issues of counselor self-care, burnout, and even impairment. We will look more carefully at these topics later in the chapter, but for now, think about how an imbalance in wanting *to help* and being willing *to be helped* could hinder the counseling process. For example, many new counselors have to confront the "savior" or the "parent" response in their work with clients, especially those whom they might see as needy, helpless, a victim, or just simply entrenched in a pattern of making poor choices that have negative consequences. This metaphorical savior or parent response can easily lead to advice-giving that is aimed at pulling clients from perilous situations or to judgmentalism. While crisis situations sometimes call for counselors to be directive with clients, the "I know what you should do" attitude does not typically build genuinely therapeutic relationships and would be seen by other counselors as unethical to the extent that it impinges on a client's autonomy. Seasoned counselors are not immune from having to evaluate their open-handedness, either. They may find themselves lulled into the belief that they do not need to receive from others (in the form of peer supervision or consultation with certain sets of clients) or even hold to the idea that because they have years of experience they should know what to do in any clinical situation. On the other hand, ethical missteps might also occur for counselors who are overly willing to be cared for by others. In these cases, counselors may end up using their clients to fulfill their own emotional or psychological needs.

In talking about excellence, Aristotle (trans. 2002) recognized that technical skills, in themselves, are good, but he did not place this type of excellence above character qualities (Stewart, 2010). To know how to use certain counseling skills, conceptualize cases, assess psychological traits, and engage in all of the other usual counselor tasks add to a helper's competence, and they are goods in themselves toward which counselors should strive. Yet, grounded in Aristotle's proposition that happiness, satisfaction, and goodness is first and foremost about character excellences, we want to emphasize the very personal components involved in becoming an ethical clinician. Counselors are their own best tools in the therapeutic encounter. Therefore, there rests a responsibility upon helpers to work diligently at developing the qualities such as courage, moderation, dignity of self, open-handedness, and so forth as these are the excellences which move helpers from being technically proficient at their jobs to being masters of the trade. We call this responsibility a commitment to excellence and a commitment to self-development. It often entails counselors working through their own life difficulties, challenging and expanding limited perceptions or knowledge bases, managing defense responses to stressful relationships and situations, valuing their own wellness, or becoming aware of anything else that might act as an unnecessary or even harmful distraction to a client's work.

Landmark 1

CASE EXAMPLE

Nicholas, a former police officer, made a career change to mental health counseling about 3 years ago. Although he had worked in law enforcement for 10 years, Nicholas was never truly at ease or happy in the job, which he believed required him to act threateningly toward citizens. The job role, as Nicholas saw it, did not fit his true personality or his desire to focus on rehabilitation, not punishment. For the past year, Nicholas has been working for a community agency as a counselor and seems to be connecting well with clients. His biggest struggle, however, relates to a persistent inability to keep to his schedule—he nearly always goes over time with clients. Nicholas's clinical supervisor meets with him to discuss client issues and raises her observation that Nicholas takes more time than is allotted for each client. Surprised, Nicholas passionately explains to his supervisor that each client is of utmost importance and that he believes it is his duty to take whatever amount of time is needed to deal with their problems. Counseling is his vocation, he tells her, further, and he needs to witness to that vocation with time and attention to every client.

1. *Considering the character excellences described by Aristotle, what potential ethical concerns might you have for Nicholas?*
2. *If you were Nicholas's supervisor, what might you want to make him aware of?*

SHARPENING THE INSTRUMENT

One's personhood is the best instrument that a counselor has at one's disposal in being able to help others in a therapeutic encounter. The responsibility a counselor has to self-development is therefore a responsibility to the whole community of persons whom one will meet as clients (Tennyson & Strom, 1986). A lot of effort must therefore be put into sharpening the therapeutic instrument that is put to work in each counseling encounter.

Many authors have described how helpers can go about making themselves into the kind of persons who are able to do good for clients. Sue and Sue (2008) and others who specialize in researching cultural competence in the mental health field (e.g., Baruth & Manning, 2012; Pedersen, Draguns, Lonner, & Trimble, 2002) have argued that a capable and ethical counselor is one who develops personal awareness, has a broad knowledge base about clients' cultural backgrounds and worldviews, and possesses a set of skills that enables them to work flexibly within the value and belief systems of diverse sets of clients. Others have pointed out that good counselors often make use of counseling themselves (Norcross & Guy, 2005). There is also widespread agreement from counselor educators, as well as licensing and certification boards, that continuing education and supervision help to ensure that counselors regularly expand their knowledge bases. Finally, life itself presents a multitude of learning opportunities which can shape us into more understanding and empathetic helpers (Skovholt & Ronnestad, 2001).

Sometimes Counselors Need Counseling

Henri Nouwen (1972) used the term "wounded healer" to describe ministers who carry their own pain and at the same time serve their communities. Of the healer, Nouwen said, "Whether he tries to enter into a dislocated world, relate to a convulsive generation, or speak to a dying man, his service will not be perceived as authentic unless it comes from a heart wounded by the suffering about which he speaks" (1972, p. xvi). The concept of the wounded healer has been widely applied to all kinds of helping professions, and especially to the mental health field. In Nouwen's estimation, the scars that come with life's suffering enhance a helper's ability to appreciate and relate authentically to others' brokenness. Counselor educators and practitioners alike recognize that there is no one who comes to the counseling profession without having been wounded in some way. Indeed, many clinicians are united in the fact that they have worked to deal with their own pain and suffering or to rise above their own shortcomings. Some estimates suggest that 75% of all mental health professionals have engaged in their own personal counseling at some point in their lives (Norcross & Guy, 2005).

Most of the time, a counselor's own woundedness advantages him or her in the therapeutic relationship because, as Nouwen pointed out, it helps others to perceive the counselor as relatable, human, and somehow equal in the therapeutic relationship—let alone in the process of living a good life. At the same time, however, wisdom among professional counselors holds that counselors' pain, suffering, and blind spots are not better off unexamined. The American Counseling Association [ACA] *Code of Ethics* describes ethical helpers as those who take their own wellness seriously and encourages all counselors to "engage in self-care activities to maintain and promote their emotional, mental, physical, and spiritual well-being to best meet their professional responsibilities" (2005, p. 9). Sometimes, then, counselors do need counseling.

Aristotle's (trans. 2002) ideas about goodness being characterized by balance make sense here. Helpers need to strike the balance between seeing their suffering as therapeutically useful and recognizing when it renders them unable or less able to deal with certain sets of issues or segments of the population. This is not always easy, especially for helpers who may believe that they always need to be emotionally strong or for helpers who miss seeing the connection between how their own unexamined areas influence the therapeutic process. Others might be concerned about how seeking counseling could negatively impact their professional development or productivity. Counselors-in-training, for example, might fear that they will be perceived by faculty as not capable of becoming a professional counselor or that their progress in the program or an internship might be stalled. While such concerns are legitimate, even counselors-in-training are not exempt from the profession's best practice recommendations that personal wellness matters and that character development is of utmost importance to ethical behavior (see ACA *Code of Ethics*, 2005, Standard F.8.b). We noted already that courageousness is a character excellence that helps counselors to bring others face-to-face with their own denial and life hurts. Likewise, courage aids clinicians in looking honestly at themselves and determining when they might benefit from therapy—whether or not there are some unpleasant side effects, such as extending or delaying a practicum or internship. Most professionals agree that the returns that accompany personal therapy for counselors far outweigh the downsides. In summarizing the research about outcomes for therapists engaging in their own counseling, Orlinsky, Norcross, Ronnestad, and Wiseman (2005) found that these therapists were aware of and better able to manage their own issues in the counseling relationship, advanced in their interpersonal skills, able to use a variety of responses and techniques to address clients' needs, and better able to handle normal stresses that accompany clinical work.

Finally, we believe it is important for counselors to think about personal therapy not only as a preventive tool to ensure that they do no harm to clients, but also as an opportunity to embrace their own lifelong, personal growth process. Sometimes, especially in graduate counseling programs, counseling can be experienced as a sanction for underdevelopment of professional behavior. While, indeed, recommendations for personal counseling can be part of a remediation plan (for licensed professionals as well as students), such recommendations must not misconstrue the inherent positive purpose of the therapeutic process. One of the great benefits of personal counseling is that it gives clients (and counselors) the chance to step back and reflect on their own life and to be challenged out of any areas of complacency. In this sense, counseling truly aims at character development and not simply symptom management. People who are relatively well thus can reap as many rewards from counseling as those who are trying to deal with unresolved hurts or an ongoing mental illness.

Landmark 2

CASE EXAMPLE

Marco recently finished graduate studies in counseling and was hired as a mobile therapist. His job duties include developing treatment plans for children and their families who have been referred for social services, sometimes through the court system. In a large percentage of his cases, the children have been exposed to abuse and neglect; some of them are living with foster parents. Marco, himself, was part of the foster system as a young boy and never really had the chance to know his parents, both of whom were drug addicted and incarcerated before he was five. After several months of working with the children and families, Marco has begun to have a flood of different emotions about his work. He often feels hopeless about the possibility of truly helping his young clients and is bitter toward the parents. At the same time, he is filled with compassion toward the youngsters and wishes he could take them home with him. More and more, he thinks about his own time in the foster system and his disappointment that his parents

(*continued*)

were not around for him. Marco has never sought counseling to explore his own growing up experience.

1. *What elements of Marco's case stand out to you?*
2. *What concerns might you have for Marco in his work and in his personal life?*
3. *If you were supervising Marco, what might you recommend to him?*

Learning Never Ends

Sharpening the therapeutic tool that is the person of the counselor involves a lifetime of learning. Graduate training in counseling is often the beginning of formalized learning, though trainees usually come to graduate studies with some personal qualities and skills already in place—the natural helping responses they have used with family and friends who turn to them for guidance (Skovholt & Ronnestad, 1992). Learning comes in various forms—some opportunities are formal, others are informal, and some come simply as life experience.

Graduate Education and Beyond

The route to becoming a professional counselor is itself a very formal process that is designed to help trainees meet certain standards. Counselor training programs help students become knowledgeable in identified content areas and have clinical experiences (i.e., practicum and internship experiences) that foster skill development and professional growth. There is often a relationship between how a program structures its course of study and the requirements made of it by an accrediting body (such as the Council for the Accreditation of Counseling and Related Educational Programs [CACREP]) or a state licensure board. A practical goal of most students who begin counselor training is professional licensure. Licensure is granted by the state and is seen as public recognition that a counselor has been sanctioned to practice one's trade. Among other things, a requirement for counselor licensure in all states is a graduate degree from a counseling program. As noted elsewhere in this text, it takes more than goodwill and a desire to help people to become a qualified and artful practitioner. The course of study in a graduate counseling program usually is aimed at fostering personal and professional competence and, hopefully, instilling in students the habits of good and ethical professional practices.

A graduate degree in counseling enables new professionals to be something akin to general practitioners more than specialists in any one area. Specialization and a deeper understanding of clinical issues come with experience, as well as ongoing education. Ethical principles encourage counselors to do good for clients, and they are a springboard for engaging in one's own personal research about clinical issues that one knows little about. Continuing education happens, therefore, every time a counselor opts to learn about a clinical issue or relationship dynamic that will broaden her knowledge base and help her to be a more prepared therapist.

In a more formal sense, professional counselors who are certified (e.g., through the National Board of Certified Counselors [NBCC]) or licensed are required to acquire a designated number of post-degree continuing education units each time their certification or license comes up for renewal. Meeting certification and licensure boards' requirements for continuing education is a duty to which counselors are bound if they are interested in maintaining their credentials. The aspirational message behind this duty, however, has more to do with reminding clinicians that professional growth is a good which they are invited to embrace out of a concern for client welfare. Skovholt and Ronnestad (2001) pointed out, interestingly, that experience alone does not propel counselors to greater levels of skill or more highly ethical and professional behavior. Rather, professional development happens with a mix of ingredients, including experience and continuing education. Without fresh insight that can be gained from fellow professionals at workshops or conferences or from reading quality literature, we counselors rely only on our personal experience (which sometimes can be biased) or prior knowledge base to work with clients who may present us with challenging or new issues. At times this is insufficient to meet clients' needs. Moreover, without engaging in lifelong continuing education either from formal trainings or informal experiences, counselors can very easily get stalled in their development process. Again, as Skovholt and Ronnestad noted in their work on counselor resilience and development, one could easily live every year of clinical work as if it were his first if he does not become a practiced, reflective learner.

Supervision and Consultation

The self-development that we propose to be at the heart of becoming an ethical counselor can be enhanced through the process of regular supervision and consultation with peers. Bernard and Goodyear (2002) described two primary purposes of supervision: to protect and monitor client safety and to add to a counselor's professional functioning. Professional functioning refers to the practical or technical skills that counselors are expected to gain with work and experience and which are necessary for licensure and certification. One might think of this as the science of good counseling (O'Sullivan & Quevillon, 1992). Professional functioning also refers, however, to a long-term goal of developing clinical wisdom and expertise. Bernard and Goodyear suggested that this aspect of professional development is an aspirational goal for counselors and one that is less tangible than becoming technically proficient. Acquiring expertise and clinical wisdom is, it seems, bound up with forming character excellences. Neither can be easily or tangibly charted, measured, or operationalized (Sternberg, 1990) and seem to be related to personal qualities, habits, and insights. One might think of this as the art of good counseling.

Supervision is at its most powerful when trainees or professionals are actively engaged in clinical work. It helps to shed light on the intersection between theory and real-life clinical issues and clients. Supervision also helps to provide supervisees (i.e., counselors) with immediate feedback about any clinical misjudgments, which increases not only their ability to recognize future similar errors in judgment but also their capacity to respond differently. Dawes (1994) suggested that supervision is crucial for clinical and professional learning because it does not necessarily come on its own through experience. Counselors might mistakenly believe, for instance, that they are correctly conceptualizing a client's problem and yet overlook crucial aspects of the client's story or behaviors; or, they might interpret an element of the relationship dynamic through a self-enhancing bias that prevents them from seeing how they unknowingly stereotyped a client. Numerous such scenarios exist, but they all remind us that counselors bring their own blind spots to the work that they do and have a learning curve to overcome in forming clinical skills.

To help counselors see themselves more clearly and move along the usual path of development, supervisors must embrace their role of providing fellow counselors with "intentional, clear feedback" (Bernard & Goodyear, 2002, p. 3). Casile, Gruber, and Rosenblatt (2007) described the supervisor's role as that of a critical friend—one who allies himself with the supervisee but who also is not unwilling to offer constructive criticism. We might think of supervisors as professional truth-tellers who themselves draw on courage to be upfront with supervisees about their strengths and areas of needed growth. For their own part, counselors, like their clients in the counseling relationship, can make the most use of supervision when they are open to receiving feedback aimed at their professional growth.

Life Opportunities

One of the often untold truths about counselor self and ethical development is that life experiences factor significantly into the process. Early in the professional development process, trainees and new counselors exert plenty of effort to make themselves into competent practitioners. Indeed, it is expected of them. Yet, only so much learning can take place within the walls of a classroom. Describing themes in counselor formation, Skovholt and Ronnestad (2001) affirmed the role that typical and atypical life experiences play in moving a helper toward expertise. They stated, "Bountiful lessons come from the practitioner's normative life events, such as the personal march through aging . . . . Equally instructive is the unusual reality, such as acute loss (e.g., job loss) or glorious success (e.g., an award for competence)" (2001, p. 32). For clinicians, part of the usual life experience also includes lessons learned from clients who teach counselors through their own lived experiences to see the intricate details related to particular struggles and about how to allow others to proceed at their own pace of growth without being critical of it or frustrated by it.

Life experience also has the effect of challenging people to more sophisticated levels of thinking. Perry (1970/1999) studied adult cognitive development and described advanced intellectual and ethical functioning as relativistic. In Perry's estimation, relativistic thinking is marked by a person's appreciation for a diversity of perspectives as well as personal ownership about what one sees as moral and good or immoral and bad. According to Perry, these types of thinkers develop a habit of exploring and researching issues of importance to them and then reasoning to their own conclusions about the question at hand. Relativistic thinkers are autonomous thinkers, and they are able to withstand a certain amount of ambiguity about complex life issues and tough choices. Perhaps more than anything else, life prompts us to this type of thinking. Like others, counselors are forced to grapple with the fact that life is full of gray areas and injustice. Friends, relatives, and clients often choose to live with pain, suffering, and oppression rather than risk the chance for a better lifestyle. There is an unequal distribution of wealth and goods in the world. Hard work sometimes does not seem to pay off. Life calls us to live somewhere in the "in-between" where absolute rights sometimes do not seem to exist, or they compete with one another. Being able to sustain ambiguity and to look at situations from various points of view is often a necessary character trait for counselors who work and empathize with clients who are faced with difficult decisions and circumstances.

ISSUES WITH THE THERAPEUTIC RELATIONSHIP

Efforts toward self-development aid counselors in tangible ways in their therapeutic encounters with clients. Personal issues can sometimes get entangled with client–therapist dynamics if counselors are not aware of their own reactions to clients (i.e., countertransference). Such issues can also affect the timing and process of termination, as well as decisions about taking on new clients or clients with challenging problems. In this section, we look at some of these common therapeutic issues and the importance of self-development to managing them in ethical ways.

Acknowledging and Using Transference and Countertransference

The idea that the personhood of the counselor matters to the way in which a clinical relationship unfolds and to its ethical quality is clearly evident as we consider the concepts of transference and countertransference. Both concepts come from Freud's understanding of human development and the interpersonal dynamics of therapy. Transference refers to the unresolved, sometimes repressed configuration of relationship dynamics that clients experience in the presence of the therapist, while countertransference refers to a counselor's unconscious or subconscious patterns of "reactivity and feelings towards the client" (Tobin & McCurdy, 2006, p. 154). Although these concepts are central to psychodynamic approaches to therapy, they are very much worth exploration for all counselors, who are expected to practice within the bounds of the profession's ethical standards. Indeed, the concept of countertransference, in particular, is now more broadly interpreted to include a variety of social, cultural, relational, and emotional responses that counselors can have toward clients, including, for example, biases or unexamined worldviews about particular clients or client traits (Hayes, Riker, & Ingram, 1997). The process of self-examination (which can be aided through supervision) helps counselors to identify when their approach or response to clients is motivated by something other than the pursuit of client growth. For instance, a counselor who is self-conscious about her weight might quietly avoid a client's desire to discuss her own struggle to manage a healthy relationship to food or, conversely, react sharply to the same client and tell her that she need not conform to societal demands on female body image. Much like ourselves when we are confronted with a moment of countertransference, the counselor in this example may be unaware of the sensitivity of the topic for herself and the somewhat extreme nature of her reactions. Yet, we can see how not facing our countertransference responses and feelings toward clients can erode the client–counselor relationship or indirectly stall clients' sincere desire for therapeutic progress in areas they deem important.

Self-development for counselors, as we have already iterated, must touch on the working through of our own personal blind spots and needed areas of growth. In one sense, countertransference is a barometer which measures the amount of healing and growth that counselors themselves still need, and countertransference responses can point clinicians in the direction on which to focus their work in personal counseling or supervision. In seeking to develop the character excellence of moderation, counselors can bring this habit to bear even on countertransference responses and feelings. Frequently, an unresolved internal or interpersonal conflict that emerges for a counselor in front of one's clients leads to an extreme reaction of some sort. In seeking moderation, counselors also are likely to place themselves on a path of resolving blind spots and countertransference responses.

Lastly, we invite you to think about the potential good that can come from a counselor's countertransference responses to clients. Most often, counselors are prompted to think about the negative side effects and the unethical missteps that are possible when a counselor's own issues are unexamined (Tobin & McCurdy, 2006). Yet, for a counselor who has such a response, especially in the more broad sense in which this concept is taken today, we might be able to envision some good also being produced. For example, a counselor who is working with a client who has a demanding and very strong and inflexible personality might feel put off by the client, in part because of the counselor's own history of poor relationships with people of a similar personality. However, there might also be an element of generalizability to the counselor's reaction to the client that might be worth sharing with the client, especially if it relates to his therapeutic goals. Thus, while it is always good practice to reflect on global reactions to clients, it is also good practice not to judge or dismiss the response immediately as bad or without use to the therapeutic dynamic.

Termination in the Counseling Relationship

Termination refers to the ending phase of the relationship between counselors and their clients. Endings are an existentially meaningful part of day-to-day life, and the same can be said for the ending of a therapeutic relationship. Therefore, as persons with the greatest power and influence in a clinical relationship, counselors must take special care to assess with clients the extent to which they are reaching their goals, prepare them for the eventual end of counseling, and facilitate opportunities that allow clients to review and solidify their therapeutic gains.

Sometimes abrupt endings in clinical relationships occur, and these can be tied to decisions on the part of the client, factors in a counselor's life, or other forces outside of both the client and the counselor's life (Vasquez, Bingham, & Barnett, 2008). It is not a secret that a sizeable number of clients (up to 50%) end counseling early in the process, even after one or two sessions (Garfield, 1994). Various pieces of research have explored reasons for early termination; these suggest that clients leave counseling due to scheduling conflicts or not being able to be seen quickly enough, uncertainty about engaging in a process that will challenge them toward change (Brogan, Prochaska, & Prochaska, 1999), issues related to race and ethnicity (Baruth & Manning, 2012), and a lack of felt connection to their therapist. Counselors themselves might encounter unforeseen circumstances that lead to premature or incomplete termination, such as relocation, job responsibility changes that decrease the amount of time they can dedicate to clients, and even death (Vasquez et al., 2008). While scenarios such as these might inhibit counselors and clients from having the most desirable termination process possible, they also prompt counselors to consider their responsibility to good client care throughout and up to the end of a clinical relationship.

In some regards, the end of the counseling relationship is best kept in mind at the beginning of the process. Most professionals agree that the informed consent process should include a discussion between counselors and clients about how long therapy typically lasts and how counselor and client together determine an appropriate time to draw the process to a close (ACA, 2005). In determining the timing of termination, counselors have a duty to assess with clients their progress or lack of movement toward goals. Making steady progress toward change usually is considered one indicator that clients are moving in the direction of termination. Likewise, when counselors and clients together notice that no concrete benefit from counseling is discernable, that, too, can prompt them to evaluate the usefulness of therapy and consider termination options. Counselors who understand the ethical value on fidelity find a way to balance their faithfulness to clients throughout the counseling process and professionally facilitate regular discussions about eventual termination (Vasquez et al., 2008). Keeping in mind their obligation to do no harm, counselors also remember that termination is primarily about the client—abruptly ending or prolonging the counseling process to meet their own needs cannot only lead to emotional or psychological pain, but it also does not help counselors forge professional and character excellence.

It is not always easy to know when it is the right time to end a counseling relationship. Corey, Corey, and Callanan (2011) recommended counselors to evaluate their own emotional responses to clients and the needs that are met from various client relationships in order to prevent unnecessarily delaying or too quickly ending a relationship. Counselors who practice habits of character excellence, such as respecting the self-worth of their clients, recognize that autonomy is an important part of self-worth, as well as psychological growth, and are careful not to foster too much client dependence.

Landmark 3

CASE EXAMPLE

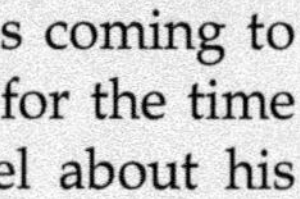

Selma has been counseling an older gentleman, Manuel, for nearly 2 months, and after their last session she began to contemplate Manuel's recent progress in therapy. She reflected that he seems happy to see her biweekly and that she herself enjoys the clinical encounter, but she is also aware that Manuel's troubling anxiety (which prompted his seeking counseling) does not really seem to have deteriorated. At their next session, Selma asks Manuel what he thinks about his overall anxiety levels, and he responds that he loves coming to see Selma—it makes him happy. Selma lets the issue subside for the time being, but 2 weeks later she again decides to talk to Manuel about his anxiousness. This time, he says, "Why are you asking me that Selma? You're not trying to make me stop coming here, are you?"

1. *If you were in Selma's position, and keeping in mind the entire counseling process, including termination, how might you respond?*

(continued)

2. *What options are at Selma's disposal?*
3. *How might you feel if you were in Selma's position?*

Working Responsibly With New Populations and Specialty Areas

Counselors work with a multitude of clients who have a variety of presenting problems. While counselor licensure and certification indicate that a person has met minimal educational and supervisory standards to allow him to use the title of counselor, these credentials do not necessarily designate a helper's areas of competence or expertise. Expertise, in fact, is carved out with years of experience, ongoing training, supervision, and consultation. The question is: How do helpers ethically forge areas of specialty or work with new client populations while accounting for the limitations in their knowledge and practice base? We believe the concepts of moderation, preparation, tentativeness, courage, and responsibleness all come to bear on this question. Perhaps the two easiest answers to the question of how to work with new populations or client issues are to make referrals or to take on clients hoping that one's current level of competence will be sufficient to do the job. These responses might in fact be ethically sound if a counselor is certain she is not qualified to handle certain client issues or if she has developed exceptional interviewing skills and a habit of reflecting on her professional work. However, they might also be reactions born either of a lack of courage or an overindulgence of one's own needs.

Aristotle's character excellences are marked by the enduring habit and quality of courage (Stewart, 2010). Without it, most counselors would practice safely with those clients whom they are sure they can help or with whom they have no value conflicts or countertransference responses. Operating from this stance can sorely limit a counselor's personal and professional growth. Indeed, encountering clients who embrace different worldviews than ourselves has the potential to stretch our abilities and our own perspectives. It is one of the most educative elements of the professional counselor's life experience. However, it is also true that counselors must be responsibly courageous. Clients are not just a testing ground for building our own competence—a firm belief in clients' self-worth reminds us of this. The *Code of Ethics* (2005) proposes concrete actions to help counselors expand the boundaries of professional competence that mesh well with clinical courage. Standard C.2.a (ACA, 2005) recommends that counselors gather education, training, and supervision before working with new specialty areas or client populations. In effect, this standard highlights the values on counselor preparation, as well as tentativeness in front of uncharted clinical waters.

SUSTAINING ONESELF FOR THE JOURNEY

Many counselors see their work as a vocation—as something that is more akin to a mission than to a job. With this comes the hope that they will be able to sustain their helping career over the course of a lifetime and that they will grow in wisdom and expertise with advancing life and work experience. Skovholt and Ronnestad (2001) used the phrase "long textured path" (p. 25) to describe the multifaceted journey toward expertise in counseling. Underscored in their descriptor, of course, is the assumption that mastery in counseling demands years of thoughtful clinical experience, which, in turn, suggests that counselors must find ways to sustain their personal and professional well-being for the trek.

Self-Care and Counselor Wellness

There are many definitions of wellness, and the concept encompasses various facets of the human experience, including those that are professional and those that are personal. Myers, Sweeney, and Witmer (2000, p. 252) described wellness as "a way of life oriented toward optimal health and well-being, in which body, mind, and spirit are integrated by the individual to live life more fully within the human and natural community." This definition is the foundation of Myer et al.'s Indivisible Self Model of Wellness, which identifies 17 dimensions of wellness that are seen as interrelated and important to overall health and wellness. Among others, these dimensions include life tasks such as work, leisure, friendship and love, as well as self-direction tasks, such as self-care, stress management, sense of worth, and problem solving skills (Myers et al., 2000). Venart, Vassos, and Pitcher-Heft (2007) suggested that most definitions of wellness bring together a balance between physical, mental, and spiritual dimensions of personhood, even while they vary on the specific descriptors they identify in each of these areas. The idea of striking a balance in meeting one's bodily, mental, emotional, spiritual, and relational needs hearkens to Aristotle's (trans. 2002) understanding of the good life as one lived in balance, harmony, and moderation. For counselors, it is important to keep in mind that when they ask themselves what it means to be a good counselor and what it means to practice counseling in a way that will help others, personal wellness is seen by most professionals to matter. As we said already, counselors themselves are their best tool in the therapeutic encounter, and they must be as healthy as possible to do good work.

To a certain degree, defining wellness and self-care is a personal endeavor, especially to the extent that one must decide for him or herself exactly how the balance among important life dimensions will be weighed. Meeting social or interpersonal needs might be more important to some, while physical exercise and activity might be more valued for others. Venart et al. (2007) reviewed the literature and summarized multiple strategies for self-care under the categories of physical, emotional, cognitive, and interpersonal wellness that are worth reviewing. Some of the recommendations culled from their review include engaging in regular exercise or body movement activities, eating a healthy diet, paying attention to bodily symptoms that indicate stress, avoiding overuse of mindless activities that can become an escape from emotional exhaustion, self-reflecting or meditating, expressing emotion with trusted family or friends, being realistic about the limits of one's ability to help others, being curious about clients' experiences, spending quality time with family and friends, seeking personal counseling if needed, and developing supportive professional peer and supervision relationships. We suggest you think about how you balance these or other dimensions of wellness in your own life. Finally, you might reflect on how you personally become aware that you are engaging a life well-lived and feel satisfied, healthy, and contented, as well as how you know that life stressors are taking an excessive toll on your well-being.

Burnout and Impairment

The ACA *Code of Ethics* (2005, C.2.g) addresses the reality of burnout and impairment for counselors and strongly recommends that professional helpers remove themselves from clinical practice when their own physical, mental, emotional, and relational well-being is severely stressed. The recommendation is a strong reminder that global well-being of counselors is important to the therapeutic process and that counselors themselves place value on personal health. Skovholt (2001, p. 56) described counseling as a "high touch human field," or one that is characterized by a repetitive cycle of forming and ending relationships. He suggested that this cycle itself (especially when the endings are abrupt or unexpected) takes a toll on helpers who invest empathy, time, interest, curiosity, and emotional energy into clinical encounters. Many helpers are able to maintain their personal wellness over time. In a national survey of ACA members, Lawson (2007) found that most counselors reported being satisfied with their work and perceived themselves to be healthy and well. However, there is a substantial body of literature that also describes the factors that lead to burnout, and counselors do well to be aware of these as they plan for a lifetime of work in the helping field.

Burnout has been characterized as an experience of depersonalization, emotional fatigue, and decreased sense of usefulness to one's clients (Lawson, 2007). Maslach (2003) noted that while the effects of burnout are primarily personal, the sources of burnout are largely related to environmental factors. These include being overworked, having a lack of control in the workplace, and being surrounded by unsupportive or negative peers and supervisors (Maslach, 2003). Skovholt, Grier, and Hanson (2001) also described some normative hazards of high touch clinical work that can slowly lead to burnout. Counselors might have higher expectations for the change process than do their clients. Counselors might perceive that they have to be able to solve every problem that their clients present to them. Counselors might be unprepared for the "failures" that accompany their work (e.g., some clients do not show tangible progress). Counselors might not be able to set appropriate and professional boundaries with clients, becoming especially invested in the client's own change process. And, finally, counselors are likely to feel the wear and tear of emotionally caring for others who cannot reciprocate the same level of interest in them.

There is special need for counselors who work with trauma victims to be alert to the signs of a related but unique phenomenon known as compassion fatigue (Figley, 2002) or vicarious trauma (McCann & Pearlman, 1990). Vicarious trauma has been described as a secondary experience of trauma that counselors have when they come in contact with people who have sustained a traumatic event, such as domestic violence, a natural or manmade disaster, atrocities of war, and the like (Craig & Sprang, 2010). In these instances, counselors themselves are susceptible to stress, disorder-like changes in their own cognitive and emotional well-being, and to the symptoms that are naturally induced in the face of trauma. They might also find it increasingly difficult to extend empathy to clients and become emotionally detached from clients, as well as family and friends. A variety of clinical experiences can increase a counselor's risk for vicarious trauma, including working regularly or primarily with trauma survivors (Adams, Figley, & Boscariono, 2008) and providing long-term treatment to sexual abuse victims (Cunningham, 2003). Whether counselors are moving toward burnout or feeling the effects of compassion fatigue, they should be cautious to regularly evaluate their well-being and muster the courage to step back from clinical work when it appears to them (or to other colleagues) that they might not be up to the task of helping others in need.

Landmark 4

RECOMMENDATIONS FOR SELF-CARE (SKOVHOLT ET AL., 2001, pp. 171–175)

1. *Maximize Experiences of Personal Success*: focus on areas of client change within your own control, such as being prepared for sessions and being knowledgeable about client issues rather than define success solely as client change.
2. *Create an Individualized Plan for Development*: be open to learning at all times from various professional sources and be willing to reinvent yourself to add vigor to the work.
3. *Reflect and Create a Plan for Self-Awareness*: find moments to introspect and reflect on your professional self, your work, and personal life.
4. *Create a Work Environment That Promotes Growth*: gather a group of professional peers and supervisors who will support and mentor you and provide honest feedback.
5. *Minimize Professional Losses*: try to ensure that as much as possible an opportunity for termination with clients is made and acknowledge the impact of not having closure.
6. *Focus on Personal Health and Wellness*: find time to spend with the people who add meaning to your life and to engage the activities that are personally enjoyable.

SIGNPOSTS FOR FUTURE TREKS

This chapter was intended to get you thinking about the personal habits and qualities of the counselor that are intimately woven into the therapeutic process. Coming to appreciate the pursuit of excellence as a cornerstone of counseling expertise might be easier to appreciate as one moves beyond the initial stages of counselor development when normative anxiety subsides and skill development advances; yet, the quest for self-development is best not overlooked, even early on in the professionalization process, as this quest is tied to the art of good counseling. In particular, we invited you to think about:

- Aristotles's character excellences as a structure for measuring ethical counselor behavior
- The role of courage, self-worth, and open-handedness in good counseling

- The reality that counselors themselves sometimes need or can benefit from personal counseling
- The lifelong process of professionalization that involves formal and information education, supervision, and life experience
- The potential drawbacks and the possible benefit of countertransference to the client growth
- Attentiveness to a planned termination process that is addressed throughout the counseling relationship
- The centrality of good self-care to counselor effectiveness and personal happiness
- Sensitivity to factors that can lead to burnout and possible impair counselors from helping clients or even cause them to do harm in some instances

INSIGHTS GAINED FROM THE JOURNEY

The first years of clinical practice are never the easiest. They are usually characterized by a certain amount of being unsettled and uncertain with oneself as a counselor. I (C. J.) can recall that during my first few years of working as a counselor I had plenty of questions about myself. Would I be able to do the job well? Would clients see me as credible? Would I actually be able to help others with their problems, especially if I myself had no personal experience of their problem? Skovholt and Ronnestad (2001, p. 33) noted that the early years of clinical practice are marked by a "series of humiliations" for the counselor. There is a phrase that will make many a counselor nervous about the work! However, I have learned that the more one comes to be at home with oneself in the counseling process and is able to focus on the client rather than one's own anxiety about figuring out a client's problem, the more one begins to look like a master counselor. I have also learned first hand that the professional development process is multifaceted. I could never have moved from being a beginning counselor without a variety of client encounters, the helpful supervision and consultation of counselors who had more experience than I did, my own study about client issues I knew little about, a reflective process by which I looked back on my own clinical techniques and overall approach to counseling, and the nerve to keep going when I was not sure I could do the job well. I have also learned how very important self-care and wellness is to the work that counselors do. This is not an aspirational goal toward which counselors reach—it is, in fact, a necessary element for all good, ethical counseling. There have been occasions, for example, when I have had learned of troubling or sad news just before seeing a client and have struggled to set aside my own personal issues in order to be present to the client. These instances remind me that I am my own best instrument in counseling, that wellness is of utmost importance, and that good counseling sometimes entails a modest admission that personal issues must be dealt with before they get in the way of good client care. Perhaps most of all, I have learned that self-development is at the heart of ethical counseling. The obligations or mandates that the counseling profession outlines in its code of ethics are really signposts for helping clinicians to engage continuously in practices that help them to be courageous, secure, balanced, giving, and humble persons who extend their goodwill and services to aid others on the process of their own self-formation.

MOVING FORWARD: CASE STUDY AND REFLECTION QUESTIONS

Eva, a pastoral counselor, has been working for about 5 years since she received her graduate degree in counseling. Among her varied pastoral duties, she primarily counsels individuals and occasionally works with couples; she sees about five clients a week. Since graduation, she has had only limited opportunities for clinical supervision due to her work environment, though she seeks out consultation when she thinks it is necessary. Eva recently received a referral from her pastor about a woman, Kacey, whom she described as emotionally unstable. Eva made an appointment to meet with Kacey, and as the course of their session unfolded, Eva noticed that Kacey's manner of speech was quite odd; she sometimes would string together words that made no sense to Eva. Eva also learned from her intake that Kacey was living on limited means and currently unemployed. Kacey described a history of abuse in her nuclear family, which led to multiple unsuccessful relationships in her adult life. Currently Kacey is living alone with her young daughter in a small apartment that they rent. At the end of the session, Eva decided to make a follow-up appointment with Kacey, but she feels some hesitancy in doing so. Reflecting on the situation, Eva knows that Kacey is not likely to be able to afford counseling services from a private practitioner and has limited means of transportation. Yet, Eva also admits to herself that she does not know what to make of Kacey's odd speech pattern and what type of serious mental health illness might be plaguing Kacey. It is a situation Eva has not encountered before.

REFLECTION QUESTIONS

- *Describe the key ethical issues in this case.*
- *What options are at Eva's disposal to resolve the ethical dilemma she is facing?*
- *What did you learn from reflecting on this case?*
- *How did your response to the case exemplify a positive approach to ethics?*

REFERENCES

Adams, R., Figley, C., & Boscariono, J. (2008). The Compassion Fatigue Scale: Its use with social workers following urban disasters. *Research in Social Work Practice, 18*, 238–250.

American Counseling Association. (2005). *ACA code of ethics*. Alexandria, VA: Author.

Aristotle. (2002). *Nicomachean ethics: Translation, introduction, and commentary (C. Rowe, Trans., & S. Broadie, Comm.)*. Oxford, UK: Oxford University Press.

Baruth, L. G., & Manning, M. L. (2012). *Multicultural counseling and psychotherapy: A lifespan perspective* (5th ed.). Upper Saddle River, NJ: Pearson Education.

Bernard, J. M., & Goodyear, R. K. (2002). *Fundamentals of clinical supervision*. Needham Heights, MA: Allyn & Bacon.

Brogan, M., Prochaska, J. O., & Prochaska, J. (1999). Predicting termination and continuation status in psychotherapy using the transtheoretical model. *Psychotherapy, 36*, 105–113.

Casile, W. J., Gruber, E. A., & Rosenblatt, S. N. (2007). Collaborative supervision for the novice supervisor. In J. Gregoire, & C. M. Jungers (Eds.), *The counselor's companion: What every beginning counselor needs to know* (pp. 86–109). Mahwah, NJ: Lawrence Erlbaum Associates.

Corey, G., Corey, M. S., & Callanan, P. (2011). *Issues & ethics in the helping professions* (8th ed.). Pacific Grove, CA: Thomson Brooks/Cole.

Craig, C. D., & Sprang, G. (2010). Compassion satisfaction, compassion fatigue, and burnout in a national sample of trauma treatment therapists. *Anxiety, Stress, & Coping, 23*, 319–339.

Cunningham, M. (2003). Impact of trauma work on social work clinicians: Empirical findings. *Social Work, 48*, 451–459.

Dawes, R. M. (1994). *House of cards: Psychology and psychotherapy built on myth*. New York: Free Press.

Figley, C. R. (2002). Compassion fatigue: Psychotherapists' chronic lack of self care. *Journal of Clinical Psychology, 58*, 1433–1441.

Garfield, S. L. (1994). Research on client variables in psychotherapy: In A. E. Bergen, & S. L. Garfield (Eds.), *Handbook of psychotherapy and behavior change* (4th ed., pp. 190–228). New York: Wiley.

Hayes, J. A., Riker, J. R., & Ingram, K. M. (1997). Countertransference behavior and management in brief counseling: A field study. *Psychotherapy Research, 7*, 145–153.

Lawson, G. (2007). Counselor wellness and impairment: A national survey. *Journal of Humanistic Counseling, Education, and Development, 46*, 20–34.

Maslach, C. (2003). *Burnout: The cost of caring*. Cambridge, MA: Malor Books.

McCann, I. L., & Pearlman, L. A. (1990). Vicarious traumatization: A framework for understanding the psychological effects of working with victims. *Journal of Traumatic Stress, 3*, 131–149.

Myers, J. E., Sweeney, T. J., & Witmer, J. M. (2000). The Wheel of Wellness counseling for wellness: A holistic model for treatment planning. *Journal of Counseling & Development, 86*, 482–493.

Norcross, J. C., & Guy, J. D. (2005). The prevalence and parameters of personal therapy in the United States. In J. D. Geller, J. C. Norcross, & D. E. Orlinsky (Eds.), *The psychotherapist's own psychotherapy: Patient and clinician perspectives* (pp. 165–176). New York: Oxford University Press.

Nouwen, H. J. M. (1972). *The wounded healer*. New York: Doubleday.

Orlinsky, D. E., Norcross, J. C., Ronnestad, M. H., & Wiseman, H. (2005). Outcomes and impacts of the psychotherapists' own psychotherapy: A research review. In J. D. Geller, J. C. Norcross, & D. E. Orlinsky (Eds.), *The psychotherapist's own psychotherapy: Patient and clinician perspectives* (pp. 214–230). New York: Oxford University Press.

O'Sullivan, J. J., & Quevillon, R. P. (1992). 40 years later: Is the Boulder model still alive? *American Psychologist, 47*, 67–70.

Pedersen, P., Draguns, J. G., Lonner, W., & Trimble, J. (2002). *Counseling across cultures* (5th ed). Thousand Oaks, CA: Sage.

Perry, W. G. (1970/1999). *Forms of ethical and intellectual development in the college years: A scheme*. San Francisco: Jossey-Bass.

Rogers, C. R. (1961). *On becoming a person: A therapist's view of psychotherapy*. New York, NY: Houghton Mifflin.

Skovholt, T. M. (2001). *The resilient practitioner: Burnout prevention and self-care strategies for counselors, therapists, teachers, and health professionals*. Boston: Allyn & Bacon.

Skovholt, T. M., Grier, T. L., & Hanson, M. R. (2001). Career counseling for longevity: Self care and burnout prevention strategies for counselor resilience. *Journal of Career Development, 27*, 167–176.

Skovholt, T. M., & Ronnestad, M. H. (1992). Themes in therapist and counselor development. *Journal of Counseling & Development, 70*, 505–515.

Skovholt, T. M., & Ronnestad, M. H. (2001). The long, textured path from novice to senior practitioner. In T. M. Skovholt, *The resilient practitioner: Burnout prevention and self-care strategies for counselors, therapists, teachers, and health professionals* (pp. 25–54). Boston: Allyn & Bacon.

Sternberg, R. J. (1990). *Wisdom: Its nature, origins, and development*. Cambridge: Cambridge University Press.

Stewart, A. E. (2010). Explorations in the meanings of excellence and its importance for counselors: The culture of excellence in the United States. *Journal of Counseling & Development, 88*, 189–195.

Sue, D. W., & Sue, D. (2008). *Counseling the culturally different: Theory & practice*. New York: Wiley.

Tennyson, W. W., & Strom, S. M. (1986). Beyond professional standards: Developing responsibleness. *Journal of Counseling & Development, 64*, 298–302.

Tobin, D. J., & McCurdy, K. G. (2006). Adlerian-focused supervision for countertransference work with counselors-in-training. *The Journal of Individual Psychology, 62*, 154–167.

Van Kaam, A. L. (1966). *The art of existential counseling. A new perspective in psychotherapy*. Denville, NJ: Dimension Book, Inc.

Vasquez, M. J. T., Bingham, R. P., & Barnett, J. E. (2008). Psychotherapy termination: Clinical and ethical responsibilities. *Journal of Clinical Psychology: In Session, 64*, 653–665.

Venart, E., Vassos, S., & Pitcher-Heft, H. (2007). What individual counselors can do to sustain wellness. *Journal of Humanistic Counseling, Education, and Development, 46*, 50–65.

9

Ethical Considerations in Counseling Practice, Research, and Education

Amy E. Alexander and Christin M. Jungers

THE FORESEEN DESTINATION

After reading this chapter, it is our hope that learners will have advanced their knowledge of:

- Some potential benefits and drawbacks of diagnosis.
- The purpose of assessment in the counseling process.
- Rights of clients in the assessment process.
- A history of social science research violations that prompted advances in research ethics guidelines.
- Rights of research study participants.
- Responsibilities of counselor educators.
- Best practices related to managing multiple relationships between educators and students.

GETTING ON THE ROAD

Throughout this book, you have been invited to engage the process of becoming an ethical counselor from a positive stance and also to think about ethics from a philosophical point of view. In this chapter, we extend the positive and philosophical perspectives to three more areas: diagnosis and assessment, research issues, and counselor education and training. The first two sections of the chapter deal with clinical practice issues related to diagnosis and assessment, while the last two sections look at two fairly common, nonclinical roles that counselors take as researchers and educators.

EXPLORING THE TERRITORY

DIAGNOSIS IN PROFESSIONAL COUNSELING

In counseling practice, assessment, diagnosis, and choice of clinical interventions are interrelated parts of the treatment process (Corey, Corey, & Callanan, 2011). Assessment helps counselors make decisions about the most fitting diagnoses, while specific diagnoses often are tied to particular evidence-based treatments. Treatment choice, however, is also influenced by a counselor's theoretical and philosophical understanding of the human person and the counseling relationship, and this must come into consideration when therapists make decisions about how to structure their work with clients. While these three areas of practice mutually inform each other, they also can be considered individually as they involve unique ethical concerns. We will look at some of the ethical considerations that surround these topics, beginning with diagnosis.

What Is Diagnosis?

Using a somewhat generic description, diagnosis refers to the process of classifying or categorizing a set of behaviors or symptoms (Dougherty, 2005; Welfel, 2010). In some counseling and most medical contexts, diagnosis refers more particularly to the identification of a *disease* based on the presence of a set of problems or symptoms. When mental health counselors talk about diagnosis, they usually mean that they will be classifying a composite of a person's behavioral, emotional, physical, cognitive, and/or spiritual experiences according to the *Diagnostic and Statistical Manual of Mental Disorders* (*DSM IV-TR*, American Psychiatric Association [APA], 2000). The *DSM IV-TR* is the most often used point of reference for making mental and behavioral health diagnoses (Dougherty, 2005; Seligman, 1999). It is widely recognized that the *DSM* seeks to parallel a medical model approach to classifying symptomology (Eriksen & Kress, 2005). As persons endowed through licensure with the privilege of describing, classifying, and, some would say, labeling clients' issues and problems, counselors ought to consider carefully (a) the underlying assumptions of diagnosis according to the *DSM*, (b) how best to communicate diagnoses to clients, and finally, (c) the more basic question of whether or not they embrace the philosophical foundations of *DSM*-based diagnoses. In day-to-day practice, most counselors use *DSM*-based diagnostic procedures; however, they may not always prefer to engage in the practice. Other clinicians and educators go a step further and contend that a *DSM*-based diagnosis is at odds with the roots of the counseling profession, which emphasize prevention and a developmental point of view regarding human wellness and pathology (Hohenshil, 1993; Ivey & Ivey, 1998, 1999). Because we believe that professional identity informs practice, we encourage you to ponder seriously the practice of diagnosis in light of your emerging professional identity.

Diagnosis: Helpful or Harmful?

We mentioned earlier that *DSM*-based diagnosis is used but not fully endorsed by all counselors. Before exploring further the potential ethical drawbacks of diagnosis, we want to ask: What are the merits of diagnosis? Welfel (2010) pointed out that there are multiple diagnostic systems that counselors use, not all of them based on the *DSM*, and that generally the classification of issues and problems can benefit client treatment. Couple, marriage, and family counselors are among the most prominent proponents of alternate diagnostic methods. (See Chapter 11 for a discussion of relationship-based understanding of client issues.) Similarly, narrative therapists affirm the usefulness of *naming the problem*, but they tend to use a collaborative process to reach this end that involves clients themselves creating a meaningful name for an externalized problem (White & Epston, 1999). Welfel (2010) proposed further that a diagnosis provides clinicians with a shared language and way of understanding clients' problems and, moreover, that objective descriptions about human experiences commonly believed to be problematic help researchers test and develop treatments that fit unique diagnoses. Corey et al. (2011) likewise pointed out a variety of pragmatic arguments used to highlight the benefits of diagnosis, including the fact that counselors rely on diagnoses to receive payment for services through managed care companies and that counselors need to be skilled in diagnosis to perform the duties required of them by many agencies and treatment facilities. Finally, as Michael Kocet and Harriet Glosoff (Kaplan et al., 2009) pointed out, some clients experience a sense of relief at having a diagnosis or name put to the experience of their problems.

Although there are numerous arguments for diagnosis, there are just as many potential drawbacks and ethical concerns, especially when diagnosis is grounded in a medical-model approach as is assumed in the *DSM*. Indeed, the ACA *Code of Ethics* (2005) includes a provision (Standard E.5.d) granting counselors permission to refrain from making a diagnosis. Members of the 2002 Ethics Revision Task Force (Kaplan et al., 2009) pointed out that diagnosis can be harmful to clients, and when it is deemed so by clinicians, they ought carefully to consider refraining from applying a *DSM*-based diagnosis. Let us explore the elements of harm further.

Harm to clients through *DSM*-based diagnosis can come in many forms. First, as numerous writers have contested (Corey et al., 2011; Dougherty, 2005; Kaplan et al., 2009; Welfel, 2010), a diagnosis can have an unintended negative impact in multiple arenas of life, including among others, career and family. Certain diagnoses may de-qualify one for one's current job. For example, fear of a diagnosis of depression or posttraumatic stress disorder (PTSD) often prohibits military personnel from seeking mental health care because evidence of such diagnoses on their record could significantly affect their ability to advance or even to serve in their current capacity (Kaplan et al.). Eriksen and Kress (2005) noted that certain diagnoses can also be potentially harmful to those applying for a job with an employer who requests the right to investigate an applicant's history of psychological diagnoses and then includes such data in hiring decisions. These authors also point out that some diagnoses can negatively impact parents who are going through custody proceedings with an estranged spouse. Others suggest that the stigma attached to a diagnostic label can be life altering in an adverse way, especially when it acts as a self-fulfilling prophesy. As narrative therapists contend, medical-model diagnoses can lead to the unfortunate blending of person and problem such that a person's identity may get lost within a diagnosis. Dorre and Kinnier (2006) referred to the dehumanizing effect that *DSM*-based diagnoses can have on people, perhaps most so for those given a diagnosis of what the *DSM* deems personality disorders.

Other ethical concerns with *DSM*-based diagnoses have to do with the overlap and lack of clarity among various diagnostic categories (Dougherty, 2005; Welfel, 2010), which present a challenge to clinicians to accurately assess a client's symptoms. It is not uncommon for practitioners to have different interpretations of a client's presenting problem, which could lead to diverse diagnoses for the same client. This becomes especially confusing when clients see more than one therapist who offer different diagnoses for what the client may experience as the same problem. Research evidence (Campbell, 1999) has suggested that practitioner bias may sometimes be at play in situations where counselors reach different diagnostic descriptions for the same client.

Numerous authors (Dougherty, 2005; Eriksen & Kress, 2005; Welfel, 2010) have pointed out, furthermore, that the process of establishing a diagnosis is often done without proper care or without gathering sufficient information on which to base a diagnosis. Counselors can be pressured from their agency or treatment facility to manage large case loads that do not allow for enough time with a client to formulate a thoughtful impression of the client, or they may be required to diagnose a client after just one 45-minute session. Neither of these situations tends to allow client or clinician the time needed to come to a fair or meaningful understanding of the client's set of issues.

Diagnosis and Philosophy

Stepping back from this brief appraisal of diagnosis, especially *DSM*-based diagnosis, we invite you to think about how your philosophical leanings help in determining the ethical quality of diagnosis. Let us clarify. First, many of the points we raised previously highlighted the *potential outcomes* (i.e., consequences) of diagnosis. Evaluating an action or practice according to its consequences is most akin to the teleological or utilitarian approach to philosophical ethics. If you tend toward this approach to moral decision making, you will want to be confident that your use of diagnosis will lead to more potential benefits for clients than to drawbacks. This might mean that you would want to identify which client groups (e.g., children in child welfare programs) are vulnerable to having a diagnosis misapplied or misused, especially by other stakeholders in the client's life, and carefully evaluate the potential for harm with such clients.

In this brief discussion, you were also invited to think about principle ethics, in particular the principles of nonmaleficence (doing no harm), beneficence (doing good), and justice relative to diagnosis. If you tend to reason through ethical dilemmas from the point of view of these and other principles, you may ask yourself some of the following questions before engaging in diagnosis. Is it possible to use *DSM*-based diagnosis and not potentially harm a client? What would this require of a counselor? Do you believe that you could fairly apply diagnoses across all client populations? How does applying a diagnosis to problems such as marital discord or family issues benefit the family unit when diagnoses tend to highlight intrapersonal problems?

It is also worth pondering whether or not there is something fundamentally incompatible with the counselor identity in the practice of *DSM*-based diagnosis by counselors. This consideration, posed from a deontological perspective on ethics, suggests that some behaviors or decisions are *in themselves* harmful and ought to be avoided. As mentioned already, for some counselors, the developmental and prevention-based identity that counselors espouse makes *DSM*-based diagnosis more incompatible than not with their overall therapeutic goals.

Finally, if you tend to use virtues to determine what it means to be an ethical practitioner, you likely would think about attitudes and dispositions associated with a virtuous therapist and how these inform your stance on, as well as your practice of, diagnosis. Cohen and Cohen (1999) identified several trust-enhancing virtues, including candor, diligence, and fairness that provide useful points of reflection on the practice of diagnosing. Because a diagnosis is usually made at the start of a clinical relationship, counselors who think about ethics from a virtue standpoint might consider how they can use diagnoses to build (rather than detract) from trust. Using candor, counselors are up front with clients about practical concerns such as the type of diagnosis that will be made, who has access to a diagnosis, and how a diagnosis is reached. Diligence suggests that counselors are thoughtful and informed when formulating a diagnosis. Diligent counselors, for example, do not just rely on a "standard" diagnosis that is used by a treatment facility or agency; they are willing to gather the necessary information within the time it takes to come to a reasonable diagnosis. Finally, fairness requires counselors to think about how they can provide the same level of openness to the diagnostic process across all sets of clients. In particular, the virtue of fairness calls counselors not to classify a client's issues according to overt or subconscious bias related to race, ethnicity, gender, or economic status.

Like many other common practices in which counselors engage, the practice of diagnosis is one that requires thoughtful and critical evaluation. We recommend that you take time to fully investigate the place of diagnosis in your future work, as it communicates an important message about your understanding of the human person and your approach to treatment. An excellent resource for an in-depth look at *DSM*-based diagnosis can be found in Eriksen and Kress's (2005) review of the subject.

Landmark 1

CASE EXAMPLE

Sandrine is a counselor at a mid-size university where she provides counseling to the student population. She is meeting with a new client who was formerly seen by another mental health professional not employed by the university. During the initial assessment, the client reveals that she believes she needs help, though she is hesitant about returning to counseling, because her last counselor told her she had narcissistic personality disorder. The client further revealed that the previous counselor informed her of the diagnosis after their initial 1-hour meeting. The client believes the diagnosis is incorrect. Protocol at the university counseling center where Sandrine works is also to

(*continued*)

formulate and input a diagnosis after the first session. Furthermore, there is no set protocol for if and how counselors reveal their diagnosis to clients.

1. *How might Sandrine best respond to the client's report and concern about her previous diagnosis?*
2. *Giving consideration to the virtues of candor, diligence, and fairness how might you approach the diagnostic process and discuss your diagnosis with the client?*
3. *Would you want to make a* DSM*-based diagnosis of the client? Describe your reasons for or against your decision.*

ASSESSMENT AND TESTING IN COUNSELING PRACTICE

In counseling, diagnosis involves practitioners in ordering sets of mental, emotional, and behavioral symptoms (or traits, or experiences) according to a recognized classification system (e.g., *DSM*). In essence, diagnosis is a part of a broad process of assessment that is aimed at providing an educated and thoughtful description of a client's personality or presenting issues in order to formulate a clinical plan that will help the client make one's desired changes (Anastasi, 1992). Methods used to gather information for an assessment are varied, and include counselor observations of the client, mental status exams, informal client interviews, formal psychological tests, and interviews with secondary sources, such as family members. In schools, counselors often administer other assessments, such as aptitude and achievement tests, the results of which are not as much about diagnosis as they are used as predictive measures.

Besides culminating in a diagnosis or an indication about potential for future academic success, assessment can lead to multiple other outcomes in clinical practice. Sometimes, assessments prompt counselors to take an immediate action, as in the case when they gather enough information to be concerned about a client's well-being and must encourage specific actions to prevent self-injury or suicide (Welfel, 2010). Assessment also informs treatment choices, and it may be the basis for recommendations to other key stakeholders (such as a court) who will make decisions that affect a client's life. Appreciating the potentially wide-reaching impact of their assessments for clients ought to spur counselors to approach this part of their work with respect and diligence. In this section, we look at some of the ethical concerns surrounding assessment practices and the use of tests.

Competence in Making Assessments

Think about these questions: What makes a counselor qualified to make an assessment of a client or to administer and interpret a test? How does a counselor decide which test or inventory to administer? What do counselors do to fairly and responsibly administer an assessment? How best can a counselor describe the results of the test? What is the client's role in the assessment process, and what rights do clients have to know about assessment outcomes? How does a counselor's ethical self (i.e., virtues and value set) play a part in the assessment process? These are a few of the many questions that ought to occupy the counselor's mind as he prepares to use testing instruments and ultimately make judgments about a client. The questions highlight, moreover, the need for counselors to be skilled in the whole process of making assessments—from determining appropriate tests, to describing the assessment or test to the client, to properly administering the test (i.e., according to test-maker's standards), to interpreting the results, and finally to sharing and explaining the results with the client and other key stakeholders (e.g., family members, courts, etc.).

The idea that ethical practice in the area of assessment demands counselors to be knowledgeable and practiced with testing and up front about the limits to their areas of experience in using certain tests or inventories is well supported (ACA, 2005; Anastasi, 1992; Naugle, 2009; Vacc, Juhnke, & Nilsen, 2001; Welfel, 2010). Before counselors use formal tests with clients, they are expected to have had a course or more in assessment, appraisal, or testing. Such courses typically introduce concepts including reliability, validity, norms, fairness to diversity, and so on, and they help counselors to develop what Anastasi called proficiency with "statistical techniques of psychometrics" and "relevant facts and principles of behavioral science" (p. 611). Simply put, counselors have to be able to understand the purposes of an instrument, the quality of the instrument, and the uses of the instrument before ever asking a client (or student) to take the test. Having a comfortable, working knowledge of the purpose of an instrument also allows counselors to make a sound determination about whether or not it will be potentially useful for a particular client and one's needs.

Competence in using psychological tests means that counselors build background knowledge about statistics and psychometrics (the study of psychological measurements), as well as about the properties of individual tests. Just as important, counselors are encouraged to understand how the results of the test factor into an overall assessment of a client's presenting problem. Counselors who aim to be the kind of practitioner who is responsible, respectful, and diligent are careful not to make sweeping conclusions about a client (or student) based on the results of one or two tests. Anastasi (1992) reminds counselors that applying tests results ethically means refraining from making clinical judgments simply on the basis of a *single source* of information, such as a test score. The temptation to see tests as a conclusive statement about an individual's psychological health or illness is strong, but counselors who use these assessments have to appreciate the fallibility of tests (Welfel, 2010). In addition, test scores can change over time as the circumstances of a person's life change or due to the process of personal growth or impairment. Keeping in mind the somewhat flexible nature of test results helps counselors to understand the value and limitations of tests in the assessment process (Anastasi, 1992).

Client Welfare and Rights

The ACA *Code of Ethics* (2005) is up front about what it means to do good by clients in the practice of using assessment techniques. First and foremost, counselors who use assessments recognize that their clients have the right to be fully informed about the tests that may be used in counseling. This includes a description about the purposes of the test(s) or assessment procedures, the best conditions for using the assessments, the role of the results in coming to an overall assessment, and the parties to whom the results may disseminated (ACA, 2005, E.1.b., E.3.a). As with the use of any specialized technique, counselors must obtain the consent of the client before proceeding with testing. Consent also must be obtained before counselors can share results with other, third parties (ACA, 2005, E.4). The obligation to gather informed consent can be interpreted as a protection for clients against the misuse of test results, as well as an implicit recommendation that counselors appreciate the collaborative nature of assessment. Inviting clients to provide their sense of the assessment results can be informative to the assessment process and communicates to them that their subjective experiences are as valuable as an objective test measure.

Often, new counselors may find that the processes surrounding the use of tests (i.e., gathering informed consent, explaining why he or she wants to use the test, describing the results, etc.) are the most challenging. The desire to "jump in" and administer an assessment may overshadow the careful guiding of the entire process. If this happens, clients can be left feeling overwhelmed, confused, uneasy about the decision to use a test, and unsure about the meaning of the results. Clients may not even know that their rights have been betrayed when counselors fail to explain the consent process. Thus, clinicians do well to remember that even with testing and assessment, the process is as important as the content.

Cultural Considerations in Assessment

Counselor educators, researchers, and practitioners have, in the last several decades, drawn increasing attention to the need for cultural awareness in the use of tests in counseling (Sue & Sue, 2008). Results of assessments and tests can be an inaccurate representation of the client's problem or abilities and aptitudes if the questions on a test are not culturally relevant or are "differently relevant" (Welfel, 2010, p. 300) to members of a particular racial, ethic, or cultural group. Anastasi (1992) points out that test bias can occur when an instrument incorporates or reflects cultural bias against a group of individuals for whom the test will eventually be used. Thus, before a counselor decides to use a test with clients from a minority group, it is best that he or she knows how the test was created and on which group it was normed. If a test is found to be valid for diverse groups of individuals, its scores are more likely to be a fair measure of the psychological construct in consideration.

Landmark 2

CASE EXAMPLE

Ashanti is a counseling intern at a high school where she sees several students each day. A number of the students, she noticed, have concerns about what to do once they graduate. Wanting to help them clarify their life goals, Ashanti decides they might benefit from a career inventory. She scans the Internet and comes across a site promoting a values-based career inventory. The site provides users with a sample copy of the inventory. Ashanti downloads the inventory, briefly looks it over, and makes a copy for the next student she is seeing. Ashanti and this student have a discussion about his lack of direction in life goals. Toward the end of the session, Ashanti tells the student that

(continued)

he might benefit from clarifying his values and that she has an assessment tool that can help. The student is excited about the inventory and is willing to complete it. Ashanti asks him to take it home, fill it out, and bring it to their next appointment.

1. *How would you evaluate the ethical quality of Ashanti's actions?*
2. *What concerns, if any, do you have about Ashanti's use of the values-based inventory?*
3. *If you were supervising Ashanti, what might you discuss with her regarding the process of using assessments in counseling?*

COUNSELOR AS RESEARCHER

Thus far, we have considered the ethics surrounding diagnosis and assessment, two common practice issues that counselors encounter in their clinical work. Now, we examine ethical issues for counselors who take on the nonclinical role of researcher. Though many counselors do not necessarily think of themselves as researchers, they do rely on research findings as an aid to formulating diagnoses, making assessments, and determining effective counseling treatments for clients. It, therefore, benefits both clinicians and researchers to recognize the awesome responsibilities that come with doing research and applying its outcomes. Before leading any investigation, for example, there are numerous ethical guidelines counselors follow to create a well-designed experiment, gain institutional support, and most importantly, protect the well-being of human participants involved in behavioral and mental health studies. In this section, we explore the basics of research ethics as they pertain to counselors, starting with a look at the development of ethical and legal guidelines in research since the 1940s.

Roots of Research Ethics

Incorporating philosophical ethics into decision-making processes is perhaps at its most critical when one considers the practice of using human participants in research. The last century has unfortunately born witness to numerous egregious acts committed in the name of science; these eventually became catalysts for much-needed attention in the area of human rights in research. Among the most well-known atrocities are those that were committed by Nazi doctors during World War II. In the aftermath of the war, the Nuremberg Trials exposed physicians for having conducted experiments on prisoners of war that involved, among other thing, injecting them with infections and surgically maiming them (National Institutes of Health [NIH], 2004). In an attempt to prevent such harm from coming to research participants again, the Nuremberg Code was written; it outlined 10 standards that must be met before researchers can use human persons in their investigations. Importantly, the code required that participants give informed consent before becoming part of any study.

The Nuremberg Code laid the groundwork for future standards and policies dealing with the use of human persons in research. For example, in the United States, the code was the foundation for NIH's first set of federal policies and regulations on the treatment of human subjects (NIH, 2004). However, with time, the code needed to be broadened and revised to reflect a growing range of practices and circumstances in medical and behavioral health sciences. The World Medical Association (WMA), while upholding the code's major sentiments, extended its guidelines to address clinical research and treatment of human participants in *The Declaration of Helsinki* in 1964. Another extension came in the 1970s when the U.S. Congress passed the National Research Act (1974). The act created a mandate for Institutional Review Boards (IRBs) to oversee research inquiries using human participants. It also established the National Commission for the Protection of Human Subjects of Biomedical and Behavioral Research (NCPHSBBR) to review U.S. federal policies on the use of human subjects (Zimmerman, 1997). The commission issued *The Belmont Report* (NCPHSBBR, 1979), a landmark document that laid out a philosophical and analytical framework that continues to be used today to help researchers reason through ethical dilemmas involving human subjects. *The Belmont Report* grounded its guidelines for human subject research in three principles: respect for human persons, beneficence, and justice (NIH, 2004).

The Belmont Report was, in large part, written as a response to revelations that the United States government had sponsored research that posed grave harm to participants in what are known as the Tuskegee experiments (Zimmerman, 1997). From 1932 to 1972, the Public Health Service of the U.S. government, along with the Tuskegee Institute, engaged in a study of 600 poor African American men in the South who were of reproductive age; two-thirds had syphilis, while the remaining one-third were not infected with the disease (Robinson & Curry, 2008). Although the purpose of the research was to try to improve the health of this specific population, the participants never provided informed consent, were not given the option to withdraw from the study, and were not given proper treatment even after it was established that current medication being used for other syphilis patients was effective in eradicating the disease (Centers for Disease Control and Prevention [CDC], 2011). The experiment was stopped after news media exposed the project in the 1970s.

This brief historical sketch reminds counselor researchers that ethical codes and federal regulations surrounding the practice of using human participants in research did not emerge without good reason. They became necessary as a result of highly egregious acts that were discovered, in some cases, after the research was concluded and at the cost of human health, welfare, dignity, and rights. As part of the body of scientist–practitioners in the behavioral and mental health fields, counselors who conduct research thus are imbued with a responsibility to design and oversee investigations that adhere to the ACA *Code of Ethics* (2005), federal and state laws, and institutional (e.g., university) policies guarding the rights of participants (see Standard G.1.a). Furthermore, the *Code of Ethics* (2005, G.1.d) clearly states, "Counselors who conduct research with human participants are responsible for the welfare of participants … and should take reasonable precautions to avoid causing injurious psychological, emotional, physical or social effects to participants." In line with the principles of *The Belmont Report*, counselor researchers have an obligation to respect their human subjects and to design and guide research efforts that are aimed at benefitting participants and the public at large. Researchers are mindful that ultimately they are charged with elevating humanity through innovative, yet competent, thoughtful, and caring approaches to inquiry and experimentation.

Landmark 3

CASE EXAMPLE

Christian is a doctoral student in a counselor education program at a prestigious university. He was invited by a well-respected professor in his program to collaborate on a research project that is near completion. The professor turned over the data culled from the experiment to Christian, whose job it is to analyze the findings. While reviewing the documents, Christian noticed that about one-quarter of the consent forms were missing. At the next project meeting with his professor, Christian mentioned his concern about the consent forms. The professor dismissed Christian's observation, saying that the data were collected from students in his class, who just assumed that they had to participate in one study over the course of their graduate training.

1. *What do you think Christian should make of his professor's response?*
2. *What potential ethical issues are Christian and his professor facing?*
3. *How do you believe you would handle the situation if you were in Christian's place?*

Being Responsible and Acting Responsibly as a Researcher

Counselors who conduct research ethically bring both character qualities and reasoning skills to bear on the work that they do. Virtues and principles help researchers to make decisions that reflect a sense of responsibleness to the dignity of the persons who are willing to act as participants. Meara, Schmidt, and Day (1996) described ethical counselors as respectful, thoughtful, and benevolent, as well as self-aware, willing to face their biases, and motivated to do good. These characteristics are compatible with the philosophical principles of respect for persons, beneficence, and justice outlined in *The Belmont Report* and recognized as cornerstones of ethical conduct for professional counselors in all areas of their work (Kitchener, 1984). Consider how these principles shed light on our understanding of ethical research.

First, the principle of respect for persons is grounded in an appreciation for others' right to autonomy or self-directedness (Zimmerman, 1997). In valuing autonomy, considerate researchers are forthright and up front with participants about the research process and how it will potentially affect them. They do not apply pressure to potential participants about their involvement in research inquiries in order to achieve their own research goals. Second, the principle of beneficence demands that the aim of research inquiries is to accomplish good for the public. This entails researchers in having to weigh the possible risks to participants against the positive gains for society that can be achieved through research. When known risks to human subjects seem to outweigh potential goods, researchers seek alternative experimental designs that place participants at less risk. Finally, research must be based on the principle of justice or fairness, which suggests that in the process of conducting research, certain group of persons (i.e., participants) must not be systematically placed at greater risk to their welfare than others. In addition, justice suggests that all persons have an equal right to benefit from research findings (Zimmerman). When counselor researchers develop the virtue of self-reflection and are aware of biases they might bring to their inquiries, they are more easily able to uphold the principle of justice by not being insensitive to vulnerable groups of people (such as the poor, children, etc.).

Participants' Rights

There are three primary rights of research participants that ought to be protected in any study: informed consent, voluntary participation, and confidentiality (Remley & Herlihy, 2010). Participants have the right to freely choose whether or not to be involved in research studies and to be informed about key aspects of the experimental process. In the spirit of protecting persons' right to autonomy (which is upheld through informed consent), the ACA *Code of Ethics* (2005, G.2.a) specifically outlines the areas of a research project about which participants must be informed. These include: the purposes of the research, the untested procedures that will be used in the study along with other procedures that participants might find helpful, possible risks and benefits of participation, a right to have questions about the study answered, knowledge about how the study's findings will be distributed, and an assurance that the participant can withdraw from the study at any time without penalty. Robinson and Curry (2008) noted that the process of obtaining consent is as important as presenting potential participants with the required information. As in gathering consent before one begins a clinical relationship, counselor researchers have to ensure that participants fully comprehend the aforementioned aspects of the study with which they are choosing to be involved. Skarbek, Henry, and Parish (2006) pointed out that numerous factors can get in the way of informed consent, such as language differences between researchers and their participants, jargon on consent forms, cognitive abilities of the participant, and differences in social standing or culture between researchers and participants. Finally, participants have the right to know that their identities will be kept anonymous throughout the research process, especially with regard to reporting of findings. Particularly in counseling research, it is not uncommon that a researcher will be interested in studying sensitive or intimate questions which may require participants to disclose highly personal information. Taking steps to ensure that participants' identities will not be revealed is of utmost importance.

Persons of Diminished or Limited Capacity to Consent

The ACA *Code of Ethics* (2005, G.2.f) specifically addresses the issue of doing research with persons whose ability to consent may be diminished or in some way limited. Some of most common examples of persons who may not be capable of consenting to participation, in addition to those noted by Skarbek et al. (2006), are children, adolescents, older adults with signs of dementia, persons who are severely mentally ill, and prisoners. Counselor researchers have a special responsibility to protect the rights of those who might easily be taken advantage of by a person or organization in a position of power and influence. As was evident in the Tuskegee experiments and those conducted by

Nazi physicians, people who are socially disadvantaged by their race, gender, ethnicity, socioeconomic status, and medical or mental status may stand a greater chance of being abused in the research process than are persons of sound cognitive abilities, privilege, financial security, and social recognition. Thus, counselor researchers have an even stronger obligation to these members of society where research ethics is concerned.

Landmark 4

CASE EXAMPLE

Mrs. Carlisle, an 88-year-old woman who is beginning to show signs of dementia, has been meeting with Raquel, a counselor at Mrs. Carlisle's assisted living facility, for the past year. Last week, Mrs. Carlisle was hospitalized. During her stay there, she was asked to participate in a clinical trial testing a new drug designed to help improve memory. Raquel was present when the clinical investigator obtained a signed informed consent from Mrs. Carlisle. However, when Raquel visited Mrs. Carlisle today and inquired about the study, she looked at Raquel blankly and seemed to have no idea what she was talking about.

1. *Ethically speaking, is there anything Raquel should do?*
2. *What concerns might you have about Mrs. Carlisle's involvement in the study?*

Deception

Consider for a moment how you understand the use of deception in research inquiries. Is it always unethical? Might there be occasions when misinforming or not providing participants with full information about a study is acceptable? These are questions that are best considered in consultation with colleagues, especially when they seem relevant to one's research proposal. The use of deception in human science research must be approached with great caution. Indeed, the ACA *Code of Ethics* (2005, G.2.b) states, "Counselors do not conduct research involving deception unless alternative procedures are not feasible and the prospective value of the research justifies the deception." Although there may be occasions when misinforming participants or not revealing full details of a study to them seems acceptable, it is never sanctioned when a participant's physical, psychological, or emotional welfare is at stake.

Institutional Review Boards (IRBs)

Institutional Review Boards (IRBs) are university-based committees made up of knowledgeable, well-trained faculty, as well as other professionals whose job it is to ensure that the rights and welfare of participants are protected (Remley & Herlihy, 2010). IRBs play a role in the ethical decision-making process by evaluating research proposals to determine if proposed projects reflect the principles of respect for persons, benevolence, and justice (Robinson & Curry, 2008). In doing this, boards must consider practical issues, such as how participants will be informed about the purpose of the investigation, what measures researchers will take to ensure that participants will be treated fairly, what research methods investigators intend to use, and what means the researcher is taking to minimize the overall risks to participants (Robinson & Curry, 2008). If an IRB rejects a proposal, it may recommend changes that will address its areas of concern. Sometimes researchers view IRBs as an obstacle to their work, however, in keeping in mind the history of abuse against human subjects that preceded their formation, we also recognize that such boards are intended to be a group of helpers who collaborate with researchers to prevent undue risks to participants in the name of human science research.

Reporting Results

At the conclusion of an investigation, researchers typically look for venues through which to publish their findings. Honest reporting of findings can be a more complex aspect of research than one initially anticipates. The general expectation is that researchers will not alter and, most importantly, will not fabricate any part of their results (ACA, 2005, G.4; Heppner, Kivlighan, & Wampold, 2008). Integrity is expected of researchers throughout the process, especially with regard to reporting. This means that investigators will accurately present and interpret their findings even if the findings are not favorable toward institutions or sponsors (ACA, 2005, G.4.b). It also suggests that researchers will enlist the consultation of other colleagues to evaluate their analyses if need be, and they will be up front about the limitations of their study (Heppner et al., 2008). Multiple factors might persuade researchers from using their best judgment in reporting. First, there are many possible unplanned or unforeseen events that can emerge during the course of an investigation that can contaminate a research project and that researchers may wish to dismiss or alter while analyzing their results. Second, researchers may face pressure from their institutions or donors to produce high impact inquiries or preferred sets of results that color their interpretation of findings. Finally, counselor researchers also have to contend with their own egos. The idea that one has spent a great deal of time and effort, personal sacrifice, and professional investment on a project one finds worthy of those investments but that turns out disappointingly, is, for some, agonizing. This may lead researchers to misrepresent or lie about their findings. Although external regulatory agents and codes of ethics help to protect the fair reporting of research findings in the counseling profession, one's personal internal gauges are also an important part of distinguishing ethical from unethical behavior and choosing to act with integrity.

COUNSELOR AS EDUCATOR

In the final section of this chapter, we turn our attention to another nonclinical role that makes up the counselor identity, and that is educator. Counselor educators are expected to live up to certain standards in their unique positions as educators, mentors (Welfel, 2010), and role models for students enrolled in counseling programs. Certain competencies accompany the educator role, and these are not necessarily present when one is involved primarily in clinical work. At the same time, many ethical issues that surround the therapeutic relationship are also relevant to the teacher–student relationship, though the implications of these relationship-based issues are not always the same in clinical and educational settings.

Fitness for the Educator Role

What endows one to be an educator? What do you expect of those whose job it is to lead others toward new levels of self and professional understanding, particularly in the mental health fields? These questions can be answered in a variety of ways, based upon where one's philosophical ideas about teaching and learning are grounded. In the counseling field, educators are often expected to balance a competent grasp of content matter with clinical skills and sensitivity to the personal growth of their students.

Counselor educators who seek to live out their role professionally and competently are expected to have an understanding of basic counseling issues and techniques, a sense of their own identity as a professional counselor, and an appreciation for ethical issues and issues of culture in counseling (ACA, 2005, F.6.b). In a sense, these are the personal responsibilities of each educator—the ones that they meet with individual study, research, and investment of time into learning about course content and advances within the field. When presenting information to students, educators aim to do so in a nonbiased way and with recognition of their own values related to the topic under study. Moreover, counselor educators are especially diligent and careful about how (or if) they introduce students to counseling techniques or methods that do not have evidence-based effectiveness and are up front with students about the lack of empirical backing for such techniques (see Standard F.6.f). Out of concern for the welfare of clients, the ACA *Code of Ethics* (2005) encourages practitioners to be wary about buying into methods of treatment that have not been thoroughly examined through research. Indeed, clients may be exposed to unnecessary harm when they are directed by a counselor toward activities that have little or no therapeutic value or that put human dignity and well-being second to unexamined biases upon which a quasi-technique may be built. Educators help their students to critically evaluate techniques and to choose those that are shown to be the most effective.

To perform one's duties as educator well, it is also necessary to step back and see the big picture of counselor training from a bird's-eye view. Educators who are dedicated to the integrity of the training experience help to orient their students to the major developmental experiences and landmarks on their training journey (ACA, 2005, F.7.a), which means they have a sense of how their program works and how it is designed to best meet the needs of students. Many counseling programs offer a formal orientation program to students which is meant to, among other things, introduce students to the faculty's expectations of them and the mission of the program, as well as to answer students' questions.

The somewhat personal nature of the professional development process of counselor trainees makes the skill set required of counselor educators unique among those of educators in other disciplines. Counselor educators have an obligation to recognize that students may, at times, be traversing the road toward personal wellness in certain areas of their life while concurrently attempting to complete graduate training in counseling. While the dual personal and professional growth processes are not typically of issue in graduate programs outside of the helping professions, they are meaningful in counseling programs where educators have the gatekeeping duty to assess students' well-being and readiness for the clinical (i.e., practicum and internship) portions of training and, eventually, for independent practice. Gatekeeping and continuous evaluation of student readiness for clinical practice is a necessary part of counselor educators' professional duties, though educators might, at times, find it difficult to assume this obligation. Welfel (2010) noted various factors that might prevent educators from fairly assessing students' professional development when it is substandard. First, professors who are untenured may fear receiving a negative course evaluation from a student who is in need of a remedial plan or who is likely not to pass a course. These professors may not give a failing grade or withhold implementing a needed remediation plan in order to protect their chances for tenure. Welfel also pointed out that some professors may be remiss in their gatekeeping duty out of an overly optimistic outlook on a student's potential for growth. Such educators may inappropriately give students the benefit of the doubt that they will develop the professionalism or skill level needed of counselors, or they may hope that students struggling to address their own lingering mental health issues will learn to manage those issues in due course. Finally, she suggested that the fear of litigation brought on by students who are dismissed from a program can prevent some professors from acting responsibly on their gatekeeping duty, and by extension, place the public at risk if they seek services from an impaired student who seems likely to become an impaired practitioner.

Relationship-Related Isssues

One of the most often written about ethical issues for counselor educators and their students revolves around boundaries and multiple relationships (Downs, 2003; Kolbert, Morgan, & Brendel, 2002). The sensitivity that counselors have toward managing multiple relationships with clients parallels the sensitivity educators must bring to handling multiple relationships with students (Baird, 1996). Indeed, at the crux of boundary issues in both educational and clinical settings is the power differential that exists between students and clients and their educators and therapists. Like clinicians, educators are seen as having the balance of power tipping in their favor and, therefore, they have a greater responsibility to exercise care and caution when navigating multiple roles with their students. Some of the indicators that educators are in a more powerful position than students are: (a) educators have the responsibility of evaluating students and assigning grades, (b) students are seeking the services of faculty and their programs to train them as counselors (Kolbert et al., 2002), and (c) there is prestige associated with the professor role that is not typically associated with the student role (Kitchener, 1988). Other factors also underline the fact that power is more explicitly granted to educators, such as the fact that they determine who is accepted into a program, and, often, they incorporate assignments into their courses that invite self-revelation from students that they themselves are not expected to reciprocate.

Given the power differential between educators and students, and the potential harm that might come to students if the professional boundaries between themselves and professors are not upheld, avoiding multiple nonprofessional relationships is the standard of best practice. The *Code of Ethics* (ACA, 2005, F.10.a) obliges educators not to form sexual relationships with students and to avoid interactions that can "compromise the training experience or grades assigned" (F.10.d). Even so, there is plenty of literature to suggest that the recommendation for counselor educators and, in a related field, psychologists, not to become sexually involved with students is sometimes overlooked (Barnett & Queen, 2000; Glaser & Thorpe, 1986). Kress and Dixon (2007) proposed recommendations for helping professors move through the decision-making process about being involved in relationships with current or even former students due to the lack of literature providing guidance in this area. They outlined various questions educators can use in self-reflection and advocated for enhanced ethics training for professors, more well-defined department policies, and the application of virtue ethics to relationship-related dilemmas.

Although the *Code of Ethics* (2005) provides a clear statement about sexual relationships between professors and students, it leaves room open for discernment related to the formation of other types of relationships between teachers and students. In counselor education (as with other types of graduate programs), professors often are expected to fulfill multiple roles with students as part of their professional role and in service to their programs. Professors might be teachers, supervisors, academic advisors, and advisors of student clubs for the trainees in their programs. In addition, they might be involved in professional mentoring activities, such as working collaboratively with students on professional presentations or publications (especially at the doctoral level). In this regard, the variety of multiple relationships that might exist between educators and students is greater than that which usually exists between therapists and their clients. Many authors (e.g., Welfel, 2010) point out that having multiple relationships with students that are aimed at professional development is often a benefit to students, and when the relationships are clearly aimed at a student's professional development, they usually are not seen as unethical. At the same time, boundary violations are one of the most recurrent causes not only of clients' complaints against service providers, but also of students' and supervisees' complaints against faculty and supervisors (Pope & Vasquez, 2007). Kolbert et al. (2002) found in their research that students and professors do not always have the same interpretation of what constitutes a helpful, professional interaction outside of the classroom setting and that students tended to have a narrower view of permissible, additional relationships than do professors. Their findings suggest that educators use caution, care, and self-reflection when considering when and in what ways to interact with students outside of the academic setting.

Landmark 5

POINT OF REFLECTION

Consider the following situations. Which of these, in your estimation, constitutes a potentially unethical situation and why?

1. Dr. Evans teaches in a master's-level graduate program. She is fairly new to the university, which is located in a small, rural town and has not yet made many social contacts. While shopping one day, she runs into a couple of her students who invite her to join them for lunch. Feeling a bit lonely, Dr. Evans decides to go.

(continued)

2. Dr. Williamson teaches a course in grief and loss counseling, and during the course of the class, he and the students develop what they believe is an innovative way of doing grief counseling from a spiritual point of view. Dr. Williamson uses the student papers to put together a poster presentation for a conference. He lists his name as the only author on the presentation.
3. Dr. Wong runs a part-time private practice in addition to teaching at the university. He is in need of another counselor to help with his growing clientele. A doctoral student in the counseling program has the experience Dr. Wong is looking for and expresses her interest in working for him. Though they are not currently in a professor–student relationship, Dr. Wong anticipates having this student in at least one class within the next year.

PERSONAL ETHICS IN COUNSELING PRACTICE, RESEARCH, AND EDUCATION

Counselors have ethical codes to guide them through the dilemmas that can arise with common clinical practices, such as diagnosing and assessing clients, and also when conducting research and teaching. Yet, counselors also need to have a solid personal ethical foundation that helps them know how to enact professional guidelines. As you continue to study the codes more closely, we invite you to take time also to reflect on how these professional guidelines interact with and are informed by your own moral standards. This means that it is important to know how your philosophical approach to ethics helps you to reason through ethical quandaries. Is your approach to ethics influenced most by projecting the outcomes (consequences) of an act and doing what produces the most happiness? Is it grounded in a sense of duty and obligation to what you see as a moral imperative? Or, is it based in the daily practice of living out the values and virtues that characterize upstanding counselors, researchers, and educators? We invite you to be steadfast in forging your personal convictions around ethics, keeping in mind the worth and dignity of each person you will encounter. As Immanuel Kant, one of the foremost authorities on early philosophical thought, exhorts us, "Act in such a way that you always treat humanity, whether in your own person or in the person of any other, never simply as a means, but always at the same time as an end." Our look at the history of research ethics, in particular, is an excellent example of our needing never to lose sight of the dignity of the persons whom we serve, especially when working through dilemmas that arise in clinical, research, or academic settings.

SIGNPOSTS FOR FUTURE TREKS

There is little doubt that you will one day be involved in the tasks of diagnosing clients and using assessments, tests, and inventories. This chapter was meant to help you begin to think about what it means to engage in these practices in as ethical a way as possible. More importantly, we wanted to invite you to think about *how* you engage these practices, what your own ethical leanings teach you about client care with regard to diagnosing and using assessments, and how your philosophical understanding of the human person is interwoven in your critical analysis of diagnosis. We also aimed to introduce some common ethical issues related to nonclinical roles that counselors take as researchers and educators. Points to keep in mind for further reflection include:

- *DSM*-based diagnosis is largely a medical-model approach to diagnosis; it is not necessarily the only diagnostic system counselors use (e.g., others include relationship-based and narrative approaches)
- *DSM*-based diagnosis has practical advantages for clinicians and clients, but it also has numerous drawbacks
- Ethical assessment practices involve counselors in having baseline knowledge about psychometrics and supervised training
- Cultural biases have the potential to skew one's interpretation of assessment results and cultural limitations of a test should be evaluated before using it with minority clients
- Best practices suggest that test scores should not be the only measure of a client's functioning or abilities
- Research ethics emphasize participants' rights, including informed consent, voluntary participation, and confidentiality
- Educators keep in mind the welfare of students' academic and professional growth when making decisions related to evaluating students and entering into multiple relationships with them

INSIGHTS GAINED FROM THE JOURNEY

In this chapter, we reviewed a broad array of topics, from diagnosis and assessment to research and counselor education. We could easily identify several ethical quandaries that we have faced related to each of these areas. We would like, however, to briefly mention our work in the area of research and how ethical issues can arise in practice. Part of our reasoning for giving a personal account of an ethical issue related to research is that it might be an area of practice about which you have not considered being involved. Thinking of oneself as a researcher can be overwhelming and daunting, but we believe that most clinicians have the abilities to advance the profession and good client care through research. If you have not entertained the idea of being a counselor-researcher, we hope you might seriously give thought to this role.

One of the lessons that I (C. J.) have taken from doing research is the importance of integrating virtues into the planning and implementation of a research investigation. A few years ago, a colleague and I conducted two studies in his country of origin (not the United States). Although it seemed likely that many of the participants would speak English, it was not a first language for any of them. This led my colleague and me to discuss how we would work through the informed consent process with potential participants. In an effort to make sure participants fully understood what we were asking of them and had the chance to freely choose to participate or not, as well as to ask questions, we decided that it would be best for my colleague (who spoke the native language of the participants) to lead the consent process. As the study began, we also discussed together our observation that some participants were clearly more comfortable answering our research questions in their own language rather than in English. We decided early on in these studies that we would also tell participants to use that language they felt most comfortable with. Although this account is not necessarily an example of a daunting ethical quandary, it is an example of how integrating virtues into research inquiries is important. Bringing virtues to bear on research (and clinical) practice means that every decision one makes has some importance and forms a person on the way of becoming a more virtuous or less virtuous researcher. In making decisions about language use in informed consent and in the study itself, my colleague and I wanted to ensure that participants felt comfortable with us as researchers, knew exactly what they were agreeing to be a part of, had the ability to be clear in their communications to us about the research questions, and did not feel as if they were just being used in order for us to complete a study that we saw as important. Creating an atmosphere in which participants could relate to us in a genuine way was important to us. Reflecting back on this aspect of these research studies, I realize that the decisions my colleague and I made marked our overall professional development, and they were occasions for us to determine the kinds of persons and researchers we want to be: persons who respect those who are willing to be a part of an investigation, persons who aim to do no harm to participants, and persons who want to show care and interest in those who help to advance our counseling profession.

MOVING FORWARD: CASE STUDY AND REFLECTION QUESTIONS

Keisha, a professional school counselor in a large urban high school, has been hearing talk that ethnic minority students in her school are disciplined at a higher rate and more severely than Caucasian students. She herself is extremely alarmed that this could be the case and decides to make a thorough review and analysis of disciplinary records and survey students and parents about their perceptions of how disciplinary action is determined. After receiving permission from the school district to review the records and to send out her survey, Keisha randomly distributes the instrument to students throughout the high school via homeroom teachers who asked for volunteers to anonymously participate in the study. She also randomly selects parents to whom she will send the survey. About 30% of the surveys were returned, and they overwhelmingly indicated that minority students believed they were treated unfairly in the disciplinary process. When Keisha reviewed student records, however, she found that the Caucasian students and minority students were nearly always given the same disciplinary action for similar infractions. Keisha was surprised by the data, especially because she personally knew of many stories from students in which they seemed to have been treated with prejudice—teachers were quicker to react negatively to minority students' misbehavior than that of the White students. Personally, she believes that teachers and administrators need diversity training and that there is an injustice occurring with regard to how disciplinary action is approached. At the next school board meeting, Keisha is called on to talk about the results of her research.

REFLECTION QUESTIONS

- *Identify any potential ethical dilemma(s) facing Keisha.*
- *To whom is her primary obligation in this situation?*
- *How might Keisha's personal values influence her decision about how to present the findings of her research?*
- *Contemplate your own philosophical approach to ethics and the ACA codes, and develop a way the counselor can handle the situation.*

REFERENCES

American Counseling Association. (2005). *ACA code of ethics*. Alexandria, VA: Author.

American Psychiatric Association. (2000). *Diagnostic and statistical manual of mental disorders*. (4th ed., rev.). Washington, DC: Author.

Anastasi, A. (1992). What counselors should know about the use and interpretation of psychological tests. *Journal of Counseling and Development, 70*, 610–615.

Baird, B. N. (1996). *The internship, practicum, and field placement handbook: A guide for the helping professions*. Upper Saddle River, NJ: Prentice-Hall.

Barnett-Queen, T. (2000). Sexually oriented relationships between educators and students in mental-health education programs. *Journal of Mental Health Counseling, 22*, 68–84.

Campbell, T. W. (1999). Challenging the evidentiary reliability of DSM-IV. *American Journal of Forensic Psychology, 17*, 47–68.

Centers for Disease Control and Prevention. (2011). *U.S. Public Health Service Syphilis Study at Tuskegee*. Retrieved from: http://www.cdc.gov/tuskegee/timeline.htm.

Cohen, E. D., & Cohen, G. S. (1999). *The virtuous therapist: Ethical practice of counseling and psychotherapy*. Pacific Grove, CA: Brooks/Cole.

Corey, G., Corey, M. S., & Callanan, P. (2011). *Issues & ethics in the helping professions*. (8th ed.). Pacific Grove, CA: Thomson Brooks/Cole.

Dorre, A., & Kinnier, R. T. (2006). The ethics of bias in counselor terminology. *Counseling and Values, 51*, 66–80.

Dougherty, J. L. (2005). Ethics in case conceptualization and diagnosis: Incorporating the medical model into the developmental counseling tradition. *Counseling and Values, 49*, 132–140.

Downs, L. (2003). A preliminary survey of the relationship between counselor educators' ethics education and ensuing pedagogy and responses to attractions to counseling students. *Counseling and Values, 48*, 2–13.

Eriksen, K., & Kress, V. E. (2005). *Beyond the DSM story: Ethical quandaries, challenges, and best practices*. Thousand Oaks, CA: Sage Publications.

Glaser, R. D., & Thorpe, J. S. (1986). Unethical intimacy: A survey of sexual contact and advances between psychology educators and female graduate students. *American Psychologist, 41*, 43–51.

Heppner, P. P., Kivlighan, D. M., & Wampold, B. E. (2008). *Research design in counseling*. Belmont, CA: Thompson Brooks/Cole.

Hohenshil, T. H. (1993). Teaching the DSM-III-R in counselor education. *Counselor Education and Supervision, 32*, 267–275.

Ivey, A. E., & Ivey, M. B. (1998). Reframing DSM-IV: Positive strategies from developmental counseling and therapy. *Journal of Counseling & Development, 76*, 334–350.

Ivey, A. E., & Ivey, M. B. (1999). Toward a developmental and diagnostic and statistical manual: The validity of a contextual framework. *Journal of Counseling & Development, 77,* 484–491.

Kaplan, D. M., Kocet, M. M., Cottone, R. R., Glosoff, H. L., Miranti, J. G., & Moll. . .Tarvydas, V. M. (2009). New mandates and imperatives in the revised ACA code of ethics. *Journal of Counseling & Development, 87,* 241–256.

Kitchener, K. S. (1984). Intuition, critical evaluation and ethical principles: The foundation for ethical decisions in counseling psychology. *The Counseling Psychologist, 12,* 43–55.

Kitchener, K. S. (1988). Dual-role relationships: What makes them so problematic. *Journal of Counseling and Development, 67,* 217–221.

Kolbert, J. B., Morgan, B., & Brendel, J. M. (2002). Faculty and student perceptions of dual relationships within counselor education: A qualitative analysis. *Counselor Education & Supervision, 41,* 193–206.

Kress, V. E., & Dixon, A. (2007). Consensual faculty–student sexual relationships in counselor education: Recommendations for counselor educators' decision making. *Counselor Education & Supervision, 47,* 110–122.

Meara, N. M., Schmidt, L. D., & Day, J. D. (1996). Principles and virtues: A foundation for ethical decisions, policies, and character. *The Counseling Psychologist, 24,* 4–77.

National Commission for the Protection of Human Subjects of Biomedical and Behavioral Research. (1979). *The Belmont report: Ethical principles and guidelines for the protection of human subjects of research.* Washington, DC: U.S. Government Printing Office.

National Institutes of Health. (2004). *Guidelines for the conduct of research involving human subjects at the National Institutes of Health.* Retrieved from: http://ohsr.od.nih.gov/guidelines/GrayBooklet82404.pdf

National Research Act of 1974, Pub, L, No, 93-348 (1974).

Naugle, K. (2009). Counseling and testing: What counselors need to know about state laws on assessment and testing. *Measurement and Evaluation in Counseling and Development, 42,* 31–45.

Pope, K. S., & Vasquez, M. J. T. (2007). *Ethics in psychotherapy and counseling: A practical guide.* San Francisco, CA: Jossey-Bass.

Remley, T., & Herlihy, B. (2010). *Ethical, legal, and professional issues in counseling.* Upper Saddle River, NJ: Prentice-Hall.

Robinson, E. H., III, & Curry, J. R. (2008). Institutional review boards and professional counseling research. *Counseling and Values, 53,* 39–53.

Seligman, L. (1999). Twenty years of diagnosis and the DSM. *Journal of Mental Health Counseling, 21,* 229–239.

Skarbek, D. M., Henry, P., & Parish, P. A. (2006). The institutional review board (IRB): Another major ingredient of our alphabet soup. *Teaching Exceptional Children, 38,* 26–30.

Sue, D. W., & Sue, D. (2008). *Counseling the culturally diverse: Theory and practice.* Hoboken, NJ: John Wiley & Sons, Inc.

Vacc, N. A., Juhnke, G. A., & Nilsen, K. A. (2001). Community mental health service providers' codes of ethics and the standards for educational and psychological testing. *Journal of Counseling & Development, 79,* 217–224.

Welfel, E. R. (2010). *Ethics in counseling & psychotherapy: Standards, research, & emerging issues* (4th ed.). Belmont, CA: Thomson Brooks/Cole.

White, M., & Epston, D. (1999). *Narrative means to therapeutic ends.* New York: W. W. Norton & Company.

Zimmerman, J. F. (1997). The Belmont Report: An ethical framework for protecting research subjects. *The Monitor.* Retrieved from: http://www.impactcg.com/docs/BelmontReport.pdf

10

ETHICAL ISSUES IN CONDUCTING CLINICAL SUPERVISION

Stephanie Helsel

THE FORESEEN DESTINATION

After reading this chapter, students will aspire to:

- Recognize the difference between laws and ethics.
- Identify ethical codes related to supervision.
- Understand how to minimize the threat of possible litigation.
- Appreciate the additional precautions dictated by FERPA and HIPAA.
- Discover how to make an ethical decision utilizing a hermeneutic model.
- Learn from the personal testimony of the contributing author.
- Reflect upon his or her ethical journey as a supervisor.

GETTING ON THE ROAD

Once counselors have begun the field placement segment of their education, they have their first experience with clinical supervision. Reviewing the counseling process as it unfolds with an experienced clinician helps to sharpen relational, technical, and conceptual skills. As counselors become more experienced, supervision often becomes a collegial forum for sharing ideas and techniques with others who are in a similar phase of their professional development. This is a time for them to process their own experiences in relation to their clients and manage countertransference issues, values clashes, and other challenges to the therapeutic relationship.

As in counseling, there are several theoretical orientations that represent different ways of conceptualizing and pacing the supervision process. The Discrimination Model (Bernard & Goodyear, 2004), Interpersonal Process Recall (Kagan, Krathwohl, & Miller, 1963), and the Reflecting Team approach (Anderson, 1987) are examples of different ways of working, which focus on the development of unique skills. Despite the abundance of such models, the practice of undergoing specific training to learn to conduct supervision is relatively recent. In fact, it was not until 1989 that the AACD (the American Association of Counseling and Development, now known as the American Counseling Association, or ACA) adopted competency areas that included supervision (ACES, 1990). In the past, most supervisors did not receive training but, rather, were promoted to supervisory levels once they were considered to be experienced clinicians. The contemporary expectation is that supervisors will maintain basic competencies in much the same way that counselors are expected to maintain a current set of skills and knowledge. This has led to an increase in training programs; in 1998, the National Board of Certified Counselors (NBCC) created an Approved Clinical Supervisor certification, which requires continuing education, as well as adherence to specific ethical guidelines related to supervision practice (CCE website, n.d.). These trends point to an increase in professional and ethical expectations that supervisors will have training and competence upon the onset of engaging in this professional practice.

Given these expectations, this chapter is meant to introduce you, who may one day become a clinical supervisor, to ethical issues in supervision. The chapter will review specific ethical guidelines that shape up supervision practice, provide scenarios to illustrate best practices and common conundrums, and include a discussion on my own philosophical approach to ethical supervision. Possessing knowledge about the codes and laws that are relevant for supervision is only part of the responsibilities that supervisors carry; in order to be truly grounded in ethical practice and able to model such things for supervisees, supervisors must reflect on their own values and find a framework that mirrors these views.

EXPLORING THE TERRITORY

ETHICAL CODES RELATED TO SUPERVISION

The behavioral guidelines that direct supervisors can be found in the ACA *Code of Ethics* (2005), the National Approved Clinical Supervisor (ACS) *Code of Ethics* (2008), client and supervisee legal rights, and the particular regulations of the agency or school within which the supervisor is working. Supervision is considered to be a crucial element of ethical decision making, often protecting counselors from litigation (Thomas, 2010). Since supervisors bear the burden of responsibility, it is important that their practice be grounded in sound ethical practice. It can be helpful for counselors to understand how their supervisors think about their work and the ethical parameters within which they work in order to take full advantage of the rich learning process that characterizes good supervision. In the following sections, you will find a discussion on relevant ethical guidelines that frame best practices in supervision.

Qualifications and Training

You can expect to engage in many different activities with your supervisors, all of which have their own set of ethical guidelines. According to the Association for Counselor Education and Supervision (1990), clinical supervision "includes the supportive and educative activities ... designed to improve the application of counseling theory and technique directly to clients" (p. 59). Supervisors are expected to refrain from acting in this role until they have undergone training dedicated to clinical supervision. Training is defined as occurring within counselor education and supervision academic programs, through continuing education seminars, and attendance at relevant conferences. The expectation described within the context of program administration, and highlighted in the ACS ethical guidelines, is that supervisors will work within the parameters of their own training and experience (ACES guideline 3.02; ACS guideline 11). This requires supervisors to refrain from assisting supervisees in diagnostic or treatment activity when working with populations to which supervisors have not been exposed. Finally, supervisors are expected to engage in ongoing peer supervision, so that they are involved in a continuous process of learning and review (ACES guideline 3.03).

Client Welfare and Supervisee Support

Supervisors' primary obligation is to ensure that their supervisees' clients are receiving appropriate care. While you the counselor are providing the day-to-day care of your clients, it is your supervisor who is considered to be the ultimate protector of your clients' welfare, well-being, and rights. This role requires the supervisor to manage a number of different counselor activities that fall within the processes of informed consent and supervisee skill building.

Confidentiality and Consent: The Client

During the initial informed consent procedure, counselors must educate their clients about their status if they are interns, the fact that they receive supervision, and what exactly this entails. Your supervisor will want to make sure that you have educated your clients about how their cases will be discussed with others, how confidentiality of their personal material will be maintained, the limits to privileged communication, and the reasons why supervision is beneficial to their care. Clients must give written consent if they will be recorded or verbal consent if supervisors will be observing sessions. It is your job to ensure that written materials related to your clients' treatment, consent forms, and recordings are protected, with signifying information removed whenever possible. A clear plan for how such materials will be destroyed or, if appropriate, stored, should be in place and known to clients.

Often your clients will need you to discuss what exactly happens during supervision and how this benefits them. This requires you to be able to describe how supervisors can ensure client well-being through a close review of counselor interventions. Since supervisors are expected to maintain knowledge of how the counselors under their direction are establishing beneficial therapeutic relationships, setting goals, and meeting outcome expectations, they might assist struggling counselors by directing treatment activities, intervening in sessions, or directing care during crisis situations. Clients should be prepared in the event that a supervisor attends a session or is present during a crisis intervention. The whole purpose of informed consent is to ensure that there are no surprises for clients and they have a sense of how the entire process works.

Confidentiality and Consent: The Supervisee

Just as you set up expectations and explanations with your clients prior to starting your counseling work together, your supervisor should do the same with you. You should expect to discuss with your supervisors how often you will meet, how you will be evaluated, how goals will be set, and what supervision model or theory is used (ACES 2.08, 2.14; 3.07, 3.09). Prior to starting supervision you can benefit from having a clear understanding of how your supervisors work, when they are available, how the treatment you are giving your clients will be reviewed and evaluated, and what will happen in the case of an emergency, whether it is related to one of your clients or to a personal issue you are having (ACES 2.05). How your supervisors will protect the confidentiality of your evaluations and other personal information along with an explanation of all possible people who would have access to such material is also good information to have. Because the supervision relationship is hierarchical in nature and requires evaluation, you also might want to inquire to whom you can report concerns you might be having with your supervisor and what due process measures you can take should you experience a problem (ACS 13). Having this information before you delve into discussing client cases and concerns will enable you to avoid having to deal with the embarrassment or tension of informing your supervisor that you are taking action against them once a problem has already developed.

Landmark 1

PREPARING SUPERVISEES FOR CLINICAL PRACTICE

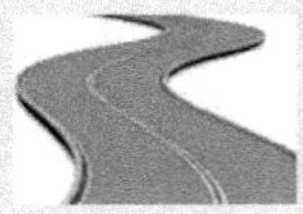

An intern begins his internship at a community mental health agency. He will be working under the daily tutelage of the primary substance abuse treatment group counselor. Upon starting at the agency, he wants to know about building security, location of fire exits, and the first-aid kit. He would also benefit from having the chain of command clearly delineated should he encounter a crisis or emergency (such as a client arrives visibly under the influence of drugs or alcohol, police arrive and ask for one of the clients, an angry spouse calls and threatens to come to the agency, or a client expresses suicidal feelings). He asks his lead therapist for this information. He is given the building security phone number, shown where the fire-exit map is posed, and where the extinguisher and first-aid kits are located. He is told that he should first go to the lead therapist if he should encounter a problem, or to the clinical supervisor if the lead therapist is unavailable. He wonders later what he should do if he encounters a problem and neither his lead therapist nor his supervisor is around. Should he try to find another therapist? Is there another supervisor in his agency? Does his academic supervisor have any involvement in an on-site problem? These are common questions that usually do not come up until there is a problem and the intern has difficulty locating someone with more experience to help.

Supervision is thought to have the most favorable outcomes when it is collaborative in nature, allowing supervisees to have input into the structure of the process (McCarthy et al., 1995). Therefore, an effective supervisory informed consent procedure allows supervisees to ask questions and discuss preferences for meeting times and frequency, topics of interest, and the roles and expectations of both parties (Thomas, 2010). Disclosure statements can provide an overview of many of these details and can serve as a springboard for discussion and negotiation. Thomas suggested that prior to a formal informed consent process, supervisors take care to obtain work samples from supervisees in order to inform requirements regarding frequency of meetings, expectations of the amount of work required by either person, and cost of supervision. Perhaps one of the most important reasons for maintaining a structured, collaborative, and comprehensive informed consent procedure that includes both formal documentation and discussion is to model for counselors how such a process can help foster a productive working relationship.

Landmark 2

SAMPLE SUPERVISION DISCLOSURE STATEMENT

Jane Smith is a private practice therapist and supervisor as well as a faculty member at Pretend University in the Counseling Psychology Department. She received her doctorate of Philosophy in Counselor Education and an MSEd in Community Counseling from Fake University. Dr. Smith is a National Certified Counselor and holds a counseling license for the state of Louisiana. She is a member of the American Counseling Association as well as the national and state divisions of counselor education and supervision. She carries the Approved Clinical Supervisor credential offered by the national counseling credentialing body NBCC.

The areas in which Dr. Smith provides supervision reflects her training and experience. She is a graduate of the Gestalt Institute of Cleveland and continues to seek training in Gestalt theory and practice. Her work experience is varied and includes employee assistance, substance abuse, and private counseling, addressing issues ranging from life-stage transitions, relational difficulties, anxiety, depression, and sexual orientation issues, as well as stress and anger management. Her clients range in age from early adolescence to late adulthood.

Dr. Smith received supervision training through coursework and supervised supervision practicum and internships in her doctoral program. She continually seeks out additional opportunities to grow as a supervisor, through national and regional conference presentations and continuing education credit courses. She also seeks her own supervision in order to obtain expanded perspectives and learn from others in the field. Jane has experience providing individual and group supervision of master's-level counseling students working in the field and following community, school, and marriage

(*continued*)

and family tracks. She also provides supervision in the form of educational consultations to doctoral students and other counselors wishing to concentrate on their Gestalt counseling orientation.

The constructivist approach Dr. Smith applies to her supervision work allows the supervisor to engage with the supervisee as an individual, taking into account the unique experience, place of employment, and culture of the counselor. Within this framework, the supervisor acts as a facilitator in the process of meaning making, using methods such as hypothesis development and testing, the application of higher-order thinking, and the use of reflective practices. The supervision process is therefore one where knowledge is coconstructed by the supervisee and supervisor and the process is tailored to meet each supervisee's individual needs.

In keeping with the collaborative learning approach used by Dr. Smith, she solicits as well as provides evaluation of distinct skill sets related to supervising and counseling, respectively. This is done both verbally at the beginning, middle, and end of the supervisory experience and in a structured format that reflects the Council for Accreditation of Counseling and Related Education Programs' (CACREP) standards for competence. When supervising in academic settings, Jane uses written evaluation to provide feedback and track progress at the middle and end of the semester. Supervisees are asked to evaluate themselves as well as provide written feedback on their supervision experience.

Dr. Smith takes care to model appropriate informed consent for her supervisees by initially establishing a clear understanding of the supervision process with her supervisees and reviewing with them their client education process. The limits of confidentiality in the supervisory context are outlined, such as when there is evidence of the client being in danger of hurting himself or another person, when there is suspicion of abuse of children, elderly, or disabled people in the client's care, or if the supervisor is required to testify during legal proceedings. Supervisees are required to inform their clients of their own supervision process and obtain releases from them when necessary. When providing supervision within an academic setting, confidentiality may be broken if it becomes evident that the supervisee's competence is insufficient to provide care to clients. Counselor impairment necessitates the supervisor's compliance with program procedure, which includes other faculty members. If Jane obtains supervision herself, her supervisees are notified that their experiences may be reviewed within this context. Dr. Smith carries liability insurance and encourages her supervisees to carry insurance as well, whether or not they are students.

Dr. Smith's fee schedule is as follows: there is no charge for supervision provided within an academic setting. When providing individual supervision in a private setting, the $___ per 50-minute session fee reflects professional standards. When providing educational consultations to doctoral students, the fee is $___ per 50-minute session.

(*continued*)

Supervisees are provided with a clear set of instructions to follow should they encounter a problem or difficulty at their place of work. Depending on the setting, this may include the contact information of their site supervisors, Dr. Smith, and their faculty advisors. In addition to providing supervisees with local crisis intervention services and their phone numbers, Dr. Smith offers cell phone availability to her supervisees, which can be used at any time.

Dr. Smith's professional supervision practices are in compliance with the codes of ethics established for counselors and supervisors by the NBCC and the ACA.

Supervisee Remediation and Gatekeeping

Supervisors are expected to rely on observation and recordings, along with the review of case notes and postsession discussion when determining quality of care being provided to clients (ACES 2.06, 3.09). Sometimes the best way your supervisor can support your development as a counselor is to provide remedial assistance and engage in gatekeeping activities (ACES 2.12; ACS 8, 10). Supervisors are expected to endorse only those clinicians who are skilled and able to provide appropriate services while adhering to ethical and legal guidelines and standards of care. Prior to failing to endorse or employ a counselor under their care, it is expected that supervisors will first provide supervisees with extra instruction should their skills be substandard and make efforts to keep the supervisee informed as to his or her status and progress. As a supervisee, you have the right to know in advance if your performance is falling shy of your agency or program's standards, and to be given a chance to improve before any other action is taken. This does not need to be punitive and, in fact, can be an enriching experience. The key is having a clear understanding that is put in writing, so you and your supervisor know what to expect.

Landmark 3

CASE EXAMPLE

A counselor was hired by a residential treatment facility that provides care for adjudicated adolescents. Despite having an internship at a similar facility, within 6 months it becomes apparent that while she performs well with the males, her relationships with the females at the facility are marked by contention and dramatic discord. She complains often of their resistance to counseling and her frustration with them. The supervisor meets with the counselor and shows her the difference in her performance evaluations as they relate to the two populations. She asks the counselor for input on how she could become more comfortable and adept at working with females. Together, they create a plan for the counselor to shadow a more experienced therapist

(*continued*)

and to colead the weekly female anger management group with this therapist. The counselor will also bring in one recorded individual session per week for detailed review with the supervisor, which will include an exploration of relevant multicultural issues. During the supervision discussion, the counselor discloses that she always had an acrimonious relationship with her sister. The supervisor suggests she begin her own counseling process to examine potential countertransference issues. The remediation plan is put in writing and signed by both parties, with a plan for the counselor's performance to be evaluated in 3 months. This is kept as a confidential document in the counselor's employment file.

Gatekeeping, or disallowing novice counselors to fully enter the field, is a controversial activity that is supported by the ACA *Code of Ethics* (2005, F5.b) as a standard of practice for counselor educators and supervisors. While models have been created for how to assist counselors in need (Frame & Stevens-Smith, 1995; Lumadue & Duffey, 1999; Wilkerson, 2006), there is no set standard of practice for remedial procedures. In general, ethical codes guide supervisors to be clear regarding all steps in a remediation process: Evaluations of student performance, feedback given to the counselor, expectations of improved competence and how that will be measured, the remediation plan, and any subsequent action taken. Documentation of all efforts, including evidence of consultation with colleagues, is also a necessary requirement.

Documentation

Regardless of whether or not supervisees are in need of remedial plans or extra instruction, it is important that supervisors maintain records of supervision meetings, issues raised, and actions taken, and can document the progress made by supervisees as well as their clients (ACS 4). Falvey and Cohen (2003) call documentation "a standard of competent supervisory practice" that aids in organizing supervision sessions, ensuring quality care for clients, building counselor skills, and "providing risk management" for the supervisor (p. 63). Maintaining evaluative, educative, and treatment-related records can be useful in the event of legal action brought against the supervisor and can aid in the supervisor's learning and growth.

There are a variety of existing supervision documentation systems, such as Focused Risk Management (Falvey & Cohen, 2003) and Case Review (Glenn & Serovich, 1994), which allow supervisors to highlight specific aspects of sessions. In general, there are four aspects of supervision that should be included regardless of system used: client status, interventions carried out by the counselor and their relationship to established treatment plans, progress made by the client, and guidance or discussion facilitated by the supervisor. Counselor reactions to the client, perceptions of the client and/or therapeutic relationship, supervisor perceptions of the client, treatment process, and/or counselor can all be included as well for a rich understanding of the care a client is receiving and the learning process of the supervisee.

Landmark 4

Supervisee: John Smith **Client ID:** Charles Q

Date: March 11, 2011

Session #: 6 **Recording #:** 4

Updated Case Information: Client no longer living with parents and is now in an apartment he shares with one male who is also a college student. Client still working part time and attending school; last week conflict with mother (via telephone) has not been resolved—no contact since argument. No increase in depression symptoms (feelings of hopelessness, anhedonia, amotivation, mild acedia).

Interventions and Client Progress: Client has responded to experiential exercises designed to evoke emotional response—client has been able to express feelings of anger toward parents for emotional neglect and has expressed grief over loss of romantic relationship (occurred 6 months prior to start of treatment); client reported a reduction in depression symptoms that correlated with emotional expression in session.

Supervisee Concerns: John reported feeling unsure of how to build on the success of the experiential activities and would like to move the client toward learning to process emotions independently.

Discussion Topics: Review of experiential exercise interventions; utility of exploring potentially maladaptive cognitions related to emotional expression; supervisee hesitancy in taking an educating role to help client understand nature and usefulness of emotional expression.

Treatment Recommendations: Create a psychoeducation module on emotional identification and expression that includes how to allow emotions to enter into awareness and how to choose a healthy way to express them; follow up with client to ensure he is keeping his regular appointments with the psychiatrist; think about building exercises toward using the empty chair technique to express anger toward mother.

Referrals: None at this time

Observations and Interpretations: John expresses a lack of confidence in stepping into the role of educator despite having experience with the topic his client is exploring. I want to follow up with him after his first attempt at providing psychoeducation and allow him to process his expectations of himself and if they were realistic.

Training Recommendations: Review EFT materials as well as the full steps involved in doing the empty chair technique; review CBT materials (thought/mood record) to see if it might be useful

Supervisor's Experience of Session: John is making progress with his client as evidenced by the decrease in depression symptoms. He is learning how to incorporate psychoeducation in with therapeutic sessions.

Helsel, S. (2011), adapted from Falvey, Caldwell & Cohen (2001) FoRMSS record.

The documentation your supervisors maintain should be designed to reflect, in a clear and concise way, that they are aware of the diagnoses, symptoms, and progress of all of your clients. If any crises or problems arise, these should be described and any action taken should be detailed according to the time and date at which it occurred. Collateral documentation should be added in order to provide a complete picture of what transpired and who was involved in the resolution of the event or situation. The burden you may feel when trying to keep up with your progress notes and other chart paperwork is often similar to what supervisors struggle with while attempting to document the client care that all their supervisees are providing, taking care to capture their supervisees' professional progress and all activities related to client treatment.

Evaluation

Supervision is a complex process that is instructive, protective, and evaluative in nature. Because supervisors have administrative as well as managerial roles and must oversee client care, it is necessary to give supervisees an idea of their status in terms of skill development, delivery of client care, and the ability to reflect on their own experience while working with clients. In order to be in compliance with the ethical codes related to feedback, supervisors must have an "established evaluation plan" (ACS 7, p. 1), and in academic settings, supervisees must have the chance to meet individually to review their progress (ACES 3.11).

Supervisors are charged with setting and maintaining the standard of professional conduct. In order to do so, they must have the ability to track counselor treatment efficacy and account for all of their participation in client welfare and care. There are no guidelines within the relevant ethical codes for how exactly supervisees' competence should be evaluated, and supervisors will have to align their practices with the institution or agency where they work. The ACA *Code of Ethics* supports "ongoing" and "periodically formal" evaluations (2005, F5.a, p. 14), while the ACS guideline requires supervisors to provide "timely feedback" to supervisees (ACS 7, p. 1).

This is where the original informed consent process you underwent with your supervisor becomes useful. You should have already seen the forms your supervisors will use to evaluate you, the dimensions along which you will be assessed, and how those manifest in concrete behavioral terms (Thomas, 2010). You should be made aware of the frequency of informal and formal evaluations and you should receive feedback regularly. Evaluation is extremely important, as this can provide further risk management for supervisors and for supervisees should a dispute develop related to performance or client treatment.

Dual Relationships

ACES guidelines 2.09 through 2.11 and ACS guideline 5 are dedicated to the sometimes tricky issue of dual relationships. The foundation for navigating such relationships is grounded in the ACA *Code of Ethics* (2005), where several limitations are placed on counselors with regard to their clients. Supervisors are expected to follow similar parameters. As with any counseling relationship, sexual and/or romantic contact with supervisees is nonnegotiable and strictly prohibited. Unlike the ACA guidelines, those pertaining to supervision do not provide instruction for how supervisors should manage relationships with former supervisees who no longer receive administrative or clinical supervision. However, it is expected that supervisors will refrain from engaging in social activities that might facilitate contact with supervisees if such contact would compromise the nature of the supervisory relationship with its inherent power differential.

Supervisors often find it necessary to maintain more than one kind of relationship with those they supervise, such as those working in an academic environment, or those with administrative and clinical supervising responsibilities. If this is the case, the guidelines require that supervisees be made aware of expectations regarding each specific role they may have (i.e., student vs. supervisee) and the supervisor may have (monitoring case load vs. professional development). The primary measure for establishing the appropriateness of different relationships is whether or not engaging in the relationship might impact on the supervisor's ability to remain unbiased, wield professional judgment, and maintain objectivity (ACES 2.09, 2.10; ACS 5). When supervisors are unsure as to the ethical dimensions of a particular dual relationship, consultation with trusted colleagues can help provide perspective and guidance (Thomas, 2010, p. 122).

Cross-Cultural Supervision

Since the early 1980s, there has been an increase in focus on the importance of counselor competence when working with clients from diverse cultural and ethnic backgrounds. Despite the emergence of multicultural counseling training courses in most counselor education programs, it is often not until supervision that counselors can gain experiential knowledge of how to navigate cross-cultural differences effectively. Addressing cultural issues in supervision can help supervisees develop awareness of their own culturally influenced beliefs, values, and biases along with how traditional counseling theories may not always be applicable to certain populations (Ancis & Marshall, 2010). Supervision that allows supervisees to explore the intersection of their identities, their supervisors' ethnic and cultural identities, and the cultural elements represented in the populations they serve is an important way to address ethical requirements in competent practice (ACS 13, ACA F.11c).

According to Borders and Brown (2005), empirical evidence supports the importance of bringing up diversity issues as early as the first supervision session in order to communicate openness and respect for the influence such elements can have on both the counseling and the supervision process. Starting with disclosing their own cultural background, values, and possible bias, supervisors can generate discussion geared toward conveying acceptance of supervisee cultural differences and in doing so, create a safe environment where supervisees feel able to ask potentially awkward or "politically incorrect" questions. Honesty and a willingness to facilitate discussion can help supervisees make connections between conceptualizing client problems and their cultural perspectives. In turn, this can help counselors work with clients' feelings toward their counselors, the impact of oppression, racism, sexism, and other institutional and social influences on their presenting problems, and decrease the possibility of counselor stereotyping (Ancis & Marshall, 2010).

Being proactive in broaching cultural differences in supervision can also help to strengthen the supervisory relationship. Ratings of supervisee satisfaction have shown that their perceptions of the efficacy of their working alliances with supervisors often was influenced by the degree to which supervisors addressed cultural issues, and especially cross-cultural issues that were present between themselves and their supervisees (Duan & Roehlke, 2001; Gatmon et al., 2001). There is no one way to broach such topics; supervisors must use their own judgment for how much to disclose about their background, when to bring diversity issues into the session, and how to invite supervisees to add to the discussion (Borders & Brown, 2005).

It is not always easy to have a direct discussion on your own values, beliefs, and life experience as a result of your ethnic background, gender, sexual orientation, or other cultural characteristics. That is why it is so useful to have supervisors initiate the conversation and model for you how to discuss this with them. You can take that experience back to your own counseling work and practice being open and comfortable with discussing the cultural elements that might be relevant in your own counseling work. However, if your supervisor fails to bring cultural topics up in conversation, it is entirely appropriate for you to do so, or to request that this be built into your supervision in some way. The following landmarks provide two examples of how this could play out in a supervision session.

Landmark 5

CASE EXAMPLE

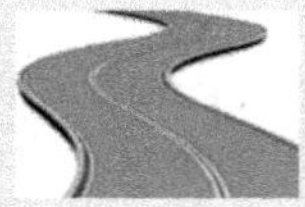

A supervisor in private practice is meeting with a potential supervisee who is working toward licensure and needs to augment the supervision he is receiving at his place of employment. The supervisor is a woman of Hispanic ethnicity, in her late 50s. The supervisee is in his mid-20s and is Caucasian in appearance. During the first session, the supervisor asks, "How do you feel it will be to work with me, as it appears that we have different ethnicities and ages?" The supervisee expresses no reservations, and tells the supervisor about his ethnic background: Italian and Polish, identified with his Polish heritage to the greatest degree. The supervisor discloses that she is Hispanic and so has some different perspectives on issues related to power, privilege, and institutional discrimination. She asks, "Do you have any questions for me regarding what you have learned about me?" The supervisee asks several questions related to personal experiences she has had dealing with sexism or racism. The supervisor explains some of the barriers she has overcome in her education and professional development. She then finishes the discussion by telling the supervisee, "Cultural issues can play a big part of all counseling processes, so I will be asking you to discuss these with me when it seems relevant. I invite you to initiate discussions and ask questions whenever you feel like you could benefit from talking about these topics."

Would you feel comfortable bringing up questions or having a conversation about cultural issues? If not, what would you need in order to do so?

Landmark 6

CASE EXAMPLE

A Caucasian supervisee discusses a new client with her supervisor, a Caucasian man. She has recently had one session with an African American adolescent, whose parents report recent changes in his behavior—volatile, angry moods, poor grades, and headaches in the morning that keep him from going to school. She assessed the adolescent and also gave him the Becks Depression Inventory, on which he scored in the moderate range. The supervisee is formulating a treatment plan that is based on using cognitive behavioral therapy to address distorted thought patterns and their influence on mood. The supervisor asks her to consider the following questions: Have you considered the role of culture in the presenting problem?; What are some ways that it might be important here?; What do you need to assess before you can create an accurate treatment plan?; To what degree is this client, or his family, dealing with instances of racism or discrimination?; and How might that effect his mood?

The supervisee admits that she had not considered the role of culture or prejudice in her client's presenting problem. She determines that she needs to ask him to tell her more about his life at school and at home, and his family's life within their community. She engages in a role-play exercise with her supervisor for how to initiate this kind of conversation with the client. Upon their next meeting, she informs the supervisor that her client had been dealing with racially based teasing and exclusion at school and he did not feel capable of going to any teachers for help. The supervisee discusses ideas she has for anger management and assertiveness skill building and how she can process how her client might feel about working with a Caucasian therapist. She also discusses with the supervisor how she can empower her client to obtain assistance from his parents and/or school personnel in managing this problem.

Do you feel that it is appropriate for counselors to help clients with institutional-level discrimination? Is it different if the client is experiencing prejudice or other damaging reactions within a relational context? Why?

Due to the evaluative and hierarchical nature of the supervisory relationship, it can be difficult for supervisees to bring topics about which they feel uncomfortable or ignorant to supervision. Therefore, it is essential that supervisors work to create a safe environment where supervisees can bring their concerns. The onus is on supervisors to continue to monitor the multicultural competency of their counselors and infuse conversations related to assessment and testing, diagnoses, and rapport building with the ways in which ethnicity, gender, and sexual orientation (among other factors) may influence the therapeutic process.

LAWS RELEVANT TO SUPERVISORS

Knowing the difference between ethical codes and laws can be confusing. Generally, legal regulations maintain the most basic level of acceptable professional behavior, whereas ethical guidelines hold professionals to the highest standard of practice (Bernard & Goodyear, 2004). Claims can be brought to a regulatory body such as the ACA and to a court of law for investigation. Supervisors are at risk of losing their licenses and supervision credentials if a professional organization finds them negligent. If harm to a client or a supervisee can be proven to have resulted from negligent behavior, legal consequences can result as well. However, these actions occur independently from one another.

First, understanding the difference between statutes and laws can be useful when investigating legal parameters of practice. Laws become written after starting as bills that are presented to state or federal Houses of Representatives and Senates. If passed, they become laws. The different provisions of the law are referred to as statutes. Statutes are also referred to as legislation, and these are what dictate specific behaviors (USLegal.com). Civil law is based upon written laws. Most of the laws related to the practice of counseling resulted from civil suits brought against psychologists and therapists, such as the infamous *Tarasoff vs. the Regents of the University of California* case that led to the duty to warn obligations.

Supervisors shoulder the burden of liability both for their own competence and vicariously the competence of the counselors they supervise (known as *respondant superior*). Therefore, it is helpful for supervisors to understand the difference between laws and ethical guidelines, and how to protect themselves from potential legal action. Since state laws can differ, it is important for supervisors to become acquainted with those specific to where they practice. In order to get a quick overview of a specific state's legal standards of conduct, consult the licensure codes, which are found online through state government websites. There, descriptions of expected behavior related to confidentiality, dual relationships, research, payment for services, and even advertising are listed. In addition to state laws, federal laws designed to protect the confidentiality of educational and medical records will take precedence over state laws except in cases where the state law is more stringent (Holloway, 2003). Compliance requires careful education and documentation which can be confusing and time consuming. Through supervisor modeling, supervisees will learn the complex practices that are necessary to meet such standards. It can be helpful for counselors to understand the legal regulations associated with supervision so that they can distinguish between ethical expectations and basic legal standards of practice. It can also help to provide an understanding of safe, legal supervision practice. To that end, legal terms related to supervision are defined below, along with explanations of their importance to supervisors and counselors who are supervised. Specific information related to confidentiality laws will also be provided, since it is such an essential client and supervisee right.

Competence

As mentioned earlier, supervisors are only allowed to supervise counselors who are treating populations or problems with which they have experience. More recently, it has become expected that supervisors will obtain training specific to their duties as supervisors rather than only in clinical issues. Failing to do so could result in charges (ethical or legal) relating to competence. It is also possible for supervisors to be reprimanded for failing to practice multiculturally competent supervision. This could manifest as making negative remarks related to the gender, ethnicity, age, or sexual orientation of a supervisee, or failing to protect clients from discriminatory behavior on the part of counselors under their care (Corey, Corey, & Callanan, 2007). If supervisors are thought to have been negligent in carrying out their professional duties (such as failing to evaluate a supervisee they terminate) or to have engaged in misconduct (such as sexual harassment), they can be sued for malpractice in addition to having ethical charges brought to their professional regulating body. State licensure codes regulate the number of continuing education requirements for clinical practice, but unless supervisors obtain related credentials (such as approved clinical supervisor) or have training requirements at their places of employment, there are no codes related specifically to ongoing supervision education.

Confidentiality

All records related to client care and the supervision process are expected to be protected and their access limited to those whose professional duties require it. The concept of privileged communication is relevant for counselors and supervisors, depending upon the situation. For example, client progress notes written by the counselor are legally considered to be the property of the client. In order for the court to have access to such records, the client must assert his or her privilege and give permission for them to be shared. Often it is up to the counselor to help clients and legal representatives understand the potential consequences of relinquishing protection, but if subpoenaed the counselor does not have the right to share such records (Remley & Herlihy, 2001).

In a supervisory context, if a supervisee brings legal action against a supervisor, evaluations and other sensitive materials generated during the supervision process are considered to belong to the supervisee. If called to share them in court, the supervisor would not be able to do so until the supervisee asserted his or her privilege to release the documents. Supervisors should keep in mind that despite the fact that most records they generate are confidential and the chance that others might read them is minimal, they should be assiduously maintained in the event that they could be required to provide legal protection.

Duty to Warn and Protect

As part of the informed consent process, this is perhaps the most important in terms of giving clients a chance to make a conscious choice about what they want to disclose. It can also provide you with guidance on how to react should a client admit that they are feeling homicidal or suicidal. It is essential that clients know prior to any such disclosure what the consequences are for doing so. Supervisors will therefore pay particular attention to this regulation and it is helpful if you can document that you reviewed this with your clients. In general, it requires that you describe for clients the limits to the confidentiality that is the hallmark of the therapeutic relationship. In particular, if it is clear that the client or another person is in imminent danger, you must inform others who are in the position to provide care and protection. This could include the intended victim, the client's parents, or the police. You are also required to report to your local children, youth, and family services agency if there is suspicion that the client is a victim or perpetrator of sexual abuse, physical or emotional abuse, and/or neglect. In all such cases, you are expected to consult with your supervisors prior to reporting any suspicions of abuse or homicidal/suicidal behavior. In order to be protected from litigation, supervisors must document such instances in detailed form, providing clear explanations of how clients were assessed, what they communicated, and how the supervisor and counselor arrived at the decision to take action or to refrain from such action. Supervisors must also be knowledgeable about the emergency guidelines for such instances set forth by their agency or place of employment. It is also advisable for supervisors to consult with "administrative superiors" in such potentially litigious situations (Borders & Brown, 2005, p. 86) and document all such feedback and directives.

HIPAA and FERPA

The Health Insurance Portability and Accountability Act, known as HIPAA, was a landmark federal law developed by the Department of Health and Human Services in 1996 that was designed to standardize how patient records were protected and confidentiality was maintained. This includes the storing and transmitting of medical and health care records, claims for reimbursement, and all related paperwork. Anyone who submits electronic claims or uses billing services to do so must comply with HIPAA regulations. In February 2009, updated standards (known as ASC X12 version 5010) were adopted that address more specifically electronic transactions and storing of client records, with clarified rules for how client information should be recorded and interpreted (Upcoming Changes to HIPAA, 2010). Supervisors working in agency settings will have privacy officers who are responsible for translating the regulations into policies and practices. However, supervisors in private practice are required to maintain compliance themselves. There are several resources available to help private practitioners, such as Edward Zuckerman's (2006) *HIPAA Help: A Compliance Toolkit for Psychotherapists*, and Internet sites where updates can be tracked (see Internet resources available in Appendix B).

For supervisors working in academic settings, The Family Educational Rights and Privacy Act (FERPA) will dictate much of how supervisee records are handled. Once students turn 18, they gain control of their educational documentation, and records must not be shared with their parents unless a consent form is signed. Most of the regulations refer to how parents or students can access school records and the process for amending errors. However, FERPA regulations can apply to generating records documenting student progress, learning, or competency. This often relates to supervision activity in the form of letters of recommendation. In order to be fully compliant, instructors should ask students to provide written consent to release information to potential internship supervisors or employers.

Protecting Yourself as a Supervisor

There is no easy process for compiling all of a state's laws regarding mental health professionals. Continuing education programs that provide overviews of relevant laws and litigation are perhaps the most efficient way of obtaining a solid working knowledge of current statutes and how they affect clinical practice of all kinds. The following are specific practices that can help increase supervisor protection from accusations of negligence, ethical violations, or illegal behavior.

- Work within the confines of the ethical guidelines for counseling and for supervising put forth by relevant credentialing and professional bodies.
- Purchase additional liability insurance specifically related to supervision and education, known as adding a "consulting endorsement."
- Make sure to avoid working with supervisees who are treating populations about which you lack expertise.
- Put forth the initial effort of becoming educated about the exact crisis or emergency response guidelines for your place of employment, or review related literature to create such policies for your private practice. Make sure that these are part of your informed consent procedure. Require your supervisees to bring written explanations of the policies in place at their internship sites or workplace.
- As part of your initial supervision sessions, review how to evaluate dangerous and suicidal behavior.
- Seek supervision or consult with experienced colleagues whenever you face a complex or difficult situation, in order to share the burden of responsibility and ensure you are acting in an ethical and appropriate manner.

CONSTRUCTIVISM AND A HERMENEUTIC DECISION-MAKING MODEL

So far, ethical guidelines and laws relating to supervisory behavior have been reviewed. While laws tell you exactly what you can and cannot do, they only direct counselors and supervisors in a small number of specific instances. Similarly, ethical codes tell you what best practice you should aim for and give you recommendations to direct you in a general sense. There is no place where counselors and supervisors are told exactly what to do for every problem. Because of this, it is useful for every counselor and every supervisor to have a structured way of working through an ethical dilemma. Often it is through supervision that counselors will see exactly how to apply a decision-making model when confronted with a real-life conundrum. Supervisors can benefit from have a structured way of working out related questions and can protect themselves from litigation by proving that they applied a model to a contested situation.

It is precisely because there is little definitive information directing counselors that I ground my work in constructivist philosophy. Constructivism is a learning theory that is informed by developmental psychologist Jean Piaget's work on individual meaning making and the tradition of social constructionism, which focuses on how learning occurs through interacting with others (McAuliffe, 2001). According to constructivist philosophy, there is no definitive truth—all reality is shaped by our perceptions of it. The fact that there are so many factors influencing our sense of reality, such as context, culture, experience, beliefs, and personality, supports the idea that there is no "black and white" version of the truth, of what is right or what is wrong. This is a useful philosophy for me since ethical dilemmas often occur in the "gray area" between laws and guidelines.

Constructivism is also applied to counseling and is considered to be a primary influence of many postmodern approaches. I find it useful since it supports the basic tenet of "meeting the clients where they are." Since each one of us has our own way of perceiving reality, we must enter into the world of our clients to understand the context within which their problems have come into being. We also must work hard to help our clients to come up with their own solutions, since there is no way we can know what is best for another person. This philosophy also informs multicultural counseling, since constructivism supports the idea that knowledge and meaning is created within us and as a result of our cultural characteristics along with personal, regional, and temporal ones.

While the constructivist philosophy acts as a lens, directing what I see and how I see when working with clients and thinking about ethical guidelines, it does not act as a model for solving ethical dilemmas. Specific models are usually introduced in ethics textbooks and students are asked to practice applying them to situations counselors frequently encounter. I use a hermeneutic model created by Houser, Wilczenski, and Ham (2006). Hermeneutics is the study of interpretation, most popularly applied to religious texts. Interpretation in this context is comprised of creating and testing hypotheses related to behavior, with the understanding that this is not a static process, and reinterpretation is always a possibility over time. The hermeneutic process involves looking at the "big picture" and then looking at specific parts of that in greater depth to enhance understanding of the entire scenario. This is called a hermeneutic circle (Houser et al., 2006). For example, a person's cultural heritage, gender, age, and geographic location could all be considered smaller parts of the larger whole of who a person is and how they behave in a specific situation.

Because hermeneutics includes the assumption that interpretation can vary depending upon the person and the factors informing the hypothesis used, it is compatible with the constructivist philosophy's assumption that meaning making is unique to the individual, influenced by their relationships and characteristics. Since we as counselors have to work within the parameters of the ethical guidelines of our profession, there are some limitations to the relativity of this model. The hermeneutic model is used to find the closest interpretation of a specific dilemma so that the most accurate interpretation of the ethical solution will emerge.

Landmark 7

APPLYING A HERMENEUTIC DECISION-MAKING MODEL

Sally is a 30-year-old Caucasian middle-class female who is working as a counselor in private practice. She receives supervision from Joann, a 50-year-old Caucasian female, also middle class. Sally originally sought out supervision from Joann due to her desire to deepen her knowledge of Gestalt counseling techniques and theory. Sally asks Joann for assistance with a Caucasian male client, Tom, who is in his 40s and who she has seen for 3 months. He originally came to her for help with problems at work and with anger

(continued)

management. His periodic bursts of anger can lead to hostile and aggressive behavior that has jeopardized his professional relationships and strained his relations with his wife of 15 years. Sally has been using some cognitive-oriented strategies for helping Tom identify what thoughts fuel his anger. She has been trying unsuccessfully to get Tom to express more emotions and tells Joann she believes if he will learn to express emotions such as hurt and fear he will not end up channeling all his emotions into anger. She has been trying to lead him to an emotional experience during therapy and he remains steadfastly resistant. To her surprise, Joann asks her to use a decision-making process to ascertain if this is the best course of therapy for Tom. They use the hermeneutic model.

The first step is to identify all of the different components at play in the dilemma of whether or not Sally's treatment goals for Tom are appropriate.

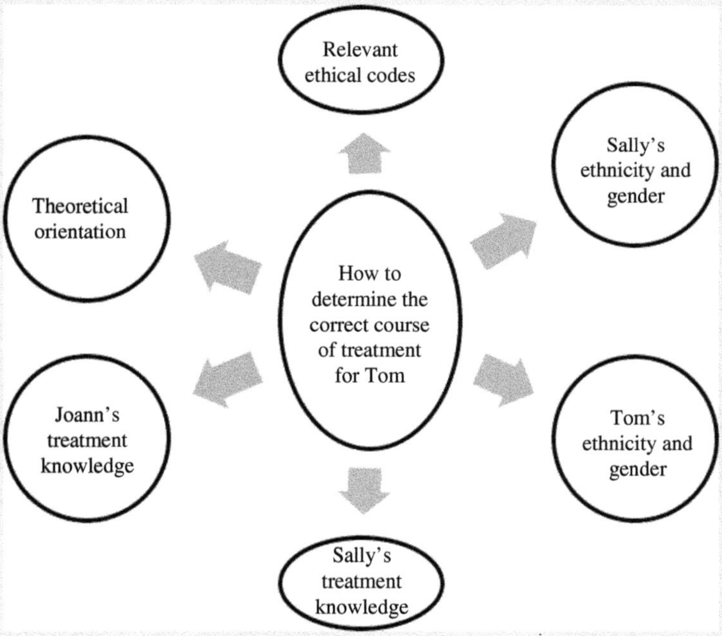

The second step is to reflect on each component as it relates to the main dilemma, then to the whole of the situation. Sally and Joann have a conversation exploring Sally and Tom's cultural, ethnic, and gender-based characteristics and role expectations. Next, they examined the Gestalt treatment interventions for developing emotional awareness. They reviewed what Sally knew about anger management and from which theoretical orientation that knowledge was derived. Next, they looked at the ethical codes related to client resistance and treatment goals: A.1.a: *respect the dignity of the client;* A.1.c: *counselors and their clients work jointly in devising integrated counseling plans;* A.4.b: *counselors are aware of their own values, attitudes, beliefs, and behaviors and avoid imposing values....* Each time they established information related to one of the

(continued)

components, they looked at how it informed the primary dilemma or question. Next, they looked at how it contributed to their understanding of the whole situation. Sally starts to understand that it was her job to work within the parameters set by her client. She can use psychoeducation to help Tom comprehend that there is a relationship between anger and more vulnerable emotions as well as why being aware of one's emotions is healthy and could serve him. However, she cannot dictate to Tom what treatment would be. If he wanted techniques to use to calm down when he felt angry and end treatment there, it would be her ethical responsibility to do so. Sally discusses with Joann how she was applying a gender-specific model to Tom's treatment, and was expecting him to respond to her the way she, as a woman, experiences emotions. Sally determines that she would need to discuss treatment with Tom and explore gender-specific themes before the two of them would be able to decide on a course of treatment. At that point, she could determine what Gestalt interventions would be appropriate.

1. *How do you find a balance between working within a client's comfort zone and culture and working with the tools you have as a counselor to help them change behavior patterns that are not healthy?*
2. *Are there differences between the way men and women are taught to experience and express emotions?*

The hermeneutic model can be a helpful tool when working with complex situations, where several different factors are influencing the question. It is also a good model to use when working within a multicultural context, such as when the client and counselor have different cultural backgrounds, genders, ages, ethnicities, and so on. This model allows for the incorporation of the personal values and knowledge of all parties and is geared toward a unified understanding of the whole and a clear interpretation of the exact nature of the issue, rather than coming to the one definitive right answer.

WORKING WITH NOVICE VERSUS EXPERIENCED COUNSELORS

Supervision will be shaped by the theoretical orientation applied; however, there are some fundamental differences between novice and experienced counselors with which all supervisors must contend. Regardless of the type of supervision offered, the intrapersonal processes of the supervisees and their conduct and work with clients must be explored. In terms of ethical practice, inexperienced supervisees require more focus on how actual ethical guidelines should be applied. Moving from the conceptual to the practical, these supervisees can feel insecure about their ability to stay grounded in ethical and legal practice and this at times requires processing on an emotional level. Managing the anxiety that comes from being a beginner is a personal journey that can require extra support and encouragement from supervisors. Reflecting on what their thought processes were when attempting to apply their orientation, ethical and legal responsibilities, agency requirements, and client needs can shed light on faults in logic and application. Reflecting on what their emotional reactions were in response to these challenges can help to illuminate times when they lose focus on clients, lose contact with the present moment, as well as with their place in the therapeutic process. Finally, working with novice supervisees often requires focusing on cultural issues and specific interventions related to their theoretical orientation.

Working with experienced counselors in a peer-supervision or a paid supervision format is a satisfying process of delving deeper into the complexity of case conceptualization. Skilled counselors may have practice in applying ethical codes, conducting effective informed consent procedures, and even dealing with emergencies. However, counselors cannot have expertise in all potential client problems, so building proficiency with specific populations is often a focus. Depending on the orientation of the supervisor, personal processes may still be present, with counselors exploring how they are responding personally to their clients, thus sifting through possible countertransference issues. Even experienced counselors need neutral observers to help identify transference within the therapeutic relationship, behaviors indicative of personality disorders, and new situations or problems presented by clients.

SIGNPOSTS FOR FUTURE TREKS

This chapter reviewed the primary ethical and legal concerns for supervisors. Codes from the American Counseling Association, the Association for Counselor Education and Supervision, and the Approved Clinical Supervisor were highlighted, with explanations given for how ethical practices manifest during supervision. I would like to share some reflections on challenges in working within an academic setting along with the parallels I have found between being a new supervisor working with novice counselors and being more experienced and working with seasoned counselors. Currently, I provide supervision at a university counseling program and within the context of private practice. I have found that much like the counseling process, where one's personal development is a continued outgrowth of being a part of a therapeutic relationship, supervisors and supervisees reciprocally learn from one another regardless of the experience level.

INSIGHTS GAINED FROM THE JOURNEY

ACADEMIC SUPERVISION

Providing supervision can require different ways of working depending on the context within which it is given. Thomas (2010) addresses some of the unique aspects of supervising in academia. In particular, she notes that there are limits to the degree supervisors could realistically intervene should a crisis or emergency arise with a client. Since academic supervisors do not have access to the client files their students are generating as interns, and they are not immediately overseeing client care, they are not qualified to assume responsibility for their students' clinical actions. Therefore, it is sometimes difficult to navigate the differences in practices that may arise between theoretical concepts such as "duty to warn" and how these actually play out in an internship setting. One such occurrence began with a supervisee who was working with an adolescent male who was in foster care. He disclosed to his counselor that he had run away from the foster home and, unbeknownst to his foster mother, was staying with a relative. During his site supervision, the supervisee disclosed this information. His site supervisor demanded that this information be reported to the foster care division of Children and Youth Services in order to protect the agency from potential litigation should anything happen to the adolescent. The supervisee had not included this in the informed consent description of limits of confidentiality and he did not have any evidence that the adolescent was in danger to himself or others. Due to these reasons, he was reluctant to tell his client that he had to report this information. He did not see how he could act against his supervisor's instructions, so he did report the information and process this with his client, who was upset at the breach of confidentiality. The supervisee brought the events to his internship course, where we explored the conundrum as a class. Since the events had already transpired, I did not feel torn between what I would have advised versus what his site supervisor had instructed. However, it was difficult to help the student explore the concepts at play—namely confidentiality and its limits, ethical guidelines and how they relate to agency policy, expected counselor behavior in the face of apparent discrepancies between ethics and policy, and informed consent practices—when he felt uncomfortable about not being well versed in the finer details of confidentiality and duty to warn. As counselors, we are told to uphold our ethical obligations even when they might be at odds with our employers' practices. However, as a supervisor, what does it mean to advise supervisees to behave in such a way when it potentially puts the supervisee at risk of disciplinary action or worse? This was an instance where I sought supervision myself from a trusted mentor and master clinician/supervisor, who also had directed an agency in the past. However, what is considered a "correct" interpretation of limits of confidentiality was not as useful as helping the supervisee process his experience and generate alternatives that addressed his feelings of discomfort and compliance with practices that seemed at odds with what he had been taught. This required delicate redirecting at times and role-playing exercises for how supervisees could handle similar situations in the future. What was ultimately the most useful was helping the students understand why it would have been in his client's best interest for him to engage in a discussion on why it would be helpful for him to notify his foster mother, and advocate for him if there were legitimate reasons why he did not feel comfortable living there.

Private Practice Supervision

I frame the supervision I provide in my private practice for community counselors seeking licensure as being consultative in nature. I take care to explain that due to reasons similar to those raised by Thomas (2010) in her description of academic supervision limitations, I cannot be considered the supervisor overseeing client care when my supervisees work in agency settings. Rather, I can provide additional consultation support. Due to the fact that our meetings are still directed toward counselor skill building, it is still considered appropriate to apply to licensure requirements. Supervisees who are working toward licensure may have started in the field prior to licensure requirements were created and are quite experienced; others may be newly graduated from their master's programs and working in their first counseling job since internship. As a result, the way in which I supervise varies depending on the developmental level of the supervisee.

Since both of these contexts share the fact that on-site supervision is being provided by a person with access to client charts, I am free to focus more on how supervisees are staying grounded in their theories, how they are conducting interventions, questions they have regarding how to manage the relationships with adolescent clients' parents, and ways to build their identities and professional development as counselors. For beginning counselors, these topics are often explored using Socratic questioning, reviewing recorded segments of sessions, and discussing personal reflections. More experienced counselors tend to be more active in presenting their own thoughts, ideas, and areas where they are seeking feedback. This requires less direction from me but poses the challenge of how to guide their reflective and problem-solving processes rather than provide answers. My ideas of what is "correct" becomes less relevant as my supervisees grow more experienced. Ultimately, they need to be clear about their values, biases, orientation, personality, way of working with clients, areas of challenge, and strengths. I feel I can best support this by reflecting patterns, themes, and parallels between what they may be struggling with in client sessions and how they are presenting during supervision sessions. This notion of parallel process, "the . . . replication of the therapeutic relationship in the supervisory situation" (Morrissey & Tribe, 2001), can be a rich area of exploration that helps build understanding of the self, of clients, and of the supervisory and therapeutic process.

The way I have practiced supervision has also transformed over time as I gained experience. There are many parallels to working with different developmental levels of counselors. For example, when I was a new supervisor, my own supervision was crucially important so I could process my own beginner anxiety, difficulty with working with supervisee personalities, and in particular knowing when to create remedial plans. As I worked to help new counselors gain proficiency in conducting informed consent procedures, I also had to give extra attention to my own procedures to ensure that they were complete. The deliberate nature of much of what counselors do to create trusting, effective therapeutic relationships is also reflected in what supervisors must do; the degree to which this took thought and planning was reflected in my own needs to be well prepared and mindful in the beginning phase of supervision. As I became more experienced and confident, these components took less time. Just as more experienced counselors spend less time on the structure of the therapeutic process in favor of the practice of therapy, I was able to turn my focus more toward the inner processes of the counselors. At this stage of my development as a supervisor, I welcome having supervisees with a variety of developmental levels, and appreciate that I can conduct supervision in academic and private practice contexts.

Supervision is an intellectually and personally gratifying process that only becomes more rich and interesting over time. All counselors can gain from a supervision process, whether it is in a peer-supervision group, contracted individually with a master supervisor-counselor, or through frequent workshops and seminars. Understanding best practices for supervisors can help all clinicians gain the most out of their supervision and challenge their supervisors to perform as ethically as possible.

MOVING FORWARD: CASE STUDY AND REFLECTION QUESTIONS

You are currently supervising four counselors at your job in a community mental health agency. One counselor seems to be performing at a level that is substandard compared to the other counselors. He seems to be more comfortable and more adept at discussing cases than providing treatment. You have listened to some recorded segments of his sessions, and he is halting, stammers, and fails to uphold standards of social convention in putting his clients at ease and building rapport. How do you know when a counselor is competent enough, and when should you intervene?

REFLECTION QUESTIONS

1. *What are the ethical codes that are relevant for your dilemma?*
2. *What type of feedback will you give to the counselor and what sources of information do you intend to consult to give an informed evaluation?*
3. *Based on what you know, might this supervisor be ethically obligated to create a remedial plan of action for the supervisee? If so, what areas of development might the remedial plan address?*
4. *What might be the best way the supervisor can relate her concerns to the supervisee in order to deal with this dilemma using a proactive, positive approach to ethics?*

REFERENCES

American Counseling Association. (2005). *ACA Code of ethics*. Retrieved March 11, 2011, from http://www.counseling.org/Resources/CodeOfEthics/TP/Home/CT2.aspx

Anderson, T. (1987). The reflecting team: Dialogue and meta-dialogue in clinical work. *Family Process, 26*(4), 415–428. Retrieved from MEDLINE.

Ancis, J. R., & Marshall, D. S. (2010). Using a multicultural framework to assess supervisees' perceptions of culturally competent supervision. *Journal of Counseling and Development, 88*(3), 277–284.

Association for Counselor Education and Supervision. (1990). Standards for counseling supervisors. *Journal of Counseling and Development, 69*, 30–32.

Bernard, J. M., & Goodyear, R. K. (2004). *Fundamentals of clinical supervision* (3rd ed.). New York: Pearson Education, Inc.

Borders, L. D., & Brown, L. L. (2005). *The new handbook of counseling supervision*. New York: Routledge, Taylor & Francis Group.

Center for Credentialing and Education. (2008). *The approved clinical supervisor (ACS) code of ethics*. Retrieved March 11, 2011, from http://www.cce-global.org/extras/cce-global/odfs/acs_codeofethics.pdf

Corey, G., Corey, M. S., & Callanan, P. (2007). *Issues and Ethics in the Helping Professions* (6th ed.). Florence, KY: Cengage Learning.

Duan, C., & Roehlke, H. (2001). A descriptive "snapshot" of cross-racial supervision in university counseling center internships. *Journal of Multicultural Counseling & Development, 29*(2), 131–146.

Falvey, J. E., & Cohen, C. R. (2003). The buck stops here: Documenting clinical supervision. *The Clinical Supervisor, 22*(2), 63–80. Retrieved from EBSCO.

Frame, M. W., & Stevens-Smith, P. (1995). Out of harm's way: Enhancing monitoring of dismissal processes in counselor education programs. *Counselor Education and Supervision, 35*, 118–129.

Gatmon, D., Jackson, D., Koshkarian, L., Martos-Perry, N., Molina, A., Patel, N. et al. (2001). Exploring ethnic, gender, and sexual orientation variables in supervision: Do they matter? *Journal of Multicultural Counseling & Development, 29*(2), 102–113. Retrieved from EBSCO.

Glenn, E., & Serovich, J. (1994). Documentation of family therapy supervision: A rationale and method. *The American Journal of Family Therapy 22*(2), 345–355.

Houser, R., Wilczenski, F. L., & Ham, M. (2006). *Culturally relevant ethical decision-making in counseling*. Thousand Oaks, CA: Sage Publications.

Holloway, J. d. (2003). What takes precedence: HIPAA or state law? *American Psychological Association Monitor on Psychology, 34*(1), 28. Retrieved from http://www.apa.org/monitor/jan03/hipaa.aspx.

Kagan, N., Krathwohl, D. R., & Miller, R. (1963). Stimulated recall in therapy using video tape: A case study. *Journal of Counseling Psychology, 10*(3), 237–243. Retrieved from EBSCO.

Lumadue, C. A., & Duffey, T. H. (1999). The role of graduate programs as gatekeepers: A model for evaluating student counselor competence. *Counselor Education and Supervision, 39*, 101–109.

McAuliffe, G. (2001). Introduction: Guidelines for constructivist teaching In K. Eriksen, & G. McAuliffe (Eds.), *Teaching counselors and therapists: Constructivist and developmental course design* (pp. 1–11). Westport, CT: Bergin & Garvey.

McCarthy, P., Sugden, S., Koker, M., Lamendola, F., Mauer, S., & Renninger, S. (1995). A practical guide to informed consent in clinical supervision. *Counselor Education and Supervision, 35*, 130–138.

Morrissey, J., & Tribe, R. (2001). Parallel process in supervision. *Counseling Psychology Quarterly, 14*(2), 103–110. Retrieved from EBSCO.

Remley, T. P., & Herlihy, B. (2001). *Ethical, legal, and professional issues in counseling*. Upper Saddle River, New Jersey: Prentice-Hall, Inc.

Thomas, J. (2010). *The ethics of supervision and consultation*. Washington, DC: American Psychological Association.

Upcoming changes to HIPAA Standards for Electronic Transactions. (March 2010). *Wisconsin Department of Health Services Forward Health Electronic newsletter*. Retrieved from https://www.forwardhealth.wi.gov/kw/pdf/2010-17.pdf

Wilkerson, K. (2006). Impaired students: Applying a therapeutic process model to graduate training programs. *Counselor Education and Supervision, 45*(3), 207–217.

Zuckerman, E. (2006). *HIPAA help: A compliance toolkit for psychotherapists for maintaining records; privacy and security, managing risks, and operating* (2nd ed.). Arnbrust, PA: Three Wishes Press.

Part III

Trekking to Special Sites in Counseling Ethics

11

Relational Ethics: Ethical Decision Making in Couple, Marriage, and Family Counseling and Therapy

Stephen Southern

THE FORSEEN DESTINATION

After reading this chapter, students will aspire to:

- Recognize and apply ethical standards with regard to couple, marriage, and family counseling and therapy (CMFT).
- Discuss how future trends affect ethical guidelines and aspirations.
- Understand problems with diagnosis and overmedicalization of counseling.
- Acquire the knowledge of confidentiality and disclosure of family secrets.
- Recognize ethical issues in working with special populations.
- Discover advances in the specialization that promote ethical practice.
- Learn from the personal testimony of the contributing author.
- Reflect upon one's ethical journey as a student in a counseling program.

GETTING ON THE ROAD

Ethical decision making in CMFT is built on a foundation of traditional ethical guidelines, but also includes aspirations and contexts associated with contemporary family life. In this chapter, I discuss the significance of ethical guidelines and aspirations for work with couples and families, trends in contemporary family life and professional perspectives, problems with diagnosis from a family systems perspective, confidentiality and disclosure of family secrets, working with special populations, and advances in the specialization of CMFT. This chapter also provides some personal testimony regarding review of ethical issues particular to CMFT. The purpose of the personal testimony is to offer a perspective of the professional journey of a specialist in CMFT and to assist counselors in serving couples and families. As you read this chapter, please refer to Appendix A at the end of the book for a complete list of ethical guidelines, including codes from the International Association of Marriage and Family Counselors (Hendricks, Bradley, Southern, Oliver, & Birdsall, 2011), a division of the American Counseling Association and the American Association for Marriage and Family Therapy (AAMFT, 2001).

EXPLORING THE TERRITORY

RELATIONAL ETHICS IN COUPLE, MARRIAGE, AND FAMILY THERAPY

CMFT is relationship oriented whether services are provided to individuals, couples, families, or groups. The relational perspective is the most distinctive feature of the specialization. Therefore, ethics in CMFT are essentially relational in nature. Clinical decisions affect clients and their family systems within the larger ecological contexts of communities and institutions. A relational perspective in ethical decision making keeps professionals mindful of the clients, families, and communities we serve (Southern, Smith, & Oliver, 2005).

Some basic definitions suggest the relational nature of the specialization, as well as the complexities in defining the field (Gladding, 2011):

> **couples counseling** The *counseling* of either *heterosexual* or *homosexual* dyadic pairs about dynamics within their *relationship*. When couples counseling is conducted exclusively with individuals who are married, it is known as *marriage counseling* or *marriage therapy*. (p. 42)
>
> **family therapy** The *treatment* of a *family* as a *client* through a number of theoretical approaches, including psychoanalytic, Bowen, structural, experiential, strategic, systemic (i.e., Milan), solution-focused, and narrative. In most family treatment, the family is seen together. (p. 63)

Based upon my experience in the specialization, *counseling* emphasizes the developmental and health-oriented aspects of working with couples and families while *therapy* refers most commonly to mental illness and disease-oriented approaches devoted to remission of symptoms. Occasionally, the systems perspective of couple, marriage and family counselors and therapists is at odds with the medical model underlying mental health counseling and other allied health professions. Specialists may choose to work with couples or married partners from a unique relational perspective or within the overall context of family systems.

Professional practice is integrally linked to ethics; work is a vocational calling. Professionals should focus on best practices and aspirations with the goal of integrating personal values and professional development in public service (Sperry, 2005). Professional practice in CMFT is informed by ethics and aspirations.

Arnold Lazarus (2001), an astute observer of changes in psychotherapy over the years, has maintained that there is no such thing as couple and family therapy (Christensen, 2001). In particular, he raised a number of issues that challenge the narrow view of codes and statutes in traditional codes of ethics.

- We work with various individuals and combinations of clients in family toward therapeutic goals

- There is no unified couple and family therapy
- Therapy involves particular methods not vague models
- Dual relationship boundaries are too restrictive and could be harmful
- Crossing boundaries with a purpose (e.g., going to a family wedding) could be therapeutic
- Divorce need not be harmful to children
- Therapists must transcend their training to reclaim natural skills and intuition
- Romance and marriage require different skills

The views of Lazarus remind specialists in the field of CMFT to examine their basic assumptions and perspectives and remain open to innovations that may better serve clients.

Relational ethics afford guidelines for practice, aspirations for justice and advocacy, and contexts for future developments in society's views on family life. Traditional guidelines for ethical practice (e.g., Jordan & Meara, 1990; Meara, Schmidt, & Day, 1996) include respect for autonomy, nonmaleficence, beneficence, justice, fidelity, and veracity (see Chapters 1 and 3 for a more in-depth description of ethical principles and virtues). These guidelines reflect underlying values of the helping professions. Perspectives and practices in professional CMFT require special considerations for each of the aforementioned ethical principles. In addition, virtue or aspirational ethics (Meara, Schmidt, & Day, 1996) encourage professionals to go beyond professional guidelines in codes of ethics and embrace ideals such as integrity, discernment, self-awareness, and interdependence. Changes in technology, cultural norms, institutions, and definitions of family life promise to challenge CMFT professionals who will find themselves in the midst of societal discourse and debate.

FUTURE CONTEXTS CMFT

The future of couple, CMFT should be considered when examining the contexts of ethical decision making. Even the inclusion of the term *couple* to the labeling of the specialization reflects efforts to recognize the increasing incidence of cohabiting partners and committed relationships among persons who are not permitted to marry or haven chosen not to embrace the institution or legal status of marriage (Wilcoxon, Remley, & Gladding, 2012). Similarly, multicultural perspectives on family life inform counselors that *family* extends far beyond genetics, legal statutes, and patriarchal kinship ties to include members who would not be considered family in a traditional nuclear family system (Wilcoxon, Remley, & Gladding, 2012).

Landmark 1

CASE EXAMPLE

Crystal is a 15-year-old Caucasian female residing in a residential treatment center for substance-use disorders. She has asked her treatment team to extend visitation to an 18-year-old African American male who she calls her "brother." He was

(*continued*)

the son of one of her mother's boyfriends who lived with them last year. Crystal's mother approved of his addition to the visitation list. A psychologist on the team confronts Crystal for calling him her brother since he is not related to her biologically or by marriage. Crystal is angry and hurt that her brother is not accepted by her caregivers.

1. *Should Crystal be allowed a family visit?*
2. *Does a teenager have a right to define her family?*
3. *What constitutes a family in contemporary America?*

Woody and Woody (2001) addressed the future of marriage and family therapy the same year the AAMFT Code of Ethics (2001) was published. They predicted some future developments that have been realized over the ensuing years. An increasing global awareness reduced some parochial Western centered views on family processes. There has been increased attention to ethnic, social class, religious, and cultural factors in identifying what is change worthy and how changes can occur. There have been significant developments in addressing gender and sexual orientation issues. In particular, legalization of gay marriage in several states including Massachusetts and New York (*New York Times*, July 25, 2011) calls into question the fundamental institution of marriage. Yet, covenant marriage, a religious innovation in which legal marriage is tied to lifelong attachment, and gay marriage each support commitment as a key to a long-lasting relationship (Southern, Cade, & Devlin, 2010). Cultural diversity in marriage and family counseling builds bridges to better communication and encourages aspirational ethics in practice.

In addition to cultural diversity and social justice concerns, sweeping changes in managed health care affect ethical decision making (Woody & Woody, 2001). Such basic issues as client identification, diagnosis, and service coding reflect daily challenges in CMFT practice. While there is greater parity in third-party payments for counseling services (Hoyt & Gurman, 2011), couple and family counseling may be viewed as elective or developmental in nature and not be covered by insurance. The relationship orientation of CMFT cautions counselors not to chase *diseased dollars* through mental health formulations, but to remain true to the systemic perspective. Similarly, ethical CMFT clinicians will not attempt to provide services outside their area of competence (e.g., testing or treating serious mental illness) although reimbursement or funding is available.

A final area of rapid development over the decade since the publication of the AAMFT Code of Ethics (2001) is technological change. Telecommunications and telehealth services expand the scope of professional CMFT practice while raising profound issues regarding confidentiality and licensure to practice in a particular geographic location (Woody & Woody, 2001).

The future of CMFT has arrived. A recent textbook focusing on ethics in marriage and family therapy (Wilcoxon, Remley, & Gladding, 2012) provided testimony and fair witness to the developments predicted in 2001. Multiculturalism, social justice, political and economic changes, and technological advances provide opportunities for us to examine ethical issues and specific cases in both ethical guidelines and aspirations.

DIAGNOSIS IN CMFT

Psychiatric diagnoses contained in the *Diagnostic and Statistical Manual of Mental Disorders* (APA, 2001) create barriers to effective practice in CMFT. Third-party payments may shape clinicians toward individual diagnoses rather than relational and contextual formulations (Crews & Hill, 2005; Hill & Crews, 2005). Psychiatric diagnoses may not reflect clinical realities encountered by counselors and therapists who serve family systems. Individual behavioral and intrapsychic descriptions are frequently stigmatizing and potentially harmful, especially for identified patients whose symptoms serve functions within their family systems. Individual-focused and medical model diagnoses also obscure cultural issues and could oppress some groups. When CMFT clinicians chase *disease-oriented dollars* in contemporary managed care, they may not be competent to make psychiatric diagnoses. In addition, they could be encouraged to commit fraud or compromise their professional identity by assisting clients in accessing third-party reimbursements for relational therapy services that are not covered in the health plans (Crews & Hill, 2005; Hill & Crews, 2005).

In a recent publication, "Wither Couple/Family Therapy," Hoyt and Gurman (2011) framed the threats to the specialization and psychotherapy in general by the overmedicalization of mental health care. The authors noted that insurance company reimbursement plans threaten to reduce or eliminate access to even evidence-based psychotherapy services in favor of medication. Similarly, Younggren and Hjelt (2010) warned of dangers affecting mental health practitioners who want to treat couples through their identified patient's health insurance policy. Increasingly, third-party payments are not provided for marital therapy services. Gurman and colleagues have demonstrated that couple, marital and family therapy interventions help not only relationships but also mental health problems presented by individuals (Gurman, 2008; Lebow & Gurman, 1995). Yet, trends toward managed care and reduced health care coverage threaten the accessibility of specialized services at a time when they may be most needed and important.

Landmark 2

CASE EXAMPLE

Jacob and Sandy attend an initial counseling session complaining of marital conflicts and sexual desire discrepancy. Each partner describes a lot of life dissatisfaction, some tearfulness at times, and difficulty sleeping. Sandy formerly had a diagnosis of dysthymic disorder, when she saw a local psychotherapist. The couple asks the counselor to treat Sandy as the client and bill for treatment of a mood disorder. Otherwise, they will not be able to afford marital counseling. Marital and sexual therapies are excluded from each of their insurance plans.

(*continued*)

1. *Should the CMFT counselor agree to identify Sandy as the client and bill her insurance company?*
2. *Does the counselor have an obligation to offer treatment to the couple without regard to their ability to pay?*
3. *How would you discuss the diagnostic issues with the couple?*

Contemporary developments in sexuality counseling and therapy suggest means for CMFT specialists to resist overmedicalization of relational issues. Leonore Tiefer and others rejected the overmedicalization of sex therapy, articulating a *New View* of female sexuality (Kaschak & Tiefer, 2001; Tiefer, 2002, 2004). As a postmodern development, *A New View of Women's Sexual Problems* (Kaschak & Tiefer, 2001), a manifesto written by clinicians and social scientists, called into question the disease-oriented, diagnosis-dependent, overmedicalized, and patriarchal model of sex therapy. Tiefer (2002), in particular, has been a persuasive critic of attempts by pharmaceutical companies to define sexuality in terms of biological reductionism. Rejecting the success of Viagra in treating male sexual dysfunction, Tiefer and colleagues resisted the attempts to find a "little pink pill" (i.e., female Viagra or another quick fix pharmaceutical) and ultimately challenged the validity of the disease-oriented diagnostic criteria of the *DSM-IV-TR* (American Psychiatric Association, 2001).

The *New View* offered a woman-centered definition of sexual problems: "... discontent or dissatisfaction with any emotional, physical, or relational aspect of sexual experience" (Kaschak & Tiefer, 2001, pp. 228–229). The *New View* emphasized the social and contextual when attempting to understand sexual concerns. Causal and curative factors may occur in one or more of the following categories: (a) sociocultural, political, or economic factors; (b) partner and relationship factors; (c) psychological factors; and (d) medical factors. By retaining a focus on intimacy and relational issues, the *New View* saved sexuality counseling and therapy from overmedicalization.

While there are benefits to the medical model, including the prescription of effective psychotropic medications, there are ethical issues implicit in psychopharmacology (Murray & Murray, 2007). In contemporary CMFT practice, most clients or family members have some experience with psychotropic medications. While there are obvious ethical benefits in terms of reducing suffering, medications may camouflage or confound the meanings and functions of mental health disorders and diagnoses in the family system (Hoyt & Gurman, 2011). There is a tension between couple and family counselors and other mental health professionals regarding whether medication is a primary treatment or inappropriate or hazardous. Murray and Murray (2007) offered some important views on medication:

- Family counselors should be knowledgeable about psychotropic medications, as well as the roles and functions of other disciplines
- Counselors may provide information that could help clients with decision making, informed consent, and compliance

Counselors may view problems in systemic context without becoming involved in "splitting" with another care provider.

Landmark 3

CASE EXAMPLE

Terry and Steven were referred by their pastor to a counselor for treatment recommendations. They have become increasingly involved in marital conflicts with some loud arguments, cursing, and recent pushing. While there are obvious relationship issues, Terry has a positive family history and signs of depression. She previously received an antidepressant medication from her family doctor. Steven says she needs to see a doctor for medication. He also thinks their fighting is related to mood changes associated with her menstrual period. The counselor is considering a referral to a psychiatrist in the group practice, but wants to consult with the referring pastor first.

1. *Should the counselor contact the pastor to discuss medication issues?*
2. *What forms or paperwork would be needed to consult with either the minister or the psychiatrist?*
3. *What would be the implications of making Terry the identified patient in this case?*

CONFIDENTIALITY AND DISCLOSURE OF FAMILY SECRETS

CMFT must protect confidentiality and do no harm by reflecting frequently on the relational elements in case formulations and recognizing that we serve family systems. Information provided by individuals is understood in the relational context of the family system. Simple record keeping must take into account the basic question, "Who is the client?"

Typically, CMFT professionals treat relationships and serve dyads or family units. There may be an identified patient, but the relationship is the client. Therefore, record keeping must take into account the confidentiality of the individuals involved in the counseling process, especially if the dissolution of the relationship, marriage, or family may produce breach of privacy. Most states do not recognize privilege for couple, marriage and family counselors. Therefore, records may be requested or demanded. Best practices require that all parties understand the limits of confidentiality and disclosure. Two recurring problems are demands for disclosure in cases involving divorce and child custody.

Occasionally, couples struggling with divorce attempt to access marriage counseling notes in building a case against one's partner. Since it unlikely that the marriage counselor enjoys privilege afforded to a psychiatrist or minister, communications may not be held confidential. There may be no protection against court-ordered disclosure of counseling communications because of the presence of more than one client in the session. It may be wise to seek a written agreement between spouses not to make or seek court disclosures when divorce is being considered (Wilcoxon, Remley, & Gladding, 2012). The partners should realize that the marriage counselor will attempt to serve the relationship as the client and address problem definition and goal setting from a relational instead of an individual focus. Nevertheless, it would still be relevant to secure informed consent for relational therapy and to record clinical notes in a manner that does no harm to either party if the records are compelled to be released.

There are similar issues in complex cases involving child custody disputes. In a previous group practice, I temporarily suspended new services to children because of custodial parents seeking "back door" custody evaluations. In some of these cases, the custodial parent would claim that the child was exhibiting various symptoms following visitation with the other parent. Otherwise, a parent would attempt to secure a formal custody evaluation in the midst of ongoing therapy for the child. It is important to recognize that there could be a conflict of interest between the roles of the counselor who is offering individual or family counseling to a child and the evaluator of parenting, residence, or other custody considerations. Child custody evaluations should be ordered by the court prior to the child seeing a counselor or therapist. The evaluator should have specialized training, supervision, and related preparation in conducting child custody evaluations. Even specialists in child custody evaluation recognize the implicit risks involved in rendering a professional opinion that could limit contact with a child. Child custody and divorce issues threaten the trust and good will required to pursue a course of counseling or therapy.

Another issue related to confidentiality and disclosure is the expression of family secrets.

"A family without secrets is like a two-year-old without tantrums: a rarity" (Fall & Lyons, 2003, p. 281) There are different types of secrets: shared family secrets, internal family secrets, individual secrets, conventional secrets, family rule violations, and taboo topics (Brendel & Nelson, 1999; Fall & Lyons, 2003). Codes of ethics are biased in favor of reviewing disclosure from the perspective of an individual client's right to confidentiality; however, marriage and family counselors recognize the essential relational contexts involved in all communications.

- Although related, secrecy, privacy, and confidentiality are separate constructs
- Generally, the more the secret relates to violation of family rules or the more extreme the taboo, the greater is the need for disclosure
- How the couple and family counselor handles secrets is the issue
- Counselors should avoid triangulation and other alignments that perpetuate family problems
- Clients have the right to informed consent regarding how disclosures will be handled
- Counselors should not harm a client system through the process of disclosure
- Codes of ethics are biased in favor of reviewing disclosure from the perspective of an individual client's right to confidentiality
- Disclosure is a process not a discrete event

Confidentiality and disclosure are key issues in counseling and therapy with couples and families. There are additional principle ethics and virtues that apply to work with special populations.

Landmark 4

CASE EXAMPLE

Sam has been involved in a 90-day residential treatment program for chemical dependence. He has made good progress in individual counseling, as well as therapy and recovery groups. Sam addressed some family-of-origin issues related to covert (indirect) incest arising from an overly close emotional and physical relationship to his mother. He also revealed in his stepwork that he had engaged in some extramarital affairs when he was active in his alcoholism and prescription drug abuse. He is scheduled to be discharged from the facility within the next three weeks. There is an upcoming family week program to which his wife, children, and parents have been invited. The family counselor advised Sam to disclose all his sexual issues to his family members. He asks his primary counselor how much he should tell during this family week program. He does not want to keep secrets, but he fears that complete disclosure will hurt his changes for bonding with his family. If he does disclose, he is concerned about whether or not he should take an overnight pass from the facility to be with his family.

1. *Should Sam disclose his sexual issues during this family week program?*
2. *How can Sam maintain an honest and open recovery process while maintaining sobriety?*
3. *How might family members be affected by the disclosures during the family week?*

WORKING WITH SPECIAL POPULATIONS

Patriarchal Traditions and Gender Issues

Gender issues affect stereotypes and values in counselor and client interactions. Ethical conduct requires careful reflection and examination of sources of biases. Frequently, value conflicts arise when helping couples whose gender role expectations place burdens on one or both members of the couple. Many couples differ in their commitment to traditional, patriarchal values. CMFT counselors also vary in their gender role perceptions and their values related to such topics as egalitarian decision-making, responsibilities at work and in the home, and autonomy versus dependence. Therefore, gender issues should be addressed in effective work with couples (Steigerwald & Forest, 2004).

A clash of values could be resolved by applying social constructivism: "... a philosophical framework that proposes that reality is the creation of individuals in interaction—a socially, consensually agreed-on definition of what is real" (Cottone, 2001, p. 454). Consensualizing could involve

- Obtaining information from those involved
- Assessing the nature of the relationships operating at that moment in time

- Consulting valued colleagues and professional expert opinion (including ethical codes and literature)
- Negotiating when there is a disagreement
- Responding in a way that allows a reasonable consensus as to what should happen or what really occurred

Issues in Working With Rural Couples and Families

There are unique issues encountered in work with couples and families in rural settings (Barnett & Yutrzenka, 2002; Weigel & Baker, 2002). Personal and professional isolation can lead to lack of referral sources. Among professional counselors, there may be a lack of opportunity for supervision, consultation, and collaboration. Dual relationships are an inevitability of practicing in rural and small town settings. Therefore, professionals must take care to do no harm and to offer safeguards to protect client confidentiality.

In some settings, it is possible to incorporate indigenous practices and resources, as well as paraprofessionals, in the counseling process. For example, in one residential treatment center in a rural area, a recovering Native American returned to the center as a clinical associate following treatment there and 2 years of sobriety. He was well-known in the community for the strength of his recovery program in overcoming alcoholism. In addition, he brought vast spiritual resources from his tribal life experience to share with suffering alcoholics and addicts. He was instrumental in building a strong therapeutic community in which clients and their families could heal.

Spiritual and Religious Issues in Marriage and Family Counseling

CMFT practice requires the competence of counselors to explore religious and theological issues (Frame, 2000; Smith & Smith, 2001). Religious reflection and spiritual development likely apply to the lives of most couples and families. Examination of religious practices in the family of origin may be especially informative when considering the well-being of couples and families. Secular counselors should possess minimal competence necessary to engage in religious exploration even among persons who present no particular expression of faith. Persons who have discontinued religious observation or institutional attendance may feel loss or lack of support. There are multiple sources of support and potential conflict when examining the religious life of those served in couple, marital, and family therapy.

When marriage and family counseling services are conducted in religious settings, such as a counseling center affiliated with a particular Protestant church, there is potential for role confusion, blurring religious and professional counseling roles. Issues of confidentiality and disclosure are presented when one receives services within a counseling ministry. Although pastoral counseling is a common function in most religious settings, ministers, priests, and other religious professionals may lack basic counseling competence by virtue of receiving little or no training in CMFT. In addition, there is the pitfall of imposing one's religious or spiritual values on clients who are seeking mental health or marriage and family counseling.

In secular settings, the professional counselor may violate work setting boundaries and expectations by incorporating religious or spiritual practices, such as praying or reading the Bible, in the marriage and family counseling process. The secular counselor could usurp religious authority by performing spiritual disciplines or rituals. Professional counselors with strong personal religious beliefs may project expectations or impose barriers to effective services delivery.

Hermann and Herlihy (2006) presented the legal and ethical implications of refusing to counsel homosexual clients. In the now famous case of *Bruff v. North Mississippi Health Services (2001)*, Bruff refused to counsel Jane Doe on how to improve her homosexual relationship because of Bruff's religious beliefs. The counselor eventually sued the company when they could not accommodate her beliefs and provide another position. She was obligated by virtue of an employee assistance program (EAP) contract to serve all clients. The case demonstrated that failure to counsel homosexual clients may constitute harm, even when a counselor argues lack of competence or tries to make a referral. Personal religious beliefs cannot overrule best practices in couple, marriage, and family counseling and therapy.

Six states, including New York effective July 24, 2011, permit gay marriage (*New York Times*, July 25, 2011). President Obama recently eliminated "Don't Ask; Don't Tell," reducing barriers to sexual minorities in the military (Bumiller, July 22, 2011). As public servants, couple, marriage, and family counselors and therapists must be adequately prepared through training and supervision, as well as reflection and self-awareness to provide helpful services to all client groups.

ADVANCES IN CMFT

Dialectics of Marriage: Commitment Is an Answer

There appears to be an irreconcilable conflict between religious conservatives, who advocate the traditional institution of marriage, and proponents of full marital rights for sexual minorities (Southern, Cade, & Devlin, 2010). According to a feminist approach, marriage is a sociopolitical institution, rooted in patriarchy and religion and connected to property and parenting rights. The nation has been engaged in heated debate over the definition of marriage. Two countervailing trends reflect the past and future of the institution. The divergent perspectives may find common ground in a shared valuing process in which commitment and devotion define marriage. Covenant marriage and gay marriage agree on the importance of commitment as a symbol and a guiding principle.

Covenant marriage refers to a traditional marital union between man and woman intended to be lifelong or even eternal. The covenant marriage movement arose in the late 1990s out of concern for no-fault divorces and erosion of the traditional or religious institution of marriage (Sanchez, Nock, Wright, & Gager, 2002). *Gay marriage* could be considered the antithesis of traditional marriage in that the union reflects the interests of persons of the same gender who wish to enjoy the rights and responsibilities of one of society's most important institutions. Covenant marriage and gay marriage appear to be irreconcilable opposites. However, the dialectics in the *revisioning* of marriage actually point toward a synthesis in which commitment is a potential solution to the problem of marital decline. Couple, marriage, and family counselors should emphasize the value of commitment in making meaning from marriage.

Whether marriage is viewed as a sacred promise or a civil contract, the central value of commitment organizes a myriad of personal and professional choices.

Commitment becomes a virtue in relational decision making. It reflects an ideal in which partners form strong bonds to define their relationship and to protect it from the trials and disorganizing influences of modern life. Commitment affords a context for establishing trust, sharing resources, enhancing intimacy, protecting vulnerability, and maintaining boundaries. The professional counselor who incorporates the virtue of commitment in ethical practice assists couples in times of need and contributes to the well-being of the community.

Covenant marriage and gay marriage can each reflect the value of commitment, reducing apparent conflicts in worldview and increasing the preparedness of counselors to serve all clients in the community. Advocates of covenant marriage and gay marriage may reflect on the meanings of commitment in making choices about their relationships. Counselors help in this process of reflection.

Sexual Rights

Sexual health is another emerging construct that promises to advance the life experiences of clients. In the specialization of CMFT, sexual health reflects a departure from an earlier model that focused on sexual dysfunction or sexual symptoms as indicators of underlying mental disorders. Today, we recognize that sexuality represents more than genital functioning and occasions choices associated with personal and relational identities (Sexuality Information and Education Council of the United States, n.d.). The expanded view of sexuality emphasizes that individuals have sexual rights, which should be acknowledged by the professional counselor. The World Health Organization (2002) asserted that sexual rights are human rights to

- Receive the highest attainable standard of sexual health, including access to sexual and reproductive health care services
- Seek, receive, and impart information related to sexuality
- Receive sexuality education
- Respect for body integrity
- Choose their partner
- Decide to be sexually active or not
- Consent to sexual relations
- Consent to marriage
- Decide whether, and when, to have children
- Pursue a satisfying, safe, and pleasurable sexual life

As individuals and couples pursue life satisfaction through sexuality, they exercise identity defining choices that can be facilitated by the reflective, self-aware counselor.

Knowledge is power, and language constructs relationships that distribute power (Foucault, 1982). Ongoing political–historical–institutional conversations or discourses are used to determine what knowledge is real, true, good, right, or proper and to determine what works. Ethical counselors use language that frees and empowers clients to exercise rights and make life-enhancing choices. Counselors who are not informed by virtue ethics may use diagnoses and other oppressive forms of language to restrict or pathologize clients.

Sexual health includes the use of empowering language to construct meaningful lived experiences. Clients discover and express their sexual rights within an ethical counseling context. Hare-Mustin (1994) said the therapy room, like a classroom, should be a "mirrored room" reflecting back all that is voiced within it. Over time, sexual terms have changed to reflect the voices of clients, especially women, who wish to exercise their rights. The oppressive patriarchal language of "frigidity" evolved into the less limiting scientific terms of "anorgasmia" or "hypoactive sexual desire," concluding with a more hopeful, woman-centered label, "preorgasmic." From this empowered feminist perspective, every woman has the right to orgasm. Sexuality counseling affords opportunities for women to discover their orgasmic potential by removing barriers. Victims of sexual violence become "survivors," who can reclaim their rights to thrive. Women and men are no longer captive to rigid gender scripts that contribute to sexual dysfunction and dissatisfaction. They are able to explore and describe their experiences with sexual joy and comfort. Postmodern constructions of sexuality shift power from the expert role of the therapist empowered by the patriarchal medical model to the co-construction of meaning by client and counselor through relational ethics.

SIGNPOSTS FOR FUTURE TREKS

Ethical practice in CMFT requires more than adherence to guidelines and principles. Attention to virtues and aspirations are essential in the rapidly changing contexts in which specialized services are rendered. CMFT is unique in the family structures presented by clients and perspectives used by counselors to select best practices. The traditional principles of autonomy, nonmaleficence, beneficence, justice, fidelity, and veracity are complemented by the virtues of integrity, discernment, self awareness, and interdependence in the acculturation of the professional counselor for ethical practice. Several generalizations summarize the findings of the journey in this chapter.

- Relational ethics that affect couples and families must take into account larger ecological contexts, institutions, and communities
- The systems perspective of specialized couple, marriage, and family counseling and therapy (CMFT) challenges the dominant medical model in mental health care and overmedicalization in services delivery
- Some basic assumptions of principle ethics have been challenged by master therapists, such as Arnold Lazarus, and informed by aspirational or virtue ethics
- Trends in CMFT are affecting the future of practice including multiculturalism, diversity, social justice, managed care, economic upheaval, and technological advances
- Changes in health insurance plans and third-party payments limit marriage counseling and therapy, encourage stigmatizing diagnoses, and overemphasize psychotropic medications that may camouflage family issues
- CMFT is willing to explore foundational issues, such as "Who is the client?"
- CMFT requires "consensualizing" and "revisioning" in order to respect the rights of minority groups and to empower those oppressed by patriarchal institutions

- CMFT has advanced through contributions of feminists to discern inappropriate labels, models, and interventions
- The specialization addresses unique concerns of rural and religious families, as well as sexual rights and health
- Commitment and freedom are virtues that guide the practice of CMFT

INSIGHTS GAINED FROM THE JOURNEY

This chapter has afforded me an opportunity to reflect on my commitment to the professional specialization of CMFT. As president of the International Association of Marriage and Family Counselors (IAMFC) and editor of *The Family Journal,* I have enjoyed many opportunities to read and discuss timely examples of ethical issues. Our specialization has resisted the trend toward overmedicalization that plagues all of the helping professions. I prefer to engage in clinical decision making and to construct case conceptualizations based on a developmentally oriented, family systems model rather than adopting a limiting medical model that seems to be guiding mental health care.

I chaired the IAMFC Ethics Committee that revised our Ethical Code in 2005 and encouraged my colleagues in an additional revision recently published in *The Family Journal* (Hendricks, Bradley, Southern, Oliver, & Birdsall, 2011). We have tried to increase attention to aspirations for justice, discernment, and interdependence. Much of my understanding of ethics has evolved over my years of involvement with IAMFC and *The Family Journal.* Therefore, many of the articles cited in this chapter were drawn from our division's publication. Recently, I attended a continuing education ethics workshop for licensed marriage and family therapists. The presenter said that he found our journal to be especially beneficial in addressing ethical issues from a practical standpoint for the practicing clinician. This observation justified the overuse of *The Family Journal* articles.

Now in my 35th year of professional practice and teaching, I am increasingly aware of my own biases. Being a Caucasian male, I have enjoyed privilege in a world of work that supported my career advancement. I continue to learn from women, minority group members, and persons living with various disabilities, who have had to struggle with patriarchal and dominant culture institutions.

I was trained as a sex therapist at Masters and Johnson Institute, which continues to contribute the foundations of most models of sexuality counseling and therapy. However, the Masters and Johnson approach has been criticized (e.g., Tiefer, 2002, 2004) for its patriarchal, heterosexist bias, particularly in advancing a male-centered model for the sexual response cycle (cf. Masters & Johnson, 1966, 1970).

I have learned a lot from students and trainees. I have been informed by comments from sexuality counseling workshop participants, who indicated that I did not adequately represent their lifestyles and relationships. For example, one participant and her partner volunteered to share from their experience the strengths of their lesbian relationship. I believe that it is important to listen, consult with colleagues, and continue learning from minority and underrepresented groups. I aspire to increase my self-awareness and discernment as I offer couple and family services.

MOVING FORWARD: CASE STUDY AND REFLECTION QUESTIONS

John is a marriage and family counselor in private practice for 20 years. He is married and has teenage children preparing to go to college. He is a Caucasian who grew up in an intact family and attended several church-related universities in route to completing his master's degree and becoming a licensed professional counselor (LPC) in a Southern state. He is an elder in his Protestant church. He derives his income from the private practice and gets referrals from doctors, colleagues, churches, and community groups. John has recently completed two intake assessment appointments with a 29-year-old African American man (Walt) who presents with sadness and despair because his family will not accept his cohabiting relationship with a 35-year-old Caucasian attorney (Ben) in town.

Walt complained of some loss of appetite and trouble sleeping, but denied suicidal ideation. He visited the college counseling center when he was an undergraduate during the coming out process. The college counselor wanted to refer him to a doctor for medication evaluation, but Walt found support on campus and in the community to support his self-exploration. He attributes his depressed feelings to the lack of support from his family of origin. Walt also noted that his relationship with Ben is becoming more conflictual. They have frequent arguments about minor concerns, but no physical altercations. Ben's ex-wife is threatening to suspend his weekend visits with his 5-year-old son if Walt continues to live in the home. Walt has argued with Ben's ex on the telephone a few times. Walt believes that he would feel better if he could improve his communication with Ben and recapture the intimacy they enjoyed in the start of their relationship last year.

John has been considering several courses of action in his clinical decision making. He may refer Walt to a doctor for psychiatric evaluation and possible psychotropic medication. He is considering offering cognitive therapy for depression since he knows that Walt's insurance company would pay for this individual therapy service. He wonders if he should have collateral contacts with Walt's family members. John would like to include Ben in at least one session, but he doubts that he can offer effective relational therapy to the couple since according to his religious beliefs the relationship is "wrong." Given the complexities of the case, he vacillates between a decision to offer individual cognitive therapy for depression or refer Walt and his partner to another counselor.

REFLECTION QUESTIONS

1. *Who is the client in this case?*
2. *What are the implications if John refers Walt for a medication evaluation?*
3. *How should John, the counselor, respond to Walt's request for couple counseling?*
4. *Should John have collateral contacts with Walt's family members or any contact with Ben's ex-wife?*
5. *What is the potential for harm in this case?*
6. *What would be the basis for referring Walt and Ben to another therapist?*
7. *How do John's family background, religious views, and current economic considerations in his private practice affect his clinical decision making?*

8. *What would you do if you were seeing Walt?*
9. *How does your series of decisions reflect a positive approach to ethics?*

REFERENCES

American Association for Marriage and Family Therapy. (2001). *AAMFT code of ethics.* Washington, DC: Author.

American Psychiatric Association. (2001). *Diagnostic and statistical manual of mental disorders.* (4th ed., text revision). Washington, DC: Author.

Barnett, J. E., & Yutrzenka, B. A. (2002). Nonsexual dual relationships in professional practice with special applications to rural and military communities. In A. A. Lazarus, & O. Zur (Eds.), *Dual relationships and psychotherapy* (pp. 273–286). New York: Springer.

Brendel, J. M., & Nelson, K. W. (1999). The stream of family secrets: Navigating the islands of confidentiality and triangulation involving family therapists. *The Family Journal, 7,* 112–117.

Bumiller, E. (July 22, 2011). Obama ends "Don't ask, don't tell" policy. Retrieved from http://www.nytimes.com/2011/07/23/us/23military.html

Christensen, T. M. (2001). A bold perspective on counseling with couples and families: An interview with Arnold A. Lazarus. *The Family Journal, 9,* 343–349.

Cottone, R. R. (2001). A social constructivist model of ethical decision making in counseling. *Journal of Counseling and Development, 79,* 39–45.

Crews, J. A., & Hill, N. R. (2005). Diagnosis in marriage and family counseling: An ethical double bind. *The Family Journal, 13,* 63–66.

Fall, K. A., & Lyons, C. (2003). Ethical considerations of family secret disclosure and post-session safety management. *The Family Journal, 11,* 281–285.

Foucault, M. (1982). *The archaeology of knowledge & the discourse on language.* New York: Vintage.

Frame, M. W. (2000). Spiritual and religious issues in counseling: Ethical considerations. *The Family Journal, 8,* 72–74.

Gladding, S. T. (2011). *The counseling dictionary: Concise definitions of frequently used terms* (3rd ed.). Boston: Pearson.

Gurman, A. S. (2008). A framework for the comparative study of couple therapy: History, models and applications. In A. S. Gurman (Ed.), *Clinical handbook of couple therapy* (pp. 1–26). New York: Guilford Press.

Hare-Mustin, R. T. (1994). Discourses in the mirrored room: A postmodern analysis of therapy. *Family Process, 33,* 19–35.

Hendricks, B., Bradley, L. J., Southern, S., Oliver, M., & Birdsall, B. (2011). Ethical code for the International Association of Marriage and Family Counselors. *The Family Journal, 19,* 217–224.

Hermann, M. A., & Herlihy, B. R. (2006). Legal and ethical implications of refusing to counsel homosexual clients. *Journal of Counseling & Development, 84,* 4414–4418.

Hill, N. R., & Crews, J. A. (2005). The application of an ethical lenses to the issue of diagnosis in marriage and family counseling. *The Family Journal, 13,* 176–180.

Hoyt, M. F., & Gurman, A. S. (2011, in press). Wither couple/family therapy? *The Family Journal, 19,* 13–17.

Jordan, A. E., & Meara, N. M. (1990). Ethics and the professional practice of psychologists: The role of virtues and principles. *Professional Psychology: Research and Practice, 21,* 107–114.

Kaschak, E., & Tiefer, L. (Eds.) (2001). *A new view of women's sexual problems.* Binghamton, NY: Haworth Press.

Lazarus, A. A. (2002). How certain boundaries and ethics diminish therapeutic effectiveness. In *Dual relationships and psychotherapy.* New York: Springer.

Lebow, J. L., & Gurman, A. S. (1995). Research assessing couple and family therapy. *Annual Review of Psychology, 46*, 27–57.
Masters, W. H., & Johnson, V. E. (1966). *Human sexual response*. Boston, MA: Little, Brown & Co.
Masters, W. H., & Johnson, V. E. (1970). *Human sexual inadequacy*. Boston, MA: Little, Brown & Co.
Meara, N. M., Schmidt, L. D., & Day, J. D. (1996). Principles and virtues: A foundation for ethical decisions, policies, and character. *Counseling Psychologist, 24*, 4–77.
Murray, C. E., & Murray, T. L. (2007). The family pharm: An ethical consideration of psychopharmacology in couple and family counseling. *The Family Journal, 15*, 65–71.
New York Times. (July 25, 2011). After long wait, same sex couples marry in New York. Retrieved from http://www.nytimes.com/2011/07/25/nyregion/after-long-wait-same-sex-couples-marry-in-new-york.html?pagewanted=all
Sanchez, L., Nock, L., Wright, J.D., & Gager, C.T. (2002). Setting the clock forward or back?: Covenant marriage and the "divorce revolution." *Journal of Family Issues, 23(1)*, 91–120.
Sexuality Information and Education Council of the United States. (n.d.). *Making the connection: Sexuality and reproductive health: Life behaviors of a sexually healthy adult*. Retrieved from http://www.siecus.com/pubs/cnct/cnct0002.html
Smith, J. A., & Smith, A. H. (2001). Dual relationships and professional integrity: An ethical dilemma case of a family counselor as clergy. *The Family Journal, 9*, 438–443.
Southern, S., Cade, R., & Devlin, J. (2010). Dialectics of marriage: Commitment as solution. *Professional Counseling Digest*, Retrieved from counselingoutfitters.com/vistas/ACAPCD-33.pdf
Southern, S., Smith, R. L., & Oliver, M. (2005). Marriage and family counseling: Ethics in context. *The Family Journal, 13*, 459–466.
Sperry, L. (2005). Health counseling with individuals, couples, and families: Three perspectives on ethical and professional practice. *The Family Journal, 13*, 328–331.
Steigerwald, F., & Forest, A. (2004). An examination of gender and ethics in family counseling—Part 2: A case study approach using a social constructionism model of ethical decision making. *The Family Journal, 12*, 278–281.
Tiefer, L. (2002). Beyond the medical model of women's sexual problems: A campaign to resist the promotion of "female sexual dysfunction". *Sexual and Relationship Therapy, 17*, 127–135.
Tiefer, L. (2004). A New View of women's sexual problems by the working group on a New View of women's sexual problems. In L. Tiefer (Ed.), *Sex is not a natural act & other essays*. (pp. 251–256). Boulder, CO: Westview Press.
Weigel, D. J., & Baker, B. G. (2002). Unique issues in rural couple and family counseling. *The Family Journal, 10*, 61–69.
Wilcoxon, S. A., Remley, T. P., Jr., & Gladding, S. T. (2012). *Ethical, legal, and professional issues in marriage and family therapy* (5th ed.). Upper Saddle River, NJ: Pearson.
Woody, R. H., & Woody, J. D. (2001). The future of marriage and family therapy. In R. H. Woody, & J. D. Woody (Eds.), *Ethics in marriage and family therapy*. Washington, DC: American Association for Marriage and Family Therapy.
World Health Organization. (January 2002). Retrieved from http://www2.hu-berlin.de/sexology/GESUND/ARCHIV/PSH.HTM
Younggren, J. N., & Hjelt, S. (2010) When marital therapy isn't. *The National Psychologist, September/October*, pp. 8–9.

12

Your Ethics: A Trip of Ethical Discovery in Addictions Counseling

Michael J. Taleff

THE FORESEEN DESTINATION

When finished with this chapter, readers may wish to:

- Reassess their addiction ethic opinions in light of today's complex ethical problems.
- Assess the suitability of their ethical thoughts and positions.
- Make an effort to uncover hidden flaws in their ethics and make corrections.
- Recalibrate their addiction ethical foundation as needed.
- Consider the position that all addiction ethics requires judgment whether you like it or not.
- Take a proactive stance and make the best addiction ethical judgments possible.
- Create a personal ethical map.

GETTING ON THE ROAD

You have to admit that learning ethics rarely tops the list of addiction professionals' interests. The latest greatest therapies usually hold that distinction. Yet, if anything is sure to make one's blood boil and spark a spirited discussion, it is a good ethical problem or dilemma. Sadly, many people just spout words and think such verbiage geysers count as an argument that resolves an addiction ethical issue. More often than not, they go on and on without really knowing what they are talking about—they just spray words. This is not a suitable way to make ethical decisions in today's addiction field. One has to learn how to make good judgments about morally and ethically sensitive matters (Grayling, 2007) and determine what should be done in difficult cases (Grayling, 2010). That is true for addiction ethical matters as well.

Now if you are really in the market to make a thoughtful stand on your ethical decisions and query others who claim to make good ethical decisions, you need *ethical maturity*. And that means you need to become responsible for your thinking to get through such dilemmas (Neiman, 2009; Taleff, 2010). A huge first step toward that maturity is acquiring clarity of thought, which seemingly in this day and age had gone out of fashion. You also need a good ethics vocabulary (Neiman, 2009). Likewise, you need the courage to come up with ethical decisions and not cop-out by offering the lame excuse of, "I don't want to judge." Finally, the last thing in the world you want to be facing today's complex addiction ethical problems is ethically lame. So, how then do you get this maturity, vocabulary, and clarity? Ah, that is where maps come into play.

EXPLORING THE TERRITORY

START WITH A GOOD MAP

To really delve into addiction ethics, you need maps. Maps have two central functions. One, they guide, direct, and funnel you from one point to another. Maps are most useful to find places to which you have never been. There is no need for maps when you know your way, only when you do not. In this case, we are talking about finding your way to new ethical destinations. Maps, then, help from wondering aimlessly in the dark, bumping into things, and morally bruising yourself. Moreover, such maps let you discover where you are.

The second major map function is that they give you the lay of the land. Good topography maps let you scan the landscape so as to say. They give you the big picture, the wide vista, all the mountains, seas, and valleys. Sometimes that vista can just take your breath away, for you can see the landscape from horizon to horizon, and even imagine beyond. In our case, it is the ethical landscape. And it is vast, absorbing, and intricate. To appreciate the map, we need only start with some core notions.

A FEW CRUCIAL, BUT NECESSARY CONCEPTS

First, you need to step back, so to say, and take in this big picture of addiction ethics. It is called *ethical perspective* (Cutler, 2004), and it gives you the distanced total view. This is akin to standing on the rim of the Grand Canyon and surveying a really big chunk of real estate. You can see all kinds of colossal things from this view.

The ethical perspective entails three big perspectives (Figure 12.1). They are metaethics, normative ethics, and practical ethics (Taleff, 2010).

Metaethics is about the very nature of right and wrong (Law, 2007) and addresses the big, big issues, such as,

- Are there such things as ethical facts?
- Can ethical issues ever be completely known?
- Are all ethical judgments merely subjective?
- How do such questions apply to addiction ethics?

In the spirit of experimentation, try to frame a past or present addiction ethical dilemma in which you were involved into one of these big questions. What did your answers do to your ethical issue? More than likely, you arrived at some big amorphous thing. That is because metaethics is a big amorphous map, but you may have begun to form some perspective, and that is the point. Let us move on.

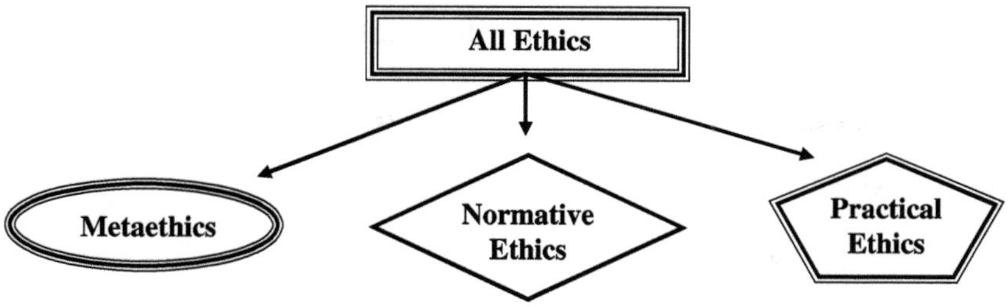

FIGURE 12.1 Ethics: The big picture.

Closing in a bit more, we go to the second big ethical view or map. It is called *normative ethics*, and it has everything to do with how you will measure or gauge right and wrong. These ideas tell you what you should do and give a few rules to do it (Law, 2007).

One big perspective within normative ethics (and there is no way getting around these terms, so bear with it) is called *utilitarianism*, and it essentially states you gauge right and wrong by whether the moral action produced the greatest happiness for all involved. So, go back to a past addiction ethical issue you encountered and assess it via this perspective. Did the final action produce the greatest happiness? If you assessed that it would, consider yourself leaning in a utilitarian direction. Consider such an assessment a little self-discovery.

Another normative perspective is called *deontology*. It means doing your duty, and if that duty is assessed as good, really good, it could be applied as a universal standard. Again, go back to your past moral issue. If you did your duty, and you felt that this duty could be applied to all people in the world (aka the *categorical imperative*), then consider yourself a deontologist. Another discovery.

There are other perspectives in the normative realm like *virtue ethics* where you make your ethical decisions based on doing the right thing because it is within your character to do so. Good virtues are honesty, having a sense of justice, and being civil. Bad virtues include such things as selfishness, sloth, and rudeness.

While space does not allow it, other perspectives include *feminist ethics* (ethics of care), *divine command* ethics (following precepts of sacred books), and *social contract theory* (live by the rules of society so we can all get along). (See Chapter 1 for a discussion of some of these perspectives.)

Landmark 1

CASE EXAMPLE

If at this point you could not recall an ethical problem or dilemma, consider whether you would report a positive urine analysis to a probation officer on a client you have been working with for some time. The client is making good progress and seems sincere, but admits he did drink about a six-pack last night after he heard his grandmother, who raised him, died. The client

(*continued*)

reports that he was really upset in that the death was sudden. However, the probation officer has made it clear that *any* slips from this client will result in 6 months in the local county jail.

What should you do; what is your ethical decision?

See that question in the Landmark box? It brings us to what is called *practical ethics* or what you consider to be your personal set of ethics. Often, the personal comes from what big perspective you favor. If, at this point, some ethical foundation is forming in your mind, then you are standing on the portion of the map that says, "You are here."

A COUPLE OF WIDE-RANGING QUESTIONS

In keeping with this big perspective theme, I need to ask you to consider a few more big questions. For instance, given what we have covered to this point, who is making your addiction ethical decisions? Yes, I know the question may sound odd, but consider it for a minute. The usual answer to that question is, "Of course I make my own ethical decisions." Really? What if many of your decisions are already made by authority figures, many of whom you have never met. For example, have you not deferred to a state code of ethics for answers? If so, that codebook was created by authority figures whom, I venture to say, you never met. Moreover, when faced with an addiction ethical problem, have you ever deferred to a sacred text (Bible, Quran) for ethical answers? Those are surely authorities created by figures long since dead, but still speaking today.

In contrast to authorities making your ethical decisions for you, is the position called the *autonomy perspective*. The assumption here is while you respect the various ethical foundations in existence today, you are self-determined and responsible for your own actions and decisions. And making your decisions is a matter of who you are (Taleff, 2010). This is a big step toward the ethical maturity mentioned above. As Kant suggests, it comes with your reflection, your self-determination, and your courage not to simply listen to others or cooperate with their answers without some thought (Hedges, 2009).

Recall the question was, who or what are making your addiction ethical decisions? You? Or is it something or somebody else? Perhaps, it is a combination. To be at the top of your ethical game, you need to figure that out. It is part of the discovery process and leaves you the choice of moving around on our metaphorical map.

Landmark 2

CASE EXAMPLE

Coming into the lunchroom of your program one day, you discover a spread of fresh pizza with all the amenities. The pizza is your favorite, and you are hungry after a tough morning. Puzzled, you turn to a colleague and inquire as to who

(*continued*)

provided the free lunch. She tells you it was from a pharmaceutical representative, who only asks that the entire staff take a few minutes of their lunch to listen to a new drug lecture. The drug in question could be helpful to some of your clients. Your hungry stomach does a little flip-flop. You have encountered this situation in the past, and partook of the feast, but felt a bit bad afterward. The thought you had was, "Am I being bribed to throw my support behind this drug?" Just then, your supervisor, always the authority, comes along and encourages all to eat. "It's okay. Don't worry about anything. Eat and just sit through the drug session."

1. *Your stomach is growling.*
2. *What do you do?*
3. *Who will make your choice?*

Okay, on to our next big question. What criteria should you use to make your ethical decisions? We covered a few of them already, but this criteria thing needs a bit more examination. We are talking about standards here, and you keenly need to be aware of yours. A way to figure this out is to assess in which of the following three broad standards you generally fall. For instance, are you a *formalist*? If so, you use established criteria to make your decisions, like the state ethical codes and the scared books we spoke of. Should this feel about right, you have made a discovery.

If you hold to a *relativist* position, you essentially believe that no one ethical position is better than another. This position does not deny ethical positions, only that one is not superior to another (Baggini & Fosl, 2003). The problem with this position lies in how you arrive at an overall ethical foundation. For instance, how would you select among the variety of positions of addiction ethical decisions you have to make without looking like you court favoritism with a particular case? Or, how do you justify switching ethical positions for different ethical cases while still holding that whatever you selected is not superior to another position that you could have chosen? Hopefully, the one you selected is the best, but as a relativist how do you justify the one you selected?

The last position is call *contextualism*. Those who hold to this position believe that the ethical context is the key factor. As such, each addiction ethical context is unique, and it is only after you have obtained sufficient information on the particular case that you then can make an informed decision.

So, which of the broad standards feels right to you? Once you decide that, you have made another self-discovery.

CRITICAL THOUGHT

The next map segment looks at how you think about ethical issues. So, how do you think about ethics? Yes, a question not often asked, but it should be. Notice the question does not ask *what* you think, but *how* you do it. If "how" sounds a bit baffling, for clarity's sake, we examine three major sections. First, we cover in what way your mind dulls thought on its own, and then we take a look at a few malicious biases and fallacies.

THE ETHICAL MAP IS FRAUGHT WITH DANGERS

Our brain evolved to think rather poorly, a sad but true fact (Gazzaniga, 2005). For example, brain research has uncovered a host of biases we all seemingly are disposed to use. Not only do such biases distort daily thinking, but they also garble good ethical judgment. In fact, you and I are hardwired for error (Buchanan, 2007). With that caveat in mind, you and I need to be aware of these biases so we do not fall prey to their tricks, or we will fall off the edge of our map.

There are a ton of these biases, but I want to outline just a few of the more significant ones (Taleff, 2006). One noteworthy bias is our propensity to make meaning out of almost anything. Be it a rationale for natural events from the other side of the world, two isolated events in time or space, or complete random events, humans will try to make some meaning out of it. Now the really big issue here is that we tend to make such connections based on the existing biases in our head. Therein lies the potential for problems. Why? Because the bias in our mind will narrow our vision and constrict the dimensions to see things clearly, and that includes ethical decisions.

How does this apply to addiction ethics? Good question. It is related this way. Say you hear of an addiction ethical problem. Let us make it a counselor who breached some boundary violation with a client. If your existing bias is a 12-Step perspective, you might see that the ethical problem came about due to a character defect as suggested by that organization. Your conclusion might be: The person who committed the ethical violation has some "character defect." That would be your bias. In a similar vein, if you hold to *virtue ethics*, you might specify what exactly the character defect is. Recall that virtue ethics specifies a number of them. For our boundary violation example, you can select from lust, covetousness, or perhaps selfishness. That would be your bias, and it would constrict ethical options. The point is for you to see how the general human propensity to make meaning works. So, with this little insight in mind, how accurate are your ethical decisions knowing they are often buried under layers of bias?

Let us look at another bias. This one is called *simplification* (Taleff, 2010). Here, we (you and I) are partial to nice, basic, packaged answers to a variety of things, including ethical issues. Forget the fuss and complications because humans are not particularly fond of complexity. Yet the reality of addiction ethical problems is that they are intricate. For example, say an addiction counselor has been found padding her time sheets to get overtime pay, arguably a small, but still an ethical violation, nonetheless. Your first simplified reaction is? (Whatever it was, it probably was not too good.) Now, what if you found out that she has financial problems? Or, she is having a tough time feeding her two young kids. At this point, you realize that your first simplified conclusion just got thrown a complex wrinkle, and you may have to reassess. But, what if now you find out she has a bit of a gambling issue and has been spending the money she could be using to feed her kids on tons of lottery tickets (next complex wrinkle). What now is your ethical assessment? You then find out she has begun treatment on her own to address the gambling issue, but the treatment is costing her money she does not have (third complex wrinkle). What now is your ethical assessment? Then, you find out she has a history of doing this from her past three jobs. Then, ... ah you get the picture.

What at first seemed fairly simple has grown into this complex monstrosity. The point is most of the addiction ethical issues we face will not have simple explanations. Yet, your propensity to simplify them (fall prey to bias) will persist. So, be on guard.

One last bias to review, from the swarm that exists out there, is called the *confirmation bias*. Here again, you and I have a natural tendency only to look for evidence that supports our particular points of view and beliefs (Taleff, 2010). The bias is so strong in us that when forced to face evidence that does not match our beliefs, we will find ways to criticize, twist, or even out and dismiss the opposing evidence.

Try now to envision what such a bias could do to addiction ethical judgments. The confirmation bias will press you to stick to an ethical conclusion despite evidence that might directly oppose that belief. Is that any way to make ethical judgments?

Landmark 3

CASE EXAMPLE

A client (Chester) comes into your care (inpatient program) with a history of stealing from others. This very same client was in your program about a year ago. At that time, your clinical team administratively discharged Chester for stealing from a number of clients. While he denied the accusation, the lost items were found in his personal locker. He claimed he was framed, but your program discharged him anyway. After Chester left, the stealing instantly stopped. Now, he is back. He claims he really wants to get sober this time, and asks for another chance.

You recall Chester from his previous admission. You felt the evidence for the discharge decision was sufficient and justified. Essentially you thought he was guilty of stealing. Moreover, you did not particularly like the fellow and was glad he was discharged, and you are not real happy that he is back.

Within 1 day of Chester's admission, Kendra (another client) complains that her purse is missing. She left it on the breakfast table this morning, and when she went back to get it, it was gone. Chester was eating breakfast about the same time.

1. *What bias do you need to watch out for in this case?*
2. *Then what would you do?*

Beware that all these biases need not skew your addiction ethical decisions. There are ways to avoid becoming entrapped in these and the variety of other innate biases, which unattended again will just drop you off the edge of our map.

A FEW MORE BIASES

Other notable bias problems are thought-stopping clichés and slogans (Hedges, 2009). And thought stopping they are. I have seen it time and again. Emotionally declared and profoundly worded slogans entrap all within earshot to agree, be it agreement via a nodding head, approving smile, or fist shot into the air. "An eye for an eye," and "do unto others . . ." are prime examples. When stated in a stirring manner, no further thought ensues and the rousing slogan is simply accepted, no questions asked. And all thought stops. People seem to be mesmerized by such simple, stirring slogans, as is a deer caught in the headlights of an oncoming car. But as we have seen, addiction ethics tends to be complex, and needs informed thought.

In a similar vein, be aware that merely to explain something is not to excuse it (Neiman, 2009). This is referred to as a *near argument* (Taleff, 2010). Near arguments are more like commentaries or observations that provide no reasons or premises to support a conclusion; just report or state what is going on. Merely reporting and stating what is going on are not reasons nor do they provide proof or evidence. This is a fine point to be sure, but many folks in our field stumble over this fine distinction.

Landmark 4

CASE EXAMPLE

You serve on a recruiting committee for your substance abuse program. You happen to be looking for a qualified counselor to fill a recent vacancy. A candidate has submitted a resumé. Among the usual items on her resume, this individual gives the impression she has 2 years of counseling experience, which would fit the needs of your program well.

You call the individual in for an interview and the applicant confirms the years of experience. At this point, you call references and find out that two of the years of experience were actually doing clerical not clinical work within the substance abuse program she worked.

You call the applicant to account for what seems to be an embellishment. She explains she really needs the job, has young children to feed, and feels she learned by talking to the counseling staff where she worked as a secretary.

Does the explanation warrant excusing the embellishment?

A SMIDGEN OF FALLACIES

We just need to review a few out-and-out fallacies before moving on. The first is the *appeal to the masses*. An example would be where most, if not all, of the staff in an addiction program does not think charging insurance companies a little extra time for their counseling sessions is bad under the guise of "everyone does it." While that may be so, it still is unethical. How about administrators pocketing money from a program and when confronted they imply you would be disloyal to report them. This is called a *red herring* because it distracts you from a real issue onto a false issue. And lastly, from the multitude of fallacies, is the ever-present *appeal to authority*. Here, addiction professionals might be tempted to take the word of certain authorities alone, without at least offering some questions or using a dram of their own critical thought. Not a good idea.

THE EMOTIONAL SIDE OF ETHICS

Ethical problems rarely come free of emotional charge. The emotional twitch or charge you feel is what tips you off that something ethical or moral is afoot. Yet, this is how many folks (Marcus, 2008), including addiction counselors, make their first and final ethical judgments. It is quick and visceral and has a certain satisfaction of certainty associated with the elicited emotion. The problem is, if you make your ethical judgments exclusively in this manner, should such emotions be your exclusive decision maker? Generally, it is not the best way to make solid ethical judgments. We need to defer to a thing called *fair mindedness*, or the ability to be intellectually honest, reasonable, and free from prejudice, strong emotion, and deception (Paul, 1993; Thomson, 1999). Yet, we do not want to entirely dump all of our emotions. They have their place in addiction ethics.

MORAL EMOTIONS THAT STIR THE SOUL: A JAUNT DOWN THIS MAP

A fellow named Pizarro (2000) maintained that emotion plays an important role in our ethical judgments. As we have seen, one such role is to heighten our awareness that an ethical situation is at hand. And while runaway emotions are not good for making ethical judgments, with just the right emotional level, we tend to focus a bit better, which gets us to attend to the specifics and the variables at hand. In addition, our moral emotions add power and energy to the desire to do good and shun things bad. Individuals have studied moral emotions, and one in particular, Haidt (2003), has actually found four broad families of moral emotions.

The first moral emotions are called *other condemning emotions*. Generally, they have a disapproving flavor about them, often directed at liars and cheaters among others. They include:

- *Anger*—An underappreciated moral emotion. Some consider it an immoral emotion associated with violence. But, anger is also the backbone of unjust indignity and standing up for what is right. The latter anger was the driving force behind Mothers Against Drunk Driving, arguably a good thing.
- *Disgust*—Moral circumstances such as betrayal, hypocrisy, and cruelty. Imagine the emotion toward someone who inflicts cigarette burns on a child, and you get this particular emotion.
- *Contempt*—A halfway emotion between anger and disgust. It is frequently directed at those who fake physical pain in order to receive insurance benefits.

Next are the *self-conscious emotions*. These feelings are meant to constrain some of our more negative thoughts and behaviors. They include:

- *Guilt*—If you harm or inflict suffering on others and do not have an antisocial personality, you will feel this. Guilt simply judges bad behavior and often motivates confession and redemption. You need only go to a 12-Step speaker's meeting and listen closely to find that this emotion has had a part in one's recovery.

- *Shame*—This is darker and abundantly more painful than guilt. While also elicited by bad behavior, it is one where others observe the moral violations. Guilt is private, shame is public; thus the extra sting.
- *Embarrassment*—This is less intense than shame or guilt, but associated with mortification and humiliation. One only needs to recall a drunken person stumbling into a wedding cake and feeling mortification of ruining a once-in-a-lifetime event.

Haidt (2003) described two groups of smaller moral emotions. Quickly, they include the *other praising emotions* and the *other suffering emotions*. As to the first, it consists of two prime emotions *gratitude* and *elevation*. The former is one of appreciation and indebtedness toward a supporter and is often found again in 12-Step groups where a sponsor is shown thanks and appreciation. Elevation is often found around holiday seasons where we are a bit more prone to be kind or where we hold one in esteem and wish to follow that example. Three emotions constitute the other suffering emotions. *Sympathy*, said to be the basis of morality, is elicited when we see others suffer. You cannot practice long in the addiction field and not experience this. *Compassion* surfaces when the suffering of others moves us. It often stirs us to be of help, as seen in the eyes of many a good addiction counselor. Lastly, *empathy*, which is not technically an emotion, but a gauge by which we try to feel what others feel. Through empathy we often become sympathetic and compassionate.

Landmark 5

POINT OF REFLECTION

Based on this moral emotions review, have you ever noticed what is your first response to addiction ethical situations you encounter?

For example, what is generally your first emotional response to:

- Counselor sexual exploitation
- Practicing elements of counseling in which one has no expertise
- Offering unequal services to clients based on race or gender
- Receiving monetary compensation for referring clients to a certain program
- Utilizing treatment interventions that lack empirical support

1. *What have you discovered?*
2. *Where are you on the moral emotional map?*

CRITICAL THINKING PRINCIPLES

Time for critical thinking! But be assured, this need not send shivers up your spine. It is not difficult; rather, there are a few basic principles that any good addiction counselor these days can easily understand and which they actually need.

First and foremost, any addiction ethical judgment you make is simply an argument. A key point of this chapter is that in order to have ethics you need to make judgments, be they about your behavior or the behavior of others. All we are asking is that the judgments you make be good ones.

So, good judgments need to be good arguments. To arrive at good arguments you first need good claims, or *reasons* (premises) that prove something on which the *conclusion* can stand. Reasons are generally recognized or implied by words such as "because," "since," and "for the reason." Conclusions are marked by words such as "therefore," "so," and "thus." A very simple addiction ethical argument (technically a syllogism) is:

> As an addiction counselor, I know not to overstep personal boundaries in counseling.
>
> One such personal boundary breach is dating a client in my care.
>
> It obscures my clinical judgment, creates power differentials, and invites the potential to take advantage of the vulnerable.
>
> Therefore, I do not date clients.

In graphic form, this argument looks like this.

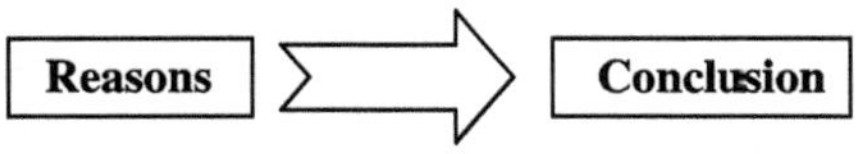

Your argument (addiction ethical judgment) also needs a dash of *clarity*. This means it should be plainly defined, understandable, and free of vague or ambiguous statements or premises (Moore & Parker, 1995). Next, we need a splash of *relevance* (Taleff, 2010). That simply means keeping the facts linked to the point of your ethical judgment. For our discussion, you would bring evidence to back your judgment, not idle speculation. Then, your conclusion needs to be quantified or specified to your particular judgment. The finer your argument (judgment) the better, because what applies to one case may not apply in another. Lastly, your ethical arguments can be *simple*, supplying one piece of evidence for your conclusion, but often they are *complex*, which means you will draw from many sources of evidence (Taleff, 2010).

Remember, the ethical conclusions you come to always reflect right and wrong. So, such conclusions need to be as solid, clear, and thoughtful as possible. Critical thinking illuminates the detail of our ethical map.

TIME TO PUT IT ALL INTO PRACTICE

Trying to make ethical decisions looks like a hodgepodge of intuitions, emotional responses, and bad thinking among others, but it is not. The final piece of our map is to bring these seemingly disparate elements into a usable process or procedure.

Yet, we first need a quick word on *open mindedness*. When making any ethical decision, keep in mind the principles that consider alternative views, a sincere dedication to the pursuit of truth, a consideration of the best evidence, tolerance, the appreciation of education, and the avoidance of indoctrination and dogma (Taleff, 2010).

AN ETHICS JUDGMENT KIT

There exists a device or formula that can help make sense of the ethical potpourri just touched on. It is called *The Addiction Ethics Judgment Kit* (Taleff, 2010). It is a decision-making format, which consists of 10 simple steps. Consider it a map compass.

1. *Collect Yourself and Settle Down.* Sometimes the ethical violations you encounter will elicit strong emotions. As noted, humans do not think well under the influence of strong emotions. So settle down, take a very deep breath, and get them under control. Use them, do not allow them to use you.
2. *Identify the Ethical Problem/Dilemma.* Ask the questions: What is it that is wrong? Does the situation stink? Should something be done?
3. *Gather Your Facts and Evidence.* Good questions are your guide. At this point, ask questions like: what do I know, what do I need to know, how reliable are the facts of the case?
4. *Consult Reliable Guidelines and Authorities.* Time to consult your state and national guidelines, rules, and available experts.
5. *Look at the Problem Through Various Ethical Perspectives.* Ask what the problem would look like through the duty perspective, or what would be the greatest happiness for all involved, among others.
6. *Think Critically.* Now you are coming close to the judgment phase and it needs solid thought. Form an argument. Make sure it has good reasons for the coming conclusion, and watch out for those pesky fallacies.
7. *Weigh Your Arguments and Make Your First Judgment.* Time to stick your neck out and make a judgment. At this point, it is only a prototype argument.
8. *Rest and Reflect.* Relax for a day, get a little distance, and put your judgment on the back burner.
9. *Retest Your First Judgment.* Review steps 2 through 7, and finalize your argument.
10. *What Now Is Your Best Course of Action?* No going back. You have thought, collected evidence, and examined the situation through different perspectives; now is the time for your decision. What is the best thing to do?

This kit is not foolproof, nothing is, but it is a reasonable compass with which to make good addiction ethical decisions.

SIGNPOSTS FOR FUTURE TREKS

Taking a look at where we have been on the journey, remember:

- Ethics is about judging
- Ethics cannot exist without judgment
- Addiction ethics needs judgment to exist as well
- So, when you judge, judge well
- To judge well, one needs a map

This chapter has been an entreaty for you to think for yourself. Judge for yourself. Question and question again. Really good ethics is about discussion, thinking, reflection, and being tolerant of other views, but still coming up with the best judgment of which you are capable.

If an ethical judgment is rendered on a client, a colleague, or yourself, you are obliged not to accept it blindly, but think the decision through, and assess if the rendering is just. If it is, by all means concur. If you discover flaws in the argument, fight for justice.

INSIGHTS GAINED FROM THE JOURNEY

Years ago, while conducting ethics workshops, the form and style I used were, shall we say, stilted, as were the many I attended. They came with ethical maps not of my own, but of others. While such views were helpful, they did not quite do the trick for me. Things were laid out too pat, too easy. When the time came to apply what I learned to real situations, I was left wanting. So, I began to think and question. Low and behold, I began to envision a new kind of addiction ethics workshop. One that raised the bar a bit and challenged participants to really ponder addiction ethics. A book followed that. All this came about because I began to think. Not a very trendy path these days, but the difference between then and now is distinctive.

I think distinctive because I have a better moral sense and do not flutter in the wind of an ethical tempest as in days past. Moreover, I trust my ethical judgment a bit more but still seek the advice of sages I have come to learn to trust because of my exploration.

Yet, this moral sense comes at a price. You have to work at it. Moral reflection, self-determination, and courage do not come easily. You do not merely read a book and absorb things like reflection, determination, or courage. Such traits are not passive, idle, or immobile. You have to work, and work, and work at it. You just need to do it. As Jack Kennedy once said, "We do these things because they are hard."

This chapter, map if you will, is just one way to get to your ethical destinations. It is erected on the shoulders of people I cannot hope to emulate. Yet, most importantly, it is my map, but I do not think necessarily yours. So, that puts you on the preverbal spot.

Your ethical map—how shall it look?

The editors asked me to present a personal ethical testimony for this section. This particular one had those subtle ethical filaments to it, not like one of those easy-to-recognize in-your-face types. I have found that over the years these subtle situations give you fits.

A long time ago, I became the clinical director of a fledging rehabilitation program. The program needed a lot of work, in terms of its physical needs and to the quality and expertise of the counselors. In discussions with the owner, I appealed to his ethical obligation to provide clients the simple things, such as bed linens, repairing dormitory doors to keep out cold air so clients could sleep comfortably, and decent food. All were soon won. That was the easy part of that job. But, persuading the staff to update their antiquated "counseling techniques" was a monumental task.

Part of my supervisory duties was to observe individual and group sessions and provide guidance. In addition, I saw part of my supervisory job as one of assessing the professional level of my staff, reinforcing quality work, and suggesting changes when needed. Of particular importance was my belief, then as now, that as an addiction counselor you have the ethical obligation to upgrade your education and professional development. And an ethical obligation it is. For example, evidence-based treatments are well known, and if not used, the addiction counselor may well be in the throngs of an ethical violation. For, if you persist on using "techniques" that have no supportive data, then continued use of such "techniques" comes under the guise of problematic treatments. We have an ethical obligation to avoid such "techniques" (Taleff, 2010).

Well, would you not know it, this program had a wasp's nest of counselors who used a host of problematic techniques and refused to use the better treatments that were available at the time.

At the pinnacle of the problematic "techniques" and of a particular stubborn nature to eradicate was the harsh confrontations these counselors used on many a client. I still recall walking around the grounds and hearing the foulest-sounding language roaring from counseling offices directed at our clients. When approached about the need to change such "techniques," I was met with the raft of rationalizations. Most notably, these counselors believed it was only through such harsh approaches that the ever-believed ubiquitous denial was to be broken.

My ethical dilemma was, do I continue to allow those counselors to verbally abuse clients (unethical), or do something to stop it despite the expected irritation and complications from this staff? I opted for the latter.

I started with petitions that indicated that there were no empirical-based data that supported the use of harsh confrontation. As expected, such information was disregarded as my naiveté and my misunderstanding of the refractory nature of addiction. "Only harsh methods would break through the entrenched denial," I was repeatedly told, often in a rather inconsiderate manner.

When I suggested these counselors apply understanding and empathy, which did have good research behind it, I was met with a firestorm of rejection and the omnipresent explanation that such "soft" approaches would merely enable clients and such approaches would result in relapse.

The end to this situation was not even or happy. Many in the nest continued those unethical if not morally repugnant treatments, but now the practices went underground. I rarely ever caught these counselors red-handed again. Moreover, their distaste for the data-driven in-services I offered, or evidence-based conferences was palpable. In addition, snide remarks for attaining state drug and alcohol certification or going back to college were a common occurrence.

A resolution did come about. This cadre of counselors, unhappy with my supervision style, slowly quit one by one. I then made sure that the replacements were willing to hold fast to modern methods and understood that I would not tolerate berating clients in the name of therapy.

In all ethical situations, one has to make a stand. I made mine and have not regretted the stance.

MOVING FORWARD: CASE STUDY AND REFLECTION QUESTIONS

Serena is an addictions counselor in a community-based treatment facility. She has worked at the agency for 5 years and usually finds the clients and the work to be invigorating. When asked, she tells her family and friends how much she loves her work because she knows she is making a difference in the lives of the clients and because it is her way of giving back. Ten years ago, Serena herself was embroiled in a battle with alcoholism. Though she was young when her drinking began, she eventually confronted the damage it was having on her personal life, especially on her relationship with her husband. Serena has been sober for the past 7 years and is proud of the hard work it took to make such an important change in her life.

Three months ago, however, Serena and her family were dealt a huge blow when her husband lost his job. They are currently struggling to make ends meet, and it looks as if they may lose their house because they cannot make the monthly payments. All of their savings are just about depleted; they are behind on multiple bills. With the stress of her financial situation weighing on her, Serena feels out of control. One night, on her way home from work, she decided to stop at the grocery store and found herself in the wine and spirits aisle. She bought a bottle of whiskey and proceeded to drink until she was drunk. The next day, she did not remember how she had even gotten home. Moreover, she was wracked with guilt over her actions, worried about the relapse turning into an ongoing pattern, and distraught over the idea of what her actions might mean for her work at the treatment facility.

REFLECTION QUESTIONS

- *What are the ethical problems for Serena in this case?*
- *What decisions might you make if you were Serena?*
- *What errors in thinking might you have to confront in the decision-making process?*
- *What does your decision tell you about your philosophical ethics leanings?*
- *How might you take a positive (nonlegalistic) approach to the case?*
- *What did you learn as a result of working through this example?*

REFERENCES

Baggini, J., & Fosl, P. S. (2003). *The philosopher's toolkit: A compendium of philosophical concepts and methods.* Madden, MA: Blackwell Publishing.

Buchanan, M. (2007). *The social atom.* New York: Bloomsbury.

Cutler, H. M. (2004). *Ethical argument: Critical thinking in ethics.* New York: Oxford.

Gazzaniga, M. C. (2005). *The ethical brain.* New York: Dana Press.

Grayling, A. C. (2007). *The choice of Hercules.* London: Phoenix.

Grayling, A. C. (2010). *Ideas that matter: The concepts that shape the 21st century.* New York: Basic Books.

Haidt, J. (2003). The moral emotions. In R. J. Davidson, K. R. Scherer, & H. H. Goldsmith (Eds.). *Handbook of affective sciences* (pp. 853–870). Oxford: Oxford University Press.

Hedges, C. (2009). *Empire of illusion: The end of literacy and the triumph of spectacle.* New York: Nation Books.

Law, S. (2007). *Philosophy*. London: DK.
Marcus, G. (2008). *Kluge*. Boston: Houghton Mifflin.
Moore, B. N., & Parker, R. (1995). *Critical thinking* (4th ed.). Mountain View, CA: Mayfield.
Neiman, S. (2009). *Moral clarity: A guide for grown-up idealists*. Princeton, NJ: Princeton University Press.
Paul, R. (1993). *Critical thinking*. Santa Rosa, CA: The Foundation of Critical Thinking.
Pizarro, D. (2000). Nothing more than feelings? The role of emotions in moral judgment. *Journal for the Theory of Social Behavior, 30*(4), 355–375.
Taleff, M. J. (2010). *Advanced ethics for addiction professionals*. New York: Springer Publishing Co.
Thomson, M. (1999). *Critical reasoning in ethics*. London: Routledge.

13

Rebellion and the Absurd: Camus's Moral Philosophy and Ethical Issues in Career Counseling

Kailla Edger

THE FORESEEN DESTINATION

After reviewing this chapter, readers will:

- Understand the purpose, practice, and value of ethical decision making in career counseling.
- Begin to develop clinical awareness of appropriate ethical decision making in career counseling.
- Be familiar with Camus's moral philosophy and how it can inform ethical decision making.
- Be able to articulate how career counseling differs in individual and group settings.
- Be able to engage in thoughtful discussion regarding issues of ethics in career counseling.

GETTING ON THE ROAD

Career counseling theory and practice are foundational to the counseling profession and actually pre-date Carl Rogers and other humanists who built on the human development focus established by career theorists. Career development is viewed as a life path, and the National Career Development Association (NCDA, 2003) defines it as "the total constellation of psychological, sociological, educational, physical, economic, and chance factors that combine to influence the nature and significance of working in the total life span of any given individual" (para. 4). While career can also be defined as "the totality of work—paid and unpaid—[that] one does in his [or] her lifetime" (NCDA, 2003, para. 5), the concept of career development is about life-career planning (Super, 1980) and goes beyond a mere focus on work activities and titles. While some may plan carefully for their career goals, others may take the jobs that come their way or that fit their standards of living. In either event, both groups involve themselves in life–career planning. A clear pattern or path becomes rather evident when an individual reviews his or her career choices. In essence, there is purpose in all of our decisions (Levoy, 1997) and, some philosophers would argue, moral responsibility, as well (Camus, 1956).

This chapter is about ethical issues and questions related to career development and the career counseling process. In order to function in a virtuous manner, career counselors have to answer various questions of ethical merit. For example, how does one use theoretical contexts, different types of career information, the results of assessments, and electronic resources in an ethical way while practicing career counseling? Furthermore, what kinds of career assessments are available, and how can one assure that he or she is using assessments appropriately? And, how can one help clients find a meaningful career path and aid them in understanding that career counseling is much more than a testing and telling process? These questions focus on some of the issues that are explored in this chapter. Throughout our reflection, Camus's philosophy of rebellion is used as the primary framework for helping career counselors make ethical decisions. Finally, the chapter explores multicultural issues with an emphasis on how these have an impact on career development for certain groups. Case studies and discussion questions are provided throughout the chapter to make the information applicable to readers.

EXPLORING THE TERRITORY

CAREER COUNSELING: A BRIEF HISTORICAL BACKGROUND

Career counseling, or vocational guidance as it was formerly known, was central to the formation of the American Counseling Association (ACA) as a professional organization and to counseling becoming recognized as a unique discipline. In 1952, the National Vocational Guidance Association (NVGA), a professional association for vocational guidance counselors, joined with three other organizations to become the American Personnel and Guidance Association (APGA), the forerunner of the ACA. By the 1950s, though, career counseling was already a well-established and researched practice. Indeed, career counseling was born out of necessity in the early 1900s due to World War I, returning veterans, increases in the demand for workers in the industrial sector, the loss of stable jobs in agriculture, and new emerging technologies. Herr and Shahnasarian (2001) contributed greatly to what we know about the evolution of career development practices. They provided a decade-by-decade record of the social, political, and economic influences that have shaped career counseling and make projections about how this counseling specialty will continue to be affected in the 21st century. Although it is difficult to calculate how career development will change in the future, it is almost certain that technology and the information age will continue to have a large impact on people's career concentrations and motivations for generations to come. Similarly, emerging technologies in the information age will continue to lead to new ethical questions and quandaries for all counselors who use technology in their counseling practices, including career counselors who frequently draw on technology-based tools to help clients learn about their vocational self-concepts and as a resource in the counseling process.

THEORETICAL CONSIDERATIONS

As counselors, it is important to understand clients' career concerns from a theoretical perspective. The theoretical perspective is the lens through which counselors view clients' career-related needs and affects how they perceive those needs. In the area of career development, theories explain the process of how individuals explore, choose, and implement career decisions. They illustrate the process of choosing a career, inform counselors about the hurdles people face in career decision making, and introduce them to methods of assisting clients with career-related issues. Good theories explain career development using the smallest number of constructs possible and are applicable to men and women of all cultural and socioeconomic groups (Brown, Brooks, & Associates, 1996).

There are essentially two types of career theories: structural and developmental. Structural theories include the trait and factor approach, Holland's typology, socioeconomic theory, and the theory of work adjustment. These theories identify characteristics of individuals and their work environments in order to find the most complementary relationship between the two. Developmental theories include Super's theory, Krumboltz's social learning theory, decision-making theories, and social-cognitive career theory. These theories define human development through stages of immaturity to maturity in the process of career development and decision making. Environment, as it influences career choice, is often taken into account in developmental theories, and some are more holistic and systems oriented.

Knowing and utilizing theory aids in ethical practice because career development theories are designed to help counselors direct clients purposefully. When utilizing a theoretical orientation in general counseling, a counselor's therapeutic orientation should complement what that counselor's belief system is about how people make changes effectively. It is true that some approaches or techniques work better with certain clients, but counselors do not need to change their orientation for every different client with whom they may engage. Therapeutic orientation defines what a counselor believes about human development and growth. Some counselors may believe that individuals change behaviors after their thought process changes (reflecting cognitive-behavioral theory), while others may believe that it is important to help clients find meaning in order to heal (reflecting existential theories). The theoretical orientation drives the therapeutic relationship, and this is no different in career counseling. Seeking to provide complete and helpful services to clients with career and lifestyle concerns, career counselors should be knowledgeable about and practice from a career-based counseling theory because these theories not only make propositions about how career decision making unfolds but also sensitize counselors to the many factors that influence career and lifestyle choices, helping them to bring depth and insight to the career counseling process. Understanding career theories, thus, is central to ethical career counseling practice, and readers are encouraged to explore these theories in depth before attempting to help clients in the career development process.

UNDERSTANDING CAREER COUNSELING THROUGH PHILOSOPHY

In the following sections, readers are introduced to the ethics of career counseling through Albert Camus's moral philosophy. Camus's central themes of the *absurd* and *rebellion* are highlighted to provide a philosophical groundwork. The discussion is followed by a demonstration of how Camus's philosophy highlights the immense responsibilities ethical career counselors have to their clients.

Albert Camus was born in 1913 in Mondovi, Algeria. His early writings were mainly short plays and journalistic manuscripts that were published locally. In 1951, Camus published his second major philosophical work, *The Rebel*, and this is where his conflict with the existentialists (particularly Jean-Paul Sartre) began (Denton, 1967). Camus was often considered an existentialist, and for good reason, since his arguments were quite compatible with existentialist thought. He upheld a frame of reference which was both humanistic and atheistic, maintained the idea that human beings have the ability to fulfill themselves, saw the foundation of values as existing in human experience, and opposed most of the same authorities and organizations that existentialists went up against (Denton, 1967). However, Camus was dissatisfied being identified as an existential, and he left the existentialist movement to study subject matter that was original to earlier existential inquiry (Barrett, 1962). Camus believed that values did not transcend humanity, and the notion that values were inherent within human existence was a consistent existential theme. He moved away from existentialism when he insisted that values did transcend the individual human being. Camus conflicted most strongly with Sartrian existentialism, so strongly in fact that he separated himself from the existential movement altogether. Camus disagreed with Sartre's notion that human beings create themselves out of nothing (Sartre, 1956). Rather, he believed that human beings have their own unique relationships with the natural world and that values are not simply outcomes of baseless choosing (Denton, 1967). The *absurd* and *rebellion* became the two foundational concepts in Camus's moral philosophy and are elucidated in further detail below.

The Absurd

In *The Myth of Sisyphus*, Camus (1959) acknowledges that the concept of the absurd is not his original idea but, unlike other philosophers, he considers the absurd the starting point of his philosophy rather than the final result. Camus also never expresses actual proof of the absurd because it was a commonly accepted idea among French scholars (Thody, 1957). For Camus, the absurd does not characterize the world; that is, the nature of the world is not absurd. Rather, the concept of the absurd aims to describe the relationship between human beings and the world. This relationship is absurd because human beings are supplied with a number of questions in their relationship with the world for which there are no answers. Camus (1959) noted that the absurd relationship "is that divorce between the mind that desires and the world that disappoints, my nostalgia for unity, this fragmented universe and the contradiction that binds them together" (p. 37). In essence, the absurd is a pattern of empty replies that human beings receive from the nature of their existence. For example, human beings seek order in the universe but no order is found. Unity is sought but only multiplicity is found. When human beings ask how to solve the problem of evil, no guarantee of goodness is ever offered (Denton, 1967). Because of the frustrating relationship human beings have with the world, they are forced into a tense situation where a confrontation is always present. This is the absurd equation with which human beings are consistently faced.

Knowing about the reality of the absurd, Camus poses the one philosophical question which supersedes all others: How does one live in this absurd relationship? Once a human being becomes aware of the absurd, he or she must decide whether life is worth living. According to Camus, human beings become aware of their absurd reality naturally and not through scholarly means. In some moment, a person wakes from the mundane habits of life and realizes that the world does not answer his or her questions. Suffering of innocent people continues. Prayers are not answered. Nothing is guaranteed except the present moment. Faced with the realization that there is no support by gods or a progressive history, a person must decide if he or she should continue living in such a world. Should I live or die? This is Camus's first philosophical question (Denton, 1967). After human beings experience the moment of conscience where a decision must be made about living or dying, they will feel a variety of emotions—scorn, sorrow, happiness. Their condition will seem futile, and they will hate life because of the plight they face. However, when individuals finally realize the essence of their lives—that their lives and their fates belong only to them—they will decide to continue living. In doing so, they will have a passion for living and experiencing the world. For Camus, the most important and enduring emotion is happiness.

Absurdity and the Limits of Knowing

Camus noted that all knowledge comes from sensory experience and that knowledge is relative. For Camus, any knowledge that is attempted to be gained outside of human consciousness is only constructed and falls prey to false impressions of the human thought process. Knowledge is limited to things that are only immediately perceivable or at least capable of being immediately perceivable. Camus rejected the errors in Western philosophy where judgments were made about the construction (namely, laws, principles, and other categories) being more real than the actual constructors (Denton, 1967). For him, knowledge that was claimed to go beyond the absurd limits of knowing usually led to murder in the name of concepts such as justice, truth, freedom, and patriotism because these abstract concepts were somehow deemed more valuable than individual human beings.

Camus noted that knowledge is possible but only within a subjective limitation. While the world is certainly absurd, this is not to say that the world is irrational. The world is neither rational nor irrational because the world does not give way to human reasoning. The world is unreasonable and, therefore, human beings cannot ever totally understand all the phenomena within the world. The limitations of absurdity preclude this possibility (Denton, 1967). Camus believed that human beings could live in an absurd existence without turning to rationalism or irrationalism (i.e., to God, to the church, to government, to suicide, etc.). He discusses a way for human beings to live their lives while facing their absurd reality and limited knowledge of the world. This is the ethics of rebellion in Camus's philosophy—how to live a moral and optimistic life in the face of the absurd.

Rebellion

Camus's philosophy of rebellion begins with the argument of the absurd reality. For Camus, human beings must recognize the absurdity of their relationship with the world and then refuse to escape the absurdity in which they exist. The two forms of escape that human beings could take are physical suicide or philosophical suicide. Physical suicide involves a human being stating "no" to the question, "Is life worth living?" Just because a person did not ask to be brought into this world certainly does not mean that he or she cannot decide to leave it. Philosophical suicide, on the other hand, involves a person accepting reassuring answers to questions which cannot be answered. This would be philosophical suicide because answers are asserted when no answers are available. Camus insisted that human beings should accept the absurd relationship between their intellectual inquiries and the silence of the world. The moral and good state of humanity occurs when individuals consciously accept their limited existence because freedom is attained. In other words, individuals must accept the absurdity of the world without accepting a need to escape from it (Reck, 1962).

Because human beings are inevitably trapped in this absurd relationship with the world and not desiring to escape, they are therefore called to change the world. Camus outlines five tenets that serve as moral guides in his ethics of rebellion. First, individuals must find a balance between complete isolation and total involvement with others. Second, moderation is the ideal for which human beings should strive. The rebellion should be against extremes. Third, trust should be held in nature and the here and now rather than history, idealism of the past, or a utopian future. Fourth, dialogue is strongly encouraged and should be pursued in as many uses as possible—not only in times of conflict. Communication should always be used to prevent conflict and promote harmony with others. Fifth, justice, fair wages, well-being, literacy, and peace should always be endorsed but never through violence. Means and ends should serve as limits on one another (Denton, 1967). With these five tenets, Camus endorses a good and moral life through the balance of components found in the here and now.

Rebellion in Career Counseling

So what does this moral philosophy have to do with ethical issues in career counseling? How is Camus's philosophy of limits relevant to the ethics of career counselors? What is the significance of the relationship with the absurd for this profession? Why rebel? Let us first start with an important point about work. "Work is one of the central components of life activities for most adults" (Brown, 2007, p. 19). For many, work is fundamental, but is it meaningful and important? That is not always the case despite research that shows this is what individuals seek. Research has shown that individuals are most satisfied with their jobs when they feel like they have the greatest degree of control and feel as if what they do is deemed important by others (Brown). It is true that not everyone has this relationship with work, but individuals who seek career counseling are looking for exactly that relationship—a career that is important and appreciated. Does this mean it is meaningful and makes a difference in some way? Camus would probably say so.

Camus's call to rebel is a call to create, a call to transform the callousness of the world (Hanna, 1958). Individuals are called to restructure the world in the here and now by looking for balance and a way to dialogue honestly and openly. The responsibility of the moral man is "to say the king is naked when he is and not [to] go into raptures over his imaginary trappings" (Camus, 1960, p. 171). Individuals must state what they see and not delude themselves in order to make life more comfortable. This is the responsibility we have toward one another in dialogue. Authentic dialogue is honest and, in addition to this, can only occur when each person realizes that he or she does not know everything and does not possess total power. The goal in dialogue can never be conversion because when a human being asserts himself to have total power or knowledge over others, he cannot hear the other in the dialogue because he has no need for it, and so the dialogue ceases to exist.

The primary goal of clinical relationships should be to help clients realize authentic living, and this is demonstrated quite clearly through Camus's description of moral philosophy. The moral person is a person who lives within the philosophy of limitation and in the face of the absurd relationship. This kind of living must imply a human being's awareness of his or her relationship with the world and the refusal to escape this world by either physical or philosophical suicide. The task of the clinician is to bring about this awareness, particularly through open and honest dialogue, which, in itself, is seen as highly moral from Camus's perspective.

Career counselors are even more specific with the task of helping clients become moral beings in the face of an absurd reality. It may seem out of place for a moral philosophy to be central in making career choices, but the affiliation of purpose and career is quite standard in Western culture. Levoy (1997) addresses career development and career choice from a philosophical and spiritual perspective that views work and career choices as inherently central to individuals' lives. He is certainly not unique in this perspective; many other authors do this as well. Career books are often located in both the psychology and the self-help sections, as well as the business sections of book stores. Why is this? Because our cultural perspective usually takes a broad view of centrality when discussing work and career in our lives. This broad view of centrality means that peoples' career choices define who they are as individuals and characterize their purpose as human beings. "Work has many other functions of equal or sometimes greater importance to both society and the individual. It is one way in which the individual relates to society. Work provides the person, and often the family, as well, with status, recognition, affiliation, and similar psychological and sociological products essential for participation in a complex society" (Brown, 2007, p. 18). Through work, individuals find purpose and have a responsibility to others.

Camus believed that if a person decided to live in the face of the absurd and revolt against the absurdity of life, he or she first needed to contemplate on what the nature of his or her rebellion would be. First, an individual must make a tension between being isolated or getting involved. With that said, if either involvement or isolation is chosen, moderation is the ideal goal. This means that a rebel must not go to extremes but, instead, should strive for balance. Preventing conflict is central to Camus's call to action and incorporating dialogue in as many ways as possible frames his moral philosophy. With that said, career counselors should judge the ethical quality of their work through these constructs when considering Camus's philosophical groundwork.

In the revolt, a career counselor must assess whether he or she is helping a client contemplate the nature of his or her rebellion (in this sense, the revolt is equivalent to the career a client chooses to pursue). In choosing a career, a client must first assess whether he or she wants to make a difference in a way that he or she feels is meaningful to self and/or others (i.e., to be *involved*) or simply make money or do what he or she may be good at but not especially passionate about (i.e., to be more or less *isolated*). However, there should be a balance between involvement and isolation that the counselor strives to help the client seek when making career choices. If a person is making a difference for others but barely meeting personal expenses because of a pay scale that does not meet his or her needs then that person would not be as effective due to those limitations. The stress of making ends meet would probably have a negative impact on his desire and ability to help others. On the other hand, if a person is making a lot of money or is doing what he or she does well but the personal fulfillment of a job is nonexistent, he or she will probably be affected in terms of mood and relationship with others. The quality of his or her life would most likely suffer. Therefore, balance is key. This is not to say a decision needs to be equally balanced, but neglecting isolation over involvement (or vice versa) can be destructive for the client (and unethical for the counselor to pursue). By utilizing dialogue, career counselors help clients strive toward balance. Within dialogue, the client should feel understood by the counselor, not judged or misunderstood. Career counselors need to strive to understand clients' lives, their needs, their wants, and their relationships in an effort to help them make the right career choices for them.

Landmark 1

FILM CASE EXAMPLE: A LITERAL CASE OF REBELLION—BILLY ELLIOT (2000)

Background

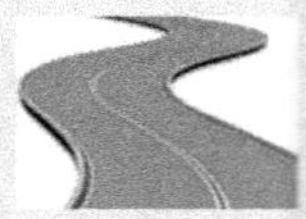

In 1984, Billy Elliot is an 11-year-old boy who lives with his father, brother, and grandmother in a small mining town in Britain. His father, along with the rest of the miners, is on strike and money is oppressively dwindling. Billy discovers ballet when he sees the ballet class going on in the same building he shares for his boxing practice. Billy, first apprehensive, is completely drawn to it and attends regularly. His father finds out about his ballet attendance and forbids him to go. Billy is very upset and thinks his dad is being unreasonable.

Career dilemma through the lens of Camus's moral philosophy

Billie has a gift for ballet. According to Camus's philosophy, he has to find a balance within his environment as he deals with his extreme love of dance and his father's extreme revolt against it. Billy's environmental conditions and events are both supportive and restrictive. His ballet teacher continues to teach him ballet for free because she believes in his ability and realizes he has a gift for dance. She is his primary supporter and mentor. Billy's father

(continued)

and brother restrict him immensely. They forbid him to practice and feel that ballet is for "poofs." They are also poor, and ballet is an expensive practice. Billy's teacher is willing to pay for his journey to the audition, but his father's pride (when he finds out about this) will not allow it. Billy's learning experiences come from his mother primarily. Billy knows that his mother would tell him to pursue his dream and would encourage him to dance if that was what he really wanted. Despite his father's homophobic beliefs about ballet, Billy is unconvinced and only stays away from ballet because he is scared of his father's reactions. Billy's task-approach skills are that of problem solver (he finds a way around his father's opposition to ballet by doing it behind his back when his father would not know it) and worker (though he needs to be pushed at times, Billy has an unshakeable drive in practicing dance despite all of the oppositions around him, including his age—what a demand on an 11-year-old boy). At this point, dialogue is still nonexistent and must be incorporated in order for Billy to rebel (i.e., choose his career).

Assisting Billy in moving through his dilemma by using Camus's moral philosophy

In talking to Billy, his career counselor assessed that Billy already knew what barriers were preventing him from taking action on his chosen career—the fear of his father. However, Billy told his counselor that he continued to persevere despite his lack of familial and monetary support from his father and brother. According to Camus's philosophy, Billy is striving toward making a difference for his quality of life (involvement) because he thinks that he is a talented dancer and that he can pursue his love of dance into a career. This is true. His primary problem is the lack of family support. How can he go to ballet school without his father's support? Billy told his counselor that instead of stopping in fear, he decided to dance for his father when he was caught in the act again. He danced his heart out. "Look what I can do, dad! I can do this!!" is what he communicated to him. And, indeed, Billy's dialogue worked—he gained the support of his father. Sneaking around was just a means to this end for Billy—he was convinced that if he could learn how to dance, he could prove to his dad that this was a possible career path for him.

ETHICAL AND LEGAL ASPECTS OF CAREER COUNSELING

Up to this point, we have looked at a brief history of career counseling and the importance of identifying a theoretical framework for career work. We also reviewed some principles from Camus's moral philosophy as a means by which career counselors can evaluate the ethical quality of their work with clients on career-related issues. In particular, Camus's philosophy provides an interesting perspective on career decision making (i.e., as an opportunity for being *involved* in one's life patterns and choices or retreating to *isolation* and, in a sense, not fully living up to the challenge of this absurd existence). In addition, Camus's philosophy highlighted several points by which career counselors evaluate what is good or upstanding in their work with others, such as creating open and honest dialogue and helping others live a balanced life with regard to life-career choices. In this discussion, it is also essential to address several other ethical issues related to career counseling. We now look at issues related to competence, confidentiality, informed consent, career assessment, best practices with electronic resources, and multicultural issues in career counseling.

Competence for Career Counselors

In order to work ethically as a career counseling professional, a clinician must demonstrate minimum competencies in working with clients on career-related issues. Like all counselors, career development professionals are responsible to perform activities only in which they are adequately prepared and trained. If a counselor does not have the necessary training or resources for the career concern a client may have, the counselor must make an appropriate referral. No counselors should attempt to use skills in which they have not been trained. The 11 competency areas in which practicing career counselors must be proficient have been defined by the National Career Development Association (NCDA, 2012) to include the following:

1. *Career Development Theory*: Theory base and knowledge considered essential for professionals engaging in career counseling and development.
2. *Individual and Group Counseling Skills*: Individual and group counseling competencies considered essential for effective career counseling.
3. *Individual/Group Assessment*: Individual/group assessment skills considered essential for professionals engaging in career counseling.
4. *Information/Resources*: Information/resource base and knowledge essential for professionals engaging in career counseling.
5. *Program Promotion, Management, and Implementation*: Skills necessary to develop, plan, implement, and manage comprehensive career development programs in a variety of settings.
6. *Coaching, Consultation, and Performance Improvement*: Knowledge and skills considered essential in enabling individuals and organizations to impact effectively upon the career counseling and development process.
7. *Diverse Populations*: Knowledge and skills considered essential in providing career counseling and development processes to diverse populations.
8. *Supervision*: Knowledge and skills considered essential in critically evaluating counselor performance, maintaining and improving professional skills, and seeking assistance for others when needed in career counseling.
9. *Ethical/Legal Issues*: Information base and knowledge essential for the ethical and legal practice of career counseling.
10. *Research/Evaluation*: Knowledge and skills considered essential in understanding and conducting research and evaluation in career counseling and development.
11. *Technology*: Knowledge and skills considered essential in using technology to assist individuals with career planning (NCDA, 2012).

In 1981, the NCDA established a certification program for career counselors who met its minimum requirements for training, knowledge, and skills to practice and who wanted to establish themselves as career specialists. The credential, known as the National Certified Career Counselor (NCCC), was managed by the National Board for Certified Counselors (NBCC) until 2000 when it was terminated. The NCDA then instituted two membership categories in 2001 so that counselors with extended training and experience in the area of career counseling could be recognized as a Master Career Counselor (MCC) or a Master Career Development Professional (MCDP). To qualify for membership in either category, counselors have to meet certain standards (seven for the MCC and four for the MCDP) which are outlined by the NCDA (Brown, 2007).

To qualify for the MCC recognition by the NCDA, counselors must meet the following requirements:

1. Be a member of the NCDA for 1 year
2. Hold a master's degree in counseling or a closely related field from an accredited institution
3. Complete 3 years of postmaster's experience in career counseling
4. Possess and maintain either the NCC credential or a state-level license as a counselor or a psychologist
5. Complete at least three credits in each of the six NCDA competency areas
6. Complete a supervised practicum in career counseling during training or 2 years of supervised postmaster's experience under a certified supervisor or a licensed counseling professional
7. Document at least 50% of job duties that are directly related to career counseling

To qualify for membership recognition in the NCDA as a MCDP, counselors must meet the following requirements:

1. Be a member of the NCDA for 1 year
2. Hold a master's degree in counseling or a closely related field from an accredited institution
3. Complete 3 years of postmaster's experience in career development experience training, teaching, program development, or materials development
4. Document at least 50% of full-time job duties that are directly related to career development

Confidentiality

Career counselors are bound to the ethical and legal guidelines surrounding confidentiality that are outlined by the ACA or the ethical code of any other organization under whose auspices they may work (e.g., American Psychological Association [APA] and National Association of Social Workers [NASW]). All 50 states have laws protecting privileged communication between mental health professionals and their clients, though the extent of a client's legal protection varies from state to state (Remley, Herlihy, & Herlihy, 1997). Given the variation in state laws, counselors are encouraged to become familiar with the bounds of confidentiality and, relatedly, privileged communication and privacy in the states within which they practice.

Informed Consent

As noted in Chapter 6, informed consent involves a discussion between counselors and their clients about the purposes, benefits and risks, and expectations of the counseling process. When meeting with clients for the first time, career counselors ought to address all of the areas traditionally reviewed in the informed consent process and, in addition, specifically talk to clients about their rights related to the use of tests and assessments because using these tools is often standard in their practices. Welfel (2010) recommended that counselors discuss nine points in informed consent, which I suggest career counselors integrate into their practice. They are

1. Goals, techniques, procedures, limitations, risks, and benefits of counseling
2. Ways in which diagnoses, tests, and written reports will be used
3. Billing and fees
4. Confidentiality rights and limitations
5. Involvement of supervisors or additional health professionals
6. Counselor's training status
7. Client's right to choose the counselor and be active in treatment planning
8. Client's right to refuse counseling and the implications of that refusal
9. Client's right to ask additional questions about counseling and to have questions answered in comprehensible language (Welfel, 2010)

Conversations about informed consent should be open, inviting, transparent, and above all respectful. Remember Camus's purpose for dialogue. The counselor must always utilize dialogue not only at times of conflict but as a way to prevent conflict. Informed consent is at the heart of this aim to prevent future conflicts. Clients should feel empowered and feel as if counselors are there to help them make the best possible decision about participating in the career counseling relationship.

Landmark 2

CASE EXAMPLE

Rachel is a 32-year-old adult with mild mental retardation (6th grade level of intelligence) who is interested in working with you on career development goals. She lives in an assisted-living housing complex and wants to begin working at a job that is more satisfying. She continues to participate in therapy groups that her assisted-living program offers and also attends weekly social skills groups to help her with her challenges.

1. *Keeping Rachel's limitations in mind, what would be your first step in the informed consent process?*

(continued)

2. *Which concepts do you think Rachel would have the most challenges with?*
3. *What interventions could you utilize if Rachel did not understand certain concepts you were discussing with her?*
4. *How is Camus's moral philosophy relevant to Rachel's case in terms of avoiding conflict?*

Career Assessment

Assessment plays a significant role in career counseling, and career counselors typically assess such traits as a client's personality, interests, values, and skills in both formal and informal ways. Formally, clients complete standardized assessments such as the *Myers-Briggs Type Indicator* ([MBTI]; 1998), *Strong Interest Inventory* ([SII]; 1994), or *Self-Directed Search* ([SDS]; Holland, 1994). Informally, career counselors use qualitative means to discuss clients' concerns and desires about their career development. Among other things, in discussing career assessment results with clients, counselors might introduce Camus's ideas about isolation and involvement. Counselors might help clients assess how they want to make meaning and also meet financial needs, for example. One may outweigh another, but both isolation and involvement would need to be incorporated in a career plan in order for the client to maintain a balance.

Zunker and Norris (1998) outlined a model for career counselors to use when assessing clients' career self-concept and career development needs. The model is meant to help counselors gain introductory knowledge about their clients' needs and then to expand their understanding of those needs by using appropriate career assessments. The stages of the career counseling process are:

1. Analyze client's needs
2. Establish a purpose for the assessment
3. Determine the instruments to be used
4. Interpret the results of the assessment
5. Make a decision about career development
6. Help the client begin to engage in work, training, and education

Career counselors formulate direction and focus for their work with clients based on the clients' career goals and on the career and lifestyle needs they express. Especially if they desire to make a career shift toward a job that is more satisfying, meaningful, or purposeful than they currently have (e.g., involvement), career counselors may decide to administer a formal assessment, such as an interest or values inventory, among other tools. They might also use informal or qualitative assessments, such as in-depth interviewing, card sorts, fantasy, and so on. Both types of assessments add to clients' vocational self-awareness. Again, if one is using Camus's philosophy as a means to reflect with clients on the ethical qualities of work, balance is the key!

There are multiple factors that play into a career counselor's ethical use of assessments. These include a counselor's thoughtful consideration about which assessment tools are most appropriate to a client's needs; knowledge about how the test was developed, standardized, and validated; consent to administer the test or inventory;

and careful processing of the results with the client. It is not necessary for career counselors to memorize the types of tests available for use in career counseling, but they should be aware of the variety of assessments that are out there to address various goals so that they can make a best choice for their client. Before using any instrument, career counselors should become very familiar with the assessment they wish to use by reviewing the administrator's manual, reading journal articles about validity and reliability testing that has been done on the assessment, and determining the assessment's applicability to various age groups, genders, races, socioeconomic statuses, and other diverse populations. After choosing an instrument that is likely to fit a client's needs, counselors must also assure that the assessment they are using is written for the client's age group, reading level, and competence level and is affordable for the client or agency.

After scoring the assessment(s), counselors should discuss the results with clients by processing what they mean to the client and determining whether or not the outcomes fit with their sense of themselves and their career goals. Again, the responsibility to dialogue in an effort to maintain harmony when striving for balance is a concept drawn from Camus's philosophy here. Pulling once again on research that suggests people seek work that is both important and that allows them to have the greatest amount of control, career counselors also consider how these notions fit with clients' assessment outcomes.

Electronic Resources

Electronic or computer-based resources and assessments are commonly used in the field of career counseling. Most colleges, universities, and high schools utilize computerized career exploration programs such as DISCOVER II and SIGI PLUS that offer students concise assessments of their personality styles, interests, values, and skills. Many electronic resources and programs use Holland's typology to determine the type of person the assessment-taker is in an effort to show which career options are best suited for that individual. Holland's theory is also often called the RIASEC theory because this is an acronym for the six types of people and environments that Holland defines in his model (R: realistic, I: investigative, A: artistic, S: social, E: enterprising, and C: conventional). Generally, individuals have a two- or three-letter Holland Code, such as RSI (realistic, social, and investigative). A person's Self-Directed Search (the test used to obtain a Holland Code) result is a combination of codes assessing a test taker's personality along with ideal work environments. The Holland Dictionary (Gottfredson & Holland, 1996) is also a useful tool for career counseling from Holland's perspective. It contains hundreds of occupations classified by a three-letter Holland Code so that career counselors can help clients process personality types and ideal careers in their search of balance.

Definitions of careers, entry level expectations, skills needed, and pay expectations are usually included in the output from electronic assessments. Career counselors can utilize these assessments as they can be very helpful to their clients, but they should only be used in conjunction with counseling. When clients take the tests alone, they tend to get a lot of helpful information about themselves in relation to possible future careers but usually do not progress beyond the information-gathering stage. Career counselors are essential in helping clients interpret the assessment results in a meaningful way, help them set goals, and determine a plan on how those goals will be accomplished. By processing results, goals, and plans in relation to clients' needs and desires, counselors can rest assured that they are striving toward ethical practice because the client is at the heart of each step in this process. The client must understand the assessment results clearly with aid from the counselor, set goals appropriate to personal desires and needs (balance), and then determine a plan on how to accomplish the goals they set. If the client is left out of any part of this process, ethics can be compromised since the client's best interest is no longer fully considered. How can it be if the client is absent? Dialogue cannot occur.

Multicultural Issues

Many scholars will agree that there are two key ways of developing cultural competency: through education and through experience. Of course, career counselors must be cautious not to stereotype certain cultural groups based on knowledge they acquire through education. Because individuals view the world differently due to their cultures and challenges, counselors may, at times, be puzzled by their clients' career decisions and goals. Counselors should consistently look at the prejudices they may have and strive to learn about cultural backgrounds that differ from their own.

Zunker (2006) outlines 20 contextual assessment areas as the key areas for exploration when assessing a client's level of acculturation, but it may still be a limited list because individuals are so diverse and are constantly influenced by different factors during their growth and development. The contextual assessment areas are:

1. Ethno-cultural heritage
2. Racial and ethno-cultural identities
3. Gender and sexual orientation
4. Socioeconomic status
5. Physical appearance, ability, or disability
6. Religion when raised and current belief and practice
7. Biological factors
8. Historical era
9. Marital status, sexual history
10. History of immigration and generations from immigration
11. Acculturation and transculturation levels
12. Family of origin and multigenerational history
13. Family scripts (roles of women and men, prescriptions for success or failure, etc.)
14. Individual and family life cycle development and stages
15. Clients' languages spoken by family of origin
16. History of individual abuse and trauma
17. History of collective trauma (colonization, slavery, etc.)
18. Gender-specific issues such as battered wife syndrome
19. Recreations and hobbies, avocations, and special social roles
20. Historical and geopolitical reality of ethnic group and relationships with dominant group

While career counselors aim to help individuals make more meaningful career choices, many clients may be significantly challenged because of their contexts. Career counselors need be sensitive to contextual influences and assist clients in becoming aware of these influences to gain understanding and mastery over them.

Landmark 3

PROFESSIONAL REFLECTION

In his article, "The Psychology of Chance Encounters and Life Paths," Bandura (1982) discusses the notion of chance encounters and its significance to chosen life paths. Bandura notes that chance encounters play a dominant role in shaping the courses of human lives. Fortuity is more probable than a deliberate plan within a string of encounters that lead a person to choose a career path. While his discussion is both interesting and probable, he misses discussing one very important point in life paths—oppression. Although Bandura touches on oppression a bit, he seems to put most of the responsibility of a life path on the individual. I think this is too simplistic. When he discusses gangs versus Ivy Leaguers, Bandura states that both these groups would be in contact with very different people due to the social circles they engage. While differential affiliations would cultivate different interests and skills, Bandura asserts that individuals contribute to their own destinies "by developing potentialities that afford access to particular social mileus" (Bandura, 1982, p. 750). While he notes that there are challenges, his tone is that the ultimate causes for running in those circles (e.g., a gang circle or an Ivy League circle) are personal skills and interests. While this is true to some degree, the social and political structure that shapes one's environment is often the bigger factor. Oppressed people do not stay in gangs only because of personal interests and skills. They stay in gangs because they cannot dig themselves out of the environment in which they live. Once you start carrying a gun at 7 and have a prison record before you even hit 18, opportunities are scarce and making an honest living is not often a realistic goal. In southern Los Angeles, hundreds of Black males are killed every year due to gang violence. If this was White-on-White crime, would the authorities intervene? Probably so. They did when the gang riots hit White areas. If you look at the creation of street gangs in Los Angeles, you will discover that they started because of an oppressive cycle of racism. Positive groups that believed in being proud of who they were as African Americans were intercepted time and time again by our government (Luczo & Peralta, 2008). Often, life paths are bigger than individual values and family dynamics. It is very often a societal issue. Career counselors must always consider culture and the oppressions of certain diverse groups when assisting clients since personal choice is not always the driving factor in someone's decision-making process. Individuals are always context bound.

ETHICAL ISSUES IN GROUP-BASED CAREER COUNSELING

Group work offers several advantages over individual counseling when working with any population and can be particularly helpful in career counseling. Although career counseling is typically practiced on an individual level, career counselors who have an opportunity to form a career development group may find that the group process further enhances what can be done on an individual level. Group work promotes personal validation and increased confidence and self-esteem (Yalom, 2005). Group work also helps individuals try out new approaches to problems that they could not solve on their own by using the knowledge, feedback, and support of their peers. The encouragement and empathy that many group members provide also lessens people's resistances so that they can begin to make more productive decisions. Career counseling groups can help clients discuss personal career-oriented needs and wants with other members. The dialogue in assisting clients toward balance is greatly strengthened here. While one group member may say, "I just want to make money!" and another may say, "I want to make a difference in people's lives. I don't care about anything else!," the counselor can bring these two together in dialogue to debate the importance of each personal goal and, in this effort, members may see others' points of views and refine theirs to create a more balanced career choice.

Ethically, the counselor must always be sure to communicate the importance of confidentiality within the group. What is said in group, stays in group is the common phrase. While confidentiality is only legally and ethically expected of the counselor, group members should be encouraged to respect one another's confidentiality in the same way they would want their information to remain confidential. Again, we come back to Camus's notion of preventing conflict and increasing solidarity among individuals by highlighting respect and expectations through dialogue.

Landmark 4
GROUP ACTIVITY

This intervention helps both men and women recognize the stereotyping that is present in the workplace. Women and men may not appreciate the different challenges that the other gender faces in the work environment. The specific tasks to this intervention are to (a) help each gender recognize stereotypes in their own gender group, (b) help each gender recognize stereotypes in the other gender group, (c) identify the effects of the stereotypes on each gender, (d) identify how one gender may contribute to a stereotype or may encourage it, and (e) discuss ways to deal with stereotyping consequences.

On index cards, all members of the group need to write down stereotypes of either gender that they have personally experienced. All the cards are collected by the counselor. Discussion groups and fish bowls will be used to help accomplish the specific tasks. For tasks:

(*continued*)

a, b, c, d: A fish bowl will be used. In their own group, the women will discuss what they have experienced as the men observe and listen around them. Then the men will go into the fish bowl and discuss their reactions to what they heard. The activity will happen again with the men discussing stereotypes and the women listening and later commenting.

e: The entire group will meet after the fish bowl activities and discuss ways that they have dealt with stereotypes, how they have contributed to them, and ways for each gender to deal with stereotypes. This will be a process and brainstorming session where each gender gives the other ideas, support, and encouragement. Different points of view of each gender should give rise to different kinds of ideas.

SIGNPOSTS FOR FUTURE TREKS

This chapter was devised not only to communicate the importance of ethical decision making in career counseling but also to discuss the meaningful journey that clients desire to take in career development. Individuals yearn to make a mark in the world in some way and most likely to do this through career choices. Camus' moral philosophy offers a way to do this through set of values that are without supernatural foundation and based within an intellectual framework. With the emphasis on legal and ethical aspects of career counseling and what *not* to do, counselors can often forget about the bigger picture. Thus, this chapter was written in such a way as to encourage counselors to look at the heart of career and the meaning-making that is essential to working in a fulfilling environment. As Camus illustrated, we are called to rebel—to create, to transform the callousness of the world. Clients yearn to do this, and career counselors can help them facilitate that process through open, honest, and respectful dialogue. Incorporating the unfairness of the world and the human desire to overcome the hurdles that oppress, career counselors are much more than assessment givers of personality, skills, and interests. They are beacons of hope and inspiration for clients that seek to make a difference in the world. To learn more about the career counseling theories and ethical guidelines discussed in this chapter, readers are encouraged to visit the websites listed in the Appendices at the end of this book.

INSIGHTS GAINED FROM THE JOURNEY

I thought that my career development had been very serendipitous, but as I looked back on my life and the events that led to my professional development, I found that they were all connected. I have to agree with Krumboltz (1998) that the "pure-luck attribution needs to be challenged" (p. 392). That is, I think that the "final product" of one's professional development is not pure luck, but I think that there are pure luck events along the way that shape who we become, and these lucky events take us to new roads that are further shaped by our personal values, beliefs, and so on. Currently, I am a university professor, a researcher, an author, and clinician specializing in sexual addictions work and religiosity.

My personal history and serendipity have shaped my professional career quite clearly. I grew up in the evangelical church and was brought up within very rigid religious beliefs and demands. As I matured into an adult, I swayed all the way over to the other side and questioned everything in theology. After graduating with an undergraduate degree in psychology, I took my first job in the counseling field as an addictions counselor because it was the only job I could find that had all daylight hours (luck!). This was my one and only reason for entering the addictions field. Over a decade later and a few job changes along the way, I continued to stay in the addictions field.

When I attended my PhD program, I was working as a manager for a rehabilitation center. A colleague of mine was fired for downloading pornography at work. After talking to him some months later, he told me he was an evangelical Christian, and he discovered that he was a sex addict. "This would be a really interesting dissertation topic!" I thought. His rigid religious beliefs about sexuality and his belief that he was a sex addict—were they connected? I wondered. I kept in touch with him through the years and then decided to do my dissertation on evangelical sexual addicts. This was a very easy decision because I had access to potential participants through my colleague and his connections. In addition to this, my student peer in the PhD program had recommended me to our professor about being a graduate assistant, and this professor specialized in sexual addictions. Luck! When my peer graduated, I took over her duties and worked very closely with my professor. His expertise was in sexual addiction, and we worked exceptionally well together, so it was an easy decision to ask him to be my chair.

After I finished my dissertation, I published a couple of articles on evangelicalism and sexual addiction, as well as a book on the topic. I remember that I got an email about submitting a book proposal, and I thought, what the heck? (Luck!)

So, as I look back on my history, everything was connected with evangelicalism (values I grew up with and then rebelled against) and addiction (pure luck with my first job). Everything else fell into place between those two themes. I think that, perhaps, my student peer may have sought me out intentionally whereas it was serendipitous for me. The addictions piece—perhaps my value system of daylight hours played a part, but if a daylight job came open in another field, I think my entire professional life would be different. And so, in the end, I have to disagree with Krumboltz in that pure luck *does* play a part, and that is just what it is—pure luck. Although the result of professional development is indefinitely shaped by one's "inner life" (Bandura, 1982, p. 747), my purpose and drive to make a difference in the world was my ultimate drive—that rebellion against a callous reality that Camus mentions. I had to find my balance in this absurd reality and making a difference (involvement) was balanced with making a living (isolation)—I had to have both! And yet, Camus's concept of involvement was always the greatest force in my final decision. I encourage you to look at your own career development and see what factors affected you—I bet you may have rebelled as well!

MOVING FORWARD: CASE STUDY AND REFLECTION QUESTIONS

Anna has been a clinical supervisor for 12 years in a female-dominant workplace where many other females held management positions. For this reason, she did not feel a lot of discrimination as a female in a leadership position. This soon changed after one of her male coworkers, Seth, was promoted to a clinical supervisor position just like hers for another part of the department. She was struck at how differently the administration treated him from the rest of the female managers. They seemed to "let him slide" on things that she felt she could not get away with. During meetings and professional interactions, Anna shared the sense with her other female supervisor coworkers that Seth talked down to her and her female colleagues. Anna stated that she and the other female supervisors complained about this to their supervisor and to the administration but that "nothing was done about it." After only 6 months in his position and much tribulation with his female coworkers, a director position opened up. "Normally, you need 3 years of supervision experience before being able to be considered for the director position," stated Anna, "but when the posting was up, we saw that the administration, namely the director above Seth, had changed the qualifications to 'one year managerial experience preferred.'" Anna decided to apply anyway despite her suspicions that the job was already targeted to be given to Seth. After a few weeks, Anna received the call that she did not get the position. Seth did. "To me, it seemed like the 'good ol' boys club' incident," said Anna. "Why did this worker who did not have enough experience and had problems with all of the other managers and his own staff get a promotion after just 6 months?" She went on to state, "I think that my frustration as a woman was that I felt that all of us female managers were not even considered for the position nor heard when we complained about this male employee and how he interacted with us. I could not prove that it was gender discrimination, and that was the most frustrating part. All of us thought it, but what could we do? I think this kind of situation is quite common for women in more male-dominated environments, and it must be difficult to go to work from day to day when you are not valued as much as you should be. I know I feel undervalued! Perhaps this is why there continue to be so many gender-oriented careers—it's just easier to 'stick to your own'—kind of how segregation works—it does not solve the problem and often makes the problem worse, or more ingrained. Now I'm just frustrated with the company and I don't know what I should do with how I'm feeling!"

REFLECTION QUESTIONS

- *What are the main dilemmas presented in this scenario?*
- *What decisions might you need to discuss with Anna as her career counselor?*
- *As a woman, how do you feel when you read over this case? What reactions did you have and how do you think they would affect your work with Anna?*
- *As a man, how do you feel when you read over this case? What reactions did you have and how do you think they would affect your work with Anna?*
- *What did you learn from reflecting on this case?*
- *How will you help resolve Anna's predicament using a positive approach to ethics?*

REFERENCES

Bandura, A. (1982). The psychology of chance encounters and life paths. *American Psychologist, 37*, 747–755.

Barrett, W. (1962). *Irrational man: A study in existentialist philosophy*. Garden City, NY: Double Day & Company, Inc.

Brown, D. (2007). *Career information, career counseling, and career development* (9th ed.). Boston, MA: Pearson.

Brown, D., Brooks, L., & Associates. (1996). *Career choice and development* (3rd ed.). San Francisco, CA: Jossey-Bass.

Camus, A. (1956). *The rebel: An essay on man in revolt*. New York: Random House.

Camus, A. (1959). *The myth of Sisyphus*. New York: Random House.

Camus, A. (1960). *Resistance, rebellion, and death*. New York: Random House.

Denton, D. E. (1967). *The philosophy of Albert Camus: A critical analysis*. Boston, MA: Prime Publishers.

Gottfredson, G. D., & Holland, J. L. (1996). *Dictionary of Holland occupational codes* (3rd ed.). Lutz, FL: PAR.

Hanna, T. (1958). *The thought and art of Albert Camus*. Chicago, IL: Henry Regnery Company.

Herr, E. L., & Shahnasarian, M. (2001). Selected milestones in the evolution of career development practices in the twentieth century. *Career Development Quarterly, 49*, 225–232.

Holland, J. L. (1994). *Self-directed search*. Odessa, FL: PAR.

Krumboltz, J. D. (1998). Counsellor actions needed for the new career perspective. *British Journal of Guidance & Counselling, 26*, 559–564.

Levoy, G. (1997). *Callings: Finding and following an authentic life path*. New York: Three Rivers Press.

Luczo, P., (Executive Producer), & Peralta, S. (Director). (2008). *Bloods and crips: Made in America*. [Motion picture]. United States: Too Easy Entertainment/LA Gangs Project.

Myers, I., & Briggs, K. (1998). *The Myers-Briggs Type Indicator®*. Palo Alto, CA: Consulting Psychologists Press.

NCDA. (2003). *Career development: A policy statement of the National Career Development Association Board of Directors*. Retrieved from http://www.ncda.org/pdf/Policy.pdf

NCDA. (2012). *Career counseling competencies*. Retrieved from http://associationdatabase.com/aws/NCDA/pt/sd/news_article/37798/_self/layout_ccmsearch/true

Reck, R. (1962, June). Albert Camus: The artist and his time. *Modern Language Quarterly, 23*(2), 129–134.

Remley, T. P., Herlihy, B., & Herlihy, S. B. (1997). The U.S. Supreme Court decision in *Jaffee v. Redmond*: Implications for counselors. *Journal of Counseling and Development, 75*, 213–218.

Sartre, J. (1956). *Being and nothingness*. New York: Washington Square Press.

Strong, E. K. (1994). *The Strong Interest Inventory*. Palo Alto, CA: Consulting Psychologists Press.

Super, D. E. (1980). A life-span, life-space approach to career development. *Journal of Vocational Behavior, 16*, 282–298.

Thody, P. (1957). *Albert Camus: A study of his work*. London: Hamish Hamilton.

Welfel, E. R. (2010). *Ethics in counseling & psychotherapy: Standards, research, and emerging issues*. Belmont, CA: Brooks/Cole.

Yalom, I. (2005). *The theory and practice of group psychotherapy*. New York: Basic Books.

Zunker, V. G. (2006). *Career counseling: A holistic approach*. Belmont, CA: Thomson Brooks/Cole.

Zunker, V. G., & Norris, D. S. (1998). *Using assessment results for career development* (5th ed.). Pacific Grove, CA: Brooks/Cole.

14

Ethics in School Counseling

Cecile Brennan

THE FORESEEN DESTINATION

After reading this chapter, students will aspire to:

- Recognize the complexity of the school counseling profession and how this impacts ethical decision making.
- Integrate the core ethical principles, the American School Counselor Association (ASCA) *Ethical Standards*, and major ethical concepts into a coherent approach to school counseling ethics.
- Discover how the personal history, emotional disposition, and functional behaviors of the school counselor can influence counseling practice and the ability to adhere to ethical principles and standards.
- Apply an ethical decision-making model when contending with complex ethical issues.

GETTING ON THE ROAD

It has been my experience that those who are attracted to school counseling are people who enjoy not knowing what each day will bring. Active and engaged school counselors do not expect to be able to hold to a regular routine. They are able to adjust to whatever arrives at their door each morning, whether it is a crying student, a concerned parent, or an administrator with a problem that could use a counselor's input. In all such circumstances, counselors need to be able to improvise: to adapt their skill and expertise to meet the need of each presenting issue. Each counseling situation truly is unique. It needs to be met by someone capable of recognizing and responding to that uniqueness. This means that school counselors must be able to apply counseling principles and guidelines in a multiplicity of circumstances with varying stakeholders. Because of this complexity, school counselors must realize that they likely will not be able to look in a book, or even ask someone for the right answer as to what is the best ethical action in a particular situation. The same set of skills that allows a school counselor to respect the perspective of a parent, yet take into consideration the concerns of a teacher, all the while focusing on the needs of a student must be brought into play when considering the ethical responsibilities of the school counseling profession.

While this may sound daunting, I view it as exciting and challenging. School counselors, like all other counselors, must be knowledgeable about the ethical codes and guidelines that govern their actions, but they must also learn how to apply those principles in multiple settings with varying constituencies. The goals of this chapter are to ground future school counselors in the codes and practices of the profession and assist in the development of a flexible decision-making process which takes into account the complex role of school counselors. Finally, all too often a discussion of professional ethics is reduced to a discussion of "how to stay out of trouble." That will not be the case with this chapter. Having a sound ethical basis goes hand in hand with being a competent professional. Ethical practice is not an add-on, a detail to be attended to so the counselor can escape trouble. Ethical practice is a prerequisite for competent and professional practice as a school counselor.

EXPLORING THE TERRITORY

CONSTRUCTING THE FOUNDATION FOR ETHICAL PRACTICE

Not surprisingly, the foundation for school counseling ethics is based on overarching ethical principles (Beauchamp & Childress, 2001; Kitchener, 2000), ethical codes and guidelines, most specifically the ASCA *Ethical Standards for School Counselors* (2010), relevant federal and state laws, and school-specific guidelines. In the following section, we will briefly review each of these foundational elements, starting with the principles of ethical practice.

Ethical Principles

The ethical principles of autonomy, beneficence, fidelity, justice, and nonmaleficence are as active for school counselors as they are for all counseling professionals and within the medical community in general. As with the entire focus on ethics, the goal of ethical principles is not merely to stay on the right side of the ethical law, but rather to ensure sound and competent professional practice. The principles (e.g., beneficence and nonmaleficence) ought to lead school counselors to act in such a way that students will benefit from their services—academically and personally. Ethical principles such as justice and fidelity also encourage counselors to be invested in offering guidance as equally as possible to all students in the school environment and to be faithful sense of trust and privacy of the helping relationship that counselors build with students. Finally, school counselors need to operate from a base of client autonomy while recognizing that many students are young and not fully autonomous. This requires that the school counselor take into consideration the student's dependency on family, and the parents' rights to participate in their child's education. In a real sense, the school counselor needs to apply ethical principles to interactions with the student, to interactions with the student's family, and to interactions with other professionals involved in the student's life. Not consulting appropriately with the family or other potentially helpful professionals is not to act in the best interest of the student.

Landmark 1

CASE EXAMPLE

Ms. Sharp, the elementary school counselor, sees Tommy crying in the hallway. She goes up to Tommy and convinces him to come with her to her office. In her office, Tommy tells her that he is being bullied by two boys in his class. He shows her where they have written on his clothes and scribbled on his books. Ms. Sharp tells Tommy that she will speak with the boys and with his classroom teacher. He agrees with this, but does not want her to tell his parents. He thinks they will blame him. She spends a good deal of time working with Tommy to convince him to let her speak with his parents. She does this because Tommy should not bear the burden of feeling he is somehow responsible for how he is being treated and Tommy's parents have a right to know what their son has been experiencing. She is acting according to the ethical principle of beneficence, the overall best interest of Tommy. Because of Tommy's youth, he is not able to assert his autonomy and make his own decision about telling his parents.

ASCA Ethical Standards

The ASCA *Ethical Standards for School Counselors* (2010) is a comprehensive instruction manual for the maintenance of a professional and ethical counseling practice. Unfortunately, many students and professionals view the *Ethical Standards* as a set of prescriptive laws which must be followed or else the counselor could "get in trouble." This is not the purpose of the *Standards*. In much the same way that instruction manuals are created for the proper operation of a new electronic device or appliance, the purpose of the *Ethical Standards* is to provide an instruction manual for the school counseling professional. Its aim is to provide guidance, not to list the ways in which a counselor could be penalized. For these reasons it should be at the school counselor's elbow as a reference to be used daily, not a rulebook to be checked only when the counselor feels threatened in a particular situation.

Ethical Standards for School Counselors (2010) is broken down into seven sections:

1. Responsibilities to students (A1–A11): This is the largest section of the *Ethical Standards* and comprehensively details the responsibilities of the school

counselor. Included is a discussion of confidentiality, dual relationships, and the duty to warn in case of danger to self or others.

2. Responsibilities to parents/guardians (B1–B2): This section tackles the difficult matter of juggling students' rights to confidentiality with parental right to information regarding their children.
3. Responsibilities to colleagues and professional associates (C1–C3): Clearly demonstrating how ethical school counseling is good professional practice, this section describes the process and procedures which should be implemented when the professional school counselor collaborates with other professionals.
4. Responsibilities to school, communities, and families (D1–D2): The role of the school counselor extends beyond meeting the needs of particular students. In this section, the school counselor's responsibility to represent and advocate for the profession within the school and the community is described.
5. Responsibilities to self (E1–E2): This section emphasizes both the need of the school counselor to put in place measures to promote self-care and avoid burn-out, and the need to establish a comprehensive plan of continued professional development. Professional development should include not just staying abreast of changes in the field, but also staying aware of the importance of social justice and advocacy for stakeholders who might be marginalized by society.
6. Responsibilities to the profession (F1–F4): This section deals with the professional school counselor as a representative of the profession who should abide by the profession's principles, and as an educator of future school counselors when acting as a supervisor for a counseling student's practicum and internship.
7. Maintenance of standards (G1–G3): This final section provides a clear blueprint for determining a course of action when confronted with an ethical dilemma. Included is a decision-making model which can be implemented when a situation is particularly difficult to assess.

Thoroughly reading the *Ethical Standards* in order to become intimately familiar with the counselor's ethical responsibilities is a requirement for all school counseling professionals. In doing so, you will discover that the guidance provided is sometimes very specific, for instance, the *Standards* specify that counselors must become knowledgeable about the laws, regulations, and policies relating to students. At other times, the guidance is more open-ended, for instance, when discussing confidentiality, the *Standards* emphasizes the need to consider multiple variables when deciding that confidentiality cannot be sustained. It is up to the counselor's judgment to assess variables such as the student's developmental level, the rights of the parent's to know about certain behaviors, and the need of the school administration to be aware of certain student activities. While this absence of absolute directives is frustrating to most students and many professionals, it is a reflection of the complexity of the school counseling profession. School counselors cannot depend on anyone or anything, such as a code of ethics, for supplying the answer to ethical dilemmas. As with most professions, arriving at a well-thought-out decision requires that the counselor bring the full weight of his or her experience and training to the decision-making process. So, while knowledge of the *Ethical Standards* is essential, it is not sufficient when attempting to resolve a dilemma.

Landmark 2

CASE EXAMPLE

The principal of Wilson Middle School felt that the school counselor's job was to schedule the students into classes, handle any instances of students getting overly emotional in the classroom, and respond to parents' concerns about their children's social lives. Miss Jackson, the new counselor, wanted to schedule a culture fest during lunchtime. Students could bring artifacts from their cultural background and display them in the cafeteria. The cafeteria staff could create an international luncheon menu. This would assist the diverse student population in learning about one another's culture. At first, the principal wondered what this had to do with school counseling. After Miss Jackson showed him the ASCA *Ethical Standards*, he realized that a school counselor's job was much broader than he thought. The *Standards* opened his eyes to the wide-ranging activities a counselor can be expected to perform.

FERPA and State Laws

Federal and state law can also impact the ethical decision process. Perhaps the most prominent federal legislation which counselors need to be aware of is the Family Education and Rights Privacy Act (FERPA, 1974). A thorough review of this act can be found at the U. S. Department of Education website (http://www2.ed.gov/policy/gen/guid/fpco/ferpa/index.html). In general, the act seeks to protect the privacy of student records. FERPA gives parents the rights to their minor child's records and then transfers that right to the student when he or she becomes 18. The importance of FERPA for school counselors is twofold. Counselors and other school officials should not be sharing student records with anyone outside of the school setting unless it is with the student's parents, or the parents have authorized the release. If counselors desire to keep a confidential record of their work with students, these records are to be kept separate from the students' other educational records and in the sole possession of the counselor. These "sole possession notes" are narrowly defined as notes which serve to assist the counselor in recollecting pertinent details about the counseling process. They should include only facts, counselor observations, and descriptions of a student's behavior. In addition, the notes should not be shared with anyone, even other school personnel. If, as an exception, there is a valid reason why these notes must be shared, they are then considered to be part of the student's educational record and subject to FERPA.

State laws can impact counselors in a number of ways. Most importantly, state laws define the legal rights of young people. For instance, what is the age a student can legally consent to sexual activity, receive information about contraception, or obtain an abortion without parental consent? Counselors need to know this information if they are going to be able to offer proper guidance to students. There is often misinformation about these issues. In my state of Ohio, many school counselors believe that an 18-year-old who engages in sexual relations with a 16-year-old is in violation of the law. However, in Ohio, the legal age of consent is 16, so no law is violated in respect to age. If this case occurred in California, these young people would be breaking the law, since the age of consent there is 18. This brief example should highlight how different state laws can be. Counselors need to proactively search out the answers to the common questions and situations they may be confronted with. A good way to accomplish this is to do an in-depth search of various state and legal databases. While this may sound difficult, it is actually quite easy using the Internet, or, if needed, consulting with a librarian.

As you are checking out various sites, keep in mind that many of the sites have a particular ideological orientation. This should not be a matter of concern, since the goal is to obtain facts about a state's legal code. What is legal and what is in the best interest of the student and his or her family are often not the same. But before a counselor can begin to assist a student in determining an appropriate course of action, the facts must be known.

School Policies

While counselors might believe that the ethical principles and the ASCA *Ethical Standards* (2010) should dictate counseling practice, school administrators and Boards of Education frequently believe that their own policies should dominate. This can put a counselor in a difficult position. The best way to avoid conflict between what the school counseling profession expects of professional school counselors and what a principal or board of education might expect is to ensure that all parties are on the same page. This can be accomplished by the counseling program sharing the ASCA *Standards* with administrators and members of the Board. Hopefully, the administration of the school will understand the importance of abiding by the *Standards.*

Realistically, we can easily imagine a situation where a particular school, whether public or private, has policies that are in conflict with the *Ethical Standards.* Common situations are school policies that require all faculty and staff to report any knowledge of student use of drugs and alcohol. If a counselor violates this policy, even if it is in service to the best practices of the profession regarding confidentiality, he or she could be reprimanded and possibly even fired by the school. Other difficult situations arise when dealing with issues of sexuality, whether it be a student's sexual expression or a student's concern that he has a sexually transmitted disease. In these circumstances, school counselors need to be aware that the school has the legal right to establish and enforce policies as long as the parents, and to a lesser extent the students, are informed about these policies.

Before being hired, prospective school counselors should ask to see any policies which they will be expected to enforce. This will not totally solve the problem of being surprised by policies after being hired, but it will provide a general overview of a particular school's understanding of a counselor's unique role. Counselors also need to be cautious about following behavioral practices that are not part of a school's written policies.

Developing a strong knowledge-based ethical foundation is essential for competent, ethical practice. Without this foundation, a counselor may be following rules, but he is not an autonomous ethical practitioner. As stated earlier, the goal is not to create mere rule-followers; the goal is to develop practitioners who are able to judge when a rule applies. Sometimes, when no rule speaks to the complexity of a particular situation, a counselor still needs to arrive at an ethically informed decision. This is possible only if that counselor has cultivated a strong ethical foundation.

Landmark 3

CASE EXAMPLE

Mr. Washington, the new 12th grade counselor, is walking down the hallway with Mrs. Bender, a longtime teacher at the high school. A girl comes up to them and tells them that another student, a senior, is pregnant. When the student leaves, Mrs. Bender tells Mr. Washington that it is school policy that parents are to be notified about pregnancy. She tells him he should meet with the student, and if she admits to being pregnant, he must notify the parents. Instead of automatically following Mrs. Bender's guidelines, he speaks with a more experienced colleague who tells him there is no such school policy. The school believes that such decisions must be individually determined after meeting with the student. The colleague agrees to assist Mr. Washington as he works through this difficult matter. This case highlights the importance of fact-finding before taking any action.

MAJOR ETHICAL CONCEPTS AND PRACTICES

Now that the ethical foundations of school counseling have been outlined, the next step is to consider how ethical principles and practices are infused in the day-to-day practice of school counseling. We will use this section to look at some of the most pertinent ethical guidelines that school counselors must understand and be able to embody in order to be considered highly ethical clinicians.

Informed Consent

One of the central principles of counseling practice is informed consent. Briefly stated, informed consent is a legal and ethical principle which requires counselors to fully explain to the client (student) and, if a minor, his or her legal guardian, the benefits, risks, and alternatives to the proposed counseling (Glosoff & Pate, 2002). The provided explanation should be geared to the individual's developmental level and intellectual ability. Oftentimes, the process of informed consent is managed by having both client and guardian sign an informed-consent statement. While this is a good practice, it is not sufficient. The informed-consent process needs to be ongoing throughout the counseling process (Glosoff & Pate, 2002; Stone, 2009).

Counselors need to be verbally checking in with both client and guardian in order to routinely update informed consent.

As with most practices, the informed-consent process is a bit more complex in a school setting because of the many different services provided by a school counselor. The first step in the informed-consent process is having a description of the comprehensive guidance program in the hands of the entire school community: parents, students, faculty, and staff. Useful information about how to construct this description can be found in ASCA print materials (ASCA, 2005) and on the ASCA website (www.schoolcounselor.org).

It is useful to have somewhat different handouts or brochures for the various stakeholders: what students need to know is different from what parents and colleagues need to know about the program. The description needs to include the scope and practice of the school counselor. The three domains of school counseling described by ASCA can provide a good starting point for describing the services of a particular program. Those three domains are academic, career, and personal/social (ASCA, 2005). The activities of each domain need to be described so everyone understands the role of the school counselor. If an activity is directly related to the educational function of the school, for instance, providing a group guidance lesson on careers or coordinating assistance for a student experiencing difficulty in a particular class, then obtaining specific parental approval is not ordinarily needed. If, however, a counselor is going to be seeing a student in one-on-one sessions, with an emotional or social issue at the heart of the encounter, then approval from the parents generally should be sought. All of this should be elaborated in the program description so parents and students understand what services the program offers.

The next step in the informed-consent process is to provide to the parents an informed-consent written document which needs to be signed by them if their child is going to participate in any activity that is not strictly a part of the academic program. This includes activities such as divorce support groups, grief groups, individual counseling, and, in some districts, classroom guidance activities dealing with sexuality. While step one is gaining parental approval, step two is providing an informed-consent form for the student if the activity is not part of the regular academic program. Students, as well as their guardians, have the right to understand the benefits, limitations, and general organization of the activity they are about to be involved in.

Having the guardians and student sign an informed-consent form is a central part of the informed-consent process. However, the process of informed consent, especially for the student, needs to be revisited. During any involvement with a student which lasts more than four or five sessions, the counselor needs to verbally check in with the student to verify that the student is still engaged in the counseling process and to ascertain whether the service is meeting the student's needs.

Confidentiality

The informed-consent process must include a discussion of the role of confidentiality in the student–counselor relationship. In the counseling profession, confidentiality is defined as the counselor's commitment not to disclose anything revealed during counseling except under "agreed-upon conditions" (Glosoff & Pate, 2002, p. 22). The "agreed-upon conditions" always include the disclosure of information when the counselor has reason to believe that the student is in danger of harming himself, being harmed or harming someone else. Of course, the difficulty is determining what constitutes being harmed or endangering self or others. While this will be discussed in more detail when the ethical decision-making process is detailed, it is helpful to note that the definition of being in harm's way will vary greatly depending on the age and the developmental level of the student.

While the ASCA *Ethical Standards* emphasize the importance of confidentiality (see section A.2. of the *Ethical Standards*) they also make clear that while the primary obligation of confidentiality is to the students, this must be balanced "with an understanding of parents/guardians' legal and inherent rights to be the guiding voice in their children's lives, especially in value-laden issues" (ASCA, 2010, A.2.d). The need to balance parents' right to know with students' right to confidentiality makes the counseling position in a school setting complicated. A further complication is the fact that most state laws support parents in their right to information about their child. Many authors have written on this subject in an attempt to guide counselors (Bodenhorn, 2006; Huss, Bryant, & Mulet, 2008; Lazovsky, 2008). If all this advice could be condensed into a single statement, it might read something like this: School counselors need to be careful not to promise more than they can deliver. The level of confidentiality that can be guaranteed depends on the age and developmental level of the student, state laws, school policies regarding parents' rights to know, and the counselor's responsibilities as a mandated reporter to report suspected abuse.

Multiple or Dual Relationships

The complexity of the school counselor's role is also evident when considering the issue of multiple relationships. For the counseling profession as a whole the ideal has always been to avoid multiple relationships whenever possible (Sommers-Flanagan & Sommers-Flanagan, 2007). Interacting with a client in multiple contexts has been viewed as potentially harmful to the primary counselor/client relationship (Sommers-Flanagan & Sommers-Flanagan, 2007). Maintaining this singularity of focus is not possible for the school counselor who almost always serves many functions within the school community. Given this reality, school counselors need to ensure, as much as possible, that the multiple roles they are placed in are complementary and do not undermine their primary role as an advocate for the student. In particular, school counselors should decline to become overt enforcers of the school's disciplinary policies; they should not be assigning punishment or monitoring detention. These roles are in conflict with the core counseling principle of fidelity.

Holding multiple roles does not necessarily undermine a counselor's effectiveness. For instance, serving as the scorer for the basketball team or the coordinator of a service project places the counselor in a position to get to know the students in a less formal setting. This can be a very useful way to build relationships with students, and it does not undermine either the core ethical principles or the counselor's future effectiveness as an advocate for students. Therefore, before engaging in a role outside the traditional practice of school counseling, counselors need to assess whether the new role would assist or undermine their ability to act as an academic advocate and personal resource for students.

Scope of Practice

A counselor's multiple roles within the school are a clear indication that a school counselor has a potentially large scope of practice. It is important for the counselor to be clear, both to herself and to her colleagues and students, what areas of school counseling she is competent to undertake. Not all school counselors are experienced enough to engage in prolonged counseling of a student with persistent emotional difficulties, or well-versed enough in college counseling to serve as the primary source of information for students applying to college.

A well-managed school counseling program clearly assesses each counselor's level of experience and expertise. However, there are many situations where one individual may be the only counselor for an entire school. In this case, if the counselor does not try to assist the student, no assistance will be forthcoming. Counselors need to manage this difficult circumstance by carefully adhering to the ethical principles, especially the injunction to "do no harm." In addition, the counselor needs to be upfront about his lack of experience or knowledge and seek out the assistance needed for a particular student.

Record Keeping

It is important that school counselors keep records of their work with students. Sometimes the school counselor will be the primary individual responsible for monitoring the progress of an academic or behavioral intervention. Not keeping clear records of such events is a violation of the ethical principle of fidelity and is potentially very harmful to the student's development.

Counselors may also be meeting with students to discuss personal issues. In these cases, record keeping is essential in order for the counselor to have an accurate understanding of the student and his or her concerns. These records should be kept separate from records dealing with academic issues or other issues which involve several people and a team approach. Many school counselors keep two sets of counseling notes (Sommers-Flanagan & Sommers-Flanagan, 2007). One set, meant to be part of a student's general counseling folder, provides limited information: date and time of appointment with a general sense of the appointment topic. The other set, referred to as sole possession notes, are meant only for the counselor's eyes. These notes may include counselor hypotheses about the student's behaviors as well as questions the counselor may want to ask the student. Sole possession notes are afforded greater protection under FERPA if they are kept in a separate file accessible only to the counselor. Sole possession records afford the student a greater level of confidentiality and so, when appropriate, are in a student's best interest.

All notes and records whether they are sole possession notes, part of a student's official academic record, or part of a counseling record should be kept in locked cabinets with restricted access. Sole possession notes are accessed only by an individual counselor. Counseling records are able to be accessed by the student's counselor, and, in some schools, by anyone on the counseling staff. Who has access to official student records should be determined by the school's administration.

Many school offices use student and/or parent volunteers. These individuals should not have access to any student files. Counselors need to be cautious about leaving folders or notes on their desks where others may see them. This would be a violation of a student's right to confidentiality as well as a violation of the student's privacy rights as guaranteed by FERPA.

How long official student records should be kept is usually determined by each school. In general, the requirement is to keep all records for at least 7 years. After that, most schools keep only the core academic record. How long a school counselor should keep sole-possession notes is up to the counselor. Again, a general rule is that these records should be kept until the counselor is confident that her work with the student has come to an end, since these notes are not meant to be shared with anyone.

RULES ARE NOT ENOUGH: SELF-AWARENESS AND THE THREE WINDOWS OF INTROSPECTION

Up to this point, the information provided has focused on establishing an ethical approach to school counseling based upon ethical codes, laws, and the best practices of the profession. Building this knowledge base is vitally important; however, it alone does not engender ethical practice. In order to be more confident about your ethical competence, an approach which stresses a more personal connection with ethical practice must be implemented. Combining self-awareness with introspection, this approach seeks to aid you in identifying potential areas of ethical vulnerability. After identifying these areas, it is up to the counselor, often in consultation with her supervisor, to proactively implement a plan to reduce personal ethical vulnerabilities.

School counselors are in particular need of this approach because of the complexity of the role of the school counselor. Unlike many other counseling professionals, the school counselor must be on duty throughout the day. In addition, the role of the school counselor can change depending on what counseling function is needed. Changing roles can require subtle adjustments in how the ethical code and principles are implemented. Finally, many individuals are the only school counselor in a building. This means that there is not someone readily available to consult who understands the issues, complexities, and ethical vulnerabilities inherent in the position of school counseling. The process of coming to an enhanced state of self-awareness is broken down into three steps. Termed the three windows of introspection, each step calls upon a counselor to introspect about a particular focus area in order to determine potential areas of ethical vulnerability.

Personal History Window

The first step in looking into the personal history window is to reflect on how your past has shaped who you are today. In particular, it is useful to spend time considering your own developmental history. What have been the principal issues at each of the major stages of your development: childhood, adolescence, and adulthood? What have been the crises and high points at each stage? Was your own family system dysfunctional? Did you have a hard time interacting with peers? Was your adolescence a time of rebellion and self-destruction?

The next step is to consider how your developmental history might impact your work with students. For example, if you as a child were taunted by members of your high school's football team, how likely is it that you will tend to bring openness and empathy to football players you may encounter in your work? What will you do to counteract a tendency to underidentify with these teens, thereby violating the ethical principles of beneficence and fidelity? Or, perhaps you grew up in a family that struggled to make ends meet, leaving you without many toys and wearing second-hand clothes. How might you tend to react when you discover that a youngster is being mocked for not having the new "in shoes" or the latest video game? How tempted might you be to violate professional boundaries in order to get the shoes or the game for this student?

Issues from our past will come back to haunt us if we are not aware of them. Many counselors have found themselves caught up in a web of countertransference. This does not need to happen. If we are aware of what is occurring, of our countertransference, we can use our identification with the client in a positive way. This is accomplished, in part, by reflecting on the circumstances and issues that shaped who we are. By reflecting on our personal history, we are able to gain a measure of control over how these issues will impact us in the present.

Landmark 3

CASE EXAMPLE

Margot, a new elementary school counselor, was physically abused as a child. She is determined to monitor students under her guidance closely for signs of abuse. Her tendency would be to question every bruise on every child. Realizing that her perspective has been shaped by her prior experience, Margot determines to observe every child, but also to check out her observations with a trusted colleague before questioning the child.

Emotional, Temperamental Window

Becoming aware of our present emotional disposition is essential if we are going to understand how we emotionally impact others and how others may be impacting us. Do you come across to others as overly assertive, insecure, stressed out, or nave? How do friends or colleagues describe your emotional disposition? Do you find yourself feeling routinely drained after working with particular student issues or concerns? Have you found yourself in tears or angry at the end of a school day?

Based upon the insights gained from such reflection, it becomes possible to determine how our dispositional style might need to be altered to accommodate a specific student or a particular circumstance. A highly extroverted counselor might need to tone down her energy level before meeting a socially anxious student. A counselor who tends toward emotional volatility may need to practice some self-calming exercises before going to the meeting with the angry teacher who does not understand why she needs to check the homework planner for the student diagnosed with attention-deficit hyperactivity disorder (ADHD).

Sometimes a counselor may be experiencing a period of particular emotional vulnerability. For example, if a counselor's spouse has just left the relationship there is a potentially heightened vulnerability. This can lead the counselor to look for emotional fulfillment from his or her students. Situations where educators and counselors have become romantically involved with students are not unknown, and by some accounts are dramatically underreported (Shakeshaft, 2004). A counselor who is self-aware is much more likely to recognize the warning signs of such involvement and seek guidance from trusted colleagues and supervisors. Ethical competence requires a counselor to be emotionally aware. In order to maintain ethical awareness, school counselors need to monitor the emotional changes in their lives as well as open themselves to feedback about how their temperament affects others.

Landmark 4

CASE EXAMPLE

Shondra, a middle-school counselor, had been leading the school's divorce support group for several years. In the middle of the school year, Shondra's husband announced he wanted a divorce. Shondra was devastated. Realizing that the depth of her emotions could interfere with the group's process, Shondra spoke with her colleagues about transitioning out of leading the group. Another counselor stepped forward and Shondra was able to transition the group into new leadership.

Conventional, Functional Window

Reflecting on how we handle the functional demands of daily life provides a window into how we will behave professionally. Have our lives been marked by lateness, procrastination, missed due dates, and avoided responsibilities? Do our friends know not to depend on us when we promise something, whether it is to return borrowed items or attend a party? Is our personal living space so chaotic that we are always looking for misplaced items? Is there a pile of unopened mail, perhaps containing bills, sitting on the counter?

An affirmative answer to the any of the above is an indication that there is likely going to be a problem maintaining the ethical principles of beneficence and fidelity. If practices that are common in our personal lives, lateness, procrastination, and lack of meeting obligations, carry over into our professional life, we will be missing appointments with students, not fully completing required paperwork and not conducting a well-organized school counseling program.

Identifying our deficits in managing daily responsibilities allows us to implement a plan to remedy these hindrances to smooth professional functioning. A school counselor cannot afford not to keep accurate and up-to-date records; nor can she afford arriving late to an important meeting or forgetting to schedule such a meeting. These ingrained habits can be difficult to change. Once a deficit in professional functioning has been identified, the school counselor needs to work with a trusted colleague on setting up a plan to correct the problem behavior.

Landmark 5

CASE EXAMPLE

Charmaine's office was a mess. She justified this to herself by saying that she had more important things to do than organize a bunch of papers. She accepted that she was just messy. Her disorganization was hidden until the day of an important meeting about the special academic needs of a student. Charmaine was in charge of presenting the student's comprehensive academic assessment to the parents. The school psychologist, coordinator of special education, and team leader for the eighth grade would also be present. The day arrived and Charmaine could not find the student's folder in the chaos of her office. She needed to delay the meeting while she frantically looked through the piles of folders. As her colleagues looked on with disgust, Charmaine realized that she could no longer accept her messiness. Not only was it impacting her ability to function, it was impacting her ability to best advocate for her students.

While it is useful to begin the process of introspection early in counseling training, this is a process which must continue to develop and mature in a counselor. Issues from the past which did not emerge as potential influences on the present may rise to the surface as a new developmental period arises or when specific student issues are confronted. The stresses and challenges of personal and professional life may impact a counselor's emotional disposition in a way that needs to be accounted for when working closely with others. This can be accomplished only if there is openness to self-examination. Using the three windows of introspection regularly will help to ensure that a counselor will bring the best, most competent, and most ethical self into each counseling situation.

THE PROCESS OF ETHICAL DECISION MAKING

Whenever a school counselor is confronted with an ethically ambiguous situation, the steps in arriving at a decision should be both deliberative and comprehensive. Fortunately, the ASCA *Ethical Standards* detail those steps (ASCA, 2010). Taken from the work of Carolyn Stone (2009), the STEPS (Solutions to Ethical Problems in Schools) model is as follows:

- Define the problem emotionally and intellectually
- Apply the ASCA *Ethical Standards* and the law
- Consider the students' chronological and developmental levels

- Consider the setting [another way of saying: What are the school policies?], parental rights, and minors' rights
- Apply the moral principles [what are referred to here as ethical principles]
- Determine your potential courses of action and their consequences
- Evaluate the selected action
- Consult
- Implement the course of action

The STEPS model guides the school counselor through a rigorous and thorough process of implementing ethical principles, guidelines, laws, and school policies while taking into consideration each student's chronological and developmental age. After an initial analysis has been completed, the school counselor needs to consult with other knowledgeable colleagues, and perhaps even obtain legal advice, before implementing a decision. The consultation may result in a need to return to the decision-making model in order to revise the decision after receiving constructive feedback.

It is important for the model to be implemented in a deliberative fashion. School counselors need to write out their response at each step in the process. Moving through the model mentally is not enough. Each step needs to be written out, using an outline format when appropriate, and the rationale behind each decision needs to be clearly stated. Finally, counselors need to document their implementation of the STEPS model in the student's counseling record.

In difficult situations it is sometimes not possible that all parties involved in the process reach consensus. For instance, a school counselor may consult with another counselor in the building and with a school administrator. There may be a split decision on what the course of action should be. The reasons for choosing the final course of action need to be documented, and the reasons for not choosing the competing course of action also need to be elaborated. Through this process, the school counselor will be documenting the rigorous process that was undertaken in order to act in the best interest of the student. If a decision is later found wanting, the school counselor can demonstrate that every attempt was made to arrive at a sound ethical decision.

SIGNPOSTS FOR FUTURE TREKS

This chapter is meant to acquaint students with the needed information to be sound ethical practitioners. For students to become competent professionals, they should

- Understand the components of a solid ethical foundation: the core ethical principles, the ASCA *Ethical Standards*, relevant state and federal laws, and school policies.
- Infuse into their lives as professional school counselors the major ethical concepts and practices.
- Attend to how their past history and personal qualities may influence their behavior as school counselors and possibly place them in an ethically vulnerable situation.

- Implement the STEPS model when confronted with a complex ethical question.

The personal testimony below is meant to assist you in seeing how I, a school counselor in a high school setting, managed a difficult ethical situation. The goal is to provide a real-life example of the need to balance various ethical principles while working toward what is in the best interest of the student.

INSIGHTS GAINED FROM THE JOURNEY

When the school nurse, Mrs. Pierro, called me into the clinic, I did not know what to expect. It was not uncommon for her to seek me out when a student presented with an illness that seemed more emotional than physical, but this time there was an urgency in her voice that was unusual. When I got to the clinic, she pulled me aside and told me that Tara, a high school junior, had shown up an hour ago saying she just could not take being in class anymore. When Mrs. Pierro tried to talk to her, Tara just cried and said she was exhausted and could not cope anymore. She also said that she was doing things she was guilty about and felt she might be "losing it." Mrs. Pierro, clearly overwhelmed by Tara's comments and behavior, led me to Tara's cot and quickly left the room.

Tara was curled up on the cot quietly sobbing. Through a process of gentle questioning I discovered that Tara was an A student, enrolled in four AP classes and active in a competitive dance program outside of school. She was also clearly overwhelmed by the amount of school work she was facing during the lead up to exams. In addition, Tara was afraid of disappointing her parents by not performing at her usual exceptional level. Although she appeared somewhat relieved to be sharing her feelings, Tara still seemed withdrawn and a bit guarded. Further probing revealed that Tara, in order to ease the pressures she felt, had been cutting herself on her thighs and upper arms. When she told me this, she looked me in the eyes for the first time and said, "Am I crazy?"

I assured Tara that while her behavior was not healthy, I did not see evidence that she was crazy. I also told her that it was going to be important for her parents to know both how overwhelmed she was feeling with school and how her feelings had led her to harm herself. Tara reacted to the mention of her parents with renewed tears. She said "They will never understand, and anyway I am too embarrassed to tell them." She pleaded with me to keep her confidence.

Knowing that I was facing a difficult and complex situation, I asked Tara if I could leave her for a few moments. Mrs. Pierro stepped back into the room and I left to seek out the dean of students, the administrator in my building, whom I worked with when making difficult decisions. I met with the dean and we decided on a course of action after weighing Tara's right to confidentiality, our concern over her physical and mental well-being, and her parent's rights to be advised as to the physical and mental condition of their child.

The first step was to ask Tara if Mrs. Pierro could look at some of the cuts. Tara agreed and Mrs. Pierro told us there were some rather deep, although not infected, cuts on her upper arms. Several of the cuts appeared new, while others were healing. After determining that Tara was actively cutting, and that the cuts were more than just scratches, I gave Tara three choices: I could call her parents and ask them to come to school to meet with Tara and myself; I could call her parents and tell them what was occurring at school and Tara would speak with them at home; or Tara could call her parents and speak with them. These three options aimed at giving Tara a choice, and so honoring her autonomy, while also ensuring that the ethical obligation to protect Tara was carried out. It was necessary to balance Tara's right to confidentiality and autonomy with the need to protect her and to advise her parents of a potentially very harmful behavior.

When presented with the three options, Tara appeared almost relieved. She said she would call her mom and tell her what was happening, but then she wanted to give me the phone so I could explain further. Tara had in fact arrived at a fourth option, one that I readily accepted.

This case highlights the need to have a process in place when confronted with a difficult and complex situation. The dean of students and I had an already-established decision-making process and a protocol which placed a student's safety at the top. Tara, in going to the nurse's office, in revealing the cutting, and in stating that she feared she was going crazy was clearly asking for an intervention. At the same time, she was insisting that her parents could not find out about her behavior. The ethical challenge was balancing Tara's stated request for confidentiality with her clear desire for help and with her parents' rights to know vital information about their child. In giving Tara the choice about how to inform her parents, and offering her support through that process, we arrived at a course of action which addressed the urgency of the situation while adhering as closely as possible to ethical principles and the *Ethical Standards*. Through this process I learned the importance of having in place a decision-making process. I was not making the decision alone. The dean of students, the school nurse, and I worked together to assess Tara and the situation. I was clear about my ethical obligations and I had assistance in weighing competing ethical principles in order to arrive at a decision that was in Tara's best overall interest.

MOVING FORWARD: CASE STUDY AND REFLECTION QUESTIONS

Marco, an energetic freshman soccer player, was a popular student among his peers and well liked by his teachers. He had come to the school 2 years ago when his family moved into town. Marco's father, originally from Chile, was a chemist at a research facility, and his mother was a college professor of Spanish. Marco, an only child, seemed to adapt well to the new school although he had a greater number of absences than usual.

Teachers and counselors became concerned when rumors circulated that Marco's dislocated shoulder and sprained wrist were not the result of an athletic injury, as Marco had originally told everyone, but instead were caused by his father who beat Marco in a fit of rage over Marco's supposedly disrespectful attitude. As the rumors were circulating, one of Marco's friends, Ryan, visited the school counselor, Mr. Brubaker, to tell him that he was worried about Marco. Marco had told Ryan that sometimes his father drank and then beat him. Marco said that he did not know how much longer he could tolerate his father and his life. Ryan was worried that Marco might do something to harm himself or his father. He asked the counselor to talk with Marco: "I don't even care if he finds out I told; I am afraid something bad is going to happen."

Mr. Brubaker called Marco into his office for a conversation. Marco appeared anxious. When Mr. Brubaker asked him how he got his injuries, Marco stated that he fell practicing soccer kicks in his backyard. Mr. Brubaker decided to ask Marco about the several students who said that Marco had received the injuries from his father. Marco, again appearing very nervous, denied this and said his friends had just misunderstood him—he just told them his father was upset because Marco was so careless to have fallen in the backyard. Mr. Brubaker was not convinced that Marco was telling the truth and suggested that perhaps he needed to meet with Marco's parents. At this point, Marco became very upset and said that this would cause a lot of trouble for him. "My father doesn't want to have anything to do with the school and would be upset to have to come here. Please don't do this to me. He will think I am causing trouble." Mr. Brubaker then suggested talking with Marco's mother. At this suggestion, Marco broke into tears and said, "You just don't understand, she would be embarrassed to come here. If you want to help, please leave me alone."

REFLECTION QUESTIONS

- *Describe the ethical issues in this case.*
- *If you were Mr. Brubaker how would you decide on your course of action?*
- *Should Marco's desire to be left alone be honored?*
- *Do you feel that the state mandate to report suspected child abuse applies here? Why or why not?*
- *How might your answers to the above change if you discovered that 6 weeks after this event Marco was hospitalized for a suicide attempt?*
- *How did your response to the case exemplify a positive approach to ethics?*

REFERENCES

American School Counselor Association. (2005). *The ASCA national model*. Alexandria, VA: Author.

American School Counselor Association. (2010). *Ethical standards for school counselors*. Alexandria, VA: Author.

Beauchamp, T., & Childress, J. (2001). *Principles of biomedical ethics* (5th ed.). New York: Oxford University Press.

Bodenhorn, N. (2006). Exploratory study of common and challenging ethical dilemmas experienced by professional school counselors. *Professional School Counseling, 10*(2), 195–202.

Family Educational Rights and Privacy Act. (1974). 20 U.S.C.A. §1232.112 ALR Fed 1.

Glosoff, H. L., & Pate, R. H. Jr. (2002). Privacy and confidentiality in school counseling. *Professional School Counseling, 6*(1), 20–28.

Huss, S. N., Bryant, A., & Mulet, S. (2008). Managing the quagmire of counseling in a school: Bringing the parents onboard. *Professional School Counseling*, *11*(6), 362–367.

Kitchener, K. S. (2000). *Foundations of ethical practice, research and teaching in psychology*. Mahwah, NJ: Erlbaum.

Lazovsky, R. (2008). Maintaining confidentiality with minors: Dilemmas of school counselors. *Professional School Counseling*, *11*(5), 335–346.

Shakeshaft, C. (2004). *Educator sexual misconduct: A synthesis of existing literature* (DOC# 2004-09). Washington, DC: United States Department of Education.

Sommers-Flanagan, R., & Sommers-Flanagan, J. (2007). *Becoming an ethical helping professional*. Hoboken, NJ: John Wiley & Sons.

Stone, C. (2009). *Ethics and law*. Alexandria, VA: American School Counselor Association.

15

GROUP COUNSELING AND COUNSELOR ETHICS

Lynn E. Linde

THE FORESEEN DESTINATION

The purpose of this chapter is to provide the reader with basic concepts related to group counseling and the special ethical issues associated with facilitating counseling groups. Additionally, it is hoped that readers will reflect upon their own ethics and style of counseling and think about how those factors influence the process and outcome of their counseling groups. After reading this chapter, readers will:

- Be familiar with the process of group counseling.
- Be able to describe the ethical issues surrounding group counseling.
- Be able to describe how their style and values influence the counseling process.
- Be able to work through a reflective process for their counseling.
- Be able to apply the reflective process to ethical decision making within groups.

GETTING ON THE ROAD

From the beginning of time, people have gathered in groups for a variety of reasons, including safety, shelter, food, intimacy, and to flourish and develop. Groups serve many purposes and sometimes the same group may serve multiple purposes. But what, exactly, is a group? Gladding (2008) defines a group as two or more individuals who meet interdependently, with the understanding that they are meeting to attain mutually agreed-upon goals. He uses the term *group work* to describe the application of skills and knowledge to help facilitate the ability of members to reach these goals. These parameters have special meaning in a counseling context, in which the counselor or group leader facilitates the growth and development of the members of the group through observation and interaction with its members.

The relationship between the counselor and the group, and among group members, has special implications for what happens in the group. The way in which the counselor selects group members, structures the sessions of the group, interacts with the group members, and processes the work of the group significantly impacts what happens in the group, the progress the group makes, the progress individual members make, and the way in which the members feel about what occurs (Gladding, 2008). Since counseling is an activity that generally occurs out of the sight of others, known as nonparticipants (Young, 2008), and may not be supervised, the way in which counselors approach their job and work with their clients is of paramount importance.

The ACA *Code of Ethics* (2005) addresses some issues regarding group work. The Association for Specialists in Group Work (ASGW), a division of the American Counseling Association (ACA), centers their efforts on promoting best practices in group work. An understanding of both of these standards is critical for practicing ethically. But it is equally important to reflect upon one's own practice. In addition to their education and training, counselors bring the sum of their experiences and who they are—that is, their values, morals, and spiritual influences—to every relationship. Professional counselors must be continually aware of how their own beliefs and values influence the way in which they perceive issues and situations, the clients and their needs, and the options that they believe to be available and viable (Linde & Erford, in press). It is not enough for counselors to know what the codes of ethics and best practices require or suggest, but they must internalize a framework for incorporating these standards into a reflective, analytical perspective that goes beyond the "musts" of counseling to what is truly in the best interests of their clients. This is particularly critical when conducting groups as the issues are more complex and multifaceted than when working with clients individually (Linde, Erford, Hayes, & Wilson, 2011).

As readers move through this chapter, this author hopes that they will keep in mind the importance of self-reflection and analysis. The goals of this chapter are to (a) describe the basic components and issues for group work, (b) describe the ethical issues associated with each of the components, and (c) provide questions to form a paradigm for reflective practice in group work. The chapter will begin with a discussion of the components of group work and the issues counselors must consider when moving through each of the components.

EXPLORING THE TERRITORY

TYPES OF GROUPS: AN OVERVIEW

ASGW defines group work as

> ... a broad professional practice involving the application of knowledge and skill in group facilitation to assist an interdependent collection of people to reach their mutual goals which may be intrapersonal, interpersonal, or work-related. The goals of the group may include the accomplishment of tasks related to work, education, personal development, personal and interpersonal problem solving, or remediation of mental and emotional disorders. (2000)

This definition covers a broad array of activities in a multitude of settings. ASGW further delineates four major types of group work: task or work groups, psychoeducational groups, counseling, and therapy groups. Each of these groups will be briefly described below. In addition, there are several other types of groups that will not be discussed but are important aspects of group work. These groups include self-help groups, personal growth groups, and T groups, sometimes known as sensitivity or basic skills training groups.

Task groups are everywhere, according to DeLucia-Waack (1996). Committees, clubs, and task forces are part of all environments: work, professional associations, faith organizations, the community, education, and probably any other environment one can name. Task group members come together with a common goal; the difference between this type of group and a counseling group is primarily that the focus of the group is on the attainment of the group's goal and not on each member's goal. Task groups are important when there is a need for multiple people to work on an issue; if the work can be done by one person, there is no need for the group. The effectiveness of the group's ability to meet their goal is often associated with the leader's or leaders' knowledge of group work and ability to facilitate the group process, understand the dynamics of the group, and move the group forward (DeLucia-Waack, 1996; Gladding, 2008). It is critical to the success of the task group that the goal(s) of the group and the guidelines for participation must be clearly established and understood by all members, there must be a structure for the group meetings to take place, and the task group leader must balance content and process. If those criteria are implemented, the group will likely accomplish its goal.

Psychoeducational groups were originally developed for use in educational settings, particularly schools. According to Gladding (2008), they tend to be time-limited, structured, and focused groups that are created to address specific issues and behavioral goals. The group's goals and activities are usually identified by the group leader and are designed to help members understand and process the information that is covered in the sessions. The goals of a psychoeducational group are usually prevention, skills acquisition, and remediation. The issues covered by such groups range from orientation sessions to concerns about identity and self-esteem, anger management, study skills or other work behaviors, friendship issues, health and nutrition issues, and academic and/or career areas. As with task groups, the skill of the group leader is essential to the successful implementation of a psychoeducational group.

Landmark 1

POINT OF INTEREST

Jesse B. Davis, principal of Grand Rapids High School, decided in 1907 that one class period each week would be devoted to guidance activities. Davis saw classroom guidance as a functional way facilitating life skills, values, and citizenship (Gladding, 2008).

The third type of group is counseling groups. Sometimes referred to as interpersonal problem-solving groups, the focus of such groups is on each member's development and behavior and change within the group and through the help of the group (Gladding, 2008). Within counseling groups, all members establish goals for themselves at the onset. The group also sets goals for the group as a whole. The goals of the group may differ somewhat from the goals of each member, particularly when the purpose of the group concerns a particular issue or behavior. In these groups, the focus is on the members and their interactions and mutual problem-solving efforts (Day, 2007). Groups tend to be time-limited. The number of members varies from 3 or 4 for groups with young children to 8 or 12 in adult groups.

Therapy groups are similar to counseling groups, but generally are used for members whose problems are more serious and longer-lasting than members of counseling groups. The sessions attempt to address severe and chronic maladjustment issues; the group is remedial in that the leader must attempt to confront the members' maladaptive behaviors and help them learn new patterns of behavior. Open-ended groups are ongoing and admit new members at any time; closed groups do not allow new members. Groups may last for months or years (Gladding, 2008).

Landmark 2

POINT OF INTEREST

The first nontask or psychoeducational group held is credited to Joseph Hersey Pratt, who ran a group for tuberculosis patients at Massachusetts General Hospital in 1905. He wrote about the dynamics of what he saw in the group—what we would now refer to as group process. His work served as the model for other leaders interested in running groups (Gladding, 2008).

THE FOUNDATION OF ETHICAL PRACTICE AND ETHICAL STANDARDS

Before we move on to look at various aspects of conducting groups and the ethical considerations, it is helpful to first look at the larger principles which undergird the development of codes of ethics. They are the moral principles of autonomy, nonmaleficence, beneficence, fidelity, and justice (Remley & Herlihy, 2010). These principles were discussed in Chapter 1 from a philosophical viewpoint; in this chapter, they will be discussed as they relate specifically to the group process, as described by Linde et al. (2011).

Autonomy refers to the members' rights to make their own decisions. Group leaders must respect the right of the members to make sound and rational decisions based on their values and beliefs and not impose their own values or beliefs about what the client should do on members. In the formation of the group, the goals should be established both by the individual members and by the group as a whole. It is critical that members for the group be selected who will not be harmed by the group, particularly if the goals of the individual are different than the goals of the group. At the same time, members should be encouraged to establish goals that can be accomplished through the group process and within the time frame of the group.

Nonmaleficence means "do no harm." Group leaders are thus charged with the responsibility to refrain from doing anything that may harm one or more of the members. However, this principle does not just refer to what the group leader must not do, but implies the precautions one must take to prevent harm from being done. Examples of preventing harm include screening potential members for the appropriateness of their inclusion in the group; preventing physical or psychological harm from the leader or any group member, or from the interactions of those other persons; or premature termination.

Beneficence refers to doing what is in the best interests of members and promoting well-being, growth, and an optimal group experience. Group leaders must plan and form the group carefully and make sure they prepare the members of the group from the beginning and have genuine informed consent. During the sessions of the group, the leader must conduct the group skillfully, provide appropriate structure, processing, and evaluation, and must prepare the members for termination and next steps.

Fidelity refers to honoring commitments and establishing a counseling relationship based on trust. The relationship a counselor has with clients is a special one, and the counselor must honor that commitment to the client as demonstrated through a variety of actions. Counselors must ensure honest and open communication in the group and throughout the process. They must also be mindful of the stress a client may experience as a result of being in the group and should address those issues.

Justice relates to the fair treatment of clients by the counselor. It is incumbent upon the counselor to do what is best for each client based on the client's needs, but also within the context of the group and the group's needs. Group leaders cannot let the needs or desires of one member of the group overtake the needs of the other members.

Moral principles are generally viewed as essential to ethical counseling practice (Herlihy & Corey, 2006). Group leaders' responsibility for their clients extends from their first encounter with the potential client, through the group process, to the termination and follow-up stages. Their behavior must be guided by the understanding and application of these principles in order to facilitate the growth and understanding of their members.

Landmark 3

CASE EXAMPLE

Joyce is a 3rd-year substance abuse counselor. She works at a center that provides counseling for clients who have been mandated to attend group sessions as a condition of getting their drivers licenses back after a conviction for driving under the influence. The center has developed a format for these mandated sessions that they believe is very effective in working with substance-using clients. Joyce is troubled by the lack of flexibility in the format and questions whether she is helping clients in the manner in which she should.

(continued)

1. *Given the moral principles of autonomy, nonmaleficence, beneficence, fidelity, and justice, is Joyce functioning in an ethical manner by following the dictates of the center?*
2. *How does the fact that she leads involuntary groups influence her practice? Does this change the ethics of the situation?*

Group leaders are expected to also abide by the ethical standards of their profession. For professional counselors, that code is the ACA *Code of Ethics* (2005). The 2007 *Best Practice Guidelines* of the ASGW were written to "clarify the application of the ACA *Code of Ethics* to the field of group work by defining Group Workers' responsibility and scope of practice involving those activities, strategies, and interventions that are consistent and current with effective and appropriate professional ethical and community standards" (ASGW, 2000). More information about ASGW and its resources can be found on their webpage; the link for it is cited at the end of this chapter.

The next section will address application of the ACA *Code of Ethics* (2005) and the ASGW 2007 *Best Practice Guidelines* to specific aspects of group counseling. These guidelines provide a framework for engaging in ethical group practice.

Landmark 4

POINT OF INTEREST

The American Personnel and Guidance Association (APGA) was founded in 1952 when four counseling groups came together to form a larger organization. This group recognized that no group of practitioners can be considered a profession without a code of ethics. This first code of ethics for APGA, now called the American Counseling Association, was created in 1961. Since then, the *ACA Code of Ethics* has been revised every 7 to 10 years. Each code has attempted to incorporate standards for the specialty areas of counseling, including group counseling. ACA has appointed the Ethics Revision Task Force which is currently working on the next iteration, expected to be adopted during 2014. ASGW developed the *Best Practice Guidelines* in 1998, following the adoption of the 1995 ACA *Code of Ethics*. The guidelines were revised in 2007.

PLANNING, FORMING, AND ORIENTING GROUPS

The two sections of the ACA *Code of Ethics* (2005) that pertain most specifically to groups are within Section A.8 and state:

> A.8.a Screening
>
> Counselors screen prospective group counseling/therapy participants. To the extent possible, counselors select members whose needs and goals are compatible with goals of the group, who will not impede the group process, and whose well-being will not be jeopardized by the group experience.

A.8.b Protecting Clients

In a group setting, counselors take reasonable precautions to protect clients from physical, emotional, or psychological trauma.

Section 8 broadly outlines the responsibilities of the group leader when identifying potential clients, to ensure the appropriateness of the members chosen, and to do what is in the best interests of the group members. The ASGW *Best Practice Guidelines*, Section A.7 Group and Member Preparation, further delineate sound practice for identifying members and forming a group, particularly in the area of informed consent. Leaders must communicate information to potential members in a culturally and developmentally appropriate manner and obtain consent from the appropriate person when working with minors. The limits of confidentiality must be explained upfront, which will be discussed later.

For the group to be successful, it is essential for the members to know and understand their rights as group members, to understand the purpose of the group, and to understand the conditions of their participation, that is whether it is voluntary or mandatory. This is generally accomplished through the prescreening interview with potential members and through the informed consent document. This document includes information such as the counselor's credentials and theoretical orientation, what the client can expect from counseling, the client's rights and safeguards that have been put in place, issues about participation and contacting the counselor outside of the group, and ending the relationship. Some, but not all, state licensing boards delineate the specifics of what must be covered in the agreement. Cottone and Taryvdas (2007) emphasize that informed consent must also address the issue of the appropriateness of the member for the group, that is the match between the member and the group and the other members. Screening must be sufficiently thorough to ensure that the client is placed in a group that is consistent with the client's goals and that the group is a good fit for the client. The ASGW 2007 Best Practice Guidelines Section A.7.b require that group workers prepare a disclosure statement specifically for their group work that includes the professional preparation of the leader, the nature of the group services provided, the role and responsibilities of the group leader and members, the limits and exceptions to confidentiality, policies regarding substance use, policies regarding contact or personal involvement of group members outside the group, policies for consultation between the group leader and group members, fees and time parameters, and the potential effects of group participation. According to Remley and Herlihy (2010), a fully developed disclosure statement that covers these points ensures that the group member's consent to join the group is truly informed consent.

Landmark 5

CASE EXAMPLE

Joseph is a counselor in private practice. As part of his practice, he runs a number of groups. He believes that the best way to help clients change is to involve them in a group. He carefully screens potential group members and makes sure that all

(*continued*)

relevant information is in his informed consent document, which the client signs before joining the group.

During a session it came out that Joseph consults with his former professor, who also has a private practice. One of the group members becomes very upset when she learns this information. It turns out that she is a former client of this counselor and had terminated her relationship as she did not believe that he was able to help her. She walks out of the session and tells Joseph she believes he was not honest with her and that she will not come back. Point of information: the name of the person with whom he consults was not on his informed consent form.

1. *Is omitting to give a client information essentially a lie, even if the licensing board did not require this information to be part of the informed consent document? In other words, did Joseph lie to the client by omitting to tell her the name of the person with whom he consults?*
2. *How do counselors know what information clients need? How could this and similar situations been avoided?*
3. *Was Joseph's behavior ethical? Does it meet the standard of care of preparing his clients for the group?*
4. *What does he do now to help his client?*

TRANSITION AND WORKING STAGES IN GROUPS

Group leaders face multiple challenges while running groups. Some of these challenges pertain to the setting in which one is practicing, such as within schools. For example, it is frequently hard to find the time within the school day to conduct counseling groups without disrupting the academic program. Other challenges may relate more to running a group when the members are mandated to attend, such as in correctional settings and as a result of court-ordered sanctions. Regardless, all groups take place within the larger context of the culture of the community and/or setting in which the group takes place. Group workers have a saying: "All group work is multicultural." To practice group work successfully, the leaders must be mindful of different points of view and world views, and their effect on group work interventions (DeLucia-Waack & Donigian, 2003).

Confidentiality is the cornerstone of counseling and helps create the trust that is essential for the members to feel comfortable sharing with leader and the other group members. Members must feel that whatever they share in the group will remain confidential and will not be shared outside the group or used against them in some way. The exceptions to confidentiality in counseling are always when the counselor feels a duty to warn or when the member or members consent to share. Unlike individual counseling, where there is a counselor and only one client, confidentiality cannot be absolute in a setting when there is more than one client. Confidentiality is an expectation in groups, which the leader reinforces, but there is no legal standard for confidentiality in groups (Remley & Herlihy, 2010). However, group leaders must uphold the standard for confidentiality. The ASGW *Best Practice Guidelines* Section A.7.d (2007) states:

> Group Workers define confidentiality and its limits (for example, legal and ethical exceptions and expectations; waivers implicit with treatment plans, documentation and insurance usage). Group Workers have the responsibility to inform all group participants of the need for confidentiality, potential consequences of breaching confidentiality and that legal privilege does not apply to group discussions (unless provided by the state statute). (p. 5)

It is the responsibility of the leader to emphasize the importance of confidentiality, and to establish it as the norm (Cottone & Tarvydas, 2007). A discussion of confidentiality should be part of the initial screening interview and the first session, and should be reinforced as necessary throughout the group sessions. However, the leader must also be honest that confidentiality is not an absolute and cannot be guaranteed. If confidentiality is broken, the group leader must address the issue with the entire group and reinforce the norm.

Working with minors in groups presents additional challenges; group leaders must work collaboratively with the parents/legal guardian to provide them with accurate and appropriate information while maintaining their ethical responsibilities to the minors. There are additional issues related to minors. Legally, the rights to confidentiality belong to the parents/guardian, but the ethical rights belong to the minor. Balancing the needs of the minor against the rights of the parents is a continuous balancing act (Linde & Erford, in press). Leaders must try to maintain confidentiality within the group, but must disclose to parents/guardians when necessary, while also being careful not to break the confidentiality of the other group members. Group leaders need to work with the parents/guardians to help them understand the importance of confidentiality in the group process and develop their trust as well as that of the group members.

Landmark 6

CASE EXAMPLE

David is a counselor in a middle school; he has been one of two counselors in this school for the past 5 years. Each year, the school counseling program sends information home to parents about the services and programs the counselors provide, including a list of groups they will be offering. The school requires parents to give passive consent for their child to be in a counseling group.

After the fifth session (of an eight session group), the parent of one of the members comes into David's office and demands to know what is going on in group and what another child in the group said/did to his child. His son came home upset yesterday and said it had something to do with what happened in group?

1. *What can David ethically tell the parent? What should he tell the parent? Are they the same thing?*

(continued)

2. *How should David work with the child?*
3. *How should David approach the group? What should he tell the other group members?*

Some of these issues can be addressed in clinical settings through the informed consent document, in which parents/guardians are made aware of the limits to their rights and the extent of the rights of their minor child. School settings prove to be more problematic, as there is a greater expectation in schools that parents/guardians have a right to be involved with their child and the consent process may look very different. When conducting groups, school counselors may wish to obtain at least passive consent from the parent/guardian, often called assent, if not informed consent. Should the parent/guardian of any child demand to know what is going on in the session, and the counselor believes that it is appropriate to share, the counselor may only divulge information about the child of the parents/guardian; information about other group members may not be shared.

The ACA *Code of Ethics* (2005) discusses limits to confidentiality. The major exception is duty to warn, which occurs when the counselor has reason to believe that a group member is being harmed, such as in cases of abuse; is in danger of harming self, such as in suicidal behavior; or threatening to harm someone else. In such cases, the leader has an ethical, and often legal, responsibility to inform the appropriate persons and/or entity. Further limitations delineated include the group member's right to privacy even after the member leaves the group or terminates counseling; sharing information with third parties, such as insurance companies; or when there is a court-ordered action. The right to confidentiality does not end with the termination of the group.

Landmark 7

CASE EXAMPLE

Aliza and Stephanie were members of the same group. They run into each other at a coffee shop near where their counselor practices and decide to have coffee together. While chatting, they start talking about what went on in the group and start gossiping about another group member.

1. *Does their behavior conform to the concept of confidentiality in groups?*
2. *Is anyone harmed if no one finds out?*

TERMINATING THE GROUP AND FOLLOW-UP

When should a group terminate? The ACA *Code of Ethics* (2005) Section A.11.c discusses termination in general, not specifically applied to groups, but the same principles apply: the group should be terminated when the services are no longer needed, there is no additional benefit to be had from the group, or when continuation would cause harm. Services could be considered ineffective if the group is not functioning well or if the content and process are no longer appropriate for the members, or if the group leader lacks skill in facilitating the group. Members entering the group come with different levels of knowledge, skill, and need, which create a tension between the needs of the individual and the needs of the group. Members develop differently over the course of the sessions; for groups that are not ongoing, not all members will be at the same point when the group ends. One of the ethical dilemmas for group leaders revolves around unfinished business. Is it acceptable to end a group because all the planned sessions have taken place but one or more members has not yet met his/her goals? Each group leader will need to decide how to handle this problem and what type of follow-up should be provided.

COUNSELOR COMPETENCE AND ETHICAL DECISION MAKING

The issue of counselor competence permeates every aspect of conducting groups, and therefore deserves to be discussed separately. The ACA *Code of Ethics* (2005) Section C.2.a states that

> Counselors practice only within the boundaries of their competence, based on their education, training, and supervised experience, state and national professional credentials, and appropriate professional experience. Counselors gain knowledge, personal awareness, sensitivity, and skills pertinent to working with a diverse client population.

While on the surface this statement seems very straightforward, like much of the application of ethics it is more complicated. Given the brief discussion about the different types of groups, is a counselor who has had a course in group counseling equally skilled developing, implementing, leading, and terminating all four types of groups? Clearly the answer is no, unless the counselor has a tremendous amount of supervised experience with all four types of groups. Corey and Corey (2007) suggest that group leaders need to recognize their limitations and not accept clients whose needs go beyond the scope of the counselor's expertise. Further, they must continue their education and training to become more expert.

Counseling students become familiar with codes of ethics and ethical decision making through their coursework; in some programs a course in ethics and professional issues is required. One of the intended outcomes of these courses is to help students become familiar with an ethical decision-making process which can be used when faced with an ethical dilemma; the process allows the counselor to identify the pertinent section(s) of the code of ethics, determine the scope of the issue, brainstorm potential courses of action, decide what to do, and evaluate the outcome. One of the steps a counselor may chose while weighing the ethical dilemma is to consult with another counselor, typically a mentor or supervisor who has more training and experience than the counselor seeking consultation.

Supervision is a particularly important process for counselors conducting groups; the concerns may multiply when multiple clients are involved and the beginning or inexperienced counselor may not be as aware or skilled at evaluating what is happening. According to Lambie, Hagedorn, and Ieva (2010), learning the ethical guidelines may happen quickly but being able to apply them to situations is a gradual developmental process. They further posit that counselor's social-cognitive development levels influence their functioning as counselors; those counselors with higher social-cognitive functioning skills developed counseling skills that enabled them to become effective counselors faster than lower functioning counselors. Thus, beginning counselors will perceive situations differently depending on their development, and more experienced counselors will demonstrate a higher level of discernment. When applied to counselor competence, it is clear that competence is not an absolute, but a variable that depends on the counselor's level of training, education, and experience. This author believes that one of the ways in which counselors monitor their competence is by becoming a reflective counselor, which is discussed in the next section.

Landmark 8

CASE EXAMPLE

Bernard is a finishing his master's program in clinical counseling and is doing his internship in a community counseling center. He is given the task of running a group for parents who have abused their children. He has never run a group like this before and has some hesitation about being the group leader on his own. When he shares his concerns with his site supervisor, he is told that practice is the only way to learn and that she will be working with him after sessions to debrief and plan for the next session.

1. *If Bernard agrees to run the counseling group for parents who abused their children, will he be practicing outside the limits of his competence?*
2. *Would the answer be different if he were going to colead the group with his site supervisor? If yes, in what way did your answer change?*
3. *Bernard was abused as a child and taken from his family and placed in foster care for a period of his childhood. This is not information he has shared with anyone. Does knowing this change your thinking about his ability to run this group? If yes, in what way has your answer changed?*
4. *What should Bernard do?*

SIGNPOSTS FOR FUTURE TREKS

This chapter reviewed types of groups and outlined the major issues concerning the ethics of group counseling. There are many excellent texts that cover groups and group counseling in thorough detail. All of these books, some of which are cited in the reference list and are written by counselors known for their knowledge of group process, cover ethics and legal issues. However, in each text, one chapter is allocated to ethical issues, particularly mandatory ethics or the "musts" of our profession. But counseling is not just about what we should do. It is also about what we "ought" to do, who we are, and how we can maximize the growth of our clients and increase the benefit they receive from counseling.

One of the ways of focusing on our clients is by examining the relationship we have with them and the interactions between us. When thinking about a group, this means examining the relationship between the counselor and each of the members, the relationship and dynamics among each of the group members with each other, and the dynamics of the group as a whole. As a counselor gains more experience, education, and training, the counselor's ability to understand group process and dynamics and consequently intervene changes and grows. As previously discussed, this is a developmental process and moves at a different rate for each counselor. But counselor self-awareness and self-knowledge is critical is one of the most important counselor characteristics; without it counselors are unlikely to develop the skills to work effectively with clients (Hagedorn & Hartwig Moorhead, 2011). As counselors we need to set aside time and opportunities on our journey to check in at the signposts to think about ourselves and the way in which we chose to practice as a counselor.

INSIGHTS GAINED FROM THE JOURNEY

The major point that I have tried to make throughout this chapter is that to be an effective counselor or group leader, one must be very self-aware and think about how who we are impacts our counseling. When was the last time you reflected on who you are as a person and as a counseling student or professional counselor? I think counselors feel so pressured to do more in less time and with fewer resources that counselor education and professional development has become focused solely on increasing knowledge, skill-building, and techniques. Such events become a series of sessions that deal with the "how-tos" of counseling, updates, and new requirements. Granted, many courses, conferences, and professional development activities include sessions on "taking care of the caregiver." But upon closer inspection, the content of these sessions generally covers time and stress management techniques and encourages counselors to give themselves permission to take time for themselves. No doubt, these are critically important to the well-being of counselors. If we cannot help ourselves, how can we help others? However, there are other, more critical actions that can assist counselors in taking care of themselves.

We sometimes lose sight of what it means to be a counselor and the qualities that make us so unique and important to our clients: for instance, our ability to develop relationships and understand what the other person is experiencing in a nonjudgmental way. We have lost our time to reflect on our practice and ourselves as counselors in a meaningful, structured way. In graduate school, particularly in ethics classes, we learn about the importance of examining our own backgrounds, values, and beliefs and to think about how that influences our interactions with others. Students are encouraged to self-reflect and question as they develop their counseling identity. Students are also challenged to move beyond the scope of their world and enter into the world as others see it, which may present a reality very different from the one so familiar to the student. But this should not be the only time in a counselor's life when such reflection occurs.

I have found that the longer I teach an ethics and professional issues class, the more time we spend discussing virtue ethics and how who we are as individuals impacts our practice as counselors. One of the questions I ask my students is, "How do you choose to live your life when no one is looking?" Many of the students have never thought about this before; they have never considered the fact that the right thing to do may not be the expected act or that there may be more than one "right" thing to do. Virtue ethics demands that we ask ourselves who we are as people, how we choose or want to be, and how we choose to treat others.

But what happens when counselors become caught up in the pressure of working? How much reflection and introspection occur then? Introspection and self-reflection are critical to discerning our values, biases, morals and influences. If we do not know who we are, how can we possibly understand our client's world and provide unbiased reflection and feedback? Ongoing self-exploration provides the impetus for helping us move ourselves and our clients further than we thought we could. As our country becomes more diverse, it also becomes more likely that the culture of our clients—and perhaps their values—will likely be different from our own, significantly increasing our need as counselors to be reflective.

The next time you are contemplating what you are going to do next, take a moment and think about yourself. Reflect, analyze, and question yourself. Perhaps this practice will take you to a new level of self-awareness and make you a more effective counselor. To help with this journey, I am proposing a set of questions that I now use, which I call "Being a Reflective Counselor."

1. Did I facilitate my clients' growth during the session?
2. What strategies did I use and what actions did I take that specifically contributed toward my clients' growth?
3. How did my personal attributes (values, spiritual influences, world view, biases, etc.) impact what occurred during the session?
4. What ethical issue(s) arose during the session? How did the client handle them? How did I handle them?
5. Was I a barrier to my clients' growth in any way? If so, in what way(s)?
6. What will I do differently next time?
7. Did anything occur during the session for which I should consult with another counselor?
8. Did I learn anything new about myself? How did/will this new knowledge inform my practice?
9. Did I ask my client(s) to do anything I was or would not be willing to do myself?
10. What behaviors did I model for my client(s)?

As a student or new counselor, it is easy to run to a code of ethics for direction regarding how to handle certain situations. As an experienced counselor I have developed an appreciation for the "grayness" of counselor behavior. I have come to believe that who we are as a person and therefore as a counselor more significantly impacts our relationship with our clients than what we do, that is the skills and techniques we use. How can we ask our clients to do things we ourselves are not willing to do? I believe that this journey has been part of my maturing as a counselor. I trust a reflective process will help many of you along your journey.

MOVING FORWARD: CASE STUDY AND REFLECTION QUESTIONS

Tony is a counseling student in the last semester of his master's program in clinical counseling. He is currently completing his second set of internship hours in a community counseling center staffed by professional counselors. He is delighted to be almost finished with his program and is looking forward to graduating in the spring. He hopes that the center where he is working will offer him a job soon; he knows there is a vacancy and has tried to make his supervisor and other counselors aware of his interest. He is well liked by center staff. They perceive him to be a capable and caring counselor who seems to do a good job with the clients assigned to him. The feedback he has received from his supervisor has been very good, and the supervisor is allowing him more independence in his work.

One of his responsibilities for his placement is conducting groups. His supervisor meets with him on a routine basis to discuss his cases and observes him on occasion, but seldom sits in on group sessions. Tony has led a number of groups previously, so he feels very comfortable with what he is doing and does not ask for additional supervision.

The center has decided it needs to offer a group for adolescents who have been referred for various reasons. Most of the teens seem to have self-esteem issues and are having a difficult time navigating adolescence and making friends. Tony has worked primarily with adolescent clients during his internship and enjoys this age group. His supervisor believes the teens will like working with someone closer to their age. Tony is asked to lead the group and he enthusiastically agrees to do it.

Tony screens all potential group members and determines that they are a good fit for the group. He believes that they will be supportive of each other and work toward individual and common goals. The parents sign the informed consent documents and the group begins. At first the group seems to be going very well. Tony meets with his supervisor after his sessions to review the group's progress and his facilitation. After the fourth session, one of the members, AJ, seems to be disengaging from the group. Tony and his supervisor decide that he should confront AJ in the next session to see what is going on.

Tony confronts AJ by relating to AJ what he has observed and asks him what is going on. AJ tells the group that a couple of weeks ago he and his father went to the house of one of the father's friends to pick something up. As they walked in the door, they watched the friend shoot himself. AJ's father called the police, who came and handled the matter. AJ is trying to deal with it, but he is finding it hard. He cannot talk to his father, who just tells him to suck it up and get over it. But AJ is having nightmares and trouble concentrating in school. Tony is shocked by the story and immediately blurts out that he is not qualified to deal with this issue. Tony then turns to another member and asks what has been going on for the past week in that person's life.

When Tony has a chance to meet with his supervisor, he tells her the group is going well. She does not ask any other questions about the group.

REFLECTION QUESTIONS

- *Describe the crucial ethical issues in this case.*
- *What are the most significant ethical issues for Tony? For the supervisor?*
- *Do the group members have any ethical responsibilities? If so, what are they?*
- *What needs to happen for AJ? For the group?*
- *Using the reflective questions outlined in the previous section, how would you approach this case?*
- *What did you learn from the case? How did reading this case inform your practice?*

REFERENCES

American Counseling Association. (2005). *ACA code of ethics*. Alexandria, VA: Author.

Association for Specialists in Group Work (ASGW). (2000). *Professional standards for the training of group workers*. Retrieved July 25, 2011 from http://www.asgw.org.

Corey, G., & Schneider Corey, M. (2007). *Groups: Process and practice* (6th ed.). Pacific Grove, CA: Brooks/Cole Publishing.

Cottone, R. R., & Tarvydas, V. M. (2007). *Counseling ethics and decision making* (3rd ed.). Columbus, OH: Pearson Merrill/Prentice Hall.

Day, S. X. (2007). *Groups in practice*. Boston: Houghton Mifflin.

DeLucia-Waack, J. L. (1996). Multiculturalism is inherent in all group work. *Journal for Specialists in Group Work, 21*, 218–223.

DeLucia-Waack, J. L., & Donigian, J. (2003). *Practice of multicultural group work: Visions and perspectives from the field*. Belmont, CA: Brooks/Cole.

Hagedorn, W. B., & Hartwig Moorhead, H. J. (2011). Counselor self-awareness: Exploring attitudes, beliefs, and values. In C. S. Cashwell, & J. S. Young (Eds.), *Integrating spirituality and religion into counseling: A guide to competent practice* (2nd ed., pp. 74–95). Alexandria, VA: American Counseling Association.

Herlihy, B., & Corey, G. (2006). *ACA ethical standards casebook* (6th ed.). Alexandria, VA: American Counseling Association.

Gladding, S. T. (2008). *Groups: A counseling specialty*. Columbus, OH: Pearson Merrill/Prentice Hall.

Lambie, G. W., Hagedorn, W. B., & Ieva, K. (2010). Social-cognitive development, ethical and legal knowledge, and ethical decision making of counselor education students. *Counselor Education and Supervision, 49*, 228–246.

Linde, L. E., Erford, B. T., Hayes, D., & Wilson, F. R. (2011). Ethical and legal foundations of group work. In B. T. Erford (Ed.), *Group work: Processes and applications* (pp. 21–38). Columbus, OH: Pearson Merrill/Prentice Hall.

Linde, L. E., & Erford, B. T. (in press). Ethical and legal issues in counseling. In B. T. Erford (Ed.), *Orientation to the counseling profession* (2nd ed.). Columbus, OH: Pearson Merrill/Prentice Hall.

Remley, T. P., Jr., & Herihy, B. (2010). *Ethical, legal, and professional issues in counseling* (3rd ed.). Columbus, OH: Pearson Merrill/Prentice Hall.

Young, M. E. (2008). *Learning the art of helping* (4th ed.). Columbus, OH: Pearson Merrill/Prentice Hall.

16

Ethical Quandary or Ethical Clarity: Ethical Conduct for Counselors Interacting with Public Systems

Nancy G. Calley

THE FORESEEN DESTINATION

After reviewing this chapter, it is hoped that readers will acquire:

- Increased understanding of the significance of ethics within the counseling profession.
- Greater familiarity with the roles of community-based counselors.
- Increased understanding of applied ethics.
- Increased knowledge about common ethical considerations for community-based counselors, and particularly, those whose work interacts with public systems.
- Understanding about some concrete methods for addressing potential ethical challenges.

GETTING ON THE ROAD

Codes of ethics communicate the values of the counseling profession, provide a framework for clinical practice, and grant guidance to counselors in their day-to-day interactions with clients, coworkers, and other social services professionals who regularly become involved in clinical work. Importantly, ethical codes must be understood not as a fixed set of standards, but as a fluid and evolving statement about what the profession understands as good and helpful behavior on the part of counselors. To start, the codes reflect a given time within the lifecycle of the profession and are amended to reflect the profession's advancing knowledge and awareness, as well as its appreciation for changing societal norms. Cultural factors, for instance, influence definitions of ethics and significantly impact revisions to ethical codes (Pack-Brown, Thomas, & Seymour, 2008). Seeing ethical standards as somewhat flexible and fluid also is necessary because norms, values, and established protocols may differ across practice settings (e.g., school counselors and community-based counselors may have slightly different understandings about various ethical standards due to the needs of their clientele). The practice setting itself can, additionally, offer unique challenges to understanding and applying ethics because it may require counselors to interact with other social systems or governing bodies (such as law enforcement or children and youth services agencies) whose needs must be considered as counselors attempt to define their own ethical best practices. Ethical codes, furthermore, tend to be sensitive and responsive to changes in professional counseling associations (Ponton & Duba, 2009). Finally, counselors themselves often have individualized interpretations about what constitutes ethical being and ethical conduct, which means that how one understands ethics is vulnerable to differences of opinion. Indeed, a recent survey found that counselors differ significantly in their beliefs about what constitutes ethical versus unethical behavior (Neukrug & Milliken, 2011). As a result of each of these factors, ethics must be understood contextually, related not only to the time in which counselors practice but also to the practice environment, the norms and values of professional organizations, the broader social, political, and legislative environment in which counselors work, and, finally, to counselors' personal opinions about ethical behavior. It is precisely the convergence of all of these elements that contributes to the complex nature of ethics and the requisite thoughtfulness and sophisticated thinking that is, therefore, needed to understand ethical standards and translate them into clinical practice. However, some would argue (me included) that this is exactly as it should be. The ethical issues we deem of particular significance in the counseling profession should require a certain degree of work to understand fully and apply effectively.

The work that is entailed in understanding and then applying ethics to clinical practice becomes perhaps most strikingly evident when counselor trainees make the transition from the classroom to professional practice. New counselors, like their seasoned mentors, are forced to appreciate ethics at a deeper level, moving from a theoretical to an applied understanding. This is no easy task, particularly because no amount of case studies can take the place of real-life opportunities for making sense of ethical standards. Yet, successfully applying ethics and ethical guidelines to clinical practice can be accomplished in such a way that, although complicated, the process need not be frightening. To make the ethical decision-making process manageable, we counselors must apply the same degree of rigor and thoughtfulness that accompanies how we go about conducting most of the rest of our professional work. That is, just as we think deeply about our clinical interventions and the potential results of those interventions for our clients, we also must take a reflective stance to the ethical decision-making process. We must bring the advanced knowledge and skills that we acquire through formal training, practice, and ongoing education into interaction with ethical principles, such as beneficence, nonmalfeasance, fidelity, justice, and autonomy, to inform our decision making. By doing so, the challenges of applying ethics to practice may not be quite so difficult.

This chapter is intended to help clarify how counselors can make the transition from a theoretical to an applied understanding of ethics. The background that I will use for exploring how ethics are applied in day-to-day practice will focus on ethical ambiguities that emerge for counselors who work in community-based settings and who have regular contact with professionals from large public systems. Working within or adjacent to public and governmental systems, such as the penal and court systems or children and youth services agencies, sometimes can be a daunting task for new counselors, and the challenge of managing clinical needs, as well as the demands placed on counselors or clients from these other systems, adds much complexity to the ethical decision-making process. This chapter is designed, therefore, to explore some of the unique challenges that community-based counselors face when they interact with public systems and provide concrete guidance in working through common ethical quandaries that arise in this work.

EXPLORING THE TERRITORY

APPLIED ETHICS IN THE COUNSELING PROFESSION

Before turning our attention directly to the ethical issues tied to working with public systems, it might be helpful to point out that counselors, especially newly practicing counselors, are not alone in their endeavors to make sense of the profession's ethical codes. While there is no substitute for live clinical experience, counselors nonetheless spend a great deal of time thinking about what it means to be an ethical clinician and how to make decisions for the good of clients. Indeed, attempts to ferret out the psychological and intellectual meaning of ethics in counseling through thoughtful examinations of the standards have long been considered course de rigor for counselors (e.g., Corey, Corey, & Callanan, 2007; Remley & Herlihy, 2010; Werth & Crow, 2009). At times, these efforts have focused on exploring specific sets of ethical guidelines, such as those that deal with counselors' responsibility with regard to end-of-life care (Werth & Crow, 2009) or their obligations related to the use of diagnosis (Dougherty, 2005; McLaughlin, 2002). More recently, literature that addresses the topic of ethics in counseling has shifted focus in order to address emerging, contemporary practice issues. For instance, today, the literature invites counselors to examine the interactions between ethics and the use of new technology in counseling, such as conducting online counseling (Barros-Bailey & Saunders, 2010; Haberstroh, Parr, Bradley, Morgan-Fleming, & Gee, 2008); the ethics related to forensic assessment and counseling (Barros-Bailey, Carlisle, & Blackwell, 2010; Day & White, 2008); the ethics of specific counseling approaches, such as family narrative therapy (Miller & Forrest, 2009); and counselors' perceptions of ethical behaviors (Neukrug & Milliken, 2011). This chapter will invite you to consider the application of ethics to the contemporary practice of working with public social systems and their professional representatives who do not always understand or appreciate the ethical standards that frame our counseling profession. When trying to take the first steps toward turning your theoretical understanding of ethics into an applied one, remember to consult the ever-growing body of scholarship related to ethics.

In addition, counselors also have at their disposal a multitude of learning tools that clinicians, educators, and researchers have developed to provide concrete assistance in applying ethics to practice. These include textbooks, videos, and decision-making models developed specifically to aid students and professional counselors in applying ethical standards to practice. In particular, case examples illustrate ethical issues that may emerge in counseling situations (Corey et al., 2007), and ethical decision-making guides provide direction and structure to counselors as they examine potential ethical issues either reactively or proactively (Calley, 2009; Lewis, Lewis, Daniels, & D'Andrea, 2003; Ridley, Liddle, Hill, & Li, 2001). Each of these efforts reflects our counseling profession's ongoing attempts to apply ethical standards effectively in practice—a feat which has become even more complex as our counseling practice environments have continued to expand. Later in the chapter, we will look more closely at one of these tools, the *Ethics into Action Map* (Calley, 2009), to see how it can guide counselors who work within or on behalf of public systems.

PRACTICE ENVIRONMENTS OF COMMUNITY-BASED COUNSELORS

Because professional counselors are trained to treat a vast array of clinical and developmental issues ranging from depression to divorce, and from autism and addiction to age-related life transitions, the scope of their practice environments naturally has been quite broad. Community-based counselors historically have practiced in settings including hospitals, outpatient clinics, and rehabilitation facilities. They also have long worked in an array of environments, such as prisons, residential treatment settings, and even client homes, that are directly or indirectly associated with large public systems. The scope of practice settings for professional counselors continues to expand. Over the last 30 years, in particular, the counseling profession has witnessed dramatic increases in growth and recognition that have significantly altered the stature of the profession—placing it in a much more prominent role than ever before. This has been a tremendous gain for the good of the profession, and more importantly, for individuals in need of therapy who are now able to benefit fully from our services.

Of the numerous changes that have occurred during the last decade, three stand out as particularly illustrative of the profession's standing today. First, with the passage of licensure in California in 2010, all 50 states, the District of Columbia, and Puerto Rico now have licensure for professional counselors. Given that states are self-governing entities, this accomplishment signifies the marking of a new era in the counseling profession—one in which the profession has full recognition across the country. Second, at a more broad-based level, the *Veterans Benefits, Healthcare, and Information Technology Act* of 2006 created occupational opportunities for professional mental health counselors within the Veteran's Administration. Third, the *Seniors Mental Health Access Improvement Act* of 2011 is intended to establish Medicare coverage of state-licensed professional counselors. Although the *Seniors Mental Health Access Improvement Act* is not yet a reality, the recent movement of the bill to the Senate makes this significant piece of legislation one step closer to becoming finalized. Again, not only do these most recent political and legislative changes reflect the significant growth of the counseling profession, each has also had dramatic effects on expanding even further the scope of counselors' clinical practice environments.

Community-based counselors whose work brings them into interaction with public systems frequently are confronted with specific sets of ethical challenges.

Broadly, these are usually related to administrative rules and regulations that may conflict with the counseling profession's ethical standards. Four of the major public systems include the adult and juvenile criminal justice system, the public mental health system, the child welfare system, and the Veteran's Administration. Working within these systems, either directly as a governmental or subcontracted employee, or indirectly as a therapist practicing in an outpatient clinic, is quite common among counselors. Therefore, I would like to highlight some of the unique ethical challenges that counselors may encounter in their interactions with public systems.

UNIQUE CHALLENGES OF COUNSELORS WORKING WITHIN PUBLIC SYSTEMS

Potential ethical quandaries arise in any mental health practice environment; however, work within public systems leads to some unique dilemmas. For instance, counselors working with mandated (i.e., court-ordered) clients are faced with determining how best to promote individual decision making and full involvement in the treatment planning process while ensuring that the individual also understands that specific treatment goals and interventions may have been preestablished by the court. Further, counselors must ensure that the individual client is fully aware of any potential consequences related to lack of treatment participation and/or progress. Such circumstances can obviously create ethical quandaries for counselors who try to balance their value on client autonomy with the restrictions and prescriptions of mandated treatment. The ethical challenges related to working with mandated clients are complicated further by the lack of scholarship in this area. Most literature on ethics in counseling has focused on general counseling practice environments rather than unique counseling settings. This is particularly unfortunate because today, more than ever before, fewer and fewer counselors find themselves practicing in what was once considered a *general* counseling environment, such as a private practice. In fact, our work occurs across so many settings, that the very terms *general* and *unique* no longer apply because much of what was once considered a unique setting (e.g., community-based practice) is now much more common, making what was once considered general no longer applicable.

In addition to the above-mentioned situation in which treatment plans are predetermined by the court or by a nonclinical professional without the participation of the client, there are four other specific incidences worthy of more detailed examination. These include the following:

- Requirements to provide a specific type of treatment or a prescribed number of sessions or length of treatment
- Requirements to fulfill more than one professional role concurrently with the same client(s)
- Required use of specific assessment instruments
- Required use of diagnostic evaluation

Each of these issues will be explored with regard to the potential ethical conflicts they pose for counselors and in an attempt to illustrate the degree of complexity associated with the incidences.

Requirement to Provide Specific Types or Length of Treatment

As already stated, working with mandated clients can pose specific ethical dilemmas for counselors. At times, these challenges may be due to the fact that jurists, lawyers, and other court representatives who have no clinical training or qualifications make recommendations and decisions regarding a mandated individual's mental health treatment. Although this type of decision making most often is done with good intentions, it is much too frequently ill informed and can result in various unintended negative consequences to the individual. For instance, in an effort to ensure that an individual receives treatment for domestic violence, a jurist may order the individual to participate in 40 sessions of *anger management*. Although the jurist's efforts to promote treatment over detention are commendable, there are two major problems that these court actions can create.

The first problem relates to ordering an individual to participate in a specific number of sessions. Predetermining the number of treatment sessions implies that mental health therapy is about quantity, not quality—a falsehood that mental health therapists corrected long ago and one that many cognitive-behavioral approaches and brief therapy models directly attest to. In addition, ordering a specific number of sessions, particularly an exorbitant number of sessions, can create significant financial hardship on the individual and, ultimately, place treatment outside of the client's reach. Not being able to afford mental health treatment can place mandated clients at risk of alternative punitive sentencing. As counselors work with mandated clients of limited financial means, and reflect on what it means to act as an ethical professional interacting with multiple systems, a point of consideration certainly arises with regard to the principle of justice and equal access to treatment.

The second major problem with this type of sentencing relates to ordering a specific type of intervention. In the case of clients being sentenced to receive anger management treatment, a major concern lies with the fact that the term *anger management* has been used regularly over the last decades by both laypersons and therapists, but it does not refer to a particular evidence-based clinical intervention. Rather, it is a popularized term that feasibly could encompass any number of approaches and interventions that have no basis in evidence. By ordering anger management treatment, jurists require individuals to participate in a treatment that has no established record of efficacy. In addition, use of the term *anger management* inaccurately communicates to individuals that their problem is related directly to anger—another falsehood that clinicians have long understood. The use of force toward another person (often present in cases in which anger management is sentenced) involves much more than one emotion; it is often related to a range of affective and cognitive factors. As a result, clinical issues related to the use of force must be treated with approaches designed to address the interactions of cognition, affect, and behavior.

While certain ethical concerns emerge for the individual client in cases of mandated treatment, counselors who treat these individuals are confronted with their own set of ethical quandaries. These include, but are not limited to, (a) clinically justifying the need for the specific number of sessions, (b) continuing counseling when all perceived gains have been made and when the risk of losing such gains may occur,

(c) establishing appropriate fees, and (d) finding treatment interventions that are evidence-based and that meet the expectations of the court. More specifically, Standard A.1.c. of the ACA *Code of Ethics* (2005) stipulates that clients and counselors work together to develop the treatment plan and that the plans are regularly reviewed to assess "their continued viability and effectiveness, respecting the freedom of choice of clients" (p. 4). When the time frame for counseling is predetermined by the court, the client and the counselor are effectively prohibited from participating in this essential component of treatment planning. Subsequently, the client's freedom of choice is restricted.

Landmark 1

CASE EXAMPLE

Katrina, a home-based therapist working contractually with the local department of social services, receives a referral for a woman, Sheila, who has recently been charged with child neglect. The neglect charge resulted when Sheila's three children were found to be unsupervised in the home. Sheila left the children unattended for an hour while she walked to the store for groceries. The home was found to have minimal food and no electricity. A court order stipulated that Sheila must participate in 20 individual sessions of counseling. Further, the court order stipulated that Sheila must obtain employment and provide at least two paystubs to the court for full consideration of reunification with her children. As Katrina begins working with Sheila, she learns that Sheila's three children are aged 4, 5, and 7. With the exception of her aunt who is currently taking care of Sheila's kids, Sheila does not have any other family or friends that can help her. She recently left her boyfriend after he "hit my son one too many times." She had tried to find work after her boyfriend moved out, but because of her criminal history (i.e., shoplifting 7 years prior) and the need to take her youngest child with her to work, she has been unsuccessful and is feeling hopeless about ever finding a way to support her family.

1. *What ethical dilemma(s) must Katrina confront?*
2. *How would you respond to these dilemma(s)?*
3. *How do you believe the ethical principles of malfeasance and beneficence can be used to guide your response to these dilemmas?*

Requirements Related to Multiple Relationships

Another ethical dilemma often inherent to working with public systems relates to the clinical role of the counselor. Counselors whose clients are part of public systems must work with other professionals who fill noncounseling roles, such as case manager, legal advocate, and jurist. At times, these other professionals make recommendations that are contrary to what counselors would consider ethical counseling practice. For instance, a counselor working within the child welfare system with children who have been removed from their parents may originally be assigned as the child's individual therapist. However, as the birth parents become involved in getting the child back, the counselor may be ordered to begin family counseling as well. Then, when it is determined by the foster care worker or representatives that the father would benefit from individual therapy, the same counselor may be ordered to provide counseling to him, too. At this point, the counselor is responsible for simultaneously providing individual counseling to the child, individual counseling to the father, and family therapy to the three of them. A counselor who is ordered to provide services to multiple clients, as in this case, inevitably find herself trying to negotiate the most effective therapeutic relationship with all three individuals, while at the same time attempting to be a strong ally to the child and father, who both are participating in individual therapy. As you can imagine, this is likely an impossible feat to accomplish, especially when the parents become separated (and may spend family therapy verbally attacking one another about the other's lack of ability to parent). Eventually, the counselor may be asked to make a recommendation to the court about which parent deserves custody of the child.

As is evident in the example above, the intentions behind requests and/or court orders for counselors to offer services to multiple clients in the same family are often guided by good faith—by what is perceived to be in the best interest of the family. Moreover, requests that place counselors in the position of being involved in multiple relationships sometimes occur because there are limited available resources. A child welfare agency responsible for providing services to the family may have only one counselor on staff, for instance. Yet, at other times, these types of court orders and requests are made as a result of ignorance about appropriate clinical roles and interventions, as well as best practices related to providing good and helpful counseling services.

The ethical quandaries and responsibilities thus confronting the counselor described in the above example are numerous. First, there is ambiguity in identifying the primary client: Is it the child, the father, or the family as a unit? Second, the counselor must ensure that she or he clearly explains any changes that occur in professional role (i.e., shifts from individual therapist for child, to individual therapist for father, to family therapist for family), the reasons for the changes, and the resulting clinical limitations (see ACA *Code of Ethics*, 2005, A.5.e). The counselor also has to receive informed consent from the parents to move forward with changes in the professional relationship. Once consent is obtained, the counselor must clarify what the specific changes to the counseling relationship are, as the counselor's role expands to encompass new individual and family counseling responsibilities. The counselor then must explain the limitations of the expanded roles, as well as potential conflicts that might arise as a result of the multiple relationships. Third, the counselor must address the issue of her ability to treat the family effectively while concurrently providing individual counseling, objectively evaluating any potential conflicts and making recommendations regarding family reunification. Finally, the counselor is faced with the personal decision to follow a court order and the expectations of her employer knowing that to do so is likely neither in the best interest of the client nor likely to be the most ethical course of action. Reflecting on the options available in light of the ethical principle of nonmalfeasance (i.e., do no harm) can provide guidance to counselors who must deal with issues pertaining to serving multiple, related clients. In fact, when counselors continuously assess their actions and decisions related to participation in multiple relationships with clients, they can more easily identify conflicts that could harm one or more of the clients and become aware of when they must withdraw from one or another of the relationships to ensure that no harm is done. As difficult as it is to believe that this type of situation can occur, it happens all too often, creating undue stress for the counselor. Thus, it is critical that counselors be knowledgeable about the potential harms that can come to clients when counselors assume multiple relationships with them and be willing to advocate for clients' best interests.

Landmark 2

CASE EXAMPLE

Rosalie, a counselor at the local Veterans Administration Hospital, has been working with Donna, a veteran from the first Gulf war for the past month. Donna has requested family counseling but also wants to continue individual counseling with Rosalie. Rosalie discussed this with her supervisor, and she was directed to begin family counseling and to continue to provide individual counseling to Donna. Rosalie's supervisor explained to her that all of the counselors currently have high caseloads and that she cannot assign another client (or family) to a different counselor right now.

1. *What ethical dilemma(s) must Rosalie confront?*
2. *How would you respond to these dilemma(s)?*
3. *How do you believe the ethical principles of malfeasance and beneficence can be used to guide your response to these dilemmas?*

Requirement to Use Specific Assessment Instruments

The standardization of specific clinical processes is highly common in many public systems, especially with regard to the use of assessment tools. Standardizing assessment procedures and instruments has its advantages; it guarantees that each client is measured by the same criteria and provides an effective means by which to compare and contrast client needs. Using the same instrument(s) to evaluate the same clinical issues across individuals also reflects some degree of equity in practices among clients. Most significantly, the use of a standard set of assessment tools reflects best practices (e.g., Grizzo & Underwood, 2004; Righthand & Welch, 2001; Skowyra & Cocozza, 2006), particularly when the tools used have a strong evidence base for assessing the psychological constructs for which they were designed.

Despite the many benefits of using of a standard set of assessment measures in clinical practice, there also can be significant problems associated with the requirement to use *specific* instruments. Typically, problems arise when the assessment instrument(s) that a counselor is obliged by the court or other public agency to use does not have sufficient evidence to support its intended use or, worse, is ineffective. For instance, a state mental health agency may require a counselor to administer a substance abuse screening test that the agency's workgroup developed but never rigorously evaluated. Counselors who work directly or indirectly with the state agency thus face an ethical dilemma related to how they will meet the counseling profession's best practice standards for testing and assessment while maintaining their relationship with an agency that necessitates substance abuse treatment providers to use an untested instrument even with the knowledge that other tools with proven efficacy exist (e.g., Substance Abuse Subtle Screening Inventory; Miller, 1994).

Public agencies also may require counselors to use an assessment tool that lacks sufficient evidence of its effectiveness because one that can evaluate a specific issue successfully has not yet been developed. For instance, you would be hard-pressed today to find a public criminal justice agency that does not require counselors to use a specified risk assessment in order to evaluate a client's potential for recidivism. In the case of evaluating recidivism risk among juveniles who have sexually offended, the need for sound assessment tools has become an issue of tremendous concern. As a result, there are now several tools that have been developed to evaluate this risk (Prentky & Righthand, 2003; Worling & Curwen, 2001). Unfortunately, none has been found to be effective in assessing sexual recidivism risk (Caldwell, Ziemke, & Vitacco, 2008; Martinez, Flores, & Rosenfeld, 2007; Viljoen, Elkovitch, Scalora, & Ullman, 2008). This of course begs the question, can there be an effective measure of sexual recidivism risk for juveniles, particularly when we know that sexual recidivism is quite small in comparison to nonsexual recidivism among juveniles who previously committed sexual offenses? (see, e.g., Caldwell, 2010).

Regardless of the myriad reasons a public agency offers for necessitating counselors to use a specific assessment instrument, the requirement creates ethical challenges for the provider and counselor when the assessment instrument lacks empirical support. (Section E of the ACA *Code of Ethics* [2005] outlines best practice standards for counselors using assessment instruments.) For one, the counselor is faced with ensuring that the assessment process meets the needs of the client, which can be difficult, at best, when the required instrument lacks an evidence base. Two, the counselor faces the responsibility of providing the client with a clear rationale for using of the instrument, which, again, is difficult when the required tool lacks effectiveness. Three, the counselor must grapple with the knowledge that the results of the assessment may be used as a critical piece of information that influences a court or state agency's decisions about the client's future. And, four, the counselor must address the fact that s/he may be required to release the assessment results to individuals who are not be qualified to interpret the data. While other ethical considerations surround the way in which assessment tools can be used in public systems, these four highlight many challenges counselors face when they are required to use identified assessment instruments or instruments lacking sufficient evidence.

Landmark 3

CASE EXAMPLE

Danielle, a therapist in a residential facility for female juvenile offenders, is required to use a risk assessment developed by the state juvenile justice agency. Although the tool has not yet been validated, the state has required all providers to begin using it and has stipulated that it must be a primary source used to guide placement decisions. Danielle is well aware of the limitations of risk assessment in general, and she knows that the required instrument has not yet been shown to have strong psychometric properties. Furthermore, Danielle realizes that she will be forced to use the results of this required instrument in decisions regarding if and when her clients can be released from residential placement and whether they will return home or to a lesser restrictive placement.

1. *What potential ethical dilemmas or conflicts does Danielle face?*
2. *How would you respond to these dilemma(s)?*
3. *How do you believe the ethical principles of malfeasance and beneficence can be used to guide your response to these dilemmas?*

Requirement to Use Diagnostic Evaluation

Another ethical issue that counselors interacting with public systems often face relates to the use of diagnosis. The fundamental purpose of diagnosis is to correctly identify mental health issues of concern in order to treat them effectively. In this regard, diagnosis of a mental health disorder is not so different from diagnosis of a physical ailment. Across fields, the more serious the diagnosis, the greater potential costs for treatment. However, unlike diagnosis of other types of problems, diagnosis of mental and primary health issues can result in inequities in accessing treatment, which ultimately can prohibit some individuals from receiving needed care. Although the *Mental Health Parity and Addiction Equity Act* of 2008 and the more recent *Affordable Care Act* of 2010 are intended to reduce inequities related to access of health care, problems related to the use of diagnosis will likely not be resolved by either of these legislative acts.

Chief among the problems that prevent some individuals from accessing mental health care is the requirement that a person be given a certain diagnosis in order to be eligible to receive specific services and/or treatment. Although this issue may also be present in other public systems, it is extremely relevant in the public mental health system, where decisions regarding eligibility for and level of treatment are often based primarily on one's diagnosis. For instance, a diagnosis of Bi-Polar I Disorder may mean that an individual is eligible for intensive and comprehensive mental health treatment. Conversely, a diagnosis of posttraumatic stress disorder (PTSD) may not be considered serious enough for the client to be eligible for mental health services through the public mental health system. Determinations about which disorders qualify for mental health treatment and about the type of treatment for which one is eligible varies from state to state and, in some states, even from region to region.

Counselors are intimately aware of the difficulties associated with attempts to place greater value on one diagnosis over another, and conversely, with the problems that arise when attempts are made to promote a simplistic view of mental health (e.g., all disorders are the same). As a result, we must appreciate the innate complexities of mental health—accepting that while differences do exist, the creation of value hierarchies among mental health disorders has significant implications. Indeed, we know that the PTSD that one individual is struggling with may be much more debilitating than the bi-polar disorder that another individual is working to manage. Armed with this knowledge, counselors charged with evaluating their clients' mental health status face significant ethical challenges, particularly when they know that the results of their assessment may mean that their client will be ineligible to receive mental health services.

Landmark 4

CASE EXAMPLE

Soyon, a counselor at the regional community mental health center, completed a diagnostic evaluation of Bradley, a young man in his early 20s. The results of the evaluation clearly support a diagnosis of acute anxiety disorder, and the degree of functional impairment that Bradley presents causes Soyon a great deal of concern. Unfortunately, anxiety disorders are not included in the list of mental health disorders the state mental health agency covers for treatment. The state has identified the following types or major categories of mental disorders: depressive disorders, panic disorder, eating disorders, autism spectrum disorders, schizophrenia, schizoaffective disorder, and obsessive compulsive disorder. Soyon is aware that Bradley does not have health insurance or any other means by which to access mental health services. However, she also knows that a diagnosis of acute anxiety disorder will not allow him to receive free mental health services through the public mental health system. Most importantly, Soyon is deeply worried about the fragile state in which Bradley appears to be in currently, and his prognosis if left untreated.

1. *What ethical dilemma(s) must Soyon confront?*
2. *How would you respond to these dilemma(s)?*
3. *How do you believe the ethical principles of malfeasance and beneficence can be used to guide your response to these dilemmas?*

In addition to the challenges counselors face when evaluating a client's mental health status for the purpose of making decisions regarding eligibility and/or level of services, there are other equally troublesome issues associated with diagnosis. One ethical issue of particular interest pertains to the lasting, negative consequences that a diagnosis can carry, especially for children and adolescents. Many factors can impede a thorough and accurate diagnosis, such as the time when the diagnostic evaluation took place and the attendant testing conditions, the limitations of the testing process, the lack of appropriate interpretation of the results, and the lack of appropriate follow-up procedures. Furthermore, if the limitations surrounding the diagnostic evaluation are not carefully noted, counselors will not be able to communicate assessment results accurately.

Unfortunately, children in the juvenile justice and child welfare systems usually experience a disproportionate level of negative consequences related to diagnosis. Rules adopted by some state and regional juvenile justice and child welfare systems, for example, require systematic mental health evaluations of all children entering care. As most mental health professionals clearly know, the manner in which a child presents immediately upon being removed from his or her home may not be an accurate representation of the child but, instead, is a representation of the child at a time during which he or she is most confused and vulnerable. However, having this knowledge at hand does not necessarily prevent counselors from conducting diagnostic evaluations during a critical or stressful time period for the child. Moreover, counselors' awareness of these limitations does not necessarily mean they will identify and thoroughly discuss the influence of factors such as timing and testing conditions on the interpretation of findings, nor will they necessarily urge caution in the use of their findings.

Most unfortunate of all is the fact that all too often diagnoses have the ability to stick. Diagnoses can remain associated with a child for years to come and play a role in the most significant aspects in the child's life (e.g., foster care placement, school placement). In extreme cases, the diagnosis can result in a child not being able to be placed in a foster home or enrolled in the local public school.

Counselors working with public systems that require systematic diagnostic evaluation face myriad challenges. They are confronted with conducting assessments during a time that may be counterproductive to accurate diagnosis. Counselors also have to thoughtfully and humbly acknowledge the deep and persisting implications that their diagnosis may carry—especially for the most vulnerable portion of their client population (i.e., children and teens). The ethical considerations surrounding diagnosis are even more critical when counselors know that there are no protocols for retesting in place and that their evaluation may be the only one the child will receive for some years to come.

Landmark 5

CASE EXAMPLE

Norman, a counselor working in a detention program for male juvenile offenders, is responsible for conducting mental health evaluations for youth within the first 48 hours of their admission to the detention facility. For Adam, Norman's client, this is the first time he has been locked up and the first time he has spent a night

(*continued*)

away from home. Adam is afraid of being in the detention facility, and he is uncertain where he will go next and what will happen to him as his legal case moves forward in court. During Norman's evaluation of Adam, Adam is largely silent—afraid that what he may say might be used against him. He is uncomfortable, moreover, because he does not know Norman, and Norman is asking him very personal questions. Norman has explained the purpose of the tests he is using to Adam, and he has told Adam that it is in his best interest to participate in the tests so that the information can be provided to the court. However, Adam is reluctant to participate, and when he does respond to Norman's questions, he decides to tell Norman what he thinks he wishes to hear rather than the truth.

1. *What potential ethical dilemmas or conflicts does Norman face?*
2. *How would you respond to these dilemmas?*
3. *How do you believe the ethical principles of malfeasance and beneficence can be used to guide your response to these dilemmas?*

Although there certainly are other challenges that counselors working with public systems face, the four areas of ethical conflict examined above illustrate the complex problems that may be encountered when counselors' practice is interwoven with public systems. It is important to keep in mind, as you ponder these very common ethical dilemmas, that though complex and challenging, these dilemmas can be effectively addressed. Moreover, counselors can and do interact with public systems while upholding their integrity and being faithful to the counseling profession's ethical standards of practice. This demands, however, that counselors remain committed to aspiring toward highly ethical conduct, value conscientiousness, and do not shy away from the often time-consuming work involved in determining the best course of action within a work environment that sometimes pressures counselors to operate at a level of practice that falls short of the profession's ethical principles.

EFFECTIVELY NEGOTIATING POTENTIAL ETHICAL CHALLENGES

For those who believe that ethical conduct requires energy and effort, clinical practice with public systems can be incredibly stimulating and rewarding. Translating ethics into practice is no small feat and one that becomes only more complex when working in practice environments whose protocols may be incongruent with professional counselors' ethical standards. One of the tools recently developed to assist counselors in taking a proactive stance to ensuring ethical conduct is the *Ethics into Action Map* (Calley, 2009). Briefly, the map guides counselors through a review of their respective code of ethics (e.g., ACA, AMCA, APA) to determine if and how relevant ethical standards can be incorporated into practice. To aid counselors, the map suggests that clinicians use the following steps:

- Review the relevant code of ethics.
- Identify two to three methods by which you actively demonstrate each standard in practice.

- If unable to identify how a standard is currently demonstrated in practice, develop methods by which the standard can be demonstrated in practice and cement these new methods into practice by incorporating them into policy and standard processes.

By engaging in a proactive and positive process of turning ethics theory into ethical practice, I anticipate that you will be better able to see how ethical standards are applicable to your work, and, thus, you will be better equipped to address potential challenges when they arise. More importantly, participating in the exercise of reviewing the code of ethics and concretely identifying how its standards are incorporated into your clinical work forces you to think about ethical standards not as potential violations that you must work to avoid, but as practice guidelines you already endorse and promote. Furthermore, by thinking about ethical standards in a non-legalistic, non-fear-based, and proactive way, you will be able to form a positive view of the professional counseling ethical codes and one that is likely much more meaningful as a result of understanding just what you do on a regular basis that reflects good ethical practice.

Landmark 6

CASE EXAMPLE

Denise, a home-based counselor affiliated with the local mental health clinic, is using the *Ethics into Action Map* to review the ACA *Code of Ethics* (2005). Standard A.1.d. requires counselors to "recognize that support networks hold various meanings in the lives of clients and consider enlisting the support, understanding and involvement of others as positive resources, when appropriate, with client consent" (ACA, 2005, p. 4). Denise thinks about this standard, trying to identify how she currently complies with it. Denise recalls that she asks specifically about support persons and the type and degree of involvement the client wishes support persons to have in their treatment planning process as part of her intake interview. These questions are included on the agency's standardized intake guide, and therefore, are already cemented into practice. Denise also recalls the *Eco-Map* exercise that she and all of the counselors facilitate during the first two sessions with clients to gain information about the role of social systems in the client's life for use in treatment planning. Having identified two concrete methods by which she is actively recognizing the importance of support networks in clients' lives, Denise is comfortable that her behaviors effectively reflect this ethical standard.

1. *In addition to the two methods that Denise identified, what else could she do to further demonstrate the intent of this ethical standard?*
2. *What do you believe are the benefits of using the Ethics into Action Map exercise?*

The *Ethics into Action Map* can assist counselors in making the transition from a theoretical to an applied understanding of ethics. However, counselor working with public systems likely will need other resources to deal with the ethical dilemmas unique to their work environments. Chief among these resources is the counselor's voice. Counselors must speak up and be assertive in order to advocate effectively for their clients, teach others about best practices for counselors, and make systemic changes when necessary that protect the ethical treatment of individuals served. This means that counselors must be able to recognize and take action to remedy any and all protocols and policies that may inadvertently contribute to unethical practice.

When this fails, counselors must negotiate within the established parameters of public systems in a manner that protects the client and maintains the ethical integrity of the counselor. This often means that counselors must follow the guidelines required by the oversight agency in a manner that upholds ethical standards of practice. Because issues related to ethics and individuals practicing within public systems are, more often than not, highly complex, this also means that it is not uncommon for counselors to take issue with a part of a requirement or decision rather than with the entire requirement. For instance, because it is not the practice of employing standard assessment processes that may be inconsistent with professional counseling ethical standards, but rather, the *type* of required assessment instrument(s) that may be of concern to the counselor, it is this element of the Order or requirement that ought to be the focus of the counselor's negotiation (see Case Study).

SIGNPOSTS FOR FUTURE TREKS

Understanding and demonstrating an ability to apply ethics effectively in practice is a highly complex process, made only more complicated by working within particular clinical settings, such as with public systems. However, counselor education and preparation is specifically designed to assist counselors (especially beginning practitioners) in accomplishing this, so that they will be ready both to identify and to effectively address any potential ethical challenges as they arise. By engaging in a reflective practice in which they bring ethical principles to bear on the often ambiguous situations that arise during work with public systems, counselors will be able to make good decisions about how to deal with the requirements to provide specific type of treatment, to fulfill more than one professional role concurrently with the same client, to use specific assessment instruments, and to use diagnostic evaluation with clients. Finally, if you find yourself one day navigating through ethical dilemmas inherent in doing community-based counseling, such as those described in this chapter, you are encouraged, again, not to lose sight of your ethical bearings (outlined in the codes of ethics) and not to be afraid to teach other professionals outside of the counseling field about the structure and process of good, ethical conduct for counselors, as it will not only strengthen your counselor identity but will also ensure that the best possible service is offered to your clients.

INSIGHTS GAINED FROM THE JOURNEY

Having spent the last 23 years working with the public systems of juvenile justice, child welfare, and mental health as an employee of subcontracted agencies, I have had numerous opportunities to learn about the myriad ways in which professional counselors' ethical standards sometimes conflict with the requirements of these systems. The learning opportunities have been rich and multifaceted, and with each, I have learned more about myself, about the individuals with whom I have worked, and about the greater meaning derived from working with marginalized populations.

At times, especially early in my career, I was convinced that other individuals working on behalf of my clients (e.g., jurists, governmental caseworkers) were not near as dedicated to helping my clients as I was; however, I quickly learned that nothing could be further from the truth. In fact, while we may often butt heads, the primary reason we did so was precisely because of the passion we each felt for our positions—and for doing what we believed to be in the best interest of our client. A good deal of the time, our conflicts arose due to what I perceived as potential ethical quandaries. However, what I learned and continue to learn to this day is that with each potential quandary, I gain clarity about exactly what constitutes ethical conduct. And I owe my deepest gratitude to those public system workers who I have had the supreme fortune to work alongside, for it is because of them that I have been able to gain such clarity.

MOVING FORWARD: CASE STUDY AND REFLECTION QUESTIONS

Regina has been working in an outpatient clinic for the past 3 years and the clinic has just been awarded a new contract to provide assessment services for adolescents who have been adjudicated. Regina and her colleagues are responsible for conducting a diagnostic interview with each referred youth and developing a summary report of findings to the court that includes a recommendation for placement of the child (e.g., home or residential facility) based on the findings. Per contractual requirements, the Millon Adolescent Clinical Inventory (MACI; Millon, 1993; Millon, Millon, Davis, & Grossman, 2006) must be used as part of the diagnostic interview.

Upon learning that she will be required to use the MACI, Regina becomes concerned about the possible ethical challenges she will face. Regina reviews the manual and research on the MACI and learns that the test is designed to assess personality traits and psychopathology in adolescents. As a counselor, Regina is familiar with current research on adolescent brain development and particularly with its implications for understanding juvenile offending behaviors (e.g., Galvan, Hare, Voss, Glover, & Casey, 2006; Steinberg, 2009). She has learned that the period of adolescence may proceed well into an individual's 20s and that differences in brain development between adolescents and adults must be understood as factors related to engaging in risky behaviors. She has further learned that during the time in which the adolescent brain is developing, adolescent behavior cannot be thought of as fixed but, rather, as dynamic and fluid—in a constant state of change. Further, Regina remembers from her earlier training in diagnosis that children under the age of 18 cannot be diagnosed with a personality disorder since personality is still developing. Regina's knowledge of diagnosis and the recent research that she has reviewed calls into question the primary premise of using the MACI with adolescents—to assess personality and psychopathology. This creates an ethical challenge for Regina. In addition to identifying this ethical challenge, Regina is equally concerned about the level of significance and implications that the results of her evaluation will have for the adolescents she will service.

Regina raises her concerns with her colleagues at the clinic during their weekly meeting, and finds that her colleagues share her concerns. Her colleagues also elect to have Regina lead the group toward an effective resolution. The group identifies addressing the issue directly with the contract manager as the necessary first step toward resolution.

The contract manager states that although she appreciates Regina's concerns, she cannot waive the requirement that the MACI be used for the assessment because it was part of the current contract language. She does, however, state that this issue could be reviewed when the contract comes up for renewal in 3 years. Having failed to resolve the issue by removing this requirement, Regina decides that she will use the assessment instrument as required. But, she will do so in a manner that will allow her to serve her clients most effectively while protecting them against any misuse of assessment results. At the same time, Regina decides to use this opportunity to teach the court representatives about clinical assessment in the hope of making systemic change.

To accomplish this, Regina meets with her first client and her client's mother to explain the purpose of the clinical interview and assessment procedures and the limitations of the process as well as to review other aspects as part of the informed consent process. Regina uses the MACI as part of the evaluation process, and, following the interview, she reviews the results and develops her report of findings. In fulfillment of one of the requirements, Regina provides a multiaxial diagnosis. Since she has no evidence of a clinical diagnosis, mental retardation or personality disorder, V71.09—No Diagnosis is listed on Axes I and II. However, on Axis III, Regina identifies Asthma, on Axis IV, she identifies specific psychosocial stressors, and on Axis V, she provides a GAF score.

In addition, Regina includes information in her report regarding the limitations of the assessment instrument, as well as clinical concerns related to personality and psychopathology assessment of children and adolescents. Further, Regina briefly summarizes research findings related to adolescent brain development and the possible implications of the research on understanding adolescent behaviors. Having developed several paragraphs regarding the limitations of the assessment and provided evidence-based data to promote increased understanding of adolescent development, Regina is comfortable that she has acted ethically while meeting the requirements of the court. Moreover, she will include the paragraphs in subsequent evaluation reports for the court and share them with her colleagues, so that they can use the same or develop similar language to meet the same needs.

REFLECTION QUESTIONS

1. *In your opinion, do you believe that Regina's behaviors demonstrated ethical conduct? Why or why not?*

2. *If you disagree with the manner in which Regina acted, how would you have responded to this dilemma?*
3. *To what degree did Regina's behaviors demonstrate the ethical principles of beneficence and nonmalfeasance?*
4. *How would you take a positive and proactive approach to working with this scenario?*

REFERENCES

American Counseling Association. (2005). *ACA code of ethics*. Alexandria, VA: Author.

Barros-Bailey, M., Carlisle, J., & Blackwell, T. L. (2010). Forensic ethics and indirect practice for the rehabilitation counselor. *Rehabilitation Counseling Bulletin, 53*, 237–242.

Barros-Bailey, M., & Saunders, J. L. (2010). Ethics and the use of technology in rehabilitation counseling. *Rehabilitation Counseling Bulletin, 53*, 255–259.

Caldwell, M. (2010). Study characteristics and recidivism base rates in juvenile sex offender recidivism. *International Journal of Offender Therapy and Comparative Criminology, 54*(2), 197–212.

Caldwell, M., Ziemke, M., & Vitacco, M. (2008). An examination of sex offender registration and notification act as applied to juveniles. *Psychology, Public Policy, and Law, 14*, 89–114.

Calley, N. G. (2009). Promoting a contextual perspective in the application of the ACA *Code of Ethics*: The ethics into action map. *Journal of Counseling and Development, 87*, 476–482.

Corey, G., Corey, M. S., & Callahan, P. (2007). *Issues and ethics in the helping professions* (7th ed.). Pacific Grove, CA: Brooks/Cole.

Day, A., & White, J. (2008). Ethical practice from the perspective of the forensic psychologist: Commentary on the uses and value of the Australian Psychological Society (2007) Code of Ethics. *Australian Psychologist, 43*, 186–193.

Dougherty, J. L. (2005). Ethics in case conceptualization and diagnosis: Incorporating a medical model into the developmental counseling tradition. *Counseling and Values, 49*, 132–140.

Galvan, A., Hare, T., Voss, H., Glover, G., & Casey, B. J. (2006). Risk-taking and the adolescent brain: Who is at risk? *Developmental Science, 10*, F8–F14.

Grisso, T., & Underwood, L. A. (2004). *Screening and assessing mental health and substance use disorders among youth in the juvenile justice system: A resource guide for practitioners*. Washington, DC: Office of Juvenile Justice and Delinquency Prevention.

Haberstroh, S., Parr, J., Bradley, L., Morgan-Fleming, B., & Gee, R. (2008). Facilitating online counseling: Perspectives from counselors in training. *Journal of Counseling and Development, 86*, 460–470.

Lewis, J. A., Lewis, M. D., Daniels, J. A., & D'Andrea, M. J. (2003). *Community Counseling* (3rd ed.). Pacific Grove, CA: Brooks/Cole.

Martinez, R., Flores, J., & Rosenfeld, B. (2007). Predictive validity of the Juvenile Sex Offender Protocol II with inner city minority youth. *Criminal Justice, 6*, 145–152.

McLaughlin, J. E. (2002). Reducing diagnostic bias. *Journal of Mental Health Counseling, 24*, 256–269.

Miller, F. (1994). *Substance abuse subtle screening inventory manual*. Bloomington, IN: SASSI Institute.

Miller, C., & Forrest, A. W. (2009). Ethics of family narrative therapy. *The Family Journal, 17*, 156–159.

Millon, T. (1993). *Millon Adolescent Clinical Inventory manual*. Minneapolis, MN: National Computer Systems.

Millon, T., Millon, C., Davis, R., & Grossman, S. (2006). *The Millon Adolescent Clinical Inventory*. Minneapolis, MN: National Computer Systems.

Neukrug, E. S., & Milliken, T. (2011). Counselors' perceptions of ethical behaviors. *Journal of Counseling and Development, 89*, 206–216.

Pack-Brown, S. P., Thomas, T. L., & Seymour, J. M. (2008). Infusing professional ethics into counselor education programs: A multicultural/social justice perspective. *Journal of Counseling and Development, 86*, 296–302.

Ponton, R. F., & Duba, J. D. (2009). The ACA Code of Ethics: Articulating counseling's professional covenant. *Journal of Counseling and Development, 87*, 117–121.

Prentky, R., & Righthand, S. (2003). *Juvenile sex offender protocol II manual*. Washington, DC: Office of Juvenile Justice and Delinquency Prevention.

Remley, T. P., & Herlihy, B. (2010). *Ethical and professional issues in counseling* (3rd ed.). Upper Saddle River, NJ: Merrill.

Ridley, C. R., Liddle, M. C., Hill, C. L., & Li, L. C. (2001). Ethical decision making in multicultural counseling. In J. G. Ponterotto, J. M. Casas, L. A. Suzuki, & C. M. Alexander (Eds.), *Handbook of Multicultural Counseling* (2nd ed., pp. 165–188). Thousand Oaks, CA: Sage.

Righthand, S., & Welch, C. (2001). *Juveniles who have sexually offended: A review of the professional literature*. Washington, DC: Office of Juvenile Justice and Delinquency Prevention.

Skowyra, K., & Cocozza, J. (2006). *Blueprint for change: A comprehensive model for identification and treatment of youth with mental health needs in contact with the juvenile justice system*. Washington, DC: US Department of Justice, Office of Justice Programs, Office of Juvenile Justice and Delinquency Prevention.

Steinberg, L. (2009). Should the science of adolescent brain development inform public policy. *American Psychologist, 64*, 739–750.

Viljoen, J. L., Elkovitch, N., Scalora, M. J., & Ullman, D. (2008). Assessment of re-offense risk in adolescents who have committed sexual offenses: Predictive validity of the ERASOR, PCL: YV, YLS/CMI and Static 99. *Criminal Justice and Behavior, 36*, 981–1000.

Werth, J. L., & Crow, L. (2009). End of life care: An overview for professional counselors. *Journal of Counseling and Development, 87*, 195–202.

Worling, J. R., & Curwen, T. (2001). *Estimate of risk of adolescent sexual offense recidivism, Ver. 2.0*. Etobicoke, ON: Thistletown Regional Centre.

17

Getting Off Track in Ethical Decision Making: Using Gestalt Principles to Understand How Ethical Missteps Occur

Maura Krushinski and Thomas Petrone

THE FORESEEN DESTINATION

It is our hope that after reading this chapter you will be able to:

- Have an increased appreciation for the myriad of ways that counselors can succumb to ethical violations.
- Identify ways in which unhealthy or stressed organizational systems contribute to ethical missteps.
- Identify the most common ethical missteps for counselors at a personal level.
- Articulate how principles of Gestalt theory, such as awareness, responsibility, and contact can help counselors avoid ethical errors.
- Appreciate the ways in which interruptions to contact boundaries, such as projection, introjection, deflection, retroflection, and confluence, can lead counselors toward ethical violations.

GETTING ON THE ROAD

Counselors have at their disposal a range of resources that are designed to help them recognize and work through ethical dilemmas in the most caring way possible. A wide body of literature (e.g., Corey, Corey, & Callanan, 2011; Meara, Schmidt, & Day, 1996; Remley & Herlihy, 2010; Welfel, 2010) describes moral and virtuous behavior for helping professionals in a variety of practice settings and encourages counselors to aspire toward these behaviors. This same literature cautions counselors against pitfalls, such as not dealing with personal pain and suffering or failing to remain current with ethical standards that can lead to harm for clients, students, and supervisees. Ethical codes are available as guides for best practice, especially with regard to common dilemmas, and in more ambiguous situations counselors have available sets of principles and shared values that can act as a backdrop for making ethical decisions. Yet, with these and many other resources available to counselors, there are all too many examples of helping professionals engaging in unethical behaviors. Violations or near violations of ethical standards are commonplace, and nonegregious missteps mark the careers of most counselors (Sherry, Teschendorf, Anderson, & Guzman, 1991; Welfel, 2005). The curious discrepancy between counselor unethical behavior and the myriad resources available for making sound ethical judgments is the focus of this chapter as we seek to examine some of the thought processes and behaviors that lie underneath, and possibly motivate, ethical missteps. We begin the chapter by looking at some common ethical violations and briefly outlining moral principles for decision making before turning to a discussion of core concepts of Gestalt theory, which we believe will help shed light on the reasons for counselors' ethical blind spots. Our goal is to help you become aware of the potential for getting off track in ethical practice and to minimize unprofessional behaviors.

EXPLORING THE TERRITORY

THE SCOPE OF ETHICAL "RULE BREAKING" IN COUNSELING

American General, Douglas MacArthur (1880–1964), was credited for saying, "Rules are mostly made to be broken and are too often for the lazy to hide behind," as well as, "You are remembered by the rules you break." In the counseling profession, the "rules" of good behavior are outlined in the ethical standards and codes, which have been developed over years of observation, research, and evaluation of how to honor the welfare of the client. Ethical standards, such as the American Counseling Association (ACA) *Code of Ethics* (2005) and the American School Counselor Association (ASCA) *Code of Ethics* (2010) are readily available to clinicians; they are discussed in great detail in counselor training classes; and they are often revisited in continuing education seminars required for certification or licensure. Contained in the codes are rules—or nuggets of wisdom—such as, "Uphold a client's right to confidential disclosures"; "Work to gain a client's trust by engaging in a forthright informed consent process"; "Be attentive to how cultural bias might skew the interpretation of an assessment"; and "Avoid multiple relationships whenever possible with clients." These "rules," in effect, help clinicians discern what constitutes ethical behavior in uncertain circumstances and point them toward professional behaviors that are likely to be confirmed as good by their colleagues.

Over the course of counselors' training and careers, they will, without a doubt, hear stories of ethical violations, or instances when professional wisdom somehow gets disregarded or misconstrued. Some of these accounts are of large-scale, egregious acts that happen in and outside of the counseling field, while other accounts are of more minor ethical missteps. State licensing boards keep a list of ethical and legal offenses, those who offend, and those who are repeat offenders. Violations are generally clustered into the following categories: boundary violations, poor practice, competency issues, record keeping violations, honesty, confidentiality, informed consent, conflicts of interest, collegial actions, reimbursement, and insufficient continuing education credits (Brohl & Ledford, 2011). In addition, there are subsets of the above categories, including inappropriate behaviors, physical contact, sexual activity, social and business relationships, and bartering. We have found that trying to make sense of the subtle violations is just as confusing as trying to understand the obvious, most dangerous ones. In either case, to act uprightly and with care for clients, counselors have to learn to develop ethical or moral sensitivity (Rest, 1994; Welfel, 2005), which is described as the ability to identify when one's actions have the potential to harm another person. We propose that developing ethical sensitivity is an ongoing process that requires counselors to come to their clinical encounters with a great deal of self-awareness and consciousness, lest they become complacent or take for granted what they believe to be or not to be ethical behavior. The concept of awareness is central to Gestalt theory, which we will describe in more detail shortly.

Landmark 1

CASE EXAMPLE

Consider the following examples and determine for yourself which you believe to be ethical violations, which stand out as most harmful, and why you believe there is a violation taking place.

1. *In a casual meeting with a fellow parent at their children's school, a counselor learns that the parent's therapist suggested she become the therapist's bookkeeper because "it would be good for her."*
2. *A doctoral student in a counseling program reports that a work colleague asked him to adjust her clinical supervision hours so she could apply for licensure early.*
3. *A client reports to her current counselor that a previous counselor had billed the insurance company for missed appointments "to help her out financially" instead of asking the client to pay a missed session fee.*
4. *A therapist does not "allow" clients to miss appointments, see other medical professionals, or go on vacation because that "would compromise their therapeutic work"; however, missed appointments are still billed.*
5. *A counselor barters massage services for therapy. After each therapy session ends, the therapist undresses to receive a full body massage from the client.*

Understanding Ethical Violations in Organizational Systems

Counselors' unethical behaviors do not have to be extreme or egregious to show questionable judgment, nor are they always just about an individual's inability to make good decisions; sometimes unhealthy organizational systems foster unethical behavior. In describing ethical violations in business settings, Bazerman and Tenbrunsel (2011) reported that people tend to overlook transgressions, bend rules to help a colleague, and disregard information that might damage the reputation of an associate if it also serves their own interest. In addition, they reported that tying financial sanctions to unethical acts only tends to increase harmful behaviors because it allows people to focus on the financial sanction without necessarily seeing or examining the reason for the sanction. Bazerman and Tenbrunsel (2011) refer to this as ethical fading, and it usually results in people condoning or engaging in compromised behaviors that they would otherwise have condemned with full conscious awareness. Finally, these authors maintained that in corporate systems people often are only held accountable if their unethical decisions appear to have been intentional, even though seemingly unintentional unethical acts can have their own damaging outcomes.

It is easy to imagine how ethical fading, or overlooking best practices, might also happen in businesses that are tied closely to or serve the mental health profession, such as managed care companies or counseling agencies themselves. Administrators and directors of mental health agencies are sometimes guilty of undertraining clinicians, which not only compromises the integrity of their agencies, but also, in turn, creates fertile ground for ethical violations. Due to high client volume, for example, agency management or directors might expect new counselors to treat clients who have issues they have never before dealt with and thus push them to practice outside their area of competence. In stressed systems, clinicians also can be encouraged to "up code" or "down code," which refers to the practice of altering a client's diagnosis to one that is more or less severe than it truly is in order to obtain additional sessions from insurance companies or to get coverage for services in the first place. Though not uncommon, this practice is considered to be both fraudulent and unethical (Daniels, 2001). Similarly, clinicians have reported that they occasionally adjust a client's Global Assessment of Functioning (GAF) score (which is a part of a *DSM*-based diagnosis) to secure more paid sessions for the client. Agencies and clinicians justify these behaviors in the name of the "best interest of the client" and helping the agency to survive. Unfortunately, these justifications divert attention from the ethical issues at hand and lead to ethical blindness, the outcome of which often is the falsification of client information.

At other times, counselors might support slightly unethical actions that take place in their organizations or overlook them in the name of maintaining employment. Counselors can easily be tempted to comply with unethical behavior rather than leave a position in an agency where unethical practices ensue, especially in a challenged economy. Relatedly, counselors who themselves are not engaging in unethical behavior sometimes will turn a blind eye to others' questionable behavior so as not to be seen as a "whistleblower."

Frequently, counselors must interact in systems with colleagues whose professions do not have an ethical code or have one that is different from their own. School counselors, for example, often face challenges because they work with others (e.g., teachers and administrators) who do not share a common code of ethics. Wardi-Zonna and Hardy (2006) discussed the difficulties for the counseling profession as it attempts to interface with the educational system. They stated, "Schools operate using an open style of communication, which is in sharp contrast to the restrictions embraced by the mental health profession" (Welfel, as cited in Wardi-Zonna & Hardy, p. 32). While collaboration among school personnel and professionals is expected and valued in order to promote student success and well-being, there is an ongoing concern among counselors in school systems related to issues of gossip or inappropriate sharing about students' personal information. Addressing these, as well as other similar examples of ethical conflicts that emerge in stressed systems or because professionals working in the same organizational system have differing codes of ethics, is vital for counselors to be able to uphold their duty to honor those whom they serve and live up to their own professional responsibilities.

Understanding Missteps at the Individual Level: Boundary Crossings and Violations

Although counselors can find themselves working in systems that allow for or encourage ethical missteps, they also have to be cognizant of ways in which their own personal blind spots can lead to ethical errors. Perhaps the most studied ethical transgression that counselors make has to do with the improper or poor management of boundaries. Awareness of boundary crossings and boundary violations are of utmost importance for ethical practice. Peterson (1992, p. 4) defined boundaries as the "limits that protect the space between the professional's power and the client's vulnerability." She maintained that many counselors are concerned about boundary violations, but the profession as a whole has been unwilling to address the overall scope of the problem. As a result, boundary violations involve a "process of disconnection" (Peterson, 1992, p. 3) that happens within the professional relationship.

The power differential between counselors and their clients creates a basic inequity in the counseling relationship, providing the professional with authority and influence over the more vulnerable client. When clinicians abuse the power ascribed to their role as helper, they violate the boundary and put the client's well-being in jeopardy. There are many ways in which a counselor could potentially harm a client with a boundary crossing or violation. When they are more concerned about using the relationship to serve their own needs, as in the case of most serious boundary violations, counselors' behavior almost inevitably communicate that a client's needs are second to their own.

Peterson (1992) outlined different types of boundary violations in which the power differential between counselors and their clients are abused. A violation characterized by a "reversal of roles" happens when the client becomes the caregiver for the counselor. With this type of blurred boundary, a client experiences a "shift in status" (Peterson, 1992, p. 78.), which can diminish the client's perception of safety and actually lead to confusion about his or her role in therapy. Another violation, which Peterson calls "the secret" (1992, p. 80), occurs when the counselor shares information with a "just between us" expectation, resulting in feelings of empowerment and vulnerability for the client. The "double bind" (1992, p. 86) violation is one that leaves the client feeling caught in a conflict of interest. In this situation, the client may feel flattered by extra personal attention that comes from a counselor, but he or she also may perceive a potential for loss that could come from trying to reestablish appropriate boundaries (e.g., the client may perceive having to choose between losing the extra attention or the counseling relationship, if not both). Finally, the "indulgence of personal privilege" (1992, p. 90) refers to a violation that emerges due to the special confluence of the counselor's own needs and the client's vulnerable position. This dynamic provides an opportunity for the client to be taken advantage of by the professional, who sees the client as a means to meet his or her own needs or desires.

Not every individual ethical violation is one that involves boundary crossings or violations. However, some of the most troubling ethical infractions for clients do involve counselors misusing the power ascribed to their professional roles. Thus, counselors must be especially aware of when their misuse of the boundary between themselves and clients is apt to occur.

MORAL PRINCIPLES: A MEANS OF ETHICAL DISCERNMENT

Ethical transgressions happen in all areas of clinical practice; they are not uncommon among helpers, and they can be encouraged by an unhealthy organizational system or because of one's own blind spots. Thus, most practitioners need some guides to follow in the ethical decision-making process. Moral principles are a helpful addition to the best practices outlined in the various codes of ethics that frame the work of helping professions. Because these principles are also described elsewhere in this book, we give just a brief overview of several key precepts counselors use to discern their moral duties when faced with dilemmas. The six most well recognized (Remley & Herlihy, 2010; Zur, 2007) are: (a) autonomy, which refers to the counselor's value on and support for the client's freedom of choice, especially with regard to decisions related to their treatment; (b) beneficence, which refers to the duty to do good and highlights the counselor's responsibility to prevent harm while attempting to benefit the client; (c) nonmaleficence, which is described as the duty to do no harm and involves the counselor in monitoring his or her own actions in order to reduce risk of harm to the client; (d) fidelity, which is the obligation to keep one's promises or commitments; (e) justice, which is the duty to treat all clients fairly; and (f) veracity, which is a responsibility to be truthful in all interactions with clients, colleagues, and professional peers.

In addition to these, there are other common duties and values that counselors tend to uphold and that are points of reflection when counselors try not to make ethical missteps. These include (a) confidentiality, or a duty to respect client privacy and protect privileged information; (b) competency, or an obligation to practice only in areas of one's expertise; (c) publicity, or a responsibility "to take actions based on ethical standards that must be known and recognized by all who are involved" (Zur, 2007, p. 58); (d) reparation, or a duty to make up for a wrong by making amends; and (d) respect for others, or a duty to honor others, and their rights and responsibilities.

GESTALT THEORY: A MEANS FOR RAISING AWARENESS AND PREVENTING ETHICAL MISSTEPS

Most ethical decision-making models recommend counselors to engage in several layers of reflection and information gathering, as well as consultation, before making decisions that have the potential to harm clients or negatively impact the counseling relationship. Using ethical codes and moral principles (described above) are part of the overall decision-making process. However, these tools are not always enough to ensure virtuous behavior from counselors. Thus, we would like to propose some additional points of reflection based on Gestalt theory that can help sensitize counselors to possible blind spots that might prevent them from perceiving that an ethical dilemma or issue has arisen. Indeed, before a counselor can begin to solve an ethical problem, he or she must recognize that it is there, which, of course, requires awareness. Awareness is a concept that is at the heart of Gestalt theory. When people are fully aware of themselves and their surroundings, they are most capable of taking responsibility for their actions and tapping into resources that will help them resolve problems. Next to awareness, the concepts of responsibility and contact are also central to Gestalt theory. We suggest that, taken together, these concepts can help counselors to expand their understanding of how ethical missteps can happen almost unforeseen, and more importantly, the concepts can offer counselors points of self-reflection not necessarily highlighted in codes of ethics or the moral principles. In this section, we briefly explain what is meant by awareness, responsibility, and contact, and then we explore various reasons, rationales, attitudes, and thinking errors that lead counselors to overlook or succumb to the lure of unethical practices.

Awareness

Gestalt theory strongly supports the idea that change and personal growth come from awareness. Awareness is "a self-process that happens at the interface of the individual and the rest of the field (one's relationship with their environment and others)" (Woldt & Toman, 2005, p. 87). In other words, when people seek awareness as it is understood by Gestalt theory, they are seeking to understand their immediate feelings, bodily experiences, and thoughts, which are belied through things such as one's tone of voice, body posture, gestures, and ways of relating to others. With awareness, people understand how they tend to behave in the here-and-now and learn about patterns of interpersonal interaction that characterize their behavior. Moreover, full awareness allows one to know the environment, be responsible for personal decisions, accept oneself, and be in genuine contact or relationship with others. A lack of awareness has the potential to impair one's ability to be in touch with present-focused emotions and thoughts that would sensitize him or her to the presence of an ethical problem and thus make it difficult to undertake a clear and informed ethical decision.

Responsibility

Responsibility, simply put, is the ability each person has to respond to his or her environment. According to Gestalt theory, people are responsible (response-able); that is, they are the primary agents in determining their own behavior. When people confuse responsibility with the act of blaming or with what they think they "should" do, they are not fully integrated or acting with sincerity. In such instances, their true wants, needs, and responses to the environment and choices in a given set of circumstances are ignored, and they overcomply or rebel against shoulds (Yontef, 1981). Not assuming responsibility for one's actions is an easy path to ethical boundary crossings and violations.

Contact

Contact and the contact boundary refer to "a quality of awareness which involves the meeting of differences (between one's self and the environment)" (Nevis, 1992, p. 23). People make contact with aspects of the physical environment and with others tangibly—through their senses. Good contact happens by seeing, hearing, smelling, touching, and moving through the world in such a way as not to lose one's individuality, but to meet the environment and others with full awareness of who one is (Corey, 2000). This type of fully aware contact brings about personal transformations. At the same time, Gestalt theorists describe what is commonly referred to as interruptions to styles of contact, or ways of resisting being fully present and aware of the world. Specifically, the interruptions in contact style or resistances are known as projection, introjection, retroflection, deflection, and confluence (Woldt & Toman, 2005). When the boundary between the counselor and the client becomes unclear, the therapeutic experience between them is also blurred, thus compromising the counselor's behavior and decision-making abilities. The counselor becomes unable to regulate him or herself appropriately in the counseling relationship, which sets the stage for possible missteps when the counselor is faced with ethical dilemmas.

INTERRUPTIONS TO STYLES OF CONTACT: LEARNING HOW ETHICAL ERRORS HAPPEN

Interruptions or resistances to contact prevent people from fully being in touch with themselves and their world if they do not have awareness of the style of contact they usually employ. Resistances to contact are not necessarily negative in that they tell us how we block our experience of the present moment, and these can become points of self-awareness if we are willing to look at them openly. However, when we do not have the disposition or ability to bring our resistances to awareness, they can become unhealthy. In this section, we examine the five interruption styles identified in Gestalt theory to help explain how counselors, in spite of what they know about professional and unprofessional behavior, still violate ethical standards. We begin by looking at projection.

Projection

Projection refers to the act of disowning or alienating parts of oneself and attributing them somewhere in the environment instead. Usually, people project onto others aspects of themselves that do not fit with their own self-image. Counselors who engage in projection as a way of breaking contact with the environment can end up attributing their own personal characteristics or qualities to the client, which can produce confusion about the counselor's self and the client's self. Counselors who are unaware of their projections run the risk of not recognizing and thereby not taking responsibility for inappropriate actions in the counseling relationship. With awareness, however, projection can be a tool that allows counselors to use their personal and professional experiences to relate to their client's world. What follows now are examples of some areas of ethical concern that occur when counselors are unaware of their projections in the counseling relationship.

Using One's Own Value System in the Absence of Clear Ethical Information

Eberlein (1987) raised concerns about ethical violations that occur when counselors experience a lack of consensus about what constitutes appropriate legal or ethical action. While some ethical standards are clear about what is or is not considered moral behavior for clinicians, the standards do leave room for personal interpretation. Moreover, counselors are always faced with the challenge of matching their unique ethical dilemmas with the recommendations of the code in light of their own perspective on the standards. Given these circumstances, Eberlein suggested that clinicians often turn to their own value systems and "their interpretation of the spirit of the code" (p. 356) in ambiguous situations. Personal interpretations can be prime examples of the Gestalt process of projection. When counselors are unaware that their ethical decision-making process is based largely on a disowned part of themselves that is being projected on to the client, this often results in ethical confusion. Consider the example in Landmark 2.

Landmark 2
CASE EXAMPLE

Dan teaches in a local university counseling program and also works in a private counseling practice. One of his clients enrolled in the program where Dan teaches a required course. As the client progressed toward her degree, a time came when she had to take her counselor's course. Dan became concerned about boundaries, confidentiality, multiple relationships, and the evaluative nature of the situation. At the same time, he was afraid that when he would have to evaluate his client in class, she might not see him as a good counselor and might even reject him, especially if he had to give her a poor evaluation on class assignments. He and the client had developed what he considered to be a strong rapport. Dan checked the ethical code to see if it strictly forbids counselors to act as a teacher to their clients but did not see any clear statements that helped him know conclusively what to do. Not wanting to jeopardize his clinical relationship, Dan hesitates about seeking consultation, figuring that he can reason through this dilemma without the input from other professionals.

1. *What unaware projections might Dan operate from?*
2. *What steps can Dan take to develop awareness of his projections in order to accurately assess the situation and then make an ethical decision?*

In the above example, Dan faces the choice of acting on his projections (related to a fear of rejection) or seeking to become self-aware about how his own feelings might get in the way of making a good decision in light of his dilemma. The situation is complicated by the fact that there is not a conclusive ethical statement in the code about what he should or should not do in this set of circumstances. Thus, he may be vulnerable to making a decision out of his own fear that the client will cut off the counseling relationship if he refuses to have her in class. Furthermore, if Dan acts on his projections, he might only rely on his own value system in coming to an ethical decision (e.g., "It is important that people like me"). However, if Dan is able to be aware of his projections and seriously ponder both the potentially negative or beneficial implications of a multiple relationship, he is more likely to be open to a host of resolutions to his dilemma.

Responding From Threat or Fear

As seen in the example from Landmark 2, counselors are susceptible to making compromised decisions based on the fear of being rejected by their clients. Similarly, counselors often feel trapped by a fear of being sued for malpractice if they refuse to comply with inappropriate requests from the client. Consider the examples of Bob and Sue offered in Landmark 3.

Landmark 3

CASE EXAMPLES

A client requested that his counselor, Bob, write a reference letter for him for a new job. The client urged Bob to present himself as his professional colleague rather than as his therapist. When Bob refused to comply, the client threatened to report Bob to the licensing or ethics board and refused to make future referrals to the counselor's practice. Bob became suddenly unsure about his decision.

1. *What unaware projections might Bob operate from?*
2. *What steps can Bob take to develop awareness of his projections in order to more accurately assess and then make an ethical decision?*

Sue was asked to submit case files to a client's attorney to prepare for a divorce settlement. Sue advised the client that there was much unrelated information in the file and release of the entire record might be a detriment to her case. As an alternative, Sue suggested the she would write a letter that would outline the relevant treatment information. The client's attorney, angry with Sue, threatened her with a subpoena.

1. *What unaware projections might Sue operate from?*
2. *What steps can Sue take to develop awareness of his projections in order to more accurately assess and then make an ethical decision?*

Imagine that in the above first example, Bob, out of panic, decided to write the letter as requested by his client in order to protect himself from the perceived consequences of his client's threats to report him or discourage others from seeking his services. His panicked response might be based, in part, on an unaware projection of fear, which Bob holds about his being strong or his not being the type of person who falls prey to others' threats. In order to make an awareness-based decision, Bob might seek peer support and supervision to help him set ethical boundaries and avoid being motivated by his projected fears.

The case of Sue is an example of how threat and fear are typical reactions counselors experience when they fail to understand how to respond to a subpoena or court order. If Sue, like many counselors, is afraid of being served with a subpoena, she might not immediately make the best ethical decisions. For example, Sue might decide not to go to work the next day because of a projected fear in which she sees herself as unable to manage the stress of responding to the subpoena and being called to court. Furthermore, Sue might be concerned that her case record will not stand up to professional or legal scrutiny and thus create additional problems for her in the future. On the other hand, if Sue decides to consult with her supervisor, review the ethical guidelines regarding responses to subpoenas, or make any similar response that will help her not to get caught up only in her projection, she likely will be able to approach the ethical dilemma in an aware manner.

"It Is Just a Little Unethical"

Very frequently, counselors who are unaware of how their projections may construct their own understanding of what constitutes ethical or unethical behavior on self-statements such as, "It will not matter," "It is a small thing," "No one is getting hurt," "Other counselors do it," and "No one will know." Operating from these beliefs, counselors make decisions to serve their own needs as opposed to upholding the ethical standards and, more importantly, acting on the best interest of the client and the profession. For example, in an attempt to gather supervised hours for state licensure, a counselor might contact a former supervisor and state, "I need a favor . . . it's a little unethical, but I need you to falsify some of my hours." The projection in this example is related to the counselor's assumption that minimizing or shaping the standards to meet her personal needs would be acceptable to her supervisor and, thus, the ethical violation is secondary.

"I Do Not Agree With the Ethics"

Counselors sometimes blindly question the profession's ethical codes and standards, believing that their understanding of a dilemma or ethical situation far exceeds the wisdom of others. This projection of "I know better" has the potential to negate the opinions of colleagues and experts in the field and when pursued without reflection leads to ethical missteps. The "I know better" projection can be illustrated by the case of a counselor who accused a university counselor education program of unethical behavior when the program utilized their doctoral students to assist in teaching courses. The inaccuracy of this accusation is based on the counselor's projection that graduate students should not be taught by anyone other than a doctoral-level educator. The accusation demonstrates a lack of understanding of the ethics and might even contribute to reputational harm toward the university counselor education program. This and other examples of unaware projections form the basis for interrupting one's relationship with self and the environment, or more specifically, the ethical standards of the profession.

Introjection

Gestalt theory describes introjection as "swallowing whole without discriminating" material that comes from outside of one's self. Commonly known as "shoulds," introjections represent the beliefs and values that others have for us. Yontef (1993) refers to introjection as ingesting foreign material or unaware internalization. Introjection can be a positive and healthy experience as the environment has many rich beliefs and values to offer. For example, with awareness, introjecting the ethical codes provides a valuable internal guideline for counselors who strive toward ethical behavior. However, without awareness, a counselor may introject inappropriate materials, which interrupt the quality of contact with the client and the standards of the profession. Similarly, counselors might introject standards of ethical practice without ever really examining for themselves why those standards are important to virtuous clinical practice or taking ownership for them. Examples related to introjection that lead to unethical missteps are described below as issues of competence.

Issues of Competence

The concept of counseling competence encompasses a wide spectrum of activities and is based on the understanding that a counselor cannot be completely competent in all areas of practice. Yet, there is a professional expectation that the counselor should have achieved at least a baseline level of expertise in the area in which he or she practices. This particular expectation is an example of an introject.

Introjections related to competence can lead to ethical missteps, however, when counselors "ingest" this practice guideline without thinking critically about what is meant by competence or how one goes about achieving professional competence. For example, counselors may possess a lack of awareness about what constitutes expertise, have an inflated sense of their abilities, believe that a brief training equals expertise, lack adequate knowledge or preparation to use certain techniques, lack needed supervision, fail to follow through with continuing education expectations, or decide to accept a referral outside of their area of expertise for financial or utilization review reasons.

Ideally, introjects or "shoulds" regarding competence serve as motivation for counselors to comply with ethical standards that recommend practice, training, and supervision as a background for competence. Unfortunately, the literature reflects inconsistent teaching and modeling of ethical behavior on the part of counselor educators, who are expected to be models of how to enact the profession's introjects around competence. For example, Downs (2003) reported that boundary violations that occur between faculty and their students influence and contribute to compromised ethical practice later in students' careers. Counselor educators sometimes feel attracted to their students and act on those feelings without regard for the short- and long-term impact on the students, their program, and the profession. Students then find themselves in a double bind, as revealing the boundary crossing places them at risk for poor grades or a compromised reputation in their educational environments. Additionally, the student may feel honored to be pursued by a faculty member.

Some counselor educators may not have kept current with emerging information about ethics that would aid them in recognizing dilemmas and making good decisions. Others may have been educated or practiced at a time when ethical standards were not as well formed or recognized as they currently are. These counselor educators may not see the significance of the professions "introjects" (standards) because they were not in place when they were emerging as professionals. As a result, they might provide inaccurate information to counselor trainees regarding the current ethical standards or introjects, which can result in the potential for ethical violations.

Retroflection

Retroflection is the ability to "hold back" when to "put out" might create a problem in the environment. It is also described as turning inward that which was intended for the environment. For example, when people harm themselves in some way when they actually have been hurt by another but are afraid to express their hurt or anger toward the deserving person, they are retroflecting. Retroflection does involve owning and accepting responsibility for the negative happenings in life; however, one should not excessively feel responsible for others' problems or for things over which one has no control (Perls, Hefferline, & Goodman, 1951). With awareness, retroflection is a vital counseling tool that can help counselors to manage the myriad of thoughts and feelings that arise in counseling sessions. For example, Yontef (1993, p. 10) stated, "biting one's lip may be more functional than saying something biting." Engaged in without awareness, retroflection is a problem for counselors that can lead to internalized resentments, as well as the inability to monitor and take responsibility for professional responses, including minor ethical infractions.

An Inability to Understand Implications

To avoid ethical violations, counselors must be able to understand the potential consequences or implications of certain behaviors and apply this understanding to their decision making. This is especially important for cases in which the ethical codes may not clearly identify an action as unethical, as such instances require counselors to think through the possible outcomes of their decisions. Consider the example of a counselor whose client asks for a ride home after the session, knowing that the counselor lives in his neighborhood. The counselor may be especially tempted to comply with the request if he has a need to be liked or accepted by the client or take care of the client. One possible result of the counselor's decision (if he gives the client a ride) is that the client could begin to misunderstand the professional nature of the relationship and become confused about the limits of the counselor–client boundary. In this case, retroflecting or containing the need to be liked, accepted, and so on can likely help the counselor take care of his client in an appropriate way.

Working in Organizations That Have Not Translated the Ethical Codes Into Their Daily Operations

School counselors regularly face challenges related to working in a system that does not always understand or support the ethical codes of the counseling profession. Frequently facing professional isolation from other clinicians (Herlihy, Gray, & McCollum, 2002), school counselors may receive little support when they have to work through ethical dilemmas in their workplace settings. Moreover, educational systems have a tendency to challenge certain standards that are central to counselors' code of ethics, which makes acting ethically difficult. An ethical dilemma that school counselors often come up against revolves around how to uphold confidentiality in a school system. The changing legal rights of school-aged children, coupled with school administrators' beliefs that they have "the right to know," complicate the practice of maintaining confidentiality in the school. Administrators, teachers, and parents expect the school counselor to reveal material related to a student client as a matter of course. It is, therefore, important that the school counselor outline the limits of confidentiality in such a way that the other professionals understand these related legal and ethical constraints. The school counselor must enter the system armed with knowledge of their ethical obligations and a commitment to uphold them in the school setting. They must also explicitly understand that they are bound by their ethical guidelines to withhold (retroflect) information that is held in confidence.

"It Does Not Apply to Me"

A primary aspect of retroflection involves the ability to create and maintain clear ethical boundaries. The counselor must know the difference between meeting their own needs as opposed to the needs of their clients. When the counselor, in an unaware way, goes to the environment (the counselor–client relationship) to meet his or her own needs, ethical dilemmas result. Consider the example in Landmark 4.

Landmark 4

CASE EXAMPLE

A client (who also happened to be a counselor) revealed to her therapist, Tauna, that when she sought spiritual advice from her pastor over a period of months she became sexually involved with him. She avowed to Tauna that because she herself is a counselor who clearly understands ethics and the notion of power differential, her pastor was not crossing any boundary. Tauna's immediate internal response was to reprimand her client for not knowing better because she was angry that another counselor would risk engaging in such a blatant boundary violation without thinking about the repercussions to the profession.

1. *In what ways does retroflection or the lack of retroflection by the client contribute to her making an ethical versus unethical decision in this situation?*
2. *How might Tauna need to practice retroflection with her client in this situation?*

Deflection

Deflection is the avoidance of contact or awareness by turning aside (Yontef, 1993), as when one is polite instead of being direct. Deflection can be useful when, with awareness, it meets the needs of the situation (e.g., where the situation needs cooling down). Other examples of deflection include not looking at a person, verbosity, vagueness, understating, and talking about rather than talking to (Polster & Polster, 1974). Avoiding or dismissing the importance of the ethical guidelines in one's professional practice can constitute deflection. This "turning aside" results in counselors ignoring or not valuing the role of ethical guidelines in their professional practice, thus creating a path to unethical behavior.

"My Friendship With My Client Is Therapeutic in Itself"

Deflection occurs when counselors make their own decisions about what is clinically indicated at the expense of the ethical codes and, more importantly, a client's well-being. For example, creating personal or professional relationships with a client as a "therapeutic method" sidesteps ethical standards that recommend counselors to avoiding multiple relationships that are not potentially beneficial. The example in Landmark 1 of the client who became the counselor's bookkeeper is an example of deflection with regard to the ethical guidelines surrounding multiple relationships.

"I Have Never Had an Ethics Class"

A current concern facing the profession involves the situation of practitioners who start a private practice or move up the ranks in agencies and hold the role or title of counselor without ever having received sufficient training, certification, or licensure. As a result, there are no governing bodies to hold these individuals accountable for ethical violations. These persons might be prone to view ethical guidelines with little esteem, and, with little or no supervision, they might ignore and deflect from the principles of best practice standards. In doing so, they fail to recognize the standards of the counseling profession. Examples of ethical violations that might ensue among those undertrained include counselors spending weekends with their clients, inviting clients to social functions, and failing to keep appropriate, if any, documentation of their therapeutic contact with clients.

Landmark 5

CASE EXAMPLE

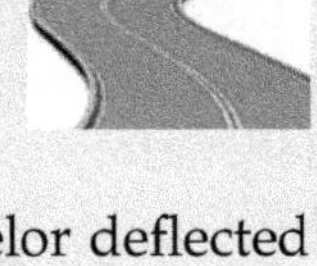

A counselor solicited private practice clients from a therapeutic training program for which she worked as a faculty member. When confronted, the counselor argued that she believed there was nothing unethical about her behavior and that she needed to build her practice. Furthermore, the counselor deflected by pointing to other ethically ambiguous situations in the program rather than address the matter at hand. She stated, "This is what counselor educators do all the time."

1. *In what ways can deflection both enhance and detract from the concerns that arise from this situation?*

Confluence

When people experience a lack of separation between themselves and others, or when the boundary becomes muted or unclear, they can be said to be experiencing confluence. When confluence exists in relationships, it can be difficult for a person to distinguish his or her own perceptions, feelings, or values from those of others. The Association for the Advancement of Gestalt Therapy states, "If we create confluence by dissolving the contact boundary without knowing we are doing so, we create a situation in which we confuse another with ourselves. We may be unable to distinguish our own thoughts and attitudes or feelings from something or someone else . . . We think we are in contact but we are not." This describes the counselor's inability to separate himself or herself from the experience of the client, and, like the other interruptions, leads to poor ethical decisions. Confluence is the basis for multiple relationships.

Temptation and Impulse Control

Counselors are frequently confronted with temptations when clients reveal personal information about their own areas of expertise and talent or about connections they have with other people who are of interest to the counselor. When counselors are prone to confluent relationships, they may find it difficult to resist temptations or practice impulse control because they do not want to hurt or offend a client. For example, a client might offer a counselor free tickets to a sold-out concert to his favorite band. If the counselor is uncertain about how to navigate his inner desire to take the tickets and the external reality that to accept the tickets might lead to a harmful multiple relationship, he is likely to be challenged in making a good ethical decision. Best practices suggest counselors to keep clear boundaries. When counselors seek awareness of their confluent behavior, they are better able to avoid blurred boundaries and questionable ethical decisions

"Practitioners Do Not Tell on Each Other"

There is debate regarding the practice of reporting a professional counseling colleague for inappropriate behavior. Ethical guidelines request that practitioners who discover peers acting unethically must institute a "cease and desist" discussion prior to reporting them to the appropriate licensing or certification board. If the offending practitioner does not change his or her behavior, there is an expectation that the peer will take the next step and report the behavior. While some practitioners will report a colleague, the occurrences of reporting are low. Peers find it challenging to determine whether they will turn a blind eye to offending behavior or turn in a fellow employee. Complicating the decision to turn in a fellow employee is the hard task of looking at one's own questionable behavior in the workplace. Finally, there may be confluent behavior based on the belief that ethics are an, us (counselors) versus them (ethics boards) relationship. All of these factors lead counselors not to challenge and to under report of ethical violations by peers.

At the same time, every profession does have employees that report their colleagues' questionable behaviors. In the counseling profession, reportable behaviors range in degree of seriousness and may include falsifying paperwork, engaging in financial indiscretions and utilizing company resources for personal gain, among the many others that we have described in this chapter. Revealing professionals' ethical missteps aids in protecting clients and allows the members of the profession's licensing boards to do their jobs and thus challenge the belief that "no one will ever know."

The counseling profession would do well to turn to the business world to learn how to support the reporting of legitimately unethical behavior. The online site Anonymous Employee Helping You Solve Your Problems at Work (www.anonymousemployee.com) outlines a model resembling common ethical decision-making model used by counselors to help determine how best to address related violations. The site recommends the following:

- Determine all aspects of the situation
- Conduct a thorough review
- Be sure of the rules and the violations
- Using ethics guidelines to ask, "Is this unethical?"

By being objective, focused on the behavior and not the person, knowing the facts, and documenting observable behavior (not assumptions), a counselor can gain clarity that will make it easier to ground a report regarding a peer's unethical conduct. To make such a report takes a lot of courage and should not be motivated by gossip or ill will. Taking such actions prior to confronting a colleague or reporting unethical actions are examples of nonconfluent and healthy procedures to cope with ethical violations.

SIGNPOSTS FOR FUTURE TREKS

The aim of this chapter was to look at some common ethical missteps that counselors make. We proposed that counselors use the most well-known resources available to them, such as codes of ethics and moral principles, to help discern the most caring actions in light of ambiguous circumstances. We also described basic tenants of Gestalt theory as a way to provide a basis for understanding the ways in which ethically informed members of the mental health profession still fall into making ethical violations. A failure to assume responsibility for one's actions, as well as maintaining an unaware stance and interrupting the connection between oneself and one's environment at the contact boundary all put counselors at risk of not enacting either the mandatory or aspirational elements of ethical standards. Thus, in closing, we recommend the following set of points found in Landmark 6 that can be used to enhance awareness of your professional behaviors. The questions are based on a helpful checklist created by Estelle Disch (2011), a professor of sociology at the University of Massachusetts Boston and co-director of Boston Associates to Stop Treatment Abuse (BASTA), for practitioners to tap into their potential for boundary crossings with clients. We have adapted it for use with educators and supervisors, as well as counselors and mental health professionals.

Landmark 6

ARE YOU IN TROUBLE WITH A CLIENT/STUDENT/SUPERVISEE?

AN ALTERNATIVE LOOK AT ETHICAL CONCERNS

These points are meant to alert professionals of boundary issues, which might be interfering with their ability to work effectively with clients, students, or supervisees. Be particularly attentive if the situation persists even after you have attempted to change it.

This client feels more like a friend than a client/student/supervisee.

I often tell my personal problems to this client/student/supervisee.

I feel sexually aroused in response to this client/student/supervisee.

I want to be friends with this client/student/supervisee when therapy ends.

I'm waiting for counseling to end in order to be lovers with this client/student/supervisee.

To be honest, I think the goodbye hugs last too long with this client/student/supervisee.

Sessions often run overtime with this client/student/supervisee.

I tend to accept gifts or favors from this client/student/supervisee without examining why the gift was given and why at that particular time.

I have had sexual contact with this client/student/supervisee.

I sometimes choose my clothing with this particular client/student/supervisee in mind.

I have attended small professional or social events at which I knew this client/student/supervisee would be present, without discussing it ahead of time.

This client/student/supervisee often invites me to social events and I do not feel comfortable saying either yes or no.

Sometimes when I am holding or hugging this client/student/supervisee during our work, I feel like the contact is sexualized for one or the other or both of us.

There is something I like about being alone in the office with this client/student/supervisee when no one else is around.

I lock the door when working with the client/student/supervisee.

The client/student/supervisee is very seductive and I often do not know how to handle it.

This client/student/supervisee owes me/the agency/the school a lot of money and I do not know what to do about it.

I have invited this client/student/supervisee to public or social events.

I am often late for sessions with this particular client/student/supervisee.

I find myself cajoling, teasing, and joking a lot with this client/student/supervisee.

I allow this client/student/supervisee to comfort me.

This client/student/supervisee scares me.

This client/student/supervisee's pain is so deep I can hardly stand it.

(*continued*)

I enjoy feeling more powerful than this client/student/supervisee.

Sometimes I feel like I am in over my head with this client/student/supervisee.

I often feel invaded or pushed by this client/student/supervisee and have a difficult time standing my ground.

I sometimes feel like punishing or controlling this client/student/supervisee.

I feel overly protective toward this client/student/supervisee.

I sometimes drink or take drugs with this client/student/supervisee.

I do not regularly check out what the physical contact I have with this client/student/supervisee means for the client.

I accommodate to this client/student/supervisee's schedule and then feel angry/manipulated.

This client/student/supervisee has invested money in an enterprise of mine or vice versa.

I find it very difficult not to talk about this client/student/supervisee with people close to me.

I find myself saying a lot about myself with this client/student/supervisee—telling stories, engaging in peer-like conversation.

If I were to list people in my caseload with whom I could envision myself in a sexual relationship, this client/student/supervisee would be on the list.

I am doing so much on this client/student/supervisee's behalf I feel exhausted.

I sometimes yell at this client/student/supervisee.

I dread seeing this client/student/supervisee.

Add your own items . . . .

INSIGHTS GAINED FROM THE JOURNEY

Even after decades of practice, it is our experience that avoiding, facing, and working through ethical concerns requires a fresh, dedicated, and collegial approach. In writing this chapter that examined how professionals can get off track and (hopefully) find their way back in their ethical decision making, we were challenged to find and employ a fresh perspective. By using core concepts of Gestalt theory we were able to develop and apply a template that we hope will both inform and support counselors in avoiding and facing the ethical challenges that inevitably occur.

As members of the counseling profession, we attempt to develop "awareness." We are challenged to have a working knowledge of the ethics standards and principles and to rely on our instincts when applying them. We are also challenged to develop our sense of responsibility into an "ability to respond" when called to action with each ethical dilemma encountered.

As authors we also looked to the concepts of "contact and the interruptions or styles of contact" and the ways in which they both enhance and detract from our ability to understand and cope with ethical decision making. The ethical standards and principles are in fact the, "Introjects" of our profession. However, "swallowing whole without chewing" on the meaning of those guidelines creates a disadvantage for our clients and us when we attempt to apply them. For us, it is the active examining, reviewing, and challenging of those guidelines that keeps them fresh and supports the flexibility that is required in making aspirational, ethically based decisions. We found this to be true as well in the concept of projection. As we developed this concept in relation to our writing, we discussed the ways that projection is so vital to our work. From our early days as counselors, projection (with awareness) has always been present as a challenge and a support in ethical practice. Perhaps our most vital insights included the importance of developing a solid theoretical approach to the ethical practice of our work as well as the need to maintain a fresh perspective toward our counseling endeavors.

MOVING FORWARD: CASE STUDY AND REFLECTION QUESTIONS

Kathy, a doctoral-level licensed professional counselor with 15 years' experience divided her professional service time between a large mental health agency and a part-time private practice. She considered herself an experienced counselor, with high standards of ethical practice but rarely availed herself of supervisory support. She believed strongly in her counseling methods, which she described as a blend of a variety of therapeutic approaches. One of Kathy's private clients was Beth, a 32-year-old, single Caucasian female. Beth sought treatment for symptoms of depression, prescription drug abuse, and relationship difficulties. Working with Kathy was her first therapy experience. After an initial assessment, Kathy suggested that Beth follow her treatment protocol of individual sessions three times per week. After 2 years of treatment, during which Beth had not missed an appointment, she reported she was still struggling with medication abuse, had developed suicidal ideation, and felt little relief from her depression.

Kathy had Beth sign a treatment contract that stipulated that she must attend treatment as indicated; 3 times per week with only a maximum of 2 weeks off from therapy per year and she was not permitted to seek services from any other helping professionals (other mental health professionals, chiropractors, meditation classes, etc.) while under her care. Kathy stated her reason for those rules was based on her professional beliefs that seeking help outside of their counseling relationship would represent a form of client resistance to treatment and undermine their therapeutic relationship.

After 2 years in treatment, Beth was invited to actualize a lifelong dream of a trip to Europe. It was a 4-week vacation. When she informed Kathy of her opportunity, Kathy responded by telling her that she would not support her trip. Kathy informed her that she believed it was a form of resistance to their therapeutic work. She further stated that as she would be holding the appointment times available for her while she was away, she would bill Beth for the missed appointments.

REFLECTION QUESTIONS

- *Describe the key ethical issues in this case.*
- *What are the ethical implications of Kathy's strict therapeutic contract?*

- *How are the Gestalt concepts of introjection, projection, and confluence helpful in understanding the ethical concerns of this case?*
- *What did you learn from reflecting on this case example?*
- *In what ways did your response reflect a positive approach to understanding the ethical considerations of this case?*

REFERENCES

American Counseling Association. (2005). *ACA code of ethics*. Alexandria, VA: Author.

American School Counselor Association. (2010). *Ethical standards for school counselors*. Retrieved from http://asca2.timberlakepublishing.com//files/EthicalStandards2010.pdf

Bazerman, M. H., & Tenbrunsel, A. E. (2011). Ethical breakdowns. *Harvard Business Review, 89*, 58–65.

Brohl, K., & Ledford, R. (2011). *Ethics and boundaries*. Ormond Beach, FL: Elite Continuing Education.

Corey, G. (2000). *Theory and practice of group counseling* (5th ed.). Belmont, CA: Brooks/Cole.

Corey, G., Corey, M., & Callanan, P. (2011). *Issues and ethics in the helping professions* (8th ed). Pacific Grove, CA: Brooks/Cole.

Daniels, J. A. (2001). Managed care, ethics, and counseling. *Journal of Counseling and Development, 79*, 119–122.

Disch, E. (2011). *Treatment abuse checklist: Is there something wrong or questionable in your treatment?* Retrieved from www.survivingtherapistabuse.com/treatment-abuse-checklist/

Downs, L. (2003). A preliminary survey of relationships between counselor educators' ethics education and ensuing pedagogy and responses to attractions with counseling students. *Counseling and Values, 48*, 2–13.

Eberlein, L. (1987). Introducing ethics to beginning psychologists: A problem-solving approach. *Professional Psychology: Research and Practice, 18*, 353–359.

Herlihy, B., Gray, N., & McCollum, V. (2002). Legal and ethical issues in school counseling supervision. *Professional School Counseling, 6*, 55–60.

Karinch, M. (2011). *How to report unethical behavior in the workplace*. Retrieved from http://www.ehow.com/how_7741792_report-unethical-behavior-workplace.html#ixzz1Mk4cgtQm

Latner, J. (1992). *The theory of Gestalt therapy*. In E. C. Nevis (Ed.), *Gestalt therapy: Perspectives, applications* (p. 23). Cleveland, Ohio: Gestalt Institute of Cleveland Press.

Meara, N. M., Schmidt, L. D., & Day, J. D. (1996). Principles and virtues: A foundation for ethical decisions, policies, and character. *The Counseling Psychologist, 24*, 4–77.

Perls, F. S., Hefferline, R., & Goodman, P. (1951). *Gestalt therapy: Excitement and growth in the human personality*. Gouldsboro, ME: The Gestalt Journal Press, Inc.

Peterson, M. R. (1992). *At personal risk*. New York, NY: W.W. Norton & Co.

Polster, E., & Polster, M. (1974). Gestalt therapy integrated: Contours of therapy and practice. New York: Vintage Books.

Remley, T., & Herlihy, B. (2010). *Ethical, legal, and professional issues in counseling*. Upper Saddle River, NJ: Prentice-Hall.

Rest, J. R. (1994). Background: Theory and research. In J. R. Rest, & D. Navarez (Eds.), *Moral development in the professions: Psychology and applied ethics* (pp. 1–26). Hillsdale, NJ: Erlbaum.

Sherry, P., Teschendorf, R., Anderson, S., & Guzman, F. (1991). Ethical beliefs and behaviors of college counseling center professionals. *Journal of College Student Development, 32*, 350–358.

Wardi-Zonna, K. L., & Hardy, J. (2006). Negotiating the crossing point: Ethical challenges in mental health school collaboration. *The Journal of the Pennsylvania Counseling Association, 8*(1), 29–41.

Welfel, E. R. (2010). *Ethics in counseling and psychotherapy: Standards, research and emerging issues*. Pacific Grove, CA: Brooks/Cole.

Welfel, E. R. (2005). Accepting fallibility: A model for personal responsibility for nonegregious ethics infractions. *Counseling and Values, 49*, 120–131.

Woldt, A., & Toman, S. (2005). *Gestalt therapy: History, theory and practice*. Thousand Oaks, CA: Sage Publications.

Yontef, G. (1981) (1993) (2005). *Awareness, dialogue and process*. Highland, NY: The Gestalt Journal Press.

Zur, O. (2007). *Boundaries in psychotherapy: Ethical and clinical exploration*. Washington, DC: American Psychological Association.

Appendix A

List of Codes of Ethics and Best Practice Guidelines for Counselors and Related Mental Health Professionals

American Association for Marriage and Family Therapy (AAMFT)
AAMFT Code of Ethics (2001)
Retrieved from: http://www.aamft.org/imis15/content/legal_ethics/code_of_ ethics.aspx

American Association of Pastoral Counselors (AAPC)
AAPC Code of Ethics (2010)
Retrieved from: http://aapc.org/content/code-ethics-1

American Counseling Association (ACA)
ACA Code of Ethics (2005)
Retrieved from: http://www.counseling.org/Resources/CodeOfEthics/TP/Home/CT2.aspx

American Mental Health Counselors Association (AMHCA)
AMHCA Code of Ethics (2000)
Retrieved from: http://www.amhca.org/assets/content/CodeofEthics1.pdf

American Psychiatric Association
APA Principles of Medical Ethics (2009)
Retrieved from: http://www.psych.org/MainMenu/PsychiatricPractice/Ethics/ResourcesStandards/PrinciplesofMedicalEthics.aspx

American Psychological Association (APA)
APA Ethical Principles of Psychologists and Code of Conduct (2010)
Retrieved from: http://www.apa.org/ethics/code/index.aspx

American School Counselor Association (ASCA)
ASCA Ethical Standards for School Counselors (2010)
Retrieved from: http://www.mnschoolcounselors.org/EthicalStandards2010.pdf

Association for Counselor Education and Supervision (ACES)
Best Practices in Clinical Supervision (2011)

Retrieved from: http://www.acesonline.net/wp-content/uploads/2011/10/ACES-Best-Practices-in-clinical-supervision-document-FINAL.pdf

Association for Specialists in Group Work (ASGW)
Best Practice Guidelines (2007)
Retrieved from: http://www.asgw.org/pdf/Best_Practices.pdf

Association for Specialists in Group Work (ASGW)
Professional Standards for the Training of Group Workers (2000)
Retrieved from: http://www.asgw.org/training_standards.htm

Association for Specialists in Group Work (ASGW)
Principles for Diversity Competent Group Workers (1998)
Retrieved from: http://www.asgw.org/diversity.htm

Center for Credentialing Education (CCE)
Approved Clinical Supervisor (ACS) Code of Ethics (2008)
Retrieved from: http://www.ncblpc.org/Laws_and_Codes/ACS_Code_of_Ethics.pdf

Commission on Rehabilitation Counselor Certification (CRCC)
Code of Professional Ethics for Rehabilitation Counselors (2010)
Retrieved from: http://www.crccertification.com/filebin/pdf/CRCCodeOfEthics.pdf

International Association of Marriage and Family Counselors (IAMFC)
IAMFC Code of Ethics
Retrieved from: http://www.iamfconline.com/PDFs/Ethical%20Codes.pdf

National Association of Social Workers (NASW)
NASW Code of Ethics (2008)
Retrieved from: http://www.naswdc.org/pubs/code/default.asp

National Board for Certified Counselors
Ethics for the Practice of Internet Counseling
Retrieved from: http://www.nbcc.org/Assets/Ethics/internetCounseling.pdf

National Board for Certified Counselors (NBCC)
NBCC Code of Ethics (2005)
Retrieved from: www.nbcc.org/Assets/Ethics/nbcc-codeofethics.pdf

National Career Development Association (NCDA)
NCDA Ethical Standards (2003)
Retrieved from: http://www.ncda.org/pdf/EthicalStandards.pdf

Appendix B

Counseling and Mental Health Web Resources

PROFESSIONAL ORGANIZATIONS

American Counseling Association
http://www.counseling.org

American School Counselor Association
http://www.schoolcounselor.org

International Association of Marriage and Family Counselors
www.iamfconline.org

American Association for Marriage and Family Therapy
www.aamft.org

Association for Counselor Education and Supervision
http://www.acesonline.net

Association for Specialists in Group Work
http://www.asgw.org

Association for Multicultural Counseling and Development
www.amcdaca.org

Association for Spiritual, Ethical, and Religious Values in Counseling
www.aservic.org

Association for Lesbian, Gay, Bisexual and Transgender Issues in Counseling
www.algbtc.org

Counselors for Social Justice
www.counselorsforsocialjustice.com

American Mental Health Counselors Association
http://www.amhca.org

International Society for Mental Health Online (ISMHO)
https://www.ismho.org

National Alliance on Mental Illness
http://www.nami.org

Chi Sigma Iota
http://csi.affiniscape.com/index.cfm

LAWS AND REGULATIONS

Family Policy Compliance Office
http://www2.ed.gov/policy/gen/guid/fpco/ferpa/index.html

Clearinghouse for HIPAA-Related Websites and American Counseling Association Resources
http://www.centerforethicalpractice.org/ethical-legal-resources/links/links-hipaa-resources-online

U.S. Department of Health and Human Services (DHHS) (provides explanations of HIPAA and privacy protection)
http://www.hhs.gov/ocr/privacy

U.S. Department of Education (provides information on FERPA)
http://www2.ed.gov/policy/gen/guid/fpco/ferpa/index.html

LICENSURE AND CERTIFICATION

National Board for Certified Counselors
http://www.nbcc.org

State Licensure Directory of Information
http://www.nbcc.org/StateLicensure

RESOURCES FOR PRACTICE, SUPERVISION, AND RESEARCH IN COUNSELING

Creating a Professional Counselor Portfolio
http://www.counseling.org/Resources/Library/VISTAS/vistas05/Vistas05.art49.pdf

Self-Care and Wellness Strategies
http://www.counseling.org/wellness_taskforce/tf_wellness_strategies.htm

Ethics, Burnout, and Self-Care
www.zurinstitute.com/ethicsofburnout.html

Termination in Counseling
http://www.divisionofpsychotherapy.org/hardy-and-woodhouse-2008

Substance Abuse and Mental Health Services Administration
http://store.samhsa.gov/home

A Guide to Clinical Supervision and Professional Development of Drug and Alcohol Counselors
http://kap.samhsa.gov/products/manuals/tips/pdf/TIP52.pdf

Supervision Training Resources (look under Health, Fitness & Wellness section of Psychological Counseling)
http://www.training-classes.com

Online Counseling and Training in Supervision Within This Context
http://counsellingresource.com/supervision

Finding and Using Ethical Counseling Supervision
http://www.mftguide.com/moreresources/tag/finding-mft-clinical-supervision

Description of the Juvenile Justice System (others can be sought from a counselor's particular state of practice)
http://www.dhs.state.mn.us/main/groups/children/documents/pub/dhs_id_008412.pdf

U.S. DHHS (provides basic information about child welfare and the courts)
http://www.childwelfare.gov/pubs/factsheets/cwandcourts.pdf

The Guttmacher Institute (a nonprofit organization that provides information about sexual and reproductive health research, policy analysis, and public education)
http://www.guttmacher.org

Legal & Ethical Issues in Counseling Resources by Carolyn Stone
http://www.counseling.org/resources/pdfs/Legal_and_Ethical_Website_Info.pdf

School Counseling Zone
http://www.school-counseling-zone.com

Leonore Tiefer Website
www.leonoretiefer.com

National Institutes of Health (NIH) Research Ethics Resources
http://www.niehs.nih.gov/research/resources/bioethics/whatis.cfm

Basics in Research Ethics
http://www.socialresearchmethods.net/kb/ethics.php

Encryption and Privacy Options for Web Communication
http://www.google.com/postini/email.html
http://www.symantec.com/business/messagelabs-hosted-email-encryption

PHILOSOPHY AND ETHICS

A Link to Aristotle's Nicomachean Ethics
http://classics.mit.edu/Aristotle/nicomachaen.html

A Copy of Bentham's Principles of Morals and Legislation
http://socserv.mcmaster.ca/econ/ugcm/3ll3/bentham/morals.pdf

A Copy of Kant's Fundamental Principles of the Metaphysics of Morals
http://www.class.uidaho.edu/mickelsen/texts/Kant%20-%20Fundamentals%20.%20.%20..txt

An Introduction to Kant's Philosophy
http://philosophy.lander.edu/ethics/kant.html

An Introduction to Ethics and Philosophical Ethics
http://philosophy.lander.edu/intro/ethics.html

Aristotle's Excellences
http://philosophy.lander.edu/ethics/ethicsbook/c5574.html

Ethics Updates (University of San Diego)
http://ethics.sandiego.edu

Internet Encyclopedia of Philosophy
http://www.iep.utm.edu/ethics

St. James Ethics Centre
http://www.ethics.org.au

Stanford Encyclopedia of Philosophy
http://plato.stanford.edu

The Free Dictionary Ethics
http://encyclopedia2.thefreedictionary.com/ethics

Index